THE CAMBRIDGE COMPANION TO SCOTTISH LITERATURE

Scotland's rich literary tradition is a product of its unique culture and landscape, as well as of its long history of inclusion and resistance to the United Kingdom. Scottish literature includes masterpieces in three languages – English, Scots and Gaelic – and global perspectives from the diaspora of Scots all over the world. This *Companion* offers a unique introduction, guide and reference work for students and readers of Scottish literature from the pre-medieval period to the post-devolution present. Essays focus on key periods and movements (the Scottish Enlightenment, Scottish Romanticism and the Scottish Renaissance), genres (the historical novel, Scottish Gothic, 'Tartan Noir') and major authors (Burns, Scott, Stevenson, MacDiarmid and Spark). A chronology and guides to further reading in each chapter make this an ideal overview of a national literature that continues to develop its own distinctive style.

GERARD CARRUTHERS is professor of Scottish Literature since 1700 at the University of Glasgow.

LIAM MCILVANNEY is Stuart Professor of Scottish Studies at the University of Otago, New Zealand.

A complete list of books in the series is at the back of this book.

D0782060

THE CAMBRIDGE
COMPANION TO

SCOTTISH LITERATURE

THE CAMBRIDGE
COMPANION TO
SCOTTISH
LITERATURE

EDITED BY
GERARD CARRUTHERS
AND LIAM MCILVANNEY

CAMBRIDGE
UNIVERSITY PRESS

CAMBRIDGE UNIVERSITY PRESS
Cambridge, New York, Melbourne, Madrid, Cape Town,
Singapore, São Paulo, Delhi, Mexico City

Cambridge University Press
32 Avenue of the Americas, New York, NY 10013-2473, USA

www.cambridge.org
Information on this title: www.cambridge.org/9780521189361

First published 2012

Printed in the United States of America

A catalog record for this publication is available from the British Library.

Library of Congress Cataloging in Publication data
The Cambridge Companion to Scottish literature / edited by Gerard Carruthers
and Liam McIlvanney.
p. cm. – (Cambridge companions to literature)
Includes bibliographical references and index.
ISBN 978-0-521-76241-0 (hardback) – ISBN 978-0-521-18936-1 (paperback)
1. English literature – Scottish authors – History and criticism.
2. Scottish literature – History and criticism. 3. Scotland – In literature.
I. Carruthers, Gerard, editor of compilation.
II. McIlvanney, Liam, editor of compilation.
PR8511.C36 2012
820.9'9411–dc23 2012003091

ISBN 978-0-521-76241-0 Hardback
ISBN 978-0-521-18936-1 Paperback

CONTENTS

NOTES ON CONTRIBUTORS

GERARD CARRUTHERS is professor (of Scottish literature since 1700) at the University of Glasgow. He is the author of *Scottish Literature: A Critical Guide* (Edinburgh University Press, 2009), editor of *The Devil to Stage: Five Plays by James Bridie* (Association for Scottish Literary Studies, 2007) and general editor of the new Oxford University Press edition of the works of Robert Burns.

THOMAS CLANCY is Chair of Celtic at the University of Glasgow. He has written extensively on both historical and literary aspects of medieval Scotland and Ireland, and is author, with Gilbert Márkus, of *Iona: The Earliest Poetry of a Celtic Monastery* (Edinburgh University Press, 1995), editor of *The Triumph Tree: Scotland's Earliest Poetry, AD 550–1350* (Interlink Pub Group Inc, 1998) and editor, with Murray Pittock, of *The Edinburgh History of Scottish Literature* Volume I, 'From Columba to the Union' (Edinburgh University Press, 2007).

CAIRNS CRAIG is Glucksman Professor of Irish and Scottish Studies at the University of Aberdeen. He is editor of the *Journal of Irish and Scottish Studies* and his most recent books are *Associationism and the Literary Imagination* (Edinburgh University Press, 2007) and *Intending Scotland* (Edinburgh University Press, 2009).

LEITH DAVIS is professor of English and director of the Centre for Scottish Studies at Simon Fraser University in Greater Vancouver, Canada. She is the author of *Acts of Union: Scotland and the Negotiation of the British Nation* (Stanford University Press, 1998) and *Music, Postcolonialism and Gender: The Construction of Irish Identity, 1725–1875* (Notre Dame University Press, 2005) and co-editor (with Ian Duncan and Janet Sorensen) of *Scotland and the Borders of Romanticism* (Cambridge University Press, 2004).

IAN DUNCAN is Florence Green Bixby Professor of English at the University of California, Berkeley. He is the author of *Scott's Shadow: The Novel in Romantic Edinburgh* (Princeton University Press, 2007) and *Modern Romance and Transformations of the Novel* (Cambridge University Press, 1992), and a co-editor of *Scotland and the Borders of Romanticism* (Cambridge University Press, 2004), *Travel Writing 1700–1830* (Oxford University Press, 2005), *Approaches to Teaching Scott's Waverley Novels* (MLA, 2009) and the *Edinburgh Companion to James Hogg* (Edinburgh University Press, forthcoming).

SARAH M. DUNNIGAN is a senior lecturer in English literature at Edinburgh University where she teaches medieval and Renaissance literature and the traditions of fantasy and fairy tale writing. She is the author of *Eros and Poetry at the Courts of Mary, Queen of Scots and James VI* (Palgrave, 2002), has edited essay collections on medieval and early modern Scottish literature and women's writing and is currently writing a book about Scottish fairy tales.

PENNY FIELDING teaches English and Scottish literature at Edinburgh University. Her books include *Scotland and the Fictions of Geography: North Britain 1760–1820* (Cambridge University Press, 2011) and *Writing and Orality: Nationality, Culture and Nineteenth-Century Scottish Fiction* (Clarendon Press, 1996). She edited the *Edinburgh Companion to Robert Louis Stevenson* (Edinburgh University Press, 2010) and is a general editor of the *New Edinburgh Edition of the Collected Works of Robert Louis Stevenson* (Edinburgh University Press, forthcoming).

DAVID GOLDIE is senior lecturer and head of the School of Humanities at Strathclyde University. He is the editor, with Gerard Carruthers and Alastair Renfrew, of *Beyond Scotland: New Contexts for Twentieth-Century Scottish Literature* (Rodopi, 2004) and *Scotland and the Nineteenth-Century World* (Rodopi, 2011).

ROBERT ELLIS HOSMER, JR, is senior lecturer in the Department of English Language & Literature, Smith College, where he teaches courses on modern and contemporary British and Irish women writers. His publications include *Contemporary British Women Writers: Texts and Strategies* (Macmillan, 1993) as well as essays, reviews and interviews for the *Chicago Tribune, America*, the *New York Times Book Review*, the *Boston Globe* and the *Paris Review*. His work on Muriel Spark includes an article, 'Writing with Intent: The Fiction of Muriel Spark' (*Commonweal*, 1988), reference book entries (*Encyclopedia of Catholic Literature*, Greenwood Publishing, 2004; *A Companion to the British and Irish Short Story*, Blackwell, 2008), as well as an interview (*London Magazine*, 2005). *'Shall we say I had fun with my imagination': Essays in Honor of Muriel Spark*, a collection of essays, is forthcoming.

NIGEL LEASK is Regius Professor of English Language and Literature at the University of Glasgow, head of the School of Critical Studies and a Fellow of the Royal Society of Edinburgh. His most recent book is *Robert Burns and Pastoral: Poetry and Improvement in Late Eighteenth-Century Scotland* (Oxford University Press, 2010).

SCOTT LYALL is lecturer in modern literature at Edinburgh Napier University, having taught previously at Trinity College, Dublin, and the University of Exeter. He is the author of *Hugh MacDiarmid's Poetry and Politics of Place: Imagining a Scottish Republic* (Edinburgh University Press, 2006) and co-editor of *The Edinburgh Companion to Hugh MacDiarmid* (Edinburgh University Press, 2011).

LIAM MCILVANNEY is the Stuart Professor of Scottish Studies at the University of Otago, New Zealand. He won the Saltire First Book Award for *Burns the Radical* in 2002, and his work has appeared in the *Times Literary Supplement* and the *London Review of Books*. A former general editor of the Association for Scottish Literary Studies, he serves on the advisory boards of *Studies in Scottish Literature* and the *International Journal of Scottish Literature*. He is co-editor of *Ireland and Scotland: Culture and Society, 1700–2000* (Four Courts Press, 2005) and *The Good of the Novel* (Faber and Faber, 2011). His first novel, *All the Colours of the Town*, was published by Faber in 2009.

PETER MACKAY has worked at Trinity College, Dublin, and the Seamus Heaney Centre for Poetry at Queen's University, Belfast. His publications include *Sorley MacLean* (RIISS, 2010), *Modern Irish and Scottish Poetry* (co-editor; Cambridge University Press, 2011) and a pamphlet of poems, *From Another Island* (Clutag, 2010). He currently works as a broadcast journalist for the BBC.

ANDREW NASH is senior lecturer in the Department of English Language & Literature at the University of Reading. He contributed several essays to Volume IV of the *Edinburgh History of the Book in Scotland* (Edinburgh University Press, 2007) and is author of *Kailyard and Scottish Literature* (Rodopi, 2007), editor of *The Culture of Collected Editions* (Palgrave Macmillan, 2003) and co-editor of *Literary Cultures and the Material Book* (British Library Publishing, 2007). He is currently co-editing a collection of essays on J. M. Barrie as well as Volume VII of *The Cambridge History of the Book in Britain* (Cambridge University Press, forthcoming), covering the period 1914 to the present.

ALESSANDRA PETRINA is associate professor of English literature at the Università degli Studi di Padova, Italy. She has written a monograph on *The Kingis Quair* (Unipress, 1997) and *Cultural Politics in Fifteenth-Century England: The Case of Humphrey, Duke of Gloucester* (Brill, 2004), together with articles on late-medieval and Renaissance literature and intellectual history, as well as on modern children's literature. Her monograph *Machiavelli in the British Isles: Two Early Modern Translations of the Prince* has been recently published (Ashgate, 2009).

MURRAY PITTOCK is Bradley Professor of English Literature at the University of Glasgow. He has held six research grants in support of his work in defining a national Scottish Romanticism, reflected in books such as *Scottish and*

Irish Romanticism (Oxford University Press, 2011 [2008]), *The Edinburgh Companion to Scottish Romanticism* (Edinburgh University Press, 2011), *Robert Burns in Global Culture* (Bucknell University Press, 2011), *The Reception of Sir Walter Scott in Europe* (Continuum, 2007) and *James Boswell* (AHRC Centre for Irish and Scottish Studies: Aberdeen, 2007). He is currently co-investigator on the AHRC Editing Burns for the 21st Century project, and is working on a study called 'Treacherous Objects: Material Culture and Sedition in Early Modern Britain and Ireland'.

DAVID PUNTER is professor of English at the University of Bristol. His most recent publications include *The Influence of Postmodernism on Contemporary Writing: An Interdisciplinary Study* (Edwin Mellen Press, 2005), *Metaphor* (Palgrave, 2007), *Modernity* (Macmillan, 2007) and *Rapture: Literature, Addiction, Secrecy* (Sussex Academic Press, 2009).

FIONA STAFFORD is professor of English at the University of Oxford. Her books include *The Sublime Savage: James Macpherson and the Poems of Ossian*, *Starting Lines in Scottish, Irish and English Poetry: From Burns to Heaney* (Oxford University Press, 2000) and *Local Attachments: The Province of Poetry* (Oxford University Press, 2010). She has recently co-edited a collection of essays and poems, *Burns and Other Poets* (Edinburgh University Press, 2011).

MATTHEW WICKMAN is senior lecturer of Scottish literature at the University of Aberdeen and associate professor of English at Brigham Young University, Utah. He is the author of *The Ruins of Experience: Scotland's 'Romantick' Highlands and the Birth of the Modern Witness* (University of Pennsylvania Press, 2007) and is working on two book-length projects which together make up a pre- and post-history of Scottish modernism.

ACKNOWLEDGEMENTS

The editors would like to thank Linden Bickett, Moira Burgess, Ian Duncan, David Goldie, Lisa Marr, Ray Ryan and Maartje Schelten.

CHRONOLOGY

AD 84/85	Tacitus claims that Calgacus leads the Caledonii, a tribe of north Britons, at the battle of Mons Graupius
c. 500	The 'Scoti' (Irish settlers) found the kingdom of Dalriada under Fergus
c. 656	The Irish St Columba founds a monastery on the island of Iona
c. 700	Adomnán of Iona's *Life of Saint Columba*
c. 700	The Virgin Mary is commemorated in a choral hymn by Cú Chuimne
8th Century	Whithorn verses on 'The Miracles of Bishop Nynia'
8th Century	The Life of St Ninian composed in Whithorn
8th Century	Hymn to St Ninian
9th Century	Scandinavian settlement begins in Scotland
9th or 10th Century	*The Book of Deer*
c. b900	Pictland is re-christened Alba
10th or 11th Century	Hymn to St Kentigern
11th Century	The *Duan Albanach* composed, perhaps by an Irish writer
11th Century	'A eolcha Alban uile' ('All ye learned men of Scotland'), also called *Duan Albanach* ('The Scottish Poem')

c. 1060	Arnor 'Earl's Poet' composes his elegy for Thorfinn the Mighty
1066	Norman victory at the Battle of Hastings cements the Norman Conquest
1093	Death of St Margaret of Scotland; her Life is written soon afterwards
12th Century	Compositions on St Kentigern and the death of Somerled by William the Clerk of Glasgow
12th Century	Lives of St Kentigern, or Mungo
c. 1150–1250	The period of compositions by Rögnvaldr Káli, earl of Orkney, Muireadhach Albanach Ó Dálaigh, Gille-Brighde Albanach and Orkney bishop Bjarni Kolbeinsson
c. 1164	Latin poem on the death of the Hebridean ruler Somerled in battle at Renfrew
13th Century	Latin hymn to St Magnus of Orkney
13th Century	The Virgin Mary is commemorated in a religious poem by Muireadhach Albanach Ó Dálaigh
†*c.* 1235	Birth of theologian and translator Michael Scot
c. 1250	Anonymous poem to Aonghas Mór, ruler of the Isles
1263	Alexander III defeats King Hakon of Norway at the Battle of Largs
c. 1265	Birth of John Duns Scotus (d.1308)
1286	King Alexander III dies after falling from his horse
1296–1328	The Scottish 'Wars of Independence' with England
1297	Scottish victory at the Battle of Stirling Bridge under William Wallace and Andrew Moray
1305	William Wallace is executed in London
1314	Scottish victory at the Battle of Bannockburn under King Robert the Bruce
c. 1320	Birth of John Barbour (d.1925)
1320	The drafting of the Declaration of Arbroath

1375	John Barbour's *The Bruce* completed
1380	John of Fordun's *Chronica Gentis Scotorum*
1400	Birth of Gilbert Hay (d.1499)
c. 1420–30	*The Kingis Quair* written; attributed to James I
1424	Andrew of Wyntoun's *Orygynale Cronykil of Scotland*
c. 1425	Birth of Robert Henryson (d.1506)
c. 1440	Walter Bower begins to write his *Scotichronicon*
1440	Birth of John of Ireland (d.1496), writes *Meroure of Wyssdome* (1490) for James IV
c. 1448	Richard Holland's *The Buke of the Howlat*
c. 1460	Birth of William Dunbar (d.1520)
1461	Production of the anonymous *Liber Pluscardensis*
c. 1474	Birth of Gavin Douglas (d.1522)
1476–8	'Blind' Harry's *Actis and Deidis of William Wallace*
1485	Beginning of the Tudor Dynasty in England with King Henry VII's victory at the Battle of Bosworth Field
c. 1486	Birth of Sir David Lyndsay (d.c.1555)
1488–1513	Reign of King James IV, killed at the Battle of Flodden in 1513
c. 1492	Robert Henryson's *The Testament of Cresseid*
1507	The first printing press in Scotland, the Chepman and Myllar press, is established in Edinburgh
1512	*The Book of the Dean of Lismore* (a collection in Gaelic of earlier lyrics)
1513	Battle of Flodden, where the English decisively defeat the Scots. James IV and many members of the Scottish nobility are killed
1513	Gavin Douglas produces his version of Virgil's *Aeneid*, the *Eneados*
c. 1520	Birth of Alexander Scott (d.1582/3)

1540	Lyndsay's *Ane Satyre of the Thrie Estaitis* first performed
1541	Birth of Mary Queen of Scots (d.1587)
1544	The translation of Euripides' *Medea* by George Buchanan (1506–82) published in Paris
c. 1548	Robert Wedderburn's *The Complaynt of Scotland*
c. 1557	Birth of Alexander Hume (d.c.1609)
c. 1560s	George Bannatyne compiles the Bannatyne Manuscript
1560	The birth of the Protestant Reformation in Scotland, mainly under the leadership of John Knox
c. 1560	Birth of William Fowler (d.1612)
1561	Mary Queen of Scots lands in Leith and takes the Scottish throne
1566	Birth of James VI of Scotland (d.1625)
1567	Publication of *The Gude and Godlie Ballads*
1570	Birth of Robert Ayton (d.1638)
c. 1580s–90s	Production of works by the 'Castalian band' in the court of James VI
1584	*The Essayes of a Prentise in the Divine Art of Poetry* written by James VI (James's *Reulis and Cautelis* also appears in this text)
1585	Birth of William Drummond of Hawthornden (d.1649)
1587	Mary Queen of Scots is executed
1594	Birth of William Mure of Rowallan (d.1657)
1597	Publication of Alexander Montgomerie's *The Cherrie and the Slae*
1599	James VI's *Basilikon Doron*
1603	Union of the Crowns, when King James VI of Scotland also takes the English throne as James I of England
1603	Elizabeth Melville writes *Ane Godlie Dreame*

1616	William Drummond of Hawthornden produces his sonnet sequence, *Flowres of Sion*
1637	Publication of the *Delitiae poetarum Scotorum* by Aberdeenshire writer Arthur Johnston
1638	The National Covenant is drawn up and signed in Greyfriars Churchyard in Edinburgh, in opposition to the religious policy of Charles I
1653	Sir Thomas Urquhart's translation of Rabelais
1681–5	'The Killing Time' when the Covenanters are persecuted
1684	Birth of Allan Ramsay (d.1758)
1688	The end of Stuart rule with the 'Glorious Revolution' in which William III replaces James II on the British throne
1692	The Glencoe Massacre
1698	William Paterson, founder of the Bank of England, spearheads the doomed Darien Scheme
1700	Birth of James Thomson (d.1748)
1706	James Watson publishes the first volume of his *Choice Collection of Comic and Serious Scots Poems both Ancient and Modern*
1706	Daniel Defoe's pamphlet *A Short Letter to the Glasgow-Men* is circulated in Scotland
1706	Anti-Union riots in Glasgow
1707	Treaty of Union. An independent Scottish parliament ceases to exist; along with England, Scotland becomes part of the United Kingdom of Great Britain, with the British parliament at Westminster
1708	James Watson prints the first volume of the *Lives and Characters of the Most Eminent Writers of the Scots Nation* by George Mackenzie
1709	Daniel Defoe's *History of the Union*
1710	Thomas Ruddiman republishes Gavin Douglas's *Eneados* under the title: *Virgil's Æneis, Translated into*

Scottish Verse, by the Famous Gawin Douglas Bishop of Dunkeld

1715	First major Jacobite rising
1718	Allan Ramsay publishes his *Scots Songs*
1720	Allan Ramsay's *Poems*. A 1721 edition of this work is published by Thomas Ruddiman
1720	Charles Edward Stuart, also known as Bonnie Prince Charlie, is born in Italy
1724	Thomas Ruddiman publishes *The Ever Green, Being a Collection of Scots Poems, Wrote by the Ingenious Before 1600*
1724	Allan Ramsay's *Tea-Table Miscellany*
1724–7	Daniel Defoe's *Tour through the Whole Island of Great Britain*
1726	James Thomson's first major publication: *Winter*
1730	James Thomson's *The Seasons* is published
1739	David Hume's *Treatise on Human Nature*
1739	Formation of Black Watch Regiment
1739	*Scots Magazine* is first published
1741	David Hume's *Essays Moral and Political*
1745	Second major Jacobite rising. The Young Pretender, Charles Edward Stuart, is defeated at the Battle of Culloden in 1746
1745	Birth of Henry Mackenzie (d.1831)
1745	Birth of James Tytler (d.1804)
1746	Battle of Culloden on 16 April, where the Jacobites are defeated by the Duke of Cumberland's army
1748	David Hume's *An Enquiry Concerning Human Understanding*
1748	Tobias Smollett's *Roderick Random*
1750	Birth of Robert Fergusson (d.1774)

1751	Alexander MacDonald's *Aiseirigh na Seann Chànain Albannaich* [The Resurrection of the Old Scottish Language]
1756–63	The Seven Years' War
1758	Birth of James Thomson Callender (d.1803), author of *The Political Progress of Britain* (1792)
1759	Birth of Robert Burns (d.1796)
1759	Adam Smith's *Theory of Moral Sentiments*
1759	William Robertson's *History of Scotland 1542–1603*
1760	James Macpherson publishes *Fragments of Ancient Poetry Collected in the Highlands of Scotland and Translated from the Gallic or Erse Language*
1761	James Macpherson's *Fingal*
1763	Adam Smith's *Lectures on Jurisprudence*
1763	James Macpherson's *Temora*
1765	James Macpherson's *The Works of Ossian*
1766	Tobias Smollett's *Travels through France and Italy*
1766	Birth of Ulster-Scots poet Samuel Thomson (d.1816)
1766	Birth of Alexander Wilson (d.1813)
1767	Adam Ferguson's *Essay on the History of Civil Society*
1767	Dugald Buchanan's *Laoidhe Spioradail* [Hymns]
1768	Duncan Bàn MacIntyre's *Orain Ghaidhealach* [Gaelic Songs]
1769	Weavers in Fenwick, Ayrshire, found the first Co-operative Society in Britain
1770	Birth of James Hogg (d.1835)
1770	Birth of Ulster-Scots poet James Orr (d.1816)
1771	Birth of Walter Scott (d.1832)
1771	Henry Mackenzie's *The Man of Feeling*
1771	Tobias Smollett's *The Expedition of Humphry Clinker*

1773	Henry Mackenzie's *The Man of the World*
1773	James Boswell and Samuel Johnson tour the Scottish Highlands and Western Isles (August–November)
1776	Adam Smith's *An Inquiry into the Nature and Causes of the Wealth of Nations*
1776	American Declaration of Independence
1778	The Highland Society of London is created
1779	Birth of John Galt (d.1839)
1780	Burns founds the Tarbolton Batchelor's Club with his brother Gilbert
1783	Burns begins his *Commonplace Book*
1785	Birth of Jacob Grimm (d.1863)
1785	James Boswell's *Journal of a Tour to the Hebrides*
1786	Birth of Wilhelm Grimm (d.1859)
1786	Robert Burns's *Poems Chiefly in the Scottish Dialect* published at Kilmarnock
1786	For a period, Robert Burns contemplates going to Jamaica to work as book-keeper in the slave plantations
1787–1803	James Johnson's six-volume *Scots Musical Museum*
1788	Thomas Reid's *Essays on the Active Powers of the Human Mind*
1788	Henry Mackenzie's lecture on German literature to the Royal Society of Edinburgh on 21 April
1789–99	The French Revolution
1791	James Boswell's *The Life of Samuel Johnson, LL.D*
1791–9	The (first) *Statistical Account of Scotland*
1792–1827	Dugald Stewart's *Elements of the Philosophy of the Human Mind*
1792	Kenneth MacKenzie's *Òrain Ghaidhealach* [Gaelic Songs]

1792	'The Year of the Sheep' (*bliadhna nan caorach*) – a significant period of land struggle that preceded the onset of the Highland Clearances
1793–1818	George Thomson's *Select Collection of Original Scottish Airs*
1795	David Macpherson's edition of Andrew of Wyntoun's *Orgynale Cronykil of Scotland*
1798	United Irishmen Rebellion against the British crown
1799	Walter Scott translates Goethe's drama *Goetz of Berlichingen*
1800	James Currie publishes the first posthumous edition of Burns's poetry and correspondence
1800	John Leyden's *Journal of a Tour of the Highlands and Western Islands of Scotland*
1800	The second edition of Wordsworth and Coleridge's *Lyrical Ballads*, including Wordsworth's 'Preface'
1802	The foundation of the *Edinburgh Review*
1802	Scott's *Minstrelsy of the Scottish Border*
1803	Dorothy Wordsworth's *Recollections of a Tour Made in Scotland*
1804	Walter Scott's edition of *Sir Tristrem*
1804	David Irving's *The Lives of the Scotis* [sic] *Poets*
1805	Walter Scott's *The Lay of the Last Minstrel*
1806	Robert Jamieson's *Popular Ballads and Songs*
1808	Elizabeth Hamilton's *The Cottagers of Glenburnie*
1808–9	John Jamieson's *Etymological Dictionary of the Scottish Language*
1809	Thomas Campbell's *Gertrude of Wyoming*
1810	Walter Scott's *The Lady of the Lake*
1812	The Grimms' *Kinder- und Hausmärchen* first printed

1813	Wilhelm Grimm publishes three 'altschottische Lieder' with translations from Scott's *Minstrelsy* and from Robert Jamieson's *Popular Ballads and Songs*
1813	James Hogg's *The Queen's Wake*
1814	Walter Scott's *Waverley*
1814	Mary Brunton's *Discipline*
1814	Highland Clearances in Sutherland begin under the Duke of Sutherland's factor, Patrick Sellar
1815	Christian Johnstone's *Clan-Albin*
1815	Walter Scott's *Guy Mannering*
1816	Walter Scott's *The Antiquary* and *Old Mortality*
1817	*Blackwood's Magazine* founded
1818	Walter Scott's *Rob Roy* and *The Heart of Midlothian*
1818	Susan Ferrier's *Marriage*
1818	James Hogg's *The Brownie of Bodsbeck*
1818	Birth of Alexander McLachlan (d.1896)
1819	John Gibson Lockhart's *Peter's Letters to His Kinsfolk*
1819	Thomas Pringle's 'The Emigrant's Farewell'
1820	Walter Scott's *Ivanhoe* and *The Bride of Lammermoor*
1820	Thomas Brown's *Lectures on the Philosophy of the Human Mind*
1820	James Hogg's *Winter Evening Tales*
1820	Walter Scott's *The Monastery*
1821	John Galt's *Annals of the Parish*
1821	James Hogg's *The Three Perils of Man: War, Women and Witchcraft*
1822	John Galt's *The Provost*
1822	John Galt's *The Entail* and *Ringan Gilhaize*

1823	James Hogg's *The Three Perils of Woman: Love, Leasing and Jealousy*
1823	William Grant Stewart's *Popular Superstitions*
1824	Hogg's *The Private Memoirs and Confessions of a Justified Sinner*. An important edition introduced by André Gide is published in 1947
1824	Walter Scott's *Redgauntlet: A Tale of the Eighteenth Century*
1824	John Galt's *Rothelan*
1824	Birth of George MacDonald (d.1905)
1825	Walter Scott's *The Talisman*
1825–8	Thomas Crofton Croker's *Fairy Legends and Traditions of the South of Ireland* (three volumes)
1827	Thomas Hamilton's *The Youth and Manhood of Cyril Thornton*
1828	Birth of Margaret Oliphant (d.1897)
1829	James Hogg's *The Shepherd's Calendar*
1829	'The Canadian Boat-Song' is published; authorship is uncertain
1829–31	Norman MacLeod edits the Gaelic periodical *An Teachdaire Gàelach* [*The Courier of the Gaels*]
1830	John Galt's *Lawrie Todd or the Settlers in the Woods*
c. 1830s	Popular poetry anthologies such as *Whistle-Binkie* are first published
1831	John Galt's *Bogle Corbet*
1831	Walter Scott's *Count Robert of Paris* (unpublished in its original form until 2006)
1832	The first Reform Bill
1832	*Chambers's Edinburgh Journal* established
1832	James Hogg's *Altrive Tales*
1833–4	Thomas Carlyle's *Sartor Resartus*

1840–3	Norman MacLeod edits the Gaelic periodical *Cuairtear nan Gleann* [*The Tourist of the Glens*]
1841	Hugh Miller's *The Old Red Sandstone*
1842	Birth of Scottish-born Canadian poet James Anderson (d.1923)
1843	The Disruption of the Church of Scotland; the United Free Church is formed
1847	Hugh Miller's *First Impressions of England and Its People*
1849	Hugh Miller's *In the Footprints of the Creator*
1849	Margaret Oliphant's *Passages in the Life of Mrs Margaret Maitland*
1850	Birth of Robert Louis Stevenson (d.1894)
1854	Hugh Miller's autobiography, *My Schools and Schoolmasters*
1854	The Crimean War begins
1857	R. M. Ballantyne's *The Coral Island*
1857	E. B. Ramsay's *Reminiscences of Scottish Life and Character*
1857	David Livingstone's *Missionary Travels and Researches in South Africa*
1858	George MacDonald's *Phantastes*
1859	Charles Darwin's *The Origin of the Species by Natural Selection*
1859	Birth of S. R. Crockett (d.1914)
1859	Foundation of the National Gallery of Scotland
1860	Birth of J. M. Barrie (d.1937)
1860	David Pae's *Lucy, The Factory Girl: Or, The Secrets of the Tontine Close*
1861–76	Margaret Oliphant's 'The Chronicles of Carlingford'
1861	Foundation of the Royal Glasgow Institute of the Fine Arts

1863	Birth of Neil Munro (d.1930)
1863	Birth of Violet Jacob (d.1946)
1863	George MacDonald's *David Elginbrod*
1864	George MacDonald's *Adela Cathcart*
1865	George MacDonald's *Alec Forbes of Howglen*
1865	Margaret Oliphant's *A Son of the Soil*
1865	Alexander Smith's *A Summer in Skye*
1866	Birth of Marion Angus (d.1946)
1866	George Mills's *The Beggar's Benison*
1867	Matthew Arnold's *On the Study of Celtic Literature*
1868	George MacDonald's *Robert Falconer*
1871	William Alexander's *Johnny Gibb of Gushetneuk*
1871	William Black's *A Daughter of Heth*
1874	Birth of Robert Service (d.1958)
1874	Birth of Lewis Spence (d.1955)
1874	James B. V. Thomson's *The City of Dreadful Night*
1878	Robert Louis Stevenson's *An Inland Voyage*
1879	Robert Louis Stevenson's *Travels with a Donkey* and *Edinburgh: Picturesque Notes*
1879	George MacDonald's *Sir Gibbie*
1882	The formation of the Scottish Text Society
1882	The 'Battle of Braes' on Skye
1883	Robert Louis Stevenson's *Treasure Island*
1883	Margaret Oliphant's *Hester*
1884	Robert Louis Stevenson's *The Silverado Squatters*
1885	Robert Louis Stevenson's *The Dynamiter* (written with his wife, Fanny van der Grift Stevenson)

1886	Robert Louis Stevenson's *The Strange Case of Dr Jekyll and Mr Hyde* and *Kidnapped*
1886	Foundation of the Scottish Home Rule Association
1887	Birth of Edwin Muir (d.1959)
1887	Arthur Conan Doyle's *A Study in Scarlet*
1888	J. M. Barrie's *Auld Licht Idylls*
1889	J. M. Barrie's *A Window in Thrums*
1889	Robert Louis Stevenson's *The Master of Ballantrae*
1889	Arthur Conan Doyle's *Micah Clarke*
1890	Arthur Conan Doyle's *The Sign of Four*
1890	Robert Louis Stevenson and his wife, Fanny van der Grift Stevenson, settle permanently in Samoa
1890	Margaret Oliphant's *Kirsteen*
1890–1915	Scottish anthropologist J. G. Frazer publishes *The Golden Bough*
1891	Oscar Wilde's *The Picture of Dorian Gray*
1891	Arthur Conan Doyle's *The White Company*
1892	Robert Louis Stevenson's 'The Beach of Falesà' is serialised in the *Illustrated London News* through July and August
1892	Robert Louis Stevenson's *A Footnote to History*
1892	Birth of Christopher Murray Grieve ('Hugh MacDiarmid') (d.1978)
1892–1904	Jonathan G. MacKinnon edits the periodical *Mac Talla* in Sydney, Cape Breton
1894	S. R. Crockett's *The Raiders*
1894	Robert Louis Stevenson's *The Ebb-Tide*
1894	John Davidson's *Ballads and Songs*
1894	Ian Maclaren's *Beside the Bonnie Briar Bush*

1895	Robert Louis Stevenson's (posthumous) *The Amateur Emigrant*
1895	George MacDonald's *Lilith*
1895	Patrick Geddes writes of a 'Scots Renascence'
1895	Ian Maclaren's *The Days of Auld Langsyne*
1895	J. H. Millar coins 'kailyard' as a derogatory description of some recent Scottish fiction
1896	Robert Louis Stevenson's *The Weir of Hermiston*
1896	S. R. Crockett's *Cleg Kelly*
1896	J. M. Barrie's *Sentimental Tommy*
1897	Robert Louis Stevenson's *St Ives*
1897	Bram Stoker's *Dracula*
1898	Birth of William Soutar (d.1943)
1898	John Buchan's *John Burnet of Barns*
1899	Joseph Conrad's *Heart of Darkness*
1900	J. M. Barrie's *Tommy and Grizel*
1900	Margaret Oliphant's *A Beleaguered City*
1900	Charles Murray's *Hamewith*
1900	Formation of the Scottish Workers' Parliamentary Committee
1901	George Douglas Brown's *The House with the Green Shutters*
1901	The University of Edinburgh establishes the Chair in Scottish History and Palaeography
1902	Arthur Conan Doyle's *The Hound of the Baskervilles*
1902	Violet Jacob's *The Sheep-stealers*
1904	J. M. Barrie's *Peter Pan* is first staged
1906	Arthur Conan Doyle's *Sir Nigel*

1906	The formation of the Scottish Federation of Women's Suffrage Societies
1907	Birth of Hugh MacLellan (d.1990)
1907	Robert Service's *Songs of a Sourdough*
1908	Birth of Robert Garioch Sutherland (d.1981)
1908	Kenneth Grahame's *The Wind in the Willows*
1909	Glasgow School of Art, designed by Charles Rennie Mackintosh, is completed
1910	Birth of Norman MacCaig (d.1996)
1911	Birth of Sorley Maclean (Somhairle MacGill-Eain) (d.1996)
1912	Joseph Conrad's *The Secret Sharer*
1912	Arthur Conan Doyle's *The Lost World*
1913	The foundation of the Chair of Scottish History and Literature at the University of Glasgow
1913	Sir Compton MacKenzie's *Sinister Street*
1914	Neil Munro's *The New Road*
1914	The Outbreak of the First World War (1914–18)
1915	Violet Jacob's *Songs of Angus*
1915	Birth of Sydney Goodsir Smith (d.1975)
1915	John Buchan's *Thirty-Nine Steps*
1916	John Buchan's *The Power House* and *Greenmantle*
1916	Robert Service's *Rhymes of a Red Cross Man*
1916	The Easter Rising in Dublin
1918	Edwin Muir's *We Moderns* (published under the pseudonym Edward Moore)
1918	Birth of W. S. Graham (d.1986)
1918	Birth of Muriel Spark (d.2006)

1918	Armistice; the end of the First World War
1919	John Buchan's *Mr Standfast*
1919	The Treaty of Versailles is signed
1919	G. Gregory Smith's *Scottish Literature: Character and Influence*
1920	The Vernacular Circle of the London Robert Burns Club is set up
1920	Birth of Edwin Morgan (d.2010)
1921	Birth of George Mackay Brown (d.1996)
1922	Foundation of the British Broadcasting Company
1922	Mussolini forms fascist government in Italy
1922	Hugh MacDiarmid's 'The Watergaw' first published in the *Dunfermline Press*
1922	James Joyce's *Ulysses*
1922	J. G. Frazer's *The Golden Bough*
1922	John Buchan's *Huntingtower*
1923	Robert Service's *The Roughneck, A Tale of Tahiti*
1923	Christopher Murray Grieve's *Annals of the Five Senses*
1924	William Bolitho's *Cancer of Empire*
1924	Denis Saurat's article: 'Le Groupe de la Renaissance Écossaise'
1924	John Buchan's *The Three Hostages*
1924	Britain's first Labour government
1925	Hugh MacDiarmid's *Sangschaw*
1925	Birth of Iain Hamilton Finlay (d.2006)
1925	Foundation of the National Library of Scotland (formerly the Advocates Library, belonging to the Faculty of Advocates and founded in 1689)
1926	Hugh MacDiarmid's *Penny Wheep* and *A Drunk Man Looks at the Thistle*

1926	Birth of James K. Baxter (d.1972)
1926	John Buchan's *The Dancing Floor*
1927	John Buchan's *Witch Wood*
1928	Nan Shepherd's *The Quarry Wood*
1928	Foundation of the National Party of Scotland (NPS)
1928	Birth of Iain Crichton Smith (Iain Mac a' Ghobhainn) (d.1998)
1929	John Buchan's *The Courts of the Morning*
1930	Nan Shepherd's *The Weatherhouse*
1930	James Bridie's *The Anatomist*
1930	Catherine Carswell's *The Life of Robert Burns*
1931	Birth of Alice Munro
1931	Willa Muir's *Imagined Corners*
1931	Hugh MacDiarmid's *First Hymn to Lenin*
1931	Naomi Mitchison's *The Corn King and the Spring Queen*
1932	Fionn Mac Colla's *The Albannach*
1932	Lewis Grassic Gibbon's *Sunset Song*
1932	Edwin Muir's *Poor Tom*
1932	Robert Craig's *O People!*
1933	J. Leslie Mitchell's *Spartacus*
1933	Neil M. Gunn's *Sun Circle*
1933	William Soutar's *Seeds in the Wind*
1933	Hitler becomes German chancellor
1933	Lewis Grassic Gibbon's *Cloud Howe*
1934	Foundation of the Scottish National Party, following the merging of the National Party and the Scottish Party
1934	Birth of Chris Wallace-Crabbe

1934	Neil Gunn's *Butcher's Broom*
1934	Helen Cruickshank's *Up the Noran Water*
1934	Eric Linklater's *Magnus Merriman*
1934	Samuel McKechnie's *Prisoners of Circumstance*
1934	John Macnair Reid's *Homeward Journey*
1934	Dot Allan's *Hunger March*
1934	Lewis Grassic Gibbon's *Grey Granite*
1934	Hugh MacDiarmid's *Stony Limits and Other Poems*
1934	Hitler becomes Führer of Germany
1935	Edwin Muir's *Scottish Journey*
1935	William Soutar's *Poems in Scots*
1935	Alexander McArthur and H. Kingsley Long's *No Mean City*
1935	George Blake's *The Shipbuilders*
1936	James Barke's *Major Operation*
1936	Birth of Alistair MacLeod
1936	Edwin Muir's *Scott and Scotland: The Predicament of the Scottish Writer*
1937	Edward Shiels's *Gael Over Glasgow*
1937	Frederick Niven's *The Staff at Simson's*
1937	Neil Gunn's *Highland River*
1937	Ewen MacLachlan's translation of the *Iliad* into Gaelic is published (although it was finished by 1816)
1938	Birth of Les Murray
1939	James Joyce's *Finnegans Wake*
1939	The outbreak of the Second World War (1939–45)
1940	Hugh MacDiarmid's *Golden Treasury of Scottish Poetry*
1941	Neil Gunn's *The Silver Darlings*

1943	Hugh MacDiarmid's *Lucky Poet*
1943	Sorley Maclean's *Dain Do Eimhir agus Dain Eile/Poems to Eimhir and Other Poems*
1944	Neil Gunn's *The Green Isle of the Great Deep*
1946	Birth of Bill Manhire
1947	The Edinburgh International Festival is established
1947	Birth of Keri Hulme
1947	Naomi Mitchison's *The Bull Calves*
1947	Sydney Goodsir Smith's *Carotid Cornucopius*
1947	J. F. Henry's *Fernie Brae*
1948	Edward Gaitens's *Dance of the Apprentices*
1948	Sydney Goodsir Smith's *Under the Eildon Tree*
1948	F. R. Leavis's *The Great Tradition*
1951	The School of Scottish Studies established at the University of Edinburgh
1952	Edwin Morgan translates *Beowulf*
1954	William Soutar's *Diaries of a Dying Man*
1954	Muriel Spark received into the Roman Catholic Church
1955	Hugh MacDiarmid's *In Memoriam James Joyce*
1955	Alistair MacLean's *HMS Ulysses*
1956	James Kennaway's *Tunes of Glory*
1957	Ian Watt's *The Rise of the Novel*
1957	Muriel Spark's *The Comforters*
1957	Alistair MacLean's *The Guns of Navarone*
1958	Muriel Spark's *Robinson*
1958	Jessie Kesson's *The White Bird Passes*
1968	Robin Jenkins's *A Very Scotch Affair*
1958	Kurt Wittig's *The Scottish Tradition in Literature*

1959	Muriel Spark's *Memento Mori*
1960	Muriel Spark's *The Ballad of Peckham Rye* and *The Bachelors*
1961	George Davie, *The Democratic Intellect*
1961	Hugh MacDiarmid's *The Kind of Poetry I Want*
1961	Muriel Spark's *The Prime of Miss Jean Brodie*
1963	Muriel Spark's *The Girls of Slender Means*
1963	The series of letters exchanged between Scott and Jacob Grimm from 1814–15 is first printed
1963	*Studies in Scottish Literature* founded by G. Ross Roy in the United States
1963	Jessie Kesson's *Glitter of Mica*
1964	James Kennaway's *Household Ghosts*
1965	Maurice Lyndsay's anthology, *Modern Scottish Poetry*
1965	Iain Crichton Smith's *The Law and the Grace*
1965	Sydney Goodsir Smith's *Kynd Kittock's Land*
1965	Muriel Spark's *The Mandelbaum Gate*
1965	Alan Sharp's *A Green Tree in Gedde*
1966	Archie Hind's *Dear Green Place*
1966	Alistair MacLean's *When Eight Bells Toll*
1967	Alan Sharp's *The Wind Shifts*
1967	Edwin Morgan's *Emergent Poems*
1967	Establishment of the Scottish Arts Council
1968	Norman MacCaig's *Rings on a Tree*
1968	Iain Crichton Smith's *Consider the Lilies*
1968	Edwin Morgan's *The Second Life*
1968	Muriel Spark's *The Public Image*
1968	Gordon Williams's *From Scenes Like These*

1970	The Association for Scottish Literary Studies (ASLS) is formed
1970	Muriel Spark's *The Driver's Seat*
1971	Foundation of the Department of Scottish Literature at the University of Glasgow; the first of its kind in the world
1971	Muriel Spark's *Not to Disturb*
1972	Liz Lochhead's *Memo for Spring*
1972	George Mackay Brown's *Greenvoe*
1972	Bill Bryden's *Willie Rough*
1972	Gordon Williams's *Walk Don't Walk*
1972	George Friel's *Mr Alfred M. A.*
1973	Muriel Spark's *The Hothouse by the East River*
1974	Muriel Spark's *The Abbess of Crewe*
1974	John McGrath's *The Cheviot, the Stag and the Black Black Oil*
1975	William McIlvanney's *Docherty*
1976	Muriel Spark's *The Takeover*
1976	Donald Campbell's *The Jesuit*
1976	Roddy McMillan's *The Bevellers*
1977	Les Murray's 'Elegy for Angus Macdonald of Cnoclinn'
1977	Adam Smith Institute, founded by Madsen Pirie and Eamonn Butler
1977	William McIlvanney's *Laidlaw*
1978	Francis Russell Hart's *The Scottish Novel: A Critical Survey*
1978	Emma Tennant's *Bad Sister*
1979	Conservative Party under Margaret Thatcher wins the general election, beating the Labour government under James Callaghan, and repeals the Scotland Act

1979	Tom Nairn's *The Break-up of Britain*
1979	The devolution referendum fails
1979	Muriel Spark's *Territorial Rights*
1979	Robin Jenkins's *Fergus Lamont*
1981	Muriel Spark's *Loitering with Intent*
1981	Allan Massie's *The Death of Men*
1981	Alasdair Gray's *Lanark*
1982	Derick Thomson's *Creachadh na Clàrsaich: Collected Poems, 1940–80*
1982	Liz Lochhead's *Dreaming Frankenstein*
1983	William McIlvanney's *The Papers of Tony Veitch*
1984	Edwin Morgan's *Sonnets from Scotland*
1984	Kathleen Jamie's *The Queen of Sheba*
1984	Muriel Spark's *The Only Problem*
1984	Allan Massie's *One Night in Winter*
1984	Iain Banks's *The Wasp Factory*
1984	James Kelman's *The Busconductor Hines*
1984	Alasdair Gray's *1982 Janine*
1984	Frederic Lindsay's *Brond*
1984	Roderick Watson's *The Literature of Scotland*
1985	Carol Ann Duffy's *Standing Female Nude*
1985	Iain Banks's *Walking on Glass*
1985	James Kelman's *A Chancer*
1986	Allan Massie's *Augustus*
1986	Iain Banks's *The Bridge*
1987	Cairns Craig's four-volume edited set *The History of Scottish Literature*

1987	Liz Lochhead's *Mary Queen of Scots Got Her Head Chopped Off*
1987	Carol Ann Duffy's *Selling Manhattan*
1987	Ian Rankin's *Knots and Crosses*
1987–8	Four-volume *History of Scottish Literature* published by Aberdeen University Press
1988	Muriel Spark's A *Far Cry from Kensington*
1988	Iain Banks's *The Player of Games*
1989	Allan Massie's *A Question of Loyalties*
1989	Janice Galloway's *The Trick Is to Keep Breathing*
1989	James Kelman's *A Disaffection*
1989	Revolutions overthrow communism in Eastern Europe
1989	Frank Kuppner's *A Very Quiet Street*
1989	James Kelman's *A Disaffection*
1990	Alexander Broadie's *The Tradition of Scottish Philosophy*
1990	Duncan Macmillan's *Scottish Art*
1990	Carol Ann Duffy's *The Other Country*
1990	Muriel Spark's *Symposium*
1990	Frank Kuppner's *The Concussed History of Scotland*
1990	Brian McCabe's *The Other McCoy*
1990	Glasgow is named European City of Culture
1991	Elspeth Barker's *O Caledonia*
1991	Allan Massie's *Sins of the Father*
1991	William McIlvanney's *Strange Loyalties*
1991	Ian Rankin's *Hide and Seek*
1992	John Purser's *Scotland's Music*
1992	Alasdair Gray's *Poor Things*

1992   Robert Crawford's *Devolving English Literature* and *Talkies*

1992   Jeff Torrington's *Swing Hammer Swing!*

1993   Don Paterson's *Nil Nil*

1993   Irvine Welsh's *Trainspotting*

1993   Iain Banks's *Complicity*

1993   Ian Rankin's *The Black Book*

1994   Allan Massie's *The Ragged Lion*

1994   James Kelman's *How Late It Was, How Late* wins the Booker Prize

1994   Frank Kuppner's *Something Very Like Murder*

1994   Janice Galloway's *Foreign Parts*

1995   A. L. Kennedy's *So I Am Glad*

1995   Mel Gibson's *Braveheart* released

1995   Christopher Whyte's *Euphemia MacFarrigle and the Laughing Virgin*

1995   Separate Chair of Scottish Literature established at the University of Glasgow

1995   Quintin Jardine's *Skinner's Round*

1995   Val McDermid's *The Mermaids Singing*

1996   Muriel Spark's *Reality and Dreams*

1996   Irvine Welsh's *Marabou Stork Nightmares*

1996   Alan Warner's *Morvern Callar*

1996   Christopher Brookmyre's *Quite Ugly One Morning*

1997   Douglas Gifford and Dorothy McMillan's edited collection *A History of Scottish Women's Writing*

1997   Don Paterson's *God's Gift to Women*

1997   Frederic Lindsay's *Kissing Judas*

1997   Ian Rankin's *Black and Blue*

1997	Scottish Devolution Referendum
1998	The establishment of Scotland's devolved parliament via the Scotland Act
1998	Jackie Kay's *Trumpet*
1998	Denise Mina's *Garnethill*
1998	Publication of *The Triumph Tree: Scotland's Earliest Poetry AD 550–1350* edited by Thomas Owen Clancy
1999	Election of new Scottish parliament
1999	Alistair MacLeod's *No Great Mischief*
1999	Andrew O'Hagan's *Our Fathers*
2000	Robert Crawford and Mich Imlah's *The New Penguin Book of Scottish Verse*
2000	James Robertson's *The Fanatic*
2000	Denise Mina's *Exile*
2001	Denise Mina's *Resolution*
2002	Christopher Brookmyre's *The Sacred Art of Stealing*
2004	Muriel Spark's *Aiding and Abetting* and *The Finishing School*
2004	Suhayl Saadi's *Psychoraag*
2004	Edwin Morgan is named by the parliament as the official Scots 'Makar'
2005	Denise Mina's *The Field of Blood*
2006	Andrew Lindsay's *Illustrious Exile*
2006	Alice Munro's *The View from Castle Rock*
2006	Foundation of the Scottish National Theatre
2006	First performance of Gregory Burke's *Black Watch*
2007	Ian Rankin's *Exit Music*
2007	The three-volume *Edinburgh History of Scottish Literature* is published by Edinburgh University Press

2007	For the first time in its history, the Scottish National Party is elected to government in Scotland
2008	The establishment of the University of Edinburgh's Scottish Centre for Diaspora Studies
2008	Mick Imlah's *The Lost Leader*
2010	James Robertson's *And the Land Lay Still*
2011	The Scottish National Party becomes the first party to win an overall majority in the Scottish Parliament

GERARD CARRUTHERS AND LIAM MCILVANNEY

Introduction

The temptation to tell, not just a history but the 'story' of Scottish literature has often been a strong one. Three watershed dates – 1560, 1603 and 1707 – invite us to plot the trajectory of Scottish literature against the nation's mutating constitutional status. The Protestant Reformation, the Union of the Crowns and the Union of the Parliaments: There is a sense in which each of these events represents a realignment and, arguably, an impairment of native cultural identity. Taken together, these events have been read as staging posts on a process of regrettable Anglicization in post-medieval Scotland. Alternatively, this timeline can be presented more positively as the story of Scotland's growing 'modernity', the emergence of a peripheral European nation into the embracing lingua franca of English. The complex arguments that swirl around Scotland's historical 'losses' and 'gains' are often coloured by particular political and cultural perspectives. We might ask, however, if these events necessarily lend themselves to one singular, overarching conclusive cultural interpretation. The Reformation has been read, most famously by twentieth-century poet Edwin Muir, as promoting an 'alien' English language and relegating Scots to a congeries of dialects.[1] For Muir, this linguistic catastrophe forecloses the possibility of an integrated, nationally confident 'Scottish literature' worthy of the name. But does a national literature require a national language? What makes a 'regional' dialect unfit for literature? Muir bemoans the cultural depredations of Calvinism but ignores the vital new prose tradition that emerges with John Knox. Alongside Knox, we might class David Lyndsay, James VI, William Drummond of Hawthornden, James Thomson, Robert Burns, Walter Scott, James Hogg, Margaret Oliphant, Robert Louis Stevenson, Hugh MacDiarmid and Muriel Spark as writers whose works are informed by the ethos and theology of Scottish Presbyterianism. Are these writers simply to be dismissed, by the inevitable logic of Muir's position, as a wrong turn in the river?

What haunts Edwin Muir, a critical follower of the ideas of T. S. Eliot, is the idea of a 'national tradition' in which literary and cultural lines remain continuous or unbroken through history. In the twenty-first century, we are more comfortable with the idea of discontinuities, of a plurality of 'traditions' rather than a singular 'tradition'. That a Catholic tradition – involving writers like William Dunbar, Alexander Geddes, Compton Mackenzie, Fionn Mac Colla, George Mackay Brown and (once again) Muriel Spark – co-exists and commingles with the Protestant tradition is an index of vitality, not of debilitating division. This brings us to another question: Need a literary culture have a solid 'centre', whatever that might be? Might it not be the case that cultures operate with a warp and woof, through debate and dialogue, and across contested rather than settled identities? In recent years, literary critics, in Scotland as elsewhere, have warned against 'essentialism', or taking a dogmatic line on what constitutes a culture and the criteria for belonging to a culture. Nevertheless, when it comes to Scottish literature (as with any other literature qualified by a national prefix) the problematic question of belonging or 'canonicity' inevitably arises. How are we to define 'Scottish literature'?

A relaxed and inclusive understanding of Scottish literature's canon is an observable late twentieth-century phenomenon. In 1998 there appeared an anthology, *The Triumph Tree: Scotland's Earliest Poetry AD 550–1350*, edited by Thomas Owen Clancy.[2] Including translations of texts originally written in Gaelic, Latin, Norse, Old English, Welsh and Scots, this anthology teaches us about a 'Scottish literature before Scottish literature', an idea developed by Clancy in his chapter in the present volume. Clancy reminds us of the relative latecoming of the Scots language to the Scottish cultural scene and of the long geographical uncertainty of 'Scotland'. Before these things began to take modern national, even 'nationalist', shape in the medieval period, what we now call Scotland had a very different if nonetheless rich creative literature. The dominant pre-twelfth-century language of Scotland, Gaelic, belongs, with its literature, to an Irish-Scottish world that straddles the North Channel. Its texts are 'Irish' as well as 'Scottish'. In other words, Gaelic is part of 'Scottish' cultural heritage but its full historical story transcends 'Scotland'.

The homogenization of language, literature and nation, it might be contended, can be traced as a serious project to the medieval period. Alessandra Petrina draws attention in the present volume to the dating by some critics of medieval Scottish literature's beginning to John Barbour's *The Bruce* (1375). She points to around 140 years from this moment, lasting until Gavin Douglas's *Eneados* (1513) where, undoubtedly, strong continuity features. We might say that this continuity is both constructed to some extent but is also natural, in the sense that successful Scottish literature clearly was inspiring subsequent texts or tradition. This period of the Scots 'Makars' sees a literature written in Middle Scots that is formally and thematically dynamic and in dialogue with the literatures of England, France and the ancient classical world. Douglas's experimental adaptation of Virgil's *Aeneid* along with Robert Henryson's new – and in many ways re-written – version of Aesop's *Fables*, show Scotland 'writing back' confidently to the centre of classical civilisation. Within this internationalism, however, we need to be aware of Scottish literature from the fourteenth century staking out distinctively national territory. Barbour's *Bruce* is one of several medieval Scots epics celebrating resistance to English military incursions. In 1314, King Robert the Bruce had defeated the English at the Battle of Bannockburn, a decisively successful event that led to the drafting of the Declaration of Arbroath in 1320. This was an address in Latin from the nobility of Scotland to the Pope suggesting that the Holy Father should recognise Scotland as an ancient and venerable nation, implicitly rejecting English claims to suzerainty.[3] Again, we see Scotland writing to the centre of civilization (in this case Roman Christianity).

Bruce's grandson, King Robert II, enthroned in a safer Scottish kingdom than his grandfather had experienced, awarded Barbour £10 in recognition of his nationalist epic. Here, in a quite direct way, we see literature involved in what might be called nation building. Barbour's *The Bruce*, written in Scots, implicitly transposes the struggle between Christian Crusaders and Muslims into the battle between righteous Scots and barbarous Englishmen. In drawing on conventions of romance and chivalry, as well as the epic mode in general, *The Bruce* asserts, as did the Declaration of Arbroath, that the Scots are a cultured and civilized people. At the same time, it propagates the martial myth of the 'fighting Scot', the freedom-loving 'barbarian' who will resist colonization even against overwhelming odds. The Declaration of Arbroath had made great play of the resistance to Roman conquest by a tribe of north Britons under the leadership of Calgacus, chief of the Caledonii in the first century AD; it is an idea also to the fore in Mel Gibson's hugely popular film *Braveheart* (1995), celebrating that other great iconic fighting hero, William Wallace. These competing versions of Scotland and Scottish literature – civilized and primitive – recur many times in the post-medieval period.[4]

Gavin Douglas's *Aeneid*, a virtuoso performance of Scots-language poetic craftsmanship in dialogue with classical literature of the ancient world, might be seen to represent the high watermark of medieval Scottish literary confidence. It was written, however, in 1513, the year of the disastrous Battle of Flodden where the English routed the Scots, killing James IV and the flower of the Scottish nobility. In enmity and friendship, Scotland historically has felt the powerful pull of England. If Flodden did not completely bring Scotland into the orbit of her southern neighbour, the Reformation a few decades later in the sixteenth century certainly did, as newly Calvinist

Scots jettisoned the 'Auld Alliance' with France in favour of closer ties with Protestant England. If this 'British' development countermanded a fully independent Scottish culture, another important cultural transformation was presenting itself. Under the leadership of John Knox, the Scottish Reformation was iconoclastic and puritanical, relegating 'profane' literature to a status far beneath the word of God. As a result of this Calvinist mentality, the reformers of Scotland were more hostile to drama than in many other places and so Edwin Muir has a point when he laments the stunted nature of the Scottish theatrical tradition from the sixteenth to the eighteenth century, especially when compared to England. We also see notorious censorship and bowdlerization in *The Gude and Godlie Ballatis* (1567), in which three reform-minded brothers, the Wedderburns, adapt Scottish folksongs and other ballads, shoehorning into these texts allegorical religious readings that evacuate any profane, worldly, bodily concerns. As Sarah Dunnigan observes in this volume, Scotland's break with European Catholicism is decisive, and it should be pointed out too that Scotland's Presbyterian Reformation is more radical than that experienced by England which maintains a church of Episcopal authority. While it marginalizes secular poetry, The Scottish Reformation gives rise to an intense kind of Protestant devotional poetry in the later sixteenth century, exemplified by Alexander Hume. In recent years, revisionist commentators have 'reclaimed' not only the prose writings of John Knox for Scottish literature, but the positive qualities of the intellectual trajectories initiated by the Reformation, which might be seen to feed into the achievement of the Scottish Enlightenment and other later periods of Scottish culture.[5] There is no doubt, however, that the cultural legacy of the Scottish Reformation remains a focus of intense controversy.

Traditionally, Scotland's seventeenth century has been viewed as a cultural wasteland. Hard on the heels of the Reformation, the Union of Crowns of 1603, when James VI of Scotland moved south to become James I of England, represents for many a further erosion of Scottish culture. While in Scotland, James's royal court provided a sanctuary for the 'profane' arts menaced by militant Calvinism. The latest in a line of artistically minded Stuart sovereigns, James authored fine sonnets and *The Essayes of a Prentise in the Divine Arte of Poesie* (1584). In James's absence, it has been argued, Scotland's 'Renaissance' is more fleeting and less fruitful than elsewhere in Europe. Perhaps this is part of the reason, as Sarah Dunnigan suggests, that the term is applied somewhat anachronistically to Scotland in the 1920s when the French critic, Denis Saurat, appropriates the term to label the poetic 'revival' led by Hugh MacDiarmid. Recent revisionist criticism has suggested that Scotland's sixteenth- and seventeenth-century Renaissance was more significant than some previous narratives attest, but it is undoubtedly true that the term 'Scottish Renaissance' denotes a twentieth-century phenomenon.

A key question arises in the twenty-first century to countervail the critical narrative of seventeenth-century absence: Did Scottish literature require a resident monarch in order to prosper? There is no doubt that literature flourished under James VI. There is no doubt, too, that the nation's literary culture was deeply affected by the fact that so many Scottish writers and artists migrated to London with James, and so we have here the diagnosis of a phenomenon that is marked throughout Scottish literary history: the migration, to England or to further afield, of the Scottish writer. James Thomson, James Boswell, Thomas Carlyle, Robert Louis Stevenson, Muriel Spark, W. S. Graham, Douglas Dunn, Alastair Reid, Andrew O' Hagan: The list of 'exiled' Scottish writers is a long one. Is the work of these individuals any less Scottish, however, due to their non-residence? Might we think not of a 'native' culture, but instead of a migratory, diasporic Scottish literary culture, embracing England, Ireland, America, Canada, South Africa, Australia, New Zealand and elsewhere (discussed in its furthest flung vestiges by Gerard Carruthers in Chapter 19)?

If anything, Scottish criticism has been less suspicious about Scottish literature overseas (the spreading of Scottish culture) than it has been about Scottish literature in England (the recession of Scottish culture). How can Scottish literature seemingly be decanted with relative ease to New Zealand, but not to England? The answer of course lies in the 'British problem', the notion that to succeed in England, Scottish writers compromise their Scottishness. This is why a poet like James Thomson, whose *The Seasons* (1726–30) is one of the most influential landscape texts across the European arts for a century and a half, is seldom taught in courses on Scottish literature. Many of the other writers listed here also struggle to hold their place in the canon of Scottish writing. Muriel Spark, perhaps the most critically and commercially successful Scottish writer of the twentieth century, is far from being accepted, one of her senior Scottish contemporaries, the novelist Robin Jenkins, going so far as to claim that it is 'very difficult … to accept' Spark as 'Scottish'.[6] But why shouldn't Scottish writers cater for an audience beyond their home country? Why shouldn't they write about non-Scottish things, or rather more generally human things? Few critics would be willing to stipulate that Scottish writers should confine themselves to Scottish subjects, but the sometimes begrudging recognition of a Thomson or a Spark seems to proceed from such an assumption.

A long line of Scottish criticism has tended to look witheringly on the slide towards Britishness facilitated by the Reformation, the Union of Crowns and, most crucially, the Union of Parliaments. The year 1707 supposedly cements and spreads what David Daiches calls the Scottish 'crisis of identity', or what David Craig refers to as an 'alienation from things native', as witnessed by everything from David Hume's anxious purging of 'Scotticisms' from his prose to the construction of Edinburgh's neoclassical New Town.[7] A split or bifurcation is diagnosed in Scottish literary culture between the languages of Scots and English, which is harmful to both sides: Authentic Scots-language literature is ghettoized, starved of a fuller, nourishing culture; neoclassical, English-language literature in Scotland is also undernourished, being too synthetic or programmatic, the result of attempts by 'enlightened' Scots to force too rapidly a cosmopolitan culture on the nation. The result is a literature that lurches between a robust but often bluff and rude demotic (as in the songs and epistles of Robert Burns) and a sterile, etiolated gentility (as in Henry Mackenzie's mannered *Man of Feeling*, 1771).

Such texts have been read as markers of a fractured, deviant, 'neurotic' culture. A little earlier in the eighteenth century, James Macpherson's 'Ossian' poetry (1760–2) inscribes in Scottish literature an attempt at cultural engineering that is inauthentic to the extent of forgery. Around the Ossian texts, a notorious literary dispute arose between activists of the Scottish Enlightenment including David Hume and England's foremost man of letters, Samuel Johnson. Hume, at least initially, endorsed Macpherson's claim to be disinterring and translating into English the genuine remains of old poetic texts in 'Erse' or Gaelic, dealing with ancient, pre-Christian warriors in the northwest part of Scotland. Johnson gleefully cried fraud. Whatever the precise truth of the Ossian texts, and the debate is not completely over today (though Macpherson was probably more creator than archaeologist of the texts), these poems, as much as Thomson's *The Seasons*, played a huge part in the European artistic imagination for at least a century following their appearance. Foreshadowing Romanticism, the Ossian texts popularised romantic landscape and sublime emotion, portraying the Celt as primitive noble savage. Despite this, there have been critics – perhaps regarding Macpherson as one of the 'sham bards of a sham nation', in Muir's description of Burns and Scott – who question the very existence of an authentic Scottish Romanticism. Given the global impact of Macpherson, Burns and Scott, however, we might be less concerned with authenticity than with appraising the achievement and legacy of these writers. As Murray Pittock also shows in the present volume, the idea of the Enlightenment and Romanticism standing in outright opposition to one another is an overdetermined critical binary that ought to be confined to the past. As Pittock points out, the universalism of the Enlightenment (its civilized cosmopolitan outlook) exists with reference to its observation of particularism (the local and even the primitive), the latter feature being a powerful motor of Romanticism. Dialogues about past and present, less developed and more sophisticated societies, are the concern of both Enlightenment and Romanticism in Scotland, as Pittock exemplifies through a reading of *Rob Roy* (1817) by Walter Scott, a writer who breathes deeply the cultural air of both milieux.

The opening poem in Robert Burns's first volume of verse, *Poems, Chiefly in the Scottish Dialect* (1786), features a talking dog named Luath in allusion to Macpherson's Ossian poems. Burns's dog speaks Scots, not Gaelic, and Burns's poem nicely illustrates something of the plural cultural valency of Macpherson's poetry. Published in English, expressing a Gaelic sensibility, promoted by Scottish Enlightenment intellectuals and adapted by vernacular poets, Macpherson's Ossian poetry attests to the inter-connection of Scotland's literatures and languages. While *The Cambridge Companion to Scottish Literature* devotes a separate chapter to 'The Gaelic Tradition', we are conscious that Gaelic literature has developed in dialogue with – and not in isolation from – literature in English and Scots. As Peter Mackay shows in Chapter 8, the first secular publication in Scottish Gaelic, Alexander MacDonald's *Aiseirigh na Seann Chànain Albannaich* (1751), contains translations from the Scots of Allan Ramsay as well as poems in conscious emulation of Thomson's *The Seasons*. Similarly, the spiritual poems of Dugald Buchanan, as in his *Laoidhe Spioradail* (1767), draw on Robert Blair and James Thomson as well as on the hymns of Isaac Watts. Later, in the twentieth-century Scottish Literary Renaissance and its aftermath, Gaelic literature and sensibilities would inflect the Scots verse of Hugh MacDiarmid and the limpid English lyrics of Norman MacCaig. As Mackay observes, 'Gaelic isolationism' is in short supply in a poetry that has from the first been involved in processes of translation and adaptation; instead, we have to do with a 'tradition of cultural negotiation, flexibility and relocation'.

The same suppleness can be witnessed in nineteenth-century Scottish literature, including Edinburgh's emergence as perhaps the world's most important metropolitan centre of periodical culture and the nation's remarkable output of short stories and novels by Walter Scott, John Galt, James Hogg and others. As Ian Duncan shows in Chapter 7, these writers are at the cutting edge of a radically new kind of anthropological 'fiction open to the intellectual currents of the age: including those that were breaking up the historical novel's philosophical foundation'. The Victorian period in Scottish literature and culture was for many years disparaged as an age of stultification and dearth, a long, dull diminuendo in which Scottish writers turned their backs on the new industrial realities and cultivated the bucolic inanities of 'cabbage-patch' fiction, if they didn't – as in the case of Thomas Carlyle and other 'exiled' writers – turn their backs on Scotland itself. In recent years, this picture has been revised, partly by the recovery of previously neglected bodies of work such as the vigorous tradition of vernacular newspaper fiction uncovered by the research of William Donaldson or the oeuvres of Victorian women writers like Margaret Oliphant and Jane Carlyle, and partly by reassessments of the extant canon, as in the partial rehabilitation of the 'Kailyard' fiction of J. M. Barrie, S. R. Crockett and Ian Maclaren. Moreover, the contention that Scotland's Enlightenment wanes in the years after 1830 has been challenged by Cairns Craig, whose work has recovered the Scottish contexts and currents in the philosophy of Sir William Hamilton and Edward Caird, the psychology of Alexander Bain, the thermodynamics of William Thomson (Lord Kelvin), the mathematical physics of James Clerk Maxwell and the social anthropology of William Robertson Smith and J. G. Frazer. Not only does this intellectual ferment amount to a 'second Scottish Enlightenment', it palpably impinges on fictions like George MacDonald's *Phantastes* (1858), Robert Louis Stevenson's *Jekyll and Hyde* (1886) and J. M. Barrie's *Peter Pan* (1906).[8] In Chapter 10, Andrew Nash interrogates the work of these writers, while also pointing to the significance of Victorian Scotland's poets of urban life, from Alexander Smith to James Thomson and John Davidson to which a renewed Scottish criticism ought to attend.

Far from ignoring modernity, Scotland's writers have made it one of their most vital concerns. The new industrial city is tackled by urban novelists from Scott to Kelman, as Liam McIlvanney shows in Chapter 15. A 'global consciousness of modernity' defines the work of Robert Louis Stevenson, as presented by Penny Fielding in Chapter 11. Of course, resistance to narratives of modernity has also characterised a strain in Scottish writing, one that insists on bringing back to disquieting life the conflicts and preoccupations of bygone ages. As David Punter shows in Chapter 9, this Scottish Gothic strain has provided a psychological scepticism in the face of the 'progress' of Scotland, and of the world, to the extent that 'if we were to search for an antonym to Gothic, it would not be realism but modernity'.

A conscious swithering between realism and fantasy, between the modern and the archaic is central to the poetry of Hugh MacDiarmid, the towering figure of twentieth-century Scottish literature and prime mover in the inter-war Risorgimento known as the Scottish Literary Renaissance. Scott Lyall's chapter takes advantage of recent advances in MacDiarmid scholarship (including the ongoing Carcanet edition of his writings and the greatly expanded body of letters and correspondence) to offer a fresh assessment of MacDiarmid's achievement. The chapter presents a MacDiarmid who is recognizably modernist (in his localism and materialism, his preoccupation with psychology and his perception of the act of poetry as 'deriving entirely from words') and at the same time distinctly conservative (in a verbal and formal archaism that takes us 'Back to Dunbar!'). We find a hugely ambitious 'project' in MacDiarmid's voluminous writings, from the early Scots lyrics and ballads, through the heterogeneous philosophical epic *A Drunk Man Looks at the Thistle* (1926) to the later modernist experiments in 'synthetic English'. MacDiarmid's importance as a cultural activist and provocateur is second to none in twentieth-century Scotland. Though Norman MacCaig described him as a 'torchlight procession of one', however, MacDiarmid was not the only significant writer of the period. MacDiarmid had precursors in the field of vernacular Scots poetry (including Charles Murray, Violet Jacob, Marion Angus and Helen Cruickshank), as well as successors in the 'Second Wave' of Scottish Renaissance poetry (William Soutar, Sydney Goodsir Smith and Robert Garioch). MacDiarmid's belief that poetry was the superior literary genre notwithstanding, the twentieth-century renaissance is also a fertile site of literary fiction, from the experimental vernacular narratives of Leslie Mitchell ('Lewis Grassic Gibbon') to the epic mythopoeia of Neil Gunn and Naomi Mitchison and the regional novels of Nan Shepherd and Willa Muir. We might also note various forms of resistance to the 'Renaissance' project, for instance in the comic scepticism of Eric Linklater, who lampoons the Scottish Renaissance in his 1934 satire *Magnus Merriman*, and in Edwin Muir, whose doubts over Scots as a viable literary language in *Scott and Scotland* (1936) prompted a famously bitter spat with MacDiarmid.

MacDiarmid's campaign for 'synthetic Scots', though it facilitated the first and second waves of the Scottish Literary Renaissance, grew less central, not merely to the poetry of MacDiarmid himself, but to that of the younger poets who emerged in the 1960s and 1970s. Scottish poets found they could be comfortably Scottish in any or all of Scotland's three indigenous languages. But whether writing in English, Scots or Gaelic, Scottish poets of the 1960s and 1970s shared with MacDiarmid a perception of language as embodied worldview, and a sense of the poetic act as finding its origin in language. Edwin Morgan, the most eclectic, energetic and experimental of the post-MacDiarmid Scottish poets, takes language as his subject and starting point in his concrete poetry, his 'sound' poetry, his 'emergent' poems and in his copious translations (from Russian, Hungarian and French, among other languages). Iain Crichton Smith (Iain Mac a' Ghobhainn), writing metaphysical poetry of the highest order in both English and Gaelic, explores his perception that 'we are born inside a language and see everything from within its parameters: it is not we who make language, it is language that makes us'. Crichton Smith's perception is shared by poets as diverse as Norman MacCaig and Tom Leonard. We might argue, then, that W. S. Graham's query – 'What is the language using us for?' – not only anticipates the insights of structuralism, but articulates the common sense of poets writing in a country with three mother tongues.

In the past three decades, Scotland has witnessed a remarkable literary resurgence. New modes of urban writing, working-class writing and women's writing have altered the landscape of Scottish literature. Much of the energy of this new mood has been political. 'POLITICS WILL NOT LEAVE ME ALONE' complains the protagonist of Alasdair Gray's novel, *1982 Janine* (1984). It would be truer to say of contemporary Scottish writers that they will not leave politics alone, and the renaissance of Scottish writing has been bound up, in complex ways, with the country's successful progress towards constitutional change. In the 1970s, the assertive Scottishness of Alan Spence, Liz Lochhead, John Byrne and others accompanied the rise to electoral respectability of the Scottish National Party. The failure of political autonomy (in the abortive Scotland Act of 1978, defeated in a controversial referendum) proved the catalyst for a 'declaration of cultural autonomy', as Scottish literature entered a phase of unprecedented vigour and accomplishment. A Scottish resistance to the 'alien' values of the Thatcher administration was asserted, as much in the novels and poems of the period as in the overt political activism of writers like James Kelman, William McIlvanney and Alasdair Gray. Surveying Scottish fiction of the 1980s and 1990s, Irish novelist Colm Tóibín argued that Scottish novels were being written, 'as in Ireland in the old days, to replace a nation'. This is true of the vernacular fiction of Kelman, Galloway and Welsh, the 'agitprop ceilidhs' produced by theatre companies like 7:84 and Wildcat, the politicized Gothic of Iain Banks and Emma Tennant, the topical detective fiction of Ian Rankin and the nationally attuned poetry of Edwin Morgan, Robert Crawford, Douglas Dunn and Kathleen Jamie.

The 1980s also saw a rejection of the rhetoric of deformity and fragmentation that until then had been the house style of Scottish cultural analysis. Scottish culture (and the very phrase risked oxymoron) was viewed as shattered, fissured, radically split – between Scottishness and Britishness, emotion and intellect, Highland and Lowland, Scots and standard English. A culture with such deep linguistic and cultural fault lines appeared hopelessly incoherent. It couldn't begin to express what Edwin Muir called 'a whole and unambiguous nationality'. From Edwin Muir in the 1930s to Tom Nairn in the 1970s, this vision of Scottish cultural debility held more or less undisputed sway. It began to be challenged from the late 1980s by a group of Edinburgh-based academics and commentators, whose ranks included Craig Beveridge, Ronald Turnbull, David McCrone, Lindsay Paterson and Cairns Craig. For these writers, the 'divided' state of Scottish culture was entirely commonplace, and it was the model of an 'organic', homogenous national culture that must be questioned. This model was inappropriate not just to Scottish but to Irish, American, Caribbean culture. If Scottish culture lacked coherence, then it was keeping distinguished company. As a result of this revisionist drive, the cultural fragmentation earlier writers deplored was recast throughout the 1980s and 90s as vital, invigorating diversity. Scotland's congeries of languages and cultures was now the strength not the weakness of its writing. It is no coincidence that, throughout this period, fragmented dialects and regional sub-cultures formed the basis of some of the nation's most successful fiction, in the work of James Kelman, Irvine Welsh, Alan Warner, Duncan McLean and others. A new cultural buzz-word – Scotlands – celebrated this pluralism and signalled the demise of any attempt to forge a coherent, unitary national identity.

Among the 'Scotlands' celebrated in this new dispensation, not much attention has been devoted to the 'Scotlands beyond our national boundaries, yet which construct their own Scotlands that in turn influence our state', which might include 'the Scotlands of … the descendants of those cleared from the Highlands, the Scotlands of Australia and New Zealand'.[9] Mass emigration is one of the definitive aspects of the modern Scottish experience. In that massive nineteenth-century exodus from the Old World to the New, Scotland played a disproportionate part. Between the 1820s and the Second World War, around 2.3 million Scots emigrated. Literature – in the form of novels and poems and stories and songs – has been central to the diaspora, both as a link to 'home' and a means for emigrant Scots to negotiate their changing relationships to the 'imagined communities' of the Old World and the New. And yet, despite the international rise of diaspora studies over the past two decades and the emergence of important works of historiography exploring the Scottish exodus, there has been little engagement with the literary productions of the diaspora. This may be changing. The recent three-volume *Edinburgh History of Scottish Literature* (2007) contains a suggestive chapter on 'Scotland's Literature of Empire and Emigration', and the establishment of the University of Edinburgh's Scottish Centre for Diaspora Studies in 2008, together with new Scottish studies centres in Canada and New Zealand, suggests that the present institutional condition of Scottish studies is an international as well as a national concern. The 'Diasporic Imagination' is a wide and fruitful field, involving not just the study of émigré Scottish writers (Stevenson in Samoa, Carlyle in London, Spark in Italy), but the excavation of a Scottish dimension in the work of Irish, North American and Australasian writers of Scottish descent. One might look at the ways in which poets from the north of Ireland – James Orr, Samuel Thomson, Hugh Porter – have used the idiom and stanza forms of the Scottish vernacular tradition.[10] One might equally explore the discourse of 'Highlandism' in the novels of Hugh MacLennan and Alistair MacLeod in Canada, or Alice Munro's fictionalized border history in *The View from Castle Rock* (2006), or the Scottish preoccupations of

Les Murray in Australia and James K. Baxter in New Zealand. In discussing these writers, the challenge is to avoid the kind of glib appropriation perpetrated by Hugh MacDiarmid when he claimed 'Hermann [*sic*] Melville, an American Scot' and 'T. S. Eliot – it's a Scottish name' – as Scottish writers.[11] Instead, we need to establish how Scottish idiom, forms, history and mythology have been adapted and customized in works that belong to more than one national literature. In the very first Scottish novel, Tobias Smollett has Lieutenant Lismahago observe that the 'spirit of rambling and adventure has been always peculiar to the natives of Scotland'; the same spirit is most certainly now abroad in the field of Scottish studies.[12]

Notes

1 Edwin Muir, *Scott and Scotland: The Predicament of the Scottish Writer* (1936; repr. Edinburgh: Polygon, 1982), p. 72.

2 Thomas Owen Clancy (ed.), *The Triumph Tree: Scotland's Earliest Poetry AD 550–1350* (Edinburgh: Canongate, 1998).

3 A translation of the Declaration of Arbroath and other historical documents of pertinence to Scottish literary studies can be found in the very useful volume edited by Gordon Donaldson, *Scottish Historical Documents* (Glasgow: Neil Wilson Publishing, 1974).

4 For extended discussion of the repeated tropes of civilisation and primitivism, see Gerard Carruthers, *Scottish Literature: A Critical Guide* (Edinburgh: Edinburgh University Press, 2009).

5 A good starting point for considering this issue is to be found in the collection edited by Crawford Gribben and David George Mullan, *Literature and the Scottish Reformation* (Aldershot: Ashgate, 2009).

6 See 'A Truthful Scot', interview with Robin Jenkins by Inga Agustdóttir, *In Scotland* (Autumn 1999), p. 13.

7 See David Daiches, *The Paradox of Scottish Culture: The Eighteenth Century Experience* (London: Oxford University Press, 1964), pp. 21–35 and throughout; David Craig, *Scottish Literature and the Scottish People 1680–1830* (London: Chatto & Windus, 1961), p. 63.

8 Cairns Craig, *Intending Scotland: Explorations in Scottish Culture since the Enlightenment* (Edinburgh: Edinburgh University Press, 2009), pp. 77–144.

9 Robert Crawford, 'Bakhtin and Scotlands', *Scotlands*, 1 (1994), pp. 56–7.

10 Liam McIlvanney, 'Across the Narrow Sea: The Language, Literature and Politics of Ulster Scots', in Liam McIlvanney and Ray Ryan (eds.), *Ireland and Scotland: Culture and Society, 1700–2000* (Dublin: Four Courts, 2005), pp. 203–26.

11 Hugh MacDiarmid, 'Scotland and Europe', in *The Raucle Tongue: Hitherto Uncollected Prose*, ed. Angus Calder, Glen Murray and Alan Riach (Manchester: Carcanet, 1997), vol. II, p. 371; *A Drunk Man Looks at the Thistle*, in *Selected Poetry*, ed. Alan Riach and Michael Grieve (Manchester: Carcanet, 1992), p. 37, line 345.

12 Tobias Smollett, *The Expedition of Humphry Clinker*, ed. Lewis M. Knapp, 2nd edn, ed. Paul-Gabriel Boucé (Oxford: Oxford University Press, 1984), p. 277.

I

THOMAS CLANCY

Scottish Literature before Scottish Literature

Knowing when to start any discussion of Scottish literature, and where to mark its boundaries, has proven increasingly problematic over the past few decades. 'Scottish Literature', as a subject of academic enquiry, emerged primarily out of the sister discipline of 'English Literature', and as such has only in recent years begun to confront two significant blind spots resulting from that evolution. The first, not directly the concern of this chapter, is the virtual exclusion of material in Scottish Gaelic from the study of Scottish Literature for much of the twentieth century.[1] The second, the topic of this chapter, is the exclusion of nearly eight centuries of literature from and about Scotland from consideration, the centuries before the middle of the fourteenth century. Scottish literature, whether we think here of its representation in anthologies or literary histories, has often been seen to begin with John Barbour (c. 1320–95) or his contemporaries. This is because theirs is the earliest substantial work we have preserved in the language of Older Scots, and thus may be seen as ancestral to the anglophone literatures of modern Scotland, those in Scots and English. Even the otherwise linguistically ecumenical Hugh MacDiarmid perpetuated this state of affairs, describing the short elegy 'When Alexander our King was Dead' as 'the earliest extant piece of Scottish verse', and only in his notes continuing this thought more subversively: 'The earliest extant that is to say except in Gaelic'.[2]

Yet Scottish literature is *not* like English literature. Despite academic habits, the term Scottish Literature cannot naturally be made subservient to one linguistically determined literary tradition. A history of English literature may be allowed, should its authors wish, to encompass all literature written in the English language and its subsidiary dialects, and thus extend to North America, Australia, India, Africa and beyond. Alternatively, it may concentrate its focus on the literature of England – arguably a political and geographical unit of considerable stability since the eighth century, and possessing since that time essentially one main vernacular literary language. Scottish literature, on the other hand, must be, if it is to make any sense as a term, the literature of Scotland as a geographical and political unit. That being so, it falls heir to, at the very least, three vernacular literatures (Gaelic, Scots and English), and several more if the chronological parameters are extended to the period before 1350.

To pose this as a historical problem by suggesting that this earlier literature belongs instead to a period before the coalescence of Scotland as a nation, and therefore is not truly Scottish, has been one way of trying to provide an excuse for the inexcusable. But when was 'before Scotland'? If by this we might mean before all the current constituent parts of Scotland fell under the dominion of the same king and became part of the Scottish nation, then we must not begin consideration of Scottish literature until the late fifteenth century (a century after Barbour), when Orkney and Shetland were ceded to the Scottish crown. If Scotland begins with the establishment of a stable dynastic kingship presiding over a core expansionist kingdom, then we must begin in the late ninth century, the period when that dynasty first comes to our attention who ruled that kingdom in fairly direct succession until 1286 (Pictland, rechristened Alba c. 900, called Scotia and Scotland by the eleventh century, generally the Kingdom of the Scots in the twelfth century and later). Kings thereafter made their claim to rule through connection to that dynasty, as, of course, does the present queen. This dynasty ruled a kingdom whose core was in eastern Scotland, but they claimed western roots, and by c. 900 had established for that kingdom a Gaelic identity. From 900 on, the kings of this kingdom took under their power, incrementally, southern Scotland (first Lothian, and then Strathclyde), northeastern Scotland (Moray, then Ross, then Caithness), the southwest and the west, and, by 1266, the Hebrides and the Isle of Man. There is no moment in this historical trajectory at which to press 'pause' and declare it the moment when Scotland came into being. Equally, this dynasty claimed descent from earlier kings in both west and east – forcing us further back into the centuries before 900.

Another way to interpret the customary framework for Scottish literature is as a response to a national narrative. The common trope of beginning Scottish literature with Barbour perhaps suggests that we should wed literary origins to the national struggle of the Wars of Independence. Certainly it is that period that sees the rise of literary Scots, and for that linguistic tradition there may be some gain in so doing, whatever its methodological failings. But to propose that this is the period when Scotland became a nation or a kingdom makes little historical sense; to propose this as a starting point for the much older Gaelic literary tradition in Scotland makes even less.

Study of Scottish literature therefore must be the study of the literature of the geographical and political unit that is now Scotland, in all its languages and its chronological depth, and despite the cultural and political realignments of much of that territory over time.[3] As we shall see, there are very significant advantages to adopting this perspective. The most important is the literary enfranchisement of all parts of Scotland. Only by adopting this view of what Scottish literature is are we able to understand the trajectory between the twelfth-century golden age of Old Norse literature in the Earldom of Orkney and the work of George Mackay Brown in the twentieth century, or to fathom the full range of literary resonances of Somhairle MacGill-Eain. Only in this way can Scots in Dumfriesshire, in Argyll, in Shetland or in Buchan be properly allowed to participate in the many local and linguistically diverse strands that make up Scotland's literary history and heritage. Doing so, however, is not without its own dilemmas. The earlier linguistic strands in Scotland's past are shared with a variety of its neighbours: Wales, Ireland, England, Iceland and Norway. Literature composed on what is now Scottish soil, or for patrons in what is now Scotland, was by and large preserved in compendia of the literature of these other countries. Reclamation of Scotland's earlier literature thereby can be seen as enacting a form of plunder on neighbours' treasuries. Deciding where and when to draw the canonical dividing lines between literatures is problematic and usually impossible. In part, however, this is simply the result of accidents of preservation of medieval texts. Only two manuscripts certainly produced before 1100 in what is now Scotland survive: the *Book of Deer*, a gospel book of the ninth or tenth century, with Gaelic notes added at Deer in the northeast from the early twelfth century; and the Schaffhausen manuscript of Adomnán of Iona's *Life of Saint Columba*, written in Iona *c.* 700 (both now preserved furth of Scotland – in England and Switzerland respectively). To this we may add the runic inscription on the Ruthwell Cross in Dumfriesshire, four verses of an Old English poem on the Crucifixion. These rare survivals by no means reflect the evident magnitude of what had once existed. Clearly, however, preservation in media on the 'national soil' cannot be our criterion for inclusion, and so we must allow ourselves to scrutinise the literature preserved elsewhere for material composed in, or for patrons in, what is now Scotland.[4]

Languages and their literatures

Between the sixth century and the fourteenth, Scotland saw identifiable literary production in seven languages (Welsh, Old English, Gaelic – Old and Middle, Old Norse, Old French, Older Scots and, of course, Latin), ranging across an array of genres: poetry of praise, religious devotion, admiration of nature, heroism; historical narrative and hagiography; and romance and saga. What we have from each of these is not equal in quantity or quality.[5] It is worth first examining the nature and extent of the linguistic traditions behind these literatures before moving on to discuss some of the literary genres and finally considering some overall aspects of this period of Scottish literature.

Up to the sixth century, the predominant languages throughout Scotland were 'Brittonic', that is they belonged to the same close family of Celtic languages as Welsh, Cornish and Breton – indeed, the language spoken in the sixth century in southern Scotland was, as far as we can see, indistinguishable from that of Wales at the time. Increasingly, scholars are coming to feel that the language of Pictland was of a similar variety. We have, however, no substantial writings in Pictish. The Britons of southern Scotland, however, may be seen as the progenitors of a problematic skein of narrative traditions and poetry preserved, but also revised and augmented, in medieval Wales. As a result it is most appropriate to describe the literature from this tradition relating to Scotland as being in Welsh. Though the great series of elegies for the dead in battle called *Y Gododdin* has been claimed as 'Scotland's Oldest Poem', it is increasingly difficult to sustain that view straightforwardly. Nonetheless, the Welsh poetry and traditions concerning 'the Men of the North', including *Y Gododdin*, are much concerned with figures and events of early southern Scotland – if they are excluded from being directly Scottish literature, they are nonetheless part of its literary history, and should be incorporated in it.[6]

The anglophone heritage of Scotland begins in the sixth or perhaps seventh century. From this point, speakers of Old English came to dominate the southeast of Scotland, an unbroken linguistic heritage in places like Berwickshire. From these roots would grow Older Scots and the foundations of modern Scottish Standard English. The earliest literary text still on Scottish soil is from this tradition: the four fragments of the 'Ruthwell Crucifixion Poem' preserved on the narrow sides of the eighth-century Ruthwell Cross. This poem lies at the heart of that great Old English masterpiece 'The Dream of the Rood', though the exact relationship is more difficult to determine. It may not be the only piece of great Old English poetry to hail from Scotland: 'The Seafarer' has been suggested as having been composed somewhere near the Bass Rock in East Lothian, owing to very specific ornithological references.[7] The record is thereafter very patchy until the fourteenth century, when a northern descendant of Old English, Older Scots, emerges as a vibrant vernacular literature closely identified with the Scottish court and kingdom. But these few early fragments allow us at least to understand that Scots literature has deeper roots.

Gaelic is the other main strand in Scottish literature. Our earliest literature in Gaelic that can be tied closely to Scotland dates from the seventh century, and is also amongst the earliest literature in Gaelic anywhere.[8] This material relates to the monastery of Iona and the wider family of monasteries owing allegiance to its founder saint, Columba. Linguistically, there is nothing to clearly separate the Gaelic languages of Ireland and Scotland in the early Middle Ages – and in any case most of our 'Scottish' texts are preserved in Ireland. Their 'Scottishness' can thus on occasion be problematic. A poem of no great literary merit written in the eleventh century, 'A eolcha Alban uile' ('All ye learned men of Scotland'), recounts the kings of Alba down to the time of Malcolm III: It has been termed *Duan Albanach* ('The Scottish Poem'), but it was more likely composed in Ireland by scholars interested in the fortunes of the Scottish royal line.[9] Two poets writing in the formal classical metres that came to dominate professional Gaelic poetry from the middle of the twelfth century illustrate the problems even further. Muireadhach Albanach ('the Scot') Ó Dálaigh was an Irishman, and was thus called because he spent much of his later life (at least fifteen years) in Scotland whither he had fled in exile from Ireland and fathered a Scottish learned family who would in time take their surname, MacMhuirich, from him. He had a companion, Gille-Brighde, also called Albanach, who we know to have been Scottish, but whose poetry as it survives is only for Irish patrons, aside from the poetry he composed during his Mediterranean adventures on the fifth crusade.[10] In these circumstances, it seems wise to be reasonably inclusive, whilst always recognising the double allegiance of this poetry and its predominantly Irish provenance in manuscript form.

The most constant of the earlier literary languages of Scotland is Latin. From Adomnán's *Life of Saint Columba* of *c.* 700 and the eighth-century Whithorn verses on 'The Miracles of Bishop Nynia', through the twelfth-century Glasgow compositions on St Kentigern and the death of Somerled, to the fourteenth-century patriotism of the hymns in the Inchcolm Antiphoner or the histories of John of Fordun, Latin is the medium for a great variety of literary production, originating from a geographically diverse set of centres. Whilst the historically crucial figure of George Buchanan and unique geniuses like Arthur Johnston have claimed some attention for neo-Latin poetry in Scotland, the earlier tradition is astonishingly neglected.[11]

Perhaps nothing demonstrates better the virtues of an inclusive approach to earlier Scottish literature than the case of Old Norse. Scandinavian settlement began in Scotland in the ninth century, and the Western and Northern Isles were under Scandinavian dominion thereafter until respectively 1266 and 1469. Although all of what we have of Old Norse literature from this part of Scotland is preserved in Scandinavian contexts, primarily Icelandic, we can build up a very coherent picture of the work of court poets from this world, poets working for the Earls of Orkney and other figures. The twelfth century in particular sees Orkney as a major literary centre, with figures such as Earl Rögnvaldr Káli and Bishop Bjarni Kolbeinsson at work. This is a major part of the cultural heritage of Orkney and Shetland, and helps underpin the modern literature of these islands as well.[12]

The language with the thinnest representation from this early period is Old French. Despite the abundant presence of men of French-speaking stock at the highest levels of Scottish nobility in Scotland from the late eleventh century on, French has left surprisingly few abiding cultural landmarks within Scotland – though there is a noticeable and distinct French contribution to the lexicon of the Scots language. In literary terms, the sixteenth century has seen some interest in Scottish literary work in French, in particular the poetry attributed to Mary, Queen of Scots, but there is some prospective earlier material too. Most notable is the Arthurian verse narrative *Roman de Fergus* ('Romance of Fergus'), by one Guillaume le Clerc, which has been claimed, to my mind very plausibly, as having been composed in Scotland with an eye to late twelfth-century concerns.[13] It joins a number of Old French lays set in a more or less nebulous Scotland; these, though undoubtedly the product of French authors, nonetheless hint at literary networks between Angevin France and southern Scotland that have not yet been sufficiently explored.[14]

Genres

There is only space to explore here a selection of genres and major themes across what we have preserved from this period. Hagiography, writing about saints, is one of the very best represented products of this period, no doubt due in part to the capacity for monasteries and cathedrals to commission and preserve ambitious works such as these.[15] In this genre, Scotland takes part in the wider culture of medieval Europe, but also contributes significantly to it. The European dimension is writ large across the spectrum of Scottish hagiography. Our earliest surviving work, Adomnán's *Life of St Columba*, takes its place as one of the three major saint's Lives of the Irish tradition, but we know it also to have been written on Iona, and one strand of its transmission was certainly through Scottish courts – a prefatory poem in one manuscript is addressed to the Scottish king Alexander I. The Life is one of the great works of medieval hagiography. Adomnán, its author, who was like his subject also the abbot of Iona (679–704), is a quirky but intelligent stylist, and although the work is structurally problematic, his vignettes of St Columba have remained imaginatively influential, in particular his tour-de-force portrayal of Columba's final hours.[16] A later reworking of the *Life of St Columba* was clearly present in Scotland as well, whence it provided the impetus for the liturgy of Columba's feast in the Inchcolm Antiphoner. Iona clearly had literary renditions, probably in Gaelic, of stories of Adomnán himself, and these contributed to the highly fabulous Irish Life of that saint, as to his office in the Aberdeen Breviary.[17]

Two other major Scottish saints can claim substantial hagiographical portfolios from this period. St Ninian (originally Nynia) has a verse Life in Latin, composed in Whithorn in the eighth century (and sent to the scholar Alcuin at the Carolingian court), as well as a prose Life by Ailred of Rievaulx (1110–67), a northern English theologian and writer who had an early presence in the Scottish court of David I.[18] These are joined by a fourteenth-century verse Life in Older Scots, which alongside transmitting the older material of the saint's actions and miracles, has an impressive description of contemporary Whithorn as a mecca for European pilgrims. That Life is found in a very extensive collection of Lives of saints in Older Scots – all but Ninian and Machar are universal rather than local saints, but the production is significant (and neglected) all the same.[19] St Kentigern or Mungo too has a considerable stable of work about him. Though his earliest Lives are both from the twelfth century (one is fragmentary), they draw on impressive streams of what appear to be folk narrative; some of these have also fed into fragments related to his Life concerning local Glasgow madman Lailoken, his adventures and his three fold death.[20] All these show an active and productive narrative tradition in Strathclyde, something that can also be glimpsed in Irish Lives of St Patrick that preserve a suite of stories about Patrick as a boy, almost certainly derived from local Dunbartonshire traditions.[21]

It is difficult completely to unpack the relationship between the largely prose hagiographical medieval material and verse in praise of God and his saints. It can also be difficult to categorise some of this poetry. The swinging Latin poem on the death of the Hebridean ruler Somerled in battle at Renfrew in 1164 was written, within two years of the event, by a clerk of Glasgow cathedral named William. On its surface it is a zingy battle poem, its narrative propelled forward by its metre, but its heroes are the bishop of Glasgow and his predecessor and patron, St Kentigern, to whose intercession the victory is ascribed: 'The Scottish saints are truly to be praised!' remarks the bishop, as he holds aloft the head of Somerled. That practical and at one level patriotic tone recurs amidst the verse of the fourteenth-century Inchcolm Antiphoner, with its reworkings of earlier tales of St Columba sitting beside clearly new prayers invoking Columba's intercession against 'the assaults of Englishmen' and praising him as the 'hope of Scots'.[22]

But other poetry is more clearly devotional, amongst it some of the early poetry relating to the monastery of Iona and Columba its founder saint. Whether Columba himself was the author of the ambitious abecedarian Latin poem 'Altus Prosator' is far from certain, but the work is a tour de force of muscular and exotic Latin. That it comes from a similar stable as the reflective and self-effacing 'Adiutor Laborantium', with its plea to 'help / [me] … a little man / trembling and most wretched, / rowing through the infinite / storm of this age' speaks volumes for the range of literary accomplishment within the Columban federation of monasteries. That accomplishment extended to the vernacular, as a difficult but important elegy on Columba, as well as two mid-seventh-century poems in his praise attest. These are important early works in Gaelic in any case, but the two latter poems, attributed to one Beccán or Bécán, are impressive pieces, drawing on native tropes and images to create Christian poems of great clarity.[23]

Columba is not the only saint to whom we have poetry addressed from this period. A hymn to Ninian exists from the eighth century; Kentigern is the subject of a hymn of uncertain date, perhaps of the tenth or eleventh century; there is a thirteenth-century Latin hymn on St Magnus of Orkney; and the Virgin Mary is commemorated in both Latin verse from *c.* 700, a delicate choral hymn by Cú Chuimne, otherwise known as a legal scholar, and in one of a number of religious poems by Muireadhach Albanach Ó Dálaigh in the early thirteenth century.[24] This poem is the earliest in a series of Gaelic poems from Scotland in classical metre in praise of the Virgin Mary which continue through to the sixteenth century, and may be seen to belong to a wider Gaelic tradition of devotional praise.[25] Muireadhach is also notable as author of a number of more reflective poems, focusing on personal spirituality, from a poem dedicating his shorn hair to Christ as he sets off on crusade, to poems of renunciation and dying.[26]

The bulk of Muireadhach's corpus of poetry, as that of his contemporary Gille-Brighde Albanach, is professional poetry of praise. Poets like Muireadhach lived by their attachment to major lords and rulers, and their literary work was predominantly attuned to the depiction of their patrons' fine qualities and lineage in intricately crafted, well-ornamented verse. For this they reaped rewards, or hoped to. Poetry from Muireadhach to one Amhlaibh of the Lennox makes clear the material transactions underlying such poetry, complaining that he is due cattle, horses and land in return for his work; another, anonymous poem to Aonghas Mór, ruler of the Isles (*c.* 1250), recounts all that Aonghas had inherited from his father: his position, his houses, his dogs and horses, his brown ivory chessmen – and his debt to the poet! The self-same poem – clearly by an Irish poet, though the patron is Scottish – demonstrates that such concentration on financial matters need not exclude artistry, or even humour. The poem's pecuniary punchlines are softened by the slapstick depiction of the poet's inability to travel by boat, uncertain where to put himself, whether to sit or lie down, gripping the boat's sides with white knuckles. Likewise, Muireadhach is able to address himself to an as yet uncontracted patron with a breezy calling card: 'Guess who I am!', before going on to trot out his literary knowledge in a long series of comparisons between the patron and heroes of Gaelic tradition. These poets were worth hiring: The poems composed for Cathal Crobhdhearg, powerful ruler of Connacht in Ireland, by Muireadhach and by Gille-Brighde Albanach are some of the finest products of this period and verse style in Gaelic.[27] It was a verse style and, indeed, a literary language (that of classical Gaelic) which would dominate both Scotland and Ireland until the sixteenth century.

A number of neglected Latin poems exist, mostly preserved in the problematic later context of Bower's *Scotichronicon* (which casts doubt on their contemporaneity). These include poetry on Robert Bruce and a celebration of the death of Edward I. More securely from an early thirteenth-century manuscript is poetry lamenting the death in 1199 of Hugh of Roxburgh, the chancellor, and a number of other poems on contemporary topics. This includes poetry addressed to William the Lion: 'Thus may the rule of the kingdom remain yours, best king of kings! / May this occasion be fixed, steadfast forever'.[28] This corpus awaits proper study, including editing and translating work, but it is evident that learned Latin verse was a feature of Scottish court circles around 1200.

Likewise, it is worth stressing the considerable amount of powerful praise poetry addressed to patrons within the Scandinavian world of Scotland and its neighbours composed in court metres in Old Norse. The genre of skaldic verse is highly crafted, intensely allusive. The allusions used in 'kennings' that make riddles out of ordinary things like a sword ('wound-etcher'), a woman clothed in linen ('flax-prop'), an arm ('hawkland') or a carrion crow ('the spear-storm cuckoo') are expansive and cryptic at once, opening out to a world of myth and lost narrative (as when a spear is 'Odin's wand' or a woman 'the wine-bowl goddess'). All of what we have from this tradition survives in Icelandic manuscripts and was largely composed by poets of Icelandic or Norwegian origin, but their (named) work for earls of Orkney and others of their ilk allows us to build up a picture of the literary world of the northern Isles during the period from 900 to 1200 especially. Poets of great skill were at work for Orkney earls, such as Arnor 'Earl's Poet', whose elegy for Thorfinn the Mighty (*c.* 1060) is one of the great examples of this court verse.[29]

Conclusions

This has been a fairly cursory examination of what is, after all, eight centuries of literature. It is worth emphasizing its fragmentary nature and the fact that certain types of literature are very patchily represented – narrative for instance. But its existence should not be ignored, and there are moments within these eight centuries when, taking Scotland as representing its modern borders, we can point to a considerable fruitfulness within the literature of a variety of languages. The period 650–800 might be one, though our evidence for this period is largely generated by one network, the monastery of Iona, and its monastic affiliates. We might instead wish to point to the period between roughly 1150 and 1250 as a fertile one across this territory, and think of Scotland as having experienced a 'twelfth-century renaissance', a term much used elsewhere in Europe. From this period we have the work of great poets, such as Rögnvaldr Káli, earl of Orkney and participant, with poet companions, on a crusading pilgrimage to the Holy Land mid-century; and Muireadhach Albanach Ó Dálaigh, likewise a crusader with his companion Gille-Brighde Albanach. From both Rögnvaldr and Muireadhach, we have tender poetry on their wives – from the former, remembering tending his sick wife's bedside; from the latter, a passionate lament for his wife of many years and mother of his eleven children. The European tropes of courtly love find their first and securest place in Scottish literature in the work of Rögnvaldr Káli, and also make an ironic appearance in the wry poetry of Orkney bishop Bjarni Kolbeinsson.[30] Sharing a page with the lament for Hugh the Chancellor in a manuscript section that otherwise contains Scottish poems in Latin is a seasonal love poem in classical mode: 'The violet's blossom purples the field, the breeze cools the fieriness of the sun above. – Whoever does not love now has a heart of iron: the air is serene, the time is made for love'.[31]

The Old French *Roman de Fergus*, with its superbly competent heroine Galiena, confirms for us that literary romance was about in Scottish courts, as does the appearance of personal names derived from romance, such as the neighbouring landowners in Strathearn, c. 1200, Tristrem of Gorthie and Ysenda (Iseult) of Kinbuck.[32] There was a wider world of literary reference available than just Arthurian material, too: The wealthy Ness of Leuchar's heiress was named Orabilis, presumably after the heroine of a popular *chanson de geste*. The son of Uchtred, lord of Galloway, later lord himself, was either named Roland or later took that name as a version of his Gaelic name Lachlann. That the legends of Roland and Charlemagne were washing about the Irish Sea in the mid- to late twelfth century is confirmed for us by our knowledge that Raghnall, King of Man and the Isles (1187–1229), had commissioned a translation of the Charlemagne cycle from French into Latin. The same king was the recipient of one of the earliest and finest full-blown Gaelic praise poems in classical metre.[33]

The cultural connections are there to see in church literature too. Glasgow's bishop Jocelin hired professional hagiographer Jocelin of Furness to refresh into elegant Latin the Life of Kentigern – the same writer wrote Lives of Waltheof of Melrose and, for John de Courcy, conqueror of Ulster, a Life of St Patrick.[34] Melrose was a centre of chronicling and, seemingly, poetry if one complex Latin poem is anything to go by. Cistercian circles may be seen at work too in Ailred of Rievaulx's Encomium on the death of King David I[35] and his revision of the Life of Ninian. The neighbouring border abbey of Dryburgh was, in the 1180s, host to some of the earliest Scottish writings of monastic and mystical theology, those of the scholar Adam of Dryburgh (c. 1140–1212). He was followed, again during our period, by two Scottish theologians whose work was highly influential in Europe as well as at home: Michael Scot (from Kirkcaldy, †c. 1235), that major translator of Greek and Arabic philosophical tracts, and John Duns Scotus (c. 1265–1308), a Franciscan whose works became cornerstones of scholastic thinking.[36]

The period before Barbour is not pre-history, nor need Scottish literature's earliest centuries, before its traditional beginnings, be a period shrouded in obscurity. To be fair, the multiple languages and scattered materials present challenges to scholarship, but it has largely been made obscure by neglect. Scotland in the late twelfth and early thirteenth century is emblematic of the period as a whole – multi-lingual, open to the wash of European trends and possessing literary traditions shared with neighbours west, north and south, indeed, shaped by individual poets and writers whose literary careers spanned countries as well as cultures. This is hardly different, in the challenges it poses to the canonicity of different authors or works, from the modern era, when Scottish authors may write for most of their lives furth of Scotland (Muriel Spark, for instance), or may be of diverse parentage and birth by background. It may be that taking Scottish literature back before 'Scottish Literature', for all its challenges of linguistic and generic unfamiliarity, presents for us a recognizable mirror to our modern, multi-cultural, hybrid-identity literary scene.

Notes

1   There have been exceptions. For anthologies with a balanced inclusion of Gaelic material, see for example Hugh MacDiarmid (ed.), *The Golden Treasury of Scottish Poetry* (London: Macmillan, 1940); Roderick Watson (ed.), *The Poetry of Scotland: Gaelic, Scots and English* (Edinburgh: Edinburgh University Press, 1995).

One chapter on Gaelic literature appears in each of the four volumes of Cairns Craig (gen. ed.), *History of Scottish Literature* (Aberdeen: Aberdeen University Press, 1987); a more generous quotient in Ian Brown, Thomas Owen Clancy, Susan Manning and Murray Pittock (eds.), *The Edinburgh History of Scottish Literature*, 3 vols. (Edinburgh: Edinburgh University Press, 2007).

2   MacDiarmid (ed.), *Golden Treasury*, pp. 2, 368.

3   A contribution towards profiling the literature of this earlier period was made by Thomas Owen Clancy (ed.), *The Triumph Tree: Scotland's Earliest Poetry AD 550–1350* (Edinburgh: Canongate, 1998); other subsequent anthologies have adopted some of this earlier material, for example Robert Crawford and Mick Imlah (eds.), *The New Penguin Book of Scottish Verse* (London: Penguin, 2001). Thomas Owen Clancy and Murray Pittock (eds.), *The Edinburgh History of Scottish Literature, Volume 1: From Columba to the Union (until 1707)* (Edinburgh: Edinburgh University Press, 2007) incorporated considerable discussion of the earlier period.

4   See 'Introduction', in Clancy (ed.), *Triumph Tree*, for further discussion of these issues.

5   There is a discussion of each of the linguistic and literary traditions in ibid.; for an overview of the linguistic history, see William Gillies, 'The Lion's Tongues: Languages in Scotland to 1314', in Clancy and Pittock (eds.), *Edinburgh History*, pp. 52–62.

6   The most recent consideration of this problematic material is in Alex Woolf (ed.), *Beyond the Gododdin: Dark-Age Scotland in Medieval Wales* (St Andrews: St John's House, 2010).

7   James Fisher, *The Shell Bird Book* (London: Ebury Press, 1966) – I am grateful to Alex Woolf for knowledge of this and the reference; for 'The Ruthwell Crucifixion Poem', see Clancy (ed.), *Triumph Tree*, p. 21 and p. 332 for sources.

8   The medieval corpus of Gaelic poetry from Scotland is well represented by Wilson McLeod and Meg Bateman (eds.), *Duanaire na Sracaire, Songbook of the Pillagers: Anthology of Scotland's Gaelic Poetry to 1600* (Edinburgh: Birlinn, 2007).

9   See Mark Zumbuhl, 'Contextualising the *Duan Albanach*', in Wilson McLeod, James E. Fraser and Anja Gunderloch (eds.), *Cànan & Cultar: Language and Culture: Rannsachadh na Gàidhlig 3* (Edinburgh: Dunedin Press, 2006), pp. 11–24.

10 For a selection of their verse and further sources, see Clancy (ed.), *Triumph Tree*, pp. 247–83; for discussion, see Katharine Simms, 'Muireadhach Albanach Ó Dálaigh and the Classical Revolution', in Clancy and Pittock (eds.), *Edinburgh History*, pp. 83–90.

11 For example, MacDiarmid (ed.), *Golden Treasury*, pp. 217–30; pp. 3–9, 25–9; Robert Crawford, *Apollos of the North: Selected Poems of George Buchanan and Arthur Johnston* (Edinburgh: Polygon, 2006). The only substantial overview of the Latin material from this period is Jack MacQueen, 'From Rome to Ruddiman: The Scoto-Latin Tradition', in Clancy and Pittock (eds.), *Edinburgh History*, pp. 184–208.

12 See Judith Jesch, 'Norse Literature in the Orkney Earldom', in Clancy and Pittock (eds.), *Edinburgh History*, pp. 77–82.

13 See D. D. R. Owen, *Fergus of Galloway: Knight of King Arthur* (London: Everyman, 1991).

14 See for example the Lays of 'Desiré' and 'Doon', in Glyn S. Burgess and Leslie C. Brook (eds.), *Arthurian Archives: French Literature IV. Old French Narrative Lays* (Cambridge: D. S. Brewer, 2007); see also R. L. Graeme Ritchie, *Chrétien de Troyes and Scotland* (Oxford: Oxford University Press, 1952). For an overview of the position of French in twelfth- and thirteenth-century Scotland, see G. W. S. Barrow, 'French after the Style of Petithachengon', in Barbara E. Crawford (ed.), *Church, Chronicle and Learning in Medieval and Early Renaissance Scotland* (Edinburgh: Mercat Press, 1999), pp. 187–93.

15 For fuller reviews, see James E. Fraser, 'Hagiography', in Clancy and Pittock (eds.), *Edinburgh History*, pp. 103–9; Alan Macquarrie, 'Medieval Scotland', in Guy Philippart (ed.), *Hagiographies: Histoire internationale de la Littérature hagiographique latine et vernaculaire en Occident des origines à 1550* (Turnhout, Belgium: Brepols, 1994), vol. I, pp. 487–501.

16 For further discussion, see Clare Stancliffe, 'Adomnán of Iona and His Prose Writings', in Clancy and Pittock (eds.), *Edinburgh History*, pp. 110–14; Richard Sharpe, *Adomnán of Iona: The Life of Saint Columba* (London: Penguin, 1995); Jonathan M. Wooding (ed.), *Adomnán of Iona: Theologian, Lawmaker, Peacemaker* (Dublin: Four Courts, 2010).

17 See Alan Macquarrie, 'The Offices for St Columba (9 June) and St Adomnán (23 September) in the Aberdeen Breviary', *Innes Review*, 51 (2000), 1–39.

18 Gilbert Márkus (trans.), in Clancy (ed.), *Triumph Tree*, pp. 126–39; John MacQueen, *St Nynia*, new edn (Edinburgh: Birlinn, 2005).

19 W. M. Metcalfe (ed.), *Legends of the Saints*, 3 vols. (Edinburgh: Scottish Texts Society, 1896); for Ninian, see vol. II, pp. 304–45.

20 For texts, see Alexander Penrose Forbes, *Lives of S. Ninian and S. Kentigern* (Edinburgh: Edmonston and Douglas, 1874); for commentary, Alan Macquarrie, *The Saints of Scotland: Essays in Scottish Church History AD 450–1093* (Edinburgh: John Donald, 1997), pp. 117–44.

21 See Thomas Owen Clancy, 'The Cults of Saints Patrick and Palladius in Early Medieval Scotland', in Steve Boardman, John Reuben Davies and Eila Williamson (eds.), *Saints' Cults in the Celtic World* (Woodbridge: Boydell, 2009), pp. 31–2, 36–8.

22 Gilbert Márkus (trans.), in Clancy (ed.), *Triumph Tree*, pp. 212–14, 317–19.

23 For this material, see Clancy (ed.), *Triumph Tree*, pp. 95–112, and Thomas Owen Clancy and Gilbert Márkus (eds.), *Iona: The Earliest Poetry of a Celtic Monastery* (Edinburgh: Edinburgh University Press, 1995).

24 Translations of all but the hymn on Kentigern in Clancy (ed.), *Triumph Tree*; for the hymn to Kentigern, see John MacQueen and Winifred MacQueen (eds.), *Scotichronicon* (Aberdeen: Aberdeen University Press, 1989), vol. II, pp. 80–2, 227–8.

25 Sim Innes, '*Is eagal liom lá na hagra*: Devotion to the Virgin in the Later Medieval Gàidhealtachd', in Steve Boardman and Eila Williamson (eds.), *The Cult of Saints and the Virgin Mary in Medieval Scotland* (Woodbridge: Boydell, 2010), pp. 125–42.

26 Clancy (ed.), *Triumph Tree*, pp. 264–6, 276–83.

27 Translations of most of these are in Clancy (ed.), *Triumph Tree*, pp. 247–83, 288–94.

28 The manuscript is Bibliotheca Apostolica Vaticana, MS Regina lat. 344, pt 2. The certainly Scottish material is on ff. 36–8 and 50. For editions of some of these poems, see W. Wattenbach, *Neues Archiv*, 2 (1876), 439–46. I hope to provide a full account of this corpus in the very near future.

29 Paul Bibire (trans.), in Clancy (ed.), *Triumph Tree*, pp. 170–5.

30 See Judith Jesch (trans.), in Clancy (ed.), *Triumph Tree*, pp. 225–35; Jesch, 'Norse Literature'; Roberta Frank, *Sex, Lies and* Málsháttakvæði: *A Norse Poem from Medieval Orkney* (Nottingham: School of English Studies, 2004).

31 The translation is from Peter Dronke, *Medieval Latin and the Rise of the European Love-Lyric* (Oxford: Oxford University Press, 1968), pp. 364–5. It is on f. 38.

32 See Owen, *Fergus of Galloway*; Ritchie, *Chrétien de Troyes and Scotland*, p. 16.

33 For the poem, see Clancy (ed.), *Triumph Tree*, pp. 236–41; for Raghnall's translation commission, see Annalee C. Rejhon, *Cân Rolant: The Medieval Welsh Version of the Song of Roland* (Berkeley: University of California Press, 1984), p. 29.

34 On Jocelin of Furness, see most recently Helen Birkett, *The Saints' Lives of Jocelin of Furness: Hagiography, Patronage & Ecclesiastical Politics* (Woodbridge: Boydell & Brewer, 2010).

35 On which, see Joanna Huntington, 'David of Scotland: "vir tam necessarius mundo"', in Boardman, Davies and Williamson (eds.), *Saints' Cults*, pp. 130–45.

36 For fuller commentary on all three of these, see Thomas O'Loughlin, 'Theology, Philosophy and Cosmography', in Clancy and Pittock (eds.), *Edinburgh History*, pp. 115–22.

Guide to Further Reading

Thomas Owen Clancy (ed.), *The Triumph Tree: Scotland's Earliest Poetry AD 550–1350* (Edinburgh: Canongate, 1998)

Thomas Owen Clancy and Gilbert Márkus (eds.), *Iona: The Earliest Poetry of a Celtic Monastery* (Edinburgh: Edinburgh University Press, 1995)

Thomas Owen Clancy and Murray Pittock (eds.), *The Edinburgh History of Scottish Literature, Volume 1: From Columba to the Union (until 1707)* (Edinburgh: Edinburgh University Press, 2007)

2

ALESSANDRA PETRINA

The Medieval Period

Attempting an assessment of medieval Scottish literature means dealing with a definition of this literature within a strongly defined national context, a topic that has drawn considerable attention in recent decades. In 1991, the journal *Studies in Scottish Literature* dedicated its twenty-sixth volume to 'The Language and Literature of Early Scotland', publishing the proceedings of the sixth conference of the International Association for Medieval and Renaissance Scottish Language and Literature, and providing a unique opportunity to assess the state of criticism on the subject; the volume attempted at the same time a definition of the Scottish literary canon in the late Middle Ages and the early modern era. Significantly, the opening contribution of the collection, by Roderick J. Lyall, was titled '"A New Maid Channoun"? Redefining the Canonical in Medieval and Renaissance Scottish Literature'.[1] From this point on, it was clear – something often repeated in recent histories of Scottish literature[2] – that medieval literature written in Older Scots could be considered the starting point of national literature, the moment of unification that determined the course of the succeeding canon. Literature and nation-building are inseparable concepts when we take into consideration late medieval English literature: from John Gower onwards, the very choice of language implies a political statement. As one surveys the Scottish literary production of the same period, it appears equally concentrated on a definition of the nation, showing a unity of purpose in excess of anything in its English counterpart. The history of Scotland up to the Union of the Crowns is of course independent of English affairs, and it is impossible to take into consideration the key dates of English history, such as the Battle of Hastings or the beginning of the Tudor dynasty, and apply them to the development of the Scottish nation: one must take into account different historical moments, and thus find different time boundaries.[3] On the other hand, the similarity in language, influences and even genres and motifs has also meant that Scottish medieval literature has often defined itself in relation to, or in opposition with, its English analogue. Critical attitudes vary from an all-enveloping acknowledgement of the weight of English masters such as Geoffrey Chaucer to a strong vindication of cultural independence that has gone hand in hand with the identification of non-English (that is to say, French or Italian) models. Recent criticism has attempted a mediation between the two views.[4] It is undeniable that there is a specificity to Scottish medieval literature that, in spite of mutual influences and cross-cultural currents, should be highlighted. The present chapter is an attempt to identify common denominators.

Any definition of medieval Scottish literature should first of all take into consideration notions of language and time range. Older Scots (a variety of Middle English, called Middle Scots by some scholars, *Scottis* by Gavin Douglas and *Inglis* by John Barbour and William Dunbar) is the language mainly used for this literature, though, like medieval England, Scotland was home to many different languages: Norman French and Latin among the aristocracy and the clergy, Scots Gaelic and Norse in various geographical areas. Gaelic literature in particular presents a strong tradition, marked by the predominance of 'bardic verse'; the earlier models can be traced to the ninth century, and one of the most relevant texts, the *Duan Albanach*, was written in the eleventh century though perhaps by an Irish writer. However, the real flourishing of Gaelic literature is in the sixteenth century; the most important early manuscript, known as *The Book of the Dean of Lismore*, is probably dated 1512, though it is a collection of earlier lyrics.[5] The precise list of literature in Gaelic that can be said to belong to Scotland is still a debatable issue. The overall picture of medieval Scotland is indeed fragmented, and such a fragmentation is rooted in geography though soon becomes an issue of politics, of ideology, where this fragmentation is perhaps artificially skated over.[6] The simple idea of 'one language, one nation' appears inappropriate.[7] One critic goes so far as to say that, with the exclusion of a handful of poets such as Henryson, Dunbar and Douglas, the term 'Middle Scots Literature' would be almost superfluous.[8]

As for the time limits, Nicola Royan's suggestion of marking the beginning of medieval literature with the completion of John Barbour's *The Bruce* (1375) and its final stage with Gavin Douglas's *Eneados* (1513) is shared by most scholars.[9] This span allows us to detect within these 140 years of literary history a series of common traits. Narrative appears to constitute the backbone of medieval Scottish literary forms, especially the narration of national history. Trends in Scottish literature often highlight strong connections between various authors: thus Barbour's *Bruce* can be seen as the natural progenitor of 'Blind' Harry's *Actis and Deidis of William Wallace* (1476–8). But the same attention to the use of history as a way to underline national identity can be found in one of the most important Latin writings of the period, Walter Bower's *Scotichronicon* (1449), which attempts a chronology of Scottish history ('history' here being almost synonymous with the history of kings) from the earliest times to the present day: the first Scottish monarchs are said to be Gathelos, from Greece, and Scota, from Egypt, as if to highlight Scotland's proud internationalism (if such a word be appropriate to such a context) and mark a distance from England's Brutus myth.

It is customary to mark the beginning of Scottish literature with the *sange* transcribed by Andrew of Wyntoun in his *Origynale Cronykil of Scotland* (1424):

Qwhen Alexander our kynge was dede,	[dead
þat Scotlande lede in lauche and le,	[that; law; protection
Away was sons of alle and brede,	[plenty; ale; bread
Off wyne and wax, of gamyn and gle.	[play; joy
Our golde was changit in to lede.	[lead
Crist, borne in virgynyte,	[Christ
Succoure Scotlande, and ramede,	[cure
þat is stade in perplexite.[10]	[that; stood

The 'Alexander' referred to is King Alexander III, who died in 1286, so this fragment may have been composed in the late thirteenth century; its importance is given not only by its presumed dating, but by the image it offers of the Scottish nation. Wyntoun includes a number of passages from other texts in his work: his history of Scotland from the beginning of the world to 1408 thus becomes an affirmation of Scottish identity through history and culture, and, judging from the number of extant manuscripts, its popularity shows also its topicality to the cultural debate in its time. The tradition of historical writing, this time based on chronicle-writing rather than focusing on individual heroes, is to be found also in a number of Latin writings, from John of Fordun's *Chronica Gentis Scotorum* (c. 1380), to its continuation, Walter Bower's *Scotichronicon* (1440–7), to the anonymous *Liber Pluscardensis* (1461). In the last instance in particular, chronicle blends easily with another literary genre, the 'advice to princes' literature.

This genre, generally popular in European medieval literature, enjoyed great popularity in Scotland, finding in Gilbert Hay (1400–99) one of its representatives. Hay, who apparently spent part of his life in France, is the author of prose translations of chivalric handbooks, such as *The Buke of the Law of Armys*, the *Buke of the Governaunce of Princis* and the *Buke of Knychthede*; though he starts from French volumes of received wisdom, his concern 'over the king's closest body of councillors gives a strongly contemporary picture of political business over the function and functioning of kingship'.[11] John of Ireland (1440–96) brought to its most articulated form the tradition of mirrors for princes in medieval Scotland, and for the first time offered with his *Meroure of Wyssdome* (1490) advice specifically addressed to a named monarch, James IV. After more than a century, another book of advice, written by a monarch for a future monarch, will echo the same issues: James VI's *Basilikon Doron* (1599). But advice literature can be found also in less obvious texts: Dunbar's *The Thrissill and the Rois*, Lyndsay's *Satyre* and Henryson's 'The Lyon and the Mouse', and even Douglas's presentation of the hero in his *Eneados*.[12] It is as if the relative smallness of the Scots-speaking community, and the closeness of many of its writers to the court and the king, made it possible to maintain an ongoing dialogue between poetry and politics.

In the two 'national' poems mentioned above, *The Bruce* and the *Wallace*, narrative history is offered in a form that does not depend on English models, but builds a genuinely Scottish tradition: this is *individual* history, focusing on the deeds of heroes rather than on the struggle of a people – the fact that the former was written for Robert II, as part of a programme of celebration of the new dynasty, may help explain this choice. Robert I and his liegeman James Douglas, who attempts to take Bruce's heart to the Holy Land, are the protagonists of Barbour's story, with the Scottish victory at Bannockburn (1314) constituting the climax of the narration. As has been observed, the House of Stewart is celebrated through the glorious achievements of their founder, even if this entailed some selection on the writer's part.[13] All the time the historical narrative, though accurate and rich in precise details, is informed by elements of romance, deriving from French literature; the metre (tetrameter couplets) helps the modern reader recapture the ballad-like rhythm. The *Actis and Deidis of William Wallace* is also an exploration of national history: the celebration of the deeds of the most popular Scottish hero helps the tale achieve a romance-like tone, in the details of the descriptions of gory battles as well as in the heroic portrayal of the central protagonist.

Romance, sometimes with more comic overtones, often with strong links to the English tradition, is a recurrent term in any analysis of Scottish medieval literature, but it is very difficult to define both the genre and its canon: even the *Bruce* calls itself a *romanys*, and often the surviving texts are much later copies. A recent survey lists *Lancelot of the Laik*, *Golagrus and Gawain*, *The Taill of Rauf Coilyear*, the Scottish *Buik of Alexander*, Gilbert Hay's *Buik of King Alexander*, *Roswall and Lillian*, *Eger and Grime*, *Clariodus*, the Scottish *Troy Book* fragments, *King Orphius*, *Sir Collinge ye Knyt*, *Florimond of Albany*, *Squyer Meldrum*, taking the genre in its broadest sense (*Freiris of Berwik* or *Colkelbie's Sow* might rather be called fabliaux)[14] – a rather meagre list, so that its author concludes by asking:

'Given the pervasive influence of particularly English models, to what extent does Scottish romance possess a distinctive identity: *is* there such a thing as Scottish romance?'[15] There is no doubt that in this case the paucity of information does not help an informed evaluation; the absence of prose romances, for instance, might indicate nothing else but a disappearance of the relevant manuscripts.

An analogous problem is evident in the case of religious poetry: a far from negligible corpus is present in the great manuscript collections of Scottish poetry, including versions of Middle English religious poetry, though these texts have so far secured little critical attention. Yet, even in the case of popular forms such as the carol, there is nothing like the wealth of material to be found in English collections: it has been suggested that 'the lacuna must be presumed to be the consequence of the Reformers' wilful destructiveness'.[16]

For all its insistence on its Scottish context, Harry's *Wallace* also shows a receptiveness to English culture highlighted by his reading of Geoffrey Chaucer: it has been argued that 'this acceptance of English cultural models ... was a concession to the reality principle; no wish-fulfilment fantasy such as *The Wallace* was going to make the English go away'.[17] This characteristic is significant as it introduces another major theme in any discussion of fifteenth-century Scottish literature, that is, its relation with its English counterpart and especially with Chaucer, possibly the most immediate model for both. The preoccupation with the identification and origin of the Scottish literary canon is a trait of a number of contemporary works: William Dunbar's *Lament for the Makars* and David Lyndsay's *Testament of the Papyngo* share a mood of self-reflexivity, at a communal rather than an individual level: Dunbar's refrain *timor mortis conturbat me* is transformed into the lament for a generation of poets whose song can be heard no more. Mortality no longer belongs to the individual, but is the concern of a community, whose most precious members, from lords to clerks to *makaris*, are progressively lost: 'Sparit is nought ther faculte.'[18] The poet's long list of dead poets becomes a precious testimony of cultural strength. In spite of its elegiac tone, the poem is also a roll-call of great poetic voices, a Scottish anthology headed by the English triad of Chaucer 'of makaris flour' (line 50), Gower and Lydgate. With a startling mirror effect, the same triad is also present in Gavin Douglas's *The Palice of Honour*, in the stanza concluding a long list of the great poets from Homer to Virgil to Petrarch;[19] the English poets share the stanza with the Scottish triad of Walter Kennedy, Dunbar and the unidentified 'Quintine'. In both cases the three English poets enter the nascent Scottish canon, and mark the passage from the classical *auctoritates* (with Douglas including a number of Italian writers in the humanist tradition) to the national voices.

Chaucer constitutes the essential watershed in medieval Scottish as well as English literature, and Chaucerian poetry is strongly bifurcated in the two very different branches. The question of Chaucer's role in Scottish literature has been a cause for long-standing controversy, in which ideology played as large a role as literary assessment; yet the writer's immense influence is acknowledged first of all by his immediate Scottish successors. He is like an immense fresco in a refectory: everyone crossing the hall must be aware of it, even if concentrating on lunch. He appears when least expected: Dunbar's *Quhen Merche wes with variand windis past* refers to the marriage between James IV and Margaret Tudor, and turns its whole attention to an exhortation to the monarchs in the form of a dream poem; yet its opening stanza elaborates on the *incipit* of the *Canterbury Tales*:

Quhen Merche wes with variand windis past,	[was; changeable
And Appryll had with hir siluer schouris	[showers
Tane leif at Nature with ane orient blast,	[taken leave of
And lusty May, that mvddir is of flouris,	[mother
Had maid the birdis to begyn their houris[20]	[*metaphorically* song alluding to church services

This use of the Chaucerian model marks the distance between Scottish and English fifteenth-century poetry, underlining the superiority of the Scottish model. The term 'Scottish Chaucerians', defining the poets 'who wrote, at least occasionally, in the formal "aureate" style and who inserted references to Chaucer into their poems', has been variously accepted and rejected;[21] it includes the author of the *Kingis Quair*, Robert Henryson, Dunbar, Douglas and perhaps Lyndsay, but in its insistence on the English model (inviting the reader to overlook the long list of Greek- and Latin-writing poets from whom Chaucer himself descended) it has perhaps narrowed the scholarly focus, inviting an unfair equation with the English Chaucerians such as Hoccleve and Lydgate, who are too often dwarfed by comparison with their master.

It does not help critical assessment to relegate Henryson or Dunbar to the status of 'an honourable footnote to the career of Chaucer',[22] which would be like saying that Wyatt and Surrey were an honourable footnote to the career of Petrarch. It is likewise absurd to deny the Chaucerian influence or concentrate exclusively on elements of independence and originality, on the assumption that originality per se is to be prized in literary evaluation; rather, there is a real risk of denying the presence of the European literary heritage in the Scottish poets, as there is in the case of Chaucer. In his pivotal *Anglo-Scottish Literary Relations (1430–1550)*, Gregory Kratzmann, beside covering the familiar ground of Chaucerian debts, considers a less obvious relation, that between Dunbar and Skelton, acknowledges Surrey's debt to Douglas when discussing the two *Aeneid* translations and analyses the relation between Lyndsay's *Satyre* and English drama on a two-way basis; but this extraordinarily useful critical path has found few followers so far, and remains to be more thoroughly explored.[23]

The strongest symbol of the continuity between Chaucer and fifteenth-century Scottish poetry is perhaps the manuscript MS Arch. Selden. B. 24, now in the Bodleian Library: as amply demonstrated, it is the prime evidence of the transmission between England and Scotland of Chaucer's poetry (as it includes, for instance, the only complete Scottish copy of *Troilus and Criseyde*), as well as of the beginning of the Chaucerian canon.[24] The centre of the collection appears to be *The Kingis Quair* (1420–30?), not only because this beautiful poem survives only in this manuscript, but also because it may be said to represent the perfect encounter between the Chaucerian canon and the Scottish literary tradition, before the latter developed along completely independent lines. The poem is attributed to James I, the king under whose reign the first Scottish University, St Andrews, was founded, and is a splendid combination of Chaucerian authority and autobiographical experience: the allegory underlying the conventional structure of the dream-vision finds an almost too precise counterpart in the experience of its presumed author. Rhyme royal, already present in Chaucer's *Troilus and Criseyde* and later used also by Henryson, here clearly indicates the debt to the tradition acknowledged in the closing lines. The result is a very sophisticated poem, showing the author's intimate knowledge of Chaucer's poetry, of Lydgate's *Temple of Glas* and of late classical philosophers such as Macrobius and Boethius; one may also find an affinity with European poetic voices that were just being imported into the British Isles, such as Dante Alighieri or Guillaume de Deguileville.[25] But even in a poem whose erudition is closely distilled through the medium of personal experience, the poet finds the occasion to evoke the golden age of a poetry-making community:

> Say on than, quhare is becummyn for schame   [where
> The songis new, the fresch carolis and dance,
> The lusty lyf, the mony change of game,   [life
> The fresche array, the lusty contenance,
> The besy awayte, the hertly obseruance   [assiduous service; heartfelt
> That quhilum was amongis thame so ryf?[26]   [formerly; plentiful

The same sophisticated, international outlook is evident in the poetry of Robert Henryson (*c.* 1425–1506), whose *Moral Fabillis*, written in the 1480s, draw on the European tradition of Aesopic fables, through the mediation of

Gualterus Anglicus and of Lydgate's and Caxton's versions.[27] Henryson's awareness of his original contribution to this century-old tradition is highlighted by the prologue, in which he describes fables as hiding in their narrative shell a sweet kernel of moral truth. In choosing the genre of the beast fable, Henryson is not unique: an earlier instance is Richard Holland's *The Buke of the Howlat* (*c.* 1448), whose more direct source is Geoffrey Chaucer's *Parlement of Foules*. Written in the alliterative stanza generally used for romance, the *Buke* is a satire on contemporary society as well as a celebration of the House of Douglas, using an immense array of birds – and a great variety of styles – to represent various aspects of the court and both religious and secular powers, that is, the pope and the emperor. In comparison with Holland (but also with Lydgate's Aesopic fables) Henryson's *Fabillis* show a more marked independence from their model, presenting the reader with a multi-layered text associating the popular appeal of the Aesopic theme with a subtle philosophical meditation in the *moralitates* following each fable: here the writer demonstrates the intricacy of allegory, using the allure of his narrations to argue the nature of truth, the insolence of power, the role of distributive justice in a fundamentally unjust world.

This is far from simple poetry. The same complexity, perhaps less elegantly couched, can be found in what is considered an earlier effort, *Orpheus and Euridice*, which offers a reading of the Orpheus myth through the lens of Nicholas Trivet's commentary on the relevant passage of Boethius' *De Consolatione Philosophiae*. Full of allusions to philosophy, astronomy, natural science and law, *Orpheus* can be quite demanding of the reader, though the display of erudition is often tempered by modesty *topoi* phrased with much good humour, as in this instance, which follows a long and complicated *excursus* into the various musical modes, according to the Greeks:

> This mery music and mellifluate,   [harmonious
> Complete and full with nowmeris od and evyn,   [numbers
> Is causit be the moving of the hevyn.
> Off sik music to wryte I do bot dote,   [but; act foolishly
> Thar-for at this mater a stra I lay,   ['I stop with regard
>   to this subject'

This contrast between the aureate tone of the conventional representation and the low-key, domestic detail is one of the characteristics we find in most fifteenth-century Scottish poets: thus Fortune tweaks the lover's ear before leaving him in *The Kingis Quair*, and Dunbar loses a slipper during the formal dance in *The Goldyn Targe*.

Henryson's masterpiece is perhaps *The Testament of Cresseid* (*c.* 1492), conceived as an answer to Chaucer's *Troilus and Criseyde*, and telling the story of Cresseid's degradation and death after her betrayal of Troilus. The Scottish writer's deviation from the model is expressed through a question ('Quha [who] wait [knows] gif all that Chaucer wrait [wrote] was trew?', line 64) expressing the freedom of the poet from the overwhelming model. Henryson's corpus marks him as perhaps the most wide-ranging among medieval Scottish poets, as well as a voice of absolute originality. The very little we know of his life and circumstances does not allow us to connect him to a court or a form of patronage, and this makes the erudition, sophistication and wit of his output even more surprising, considering the relative isolation in which he appears to have worked.

The reign of James IV marks the most splendid period of the medieval Scottish court,[28] and the two poets who may be said to close the fifteenth century – William Dunbar and Gavin Douglas, both university graduates (probably of St Andrews) – move in a different milieu from their predecessors. William Dunbar (*c.* 1460–1520) acknowledges the patronage he enjoys through poems such as *The Thrissill and the Rois*, a dream-vision celebrating the marriage of Margaret Tudor and James IV, symbolised by the two plants, or *The Goldyn Targe*, a dream-vision conventionally set in May and evidently owing a debt to Chaucer, though working also as a celebration of James IV in its allusion to the ship and the gun, emblems of military power, and its use of heraldic colours. As in the case of Henryson, however, Dunbar's curiosity and experimentation with different genres and modes stop him from being simply a courtly writer of occasional poetry. His *Tretis of the Tua Mariit Wemen and the Wedo*, 530 lines of anti-feminist invective in the form of a dialogue between three women, has evoked comparisons with Boccaccio's *Decameron*;[29] the poem shares with the Italian masterpiece a deceptively domestic environment giving space to a multi-layered narration, but this very characteristic also shows how Henryson's lesson did not go unheard. On the other hand, *The Flyting of Dunbar and Kennedie* is one of the best instances of a fully 'national' mode of poetry: Dunbar's flyting with Walter Kennedy owes much to the European tradition of the *tenzone*, but probably even more to a Gaelic tradition of oral contest. This poetic invective, characterising Scottish poetry in the fifteenth and sixteenth century up to the *Invectiues Capitane Allexander Montgomeree and Pollvart* (1582), takes its strength also from the alliterative stanza it uses. While this form was declining in contemporary English poetry, in Scotland alliteration was used in complex stanzas, as shown in *The Buke of the Howlat* as well as in Henryson's *Sum Practysis of Medecyne*, and to be found in widely different texts, from *The Awntyrs of Arthure* to *The Taill of Rauf Coilyear*; James VI still recommends alliterative (or 'tumbling') verse in his *Reulis and Cautelis*.[30]

Dunbar therefore balances his poetic exploration between the courtly and the popular, disguising erudition under the latter and freeing the former from abject convention through his curiosity and sophistication. The case of Gavin Douglas (1474–1522) is somewhat different. Here the influence of humanism is most evident, especially if we consider his *Eneados* (1513), a translation of Virgil's *Aeneid*. This is a fascinating instance of slow development in the medieval to a humanistic approach to classical texts. The use of Maphaeus Vegius' thirteenth book or *Supplementum* to Virgil, like his drawing on Landino's Neoplatonic reading of the epic matter, has been read as proof both of Douglas's humanism,[31] as well as of his penchant for Christian allegorising and for a traditionally moral reading of Virgil.[32] At the same time, Douglas's translation, as he proudly affirms, 'Writtin in the langage of the Scottis natioun' (Prologue, line 103), appropriates this most famous of classical texts and makes it part of the national culture. His literary consciousness is evident in the prologues to the various books, original and exceptional statements on the nature of translation and literary recreation written in various metrical forms and offering a sort of creative comment to Virgil's monument.[33]

Douglas therefore appears to mark a point of transition between medieval and Renaissance in Scottish literature; the very fact that his other great work, *The Palice of Honour*, may be said to draw on Chaucer's *House of Fame* and to inspire Skelton's *Garlande of Laurell* is significant of the extent to which this poet transcends the boundaries of national literature in order to set his work at a challengingly international level: as he writes towards the end of the *Eneados*, his expected audience is not limited to Scotland: 'Throw owt the ile yclepit [called] Albyon / Red [read] sall [shall] I be, and sung with many one' (*Conclusio*, lines 11–12). It is therefore appropriate to propose him as the poetic voice who concludes the great, if short, season of medieval poetry in Scotland. The *Eneados* was concluded in 1513, a portentous year for Scottish history, since this was the year in which James IV's reign reached its apogee only to conclude disastrously with his attempted invasion of England and the disastrous defeat at Flodden. It is remarkable that we have no record of Dunbar's poetry after 1513, though he presumably lived on, and that even Douglas wrote his most famous works before that date. King James's interest in literacy may also be demonstrated by his role in the setting up of the Chepman and Myllar press in Edinburgh in 1508: it could be said that the culture of early modern Scotland found its starting point here.[34]

These two dates and their overlapping underline the continuity between medieval and Renaissance in Scottish culture: Older Scots continued to be the language employed for literary texts until the end of the seventeenth century, while some of the key topics we associate with medieval Scottish literature, from its metrical preferences to its attention to foreign models, would find a resonant if belated echo in James VI's literary renaissance. Unlike its English counterpart, Scottish literature does not seem to suffer from the long-fifteenth-century syndrome, that period of understudied and much abused 'drab' writing;[35] as a consequence, the transition into early modern literature is seamless, and the concept of Renaissance, here associated with the reign of James VI, takes on political rather than literary overtones. The Scottish literary fifteenth century looks certainly more attractive than its English counterpart, and is in fact the high point of medieval Scottish literature. If the two have in common the overhanging shadow of Chaucer and the first tentative approaches of European humanism, Scottish poets appear to have struck upon a vein of originality that is absent in English poetry at the time: the key word to understand the 'matter of Scotland' in this comparison is probably *makar*, the word chosen by William Dunbar to designate himself and his fellow poets in his *Lament*, but also appearing in Harry's *Wallace* to evoke the times 'Quhen gud makaris rang weill in-to Scotland' (XI.1455). Denton Fox's suggestion that the word might be considered the Scottish equivalent of Dante Alighieri's *miglior fabbro* offers a fascinating reading of the literature discussed in this chapter: drawing on the wealth of the European cultural inheritance, the Scottish medieval poets, in the best instances, propose a fruitful marriage of *auctoritee* and *experience*, inscribing received wisdom within a domestic context of unique topicality. The image proposed by the writer of *The Kingis Quair* is particularly significant here:

> I set me doun,
> And furthwithall my pen in hand I tuke [shortly
> And maid a [cros], and thus begouth my buke. (lines 89–91) [began

Echoed also in the opening stanzas of Henryson's *Testament*, it pinpoints the personal, immediate, almost domestic approach to literary matter that characterises most of Scottish medieval literature, and gives a unique overtone to the poetry 'Writtin in the langage of the Scottis natioun.'

Notes

1 Roderick J. Lyall, '"A New Maid Channoun"? Redefining the Canonical in Medieval and Renaissance Scottish Literature', *Studies in Scottish Literature*, 26 (1991), 1–18.

2 Among recent instances, see Marco Fazzini (ed.), *Alba Literaria: A History of Scottish Literature* (Mestre: Amos Edizioni, 2005); Douglas Gifford, Sarah Dunnigan and Allan MacGillivray (eds.), *Scottish Literature: In English and Scots* (Edinburgh University Press, 2002).

3 R. James Goldstein, 'Writing in Scotland, 1058–1560', in David Wallace (ed.), *The Cambridge History of Medieval English Literature* (Cambridge and New York: Cambridge University Press, 1999), pp. 229–54.

4 Nicola Royan, 'Scottish Literature', in David F. Johnson and Elaine Treharne (eds.), *Readings in Medieval Texts: Interpreting Old and Middle English Literature* (Oxford University Press, 2005), pp. 354–69; Priscilla Bawcutt and Janet Hadley Williams, 'Introduction: Poets "of this Natioun"', in Priscilla Bawcutt and Janet Hadley Williams (eds.), *A Companion to Medieval Scottish Poetry* (Cambridge: D. S. Brewer, 2006), pp. 1–18.

5 For further information, especially on historical writing, see Benjamin T. Hudson, 'The Scottish Gaze', in R. Andrew McDonald (ed.), *History, Literature, and Music in Scotland, 700–1560* (University of Toronto Press, 2002), pp. 29–59.

6 Richard J. Moll, '"Off Quhat Nacioun Art Thow?" National Identity in Blind Hary's *Wallace*', in McDonald (ed.), *History, Literature, and Music*, p. 121. Harry solves the problem by describing 'all of the ethnic groups of Scotland as "trew Scottis," as long as they support the ideological ideal of Scottish independence' (126–7).

7 Joachim Schwend, 'Nationalism in Scottish Medieval and Renaissance Literature', in Horst W. Drescher and Hermann Völkel (eds.), *Nationalism in Literature – Literarischer Nationalismus: Literature, Language and National Identity* (Frankfurt am Main: Peter Lang, 1989), pp. 29–42.

8 Denton Fox, 'Middle Scots Poets and Patrons', in V. J. Scattergood and J. W. Sherborne (eds.), *English Court Culture in the Later Middle Ages* (London: Duckworth, 1983), pp. 109–27.

9 Royan, 'Scottish Literature', pp. 354–69. But see Benjamin T. Hudson, 'The Literary Culture of the Early Scottish Court', in Graham Caie, Roderick J. Lyall, Sally Mapstone and Kenneth Simpson (eds.), *The European Sun* (East Linton: Tuckwell Press, 2001), pp. 156–65, for a reconstruction of early Scottish literature.

10 F. J. Amours (ed.), *The Original Chronicle of Andrew of Wintoun* (Edinburgh and London: Blackwood, 1907), Book VII, Part X, lines 3621–8.

11 Sally Mapstone, 'The Advice to Princes Tradition in Scottish Literature', unpublished D.Phil. thesis, University of Oxford (1986), p. 141. This remains the most complete study on the genre.

12 *Ibid.*, pp. 454–63.

13 Derrick McClure, 'Barbour's *Brus*: Epic Poetry and the National Resistance of the Admirable Warrior King', in Fazzini (ed.), *Alba Literaria*, pp. 9–18.

14 A. S. G. Edwards, 'Contextualising Middle Scots Romance', in L. A. J. R. Houwen, A. A. MacDonald and S. L. Mapstone (eds.), *A Palace in the Wild: Essays on Vernacular Culture and Humanism in Late-Medieval and Renaissance Scotland* (Leuven: Peeters, 2000), pp. 61–73.

15 *Ibid.*, p. 69.

16 Alasdair A. MacDonald, 'Religious Poetry in Middle Scots', in R. D. S. Jack (ed.), *The History of Scottish Literature*, vol. I, *Origins to 1660 (Mediaeval and Renaissance)* (Aberdeen University Press, 1988), p. 92.

17 R. James Goldstein, *The Matter of Scotland: Historical Narrative in Medieval Scotland* (Lincoln: University of Nebraska Press, 1993), pp. 282–3. See also Walter Scheps, 'Chaucer and the Middle Scots Poets', *Studies in Scottish Literature*, 22 (1987), 55–8.

18 Line 47. The edition used is Priscilla Bawcutt (ed.), *The Poems of William Dunbar* (Glasgow: Association for Scottish Literary Studies, 1998).

19 *The Palice of Honour*, lines 916–24. The edition used is Priscilla Bawcutt (ed.), *The Shorter Poems of Gavin Douglas* (Edinburgh: The Scottish Text Society, 2003).

20 Bawcutt (ed.), *Poems of William Dunbar*, p. 163, lines 1–5.

21 Denton Fox, 'The Scottish Chaucerians', in D. S. Brewer (ed.), *Chaucer and Chaucerians: Critical Studies in Middle English Literature* (London: Nelson, 1966), p. 164.

22 Lyall, 'A New Maid Channoun?', 12.

23 Gregory Kratzmann, *Anglo-Scottish Literary Relations (1430–1550)* (Cambridge University Press, 1980).

24 Julia Boffey and A. S. G. Edwards (eds.), *The Works of Geoffrey Chaucer and 'The Kingis Quair': A Facsimile of Bodleian Library, Oxford, MS Arch. Selden. B. 24* (Cambridge: D. S. Brewer, 1997). See also Sally Mapstone, 'Introduction: Older Scots and the Fifteenth Century', and Julia Boffey and A. S. G. Edwards, 'Bodleian MS Arch. Selden. B. 24: The Genesis and Evolution of a Scottish Poetic Anthology', in Sally Mapstone (ed.) *Older Scots Literature* (Edinburgh: John Donald, 2005), pp. 3–13; 14–29.

25 See Alessandra Petrina, *The Kingis Quair of James I of Scotland* (Padova: Unipress, 1997).

26 John Norton-Smith (ed.), *James I of Scotland: The Kingis Quair* (Leiden: Brill, 1981), lines 841–6.

27 Denton Fox, 'The Sources', in Denton Fox (ed.), *The Poems of Robert Henryson* (Oxford: Clarendon Press, 1981), pp. xliv–l.

28 On the issue of royal patronage, see Sally Mapstone, 'Was There a Court Literature in Fifteenth-Century Scotland?', *Studies in Scottish Literature*, 26 (1991), 410–22.

29 Priscilla Bawcutt, 'William Dunbar and Gavin Douglas', in Jack (ed.), *History of Scottish Literature*, vol. I, p. 78.

30 One is tempted to think that Chaucer's Parson, who observes that as a 'Southren man' he cannot 'geeste "rum, ram, ruf" by lettre', is mockingly alluding to Scottish poetry.

31 Priscilla Bawcutt, *Gavin Douglas: A Critical Study* (Edinburgh University Press, 1976), pp. 73–8.

32 Anna Torti, 'The Poetry of Gavin Douglas: Memory, Past Tradition and Its Renewal', in Fazzini (ed.), *Alba Literaria*, pp. 75–6.

33 Fox, 'Scottish Chaucerians', pp. 188–92.

34 Mapstone underlines also the role of the Sinclair family as patrons of literature in the late fifteenth century ('Introduction', pp. 3–9).

35 The key study on the subject is David Lawton, 'Dullness and the Fifteenth Century', *ELH*, 54 (1987), 761–99.

Guide to further reading

Bawcutt, Priscilla, *Gavin Douglas: A Critical Study* (Edinburgh: Edinburgh University Press, 1976)

Bawcutt, Priscilla and Janet Hadley Williams (eds.), *A Companion to Medieval Scottish Poetry* (Cambridge: D. S. Brewer, 2006)

Fox, Denton, 'The Scottish Chaucerians', in D. S. Brewer (ed.), *Chaucer and Chaucerians: Critical Studies in Middle English Literature* (London: Nelson, 1966), pp. 164–200

Fox, Denton and William A. Ringler (eds.), *The Bannatyne Manuscript: National Library of Scotland Advocates' Ms.1.1.6* (London: Scolar Press, 1980)

Goldstein, R. James, *The Matter of Scotland: Historical Narrative in Medieval Scotland* (Lincoln: University of Nebraska Press, 1993)

Jack, R. D. S., *The Italian Influence on Scottish Literature* (Edinburgh University Press, 1972)

Jack, R. D. S. (ed.), *The History of Scottish Literature*, vol. 1, *Origins to 1660 (Mediaeval and Renaissance)* (Aberdeen University Press, 1988)

Kratzmann, Gregory, *Anglo-Scottish Literary Relations 1430–1550* (Cambridge University Press, 1980)

Mapstone, Sally, 'The Advice to Princes Tradition in Scottish Literature', unpublished D.Phil. thesis, University of Oxford (1986)

Royan, Nicola, 'Scottish Literature', in David F. Johnson and Elaine Treharne (eds.), *Readings in Medieval Texts: Interpreting Old and Middle English Literature* (Oxford University Press, 2005), pp. 354–69

Schwend, Joachim, 'Nationalism in Scottish Medieval and Renaissance Literature', in Horst W. Dresher and Hermann Völkel (eds.), *Nationalism in Literature – Literarischer Nationalismus: Literature, Language and National Identity* (Frankfurt am Main: Peter Lang, 1989), pp. 29–42

Smith, Janet M., *The French Background of Middle Scots Literature* (Edinburgh: Oliver & Boyd, 1934)

Studies in Scottish Literature, 26 (1991)

3

SARAH DUNNIGAN

Reformation and Renaissance

In a curious twist of cultural history, Scotland enjoys a 'Renaissance' that began in the twentieth century rather than at some point between the fourteenth and the sixteenth centuries. Denis Saurat's term for the cultural energies of the movement associated with Hugh MacDiarmid renders the fate of earlier Scottish literature 'curiouser' still: an anomaly in both Scottish and European literary history. Even in the wake of a new 'British history' which recognises the separate and interlinked cultures of the four nations, and of renewed sympathy towards the idea of a 'northern' Renaissance, the depths of the literature associated, for example, with Mary, Queen of Scots (1542–87), and her son, James (1566–1625) – poets themselves – remain uncharted beyond specialist critical studies. Instead, a story about an impossible, or improbable, first Scottish Renaissance is told, woven out of two historical events, often perceived as culturally calamitous: the mid-sixteenth-century Reformation, and the Union of the Crowns in 1603. Yet Edwin Muir's powerfully emotive visions of the hollowed-out culture resulting from Scotland's violent Reformation, for example, should not prevent us from seeing interesting redirections and reconceptualisations of artistic expression rather than its complete extinction.

The very term 'Renaissance' is perhaps a distorted looking-glass through which to view artistic and intellectual changes which assume different forms in different cultures. Coined by the French writer Jules Michelet in 1855, then famously used by Jacob Burckhardt in *The Civilization* [or *Culture*] *of the Renaissance in Italy* (1860), it embodied the monumental processes of intellectual, artistic and cultural renewal or rebirth which could collectively be judged a self-conscious or purposeful negation of an earlier *medium aevum* or 'middle age'. This idea of Renaissance spawns its own myth (an illuminatory Renaissance versus the medieval 'dark ages') but might be preferable to the alternative periodisation of 'early modern', which unhelpfully foregrounds the notion of a prescient, welcome 'modernity'. The term 'Renaissance' does not refer to a homogeneous movement; it did not suddenly begin with the art of Giotto (*c.* 1266–1337) in Florence, or at any other single, fixed point. This is helpful to remember when trying to pinpoint a 'Renaissance' across the variegated landscapes of sixteenth- and early seventeenth-century Scottish literature. The translation of Euripides' *Medea* by the Neo-Latin poet, polemicist, historian and educationalist George Buchanan (1506–82), published in Paris in 1544 and vital in the development of European drama, is a founding moment in 'the Scottish Renaissance'. Yet it arises out of a whole series of artistic and intellectual currents which interlocked Scotland with Europe from the late fifteenth century onwards. Literary texts, enfolded in complex patterning of cultural diffusion, development and exchange, challenge and resist the very categories which we impose. Gavin Douglas's translation of Virgil's *Aeneid* into Scots, completed by 1513, before Flodden, but not printed until 1553, fuses both 'medieval' and 'Renaissance' traditions: faithful to allegorical, Christian exposition but expressive of human-istic ideals, it strives for a new kind of *eloquentia*, anticipating the use of translation by later sixteenth-century Scottish writers as a means of forging and renewing literary and cultural identities (this is, after all, the century in which Ariosto, Petrarch and Machiavelli are translated into Scots).

Despite awareness of the restrictive as well as helpful nature of histor-ical and cultural categories, this chapter has inevitably been selective in its choice of writers and subjects. It is impossible to do justice to the linguis-tically and culturally distinct traditions of Gaelic writing in the period;[1] oral and popular traditions have not been included here, though that is not intended to suggest any kind of unbreachable boundary between oral and literary cultures.[2] In focusing on literary texts (those which are explicitly fictional or imaginative in scope and intent), the chapter excludes a strong vein of historiographical writing. Yet this period acutely exemplifies how literary texts are always enfolded within other contexts – social, political and religious. Buchanan's *oeuvre* alone provides an extraordinary testament of how a writer's political and religious affiliations are rarely consistent: once the composer of masques and celebratory verse for Mary Stewart's marriage, his Protestant 'conversion' helped turn him into the most vocif-erous of her public and polemical detractors. It is also worth noting that much of the literature mentioned here survives in manuscript rather than print, and that this impinges on our reading of such texts: a manuscript is usually intended for private as opposed to 'public' reading; belongs to a more 'active' process of circulation, reception and transmission; and lacks the 'permanency' or 'sealed off' nature of print. Although this chapter largely focuses on courtly literature, the importance of wider manuscript cultures must be recognised; several major manuscript miscellanies survive which belong to different families or to particular owners, and suggest the literary interests and reading preoccupations of communities and households beyond the royal court which governs production.[3] Arguably, the single most important literary source of the period is the vast manuscript compiled by one George Bannatyne, an Edinburgh merchant, in the 1560s, the richest cultural monument of sixteenth-century Scotland, into which might be read various impulses of religious and political sympathy, toleration and disquiet; it also captured the fascination of Romantic scholars and antiquarians, including Walter Scott. Cultural taste can also be gleaned from knowledge of what books were printed throughout the period. The first printing press in Scotland had been set up by Walter Chepman and Andrew Myllar in Edinburgh in 1508, thirty-two years after Caxton's English press. Later printers such as Robert Lekprevik provided a means of producing immediate and popular literary responses to the crises of Mary, Queen of Scots' reign. Poetic broadsides were deliberately designed to provoke dissent within an increasingly literate populace. Although such broadsides and the religious material from both Reformed and Catholic communities constitute the bulk of printed literature in the mid sixteenth century, secular literary tastes are suggested by the frequent reprinting of David Lyndsay's work,[4] and of Blind Harry's *Wallace*; so too can be found the earliest prints of romances which belong to the late fifteenth- and earlier sixteenth-century periods, such as *Rauf Coilyear* and *Clariodus*. This suggests a print culture by no means dominated by contemporary religious dictates, whilst the fact that printed romance survives well into the early seventeenth century, in the work of Patrick Gordon, for example, suggests an enduring readerly appetite for such labyrinthine, fantastical fictions.

Literature of the spirit

Religion can have artistic consequences, both inhibitive and nurturing; in Scotland the European religious movement known as the Reformation, which saw the universalism of the Catholic church broken apart from the early part of the century, proved to be both. The violent purgation of churches (together with their visual and musical cultures),[5] and the hostility towards popular cultural traditions, is well attested but new forms of cultural expression emerged which reflected emotional and popular support for this religious movement. Dissatisfaction with spiritual authority and the corruption of the church had been articulated before, but from the early 1500s the need for reform acquired a new moral urgency. David Lyndsay's virtuosic play, *Ane Satyre of the Thrie Estaitis* (first performed in 1540), blends the traditions of late medieval anticlerical satire with the urgent impulses of a newer 'reformist message',[6] whilst the Franciscan order was the target of George

Buchanan's lacerating Neo-Latin satires. The cumulative force of the preach-ings and writings of different Reformed thinkers such as Luther, Zwingli and Calvin demanded a profound renewal of spiritual life. Reformation did not 'suddenly' occur but in Scotland, as elsewhere, unfolded across several dec-ades (which witnessed the making of both Catholic and Protestant martyrs) before culminating in the period between 1558and 1565 where political and spiritual schisms were cut most deeply: the first statutes of a Reformed par-liament had been passed by the time a devoutly Catholic queen had come to power. This was a religious revolution which renewed and redefined the relationship between devotional belief, practice and literature.[7] Many of the religious lyrics preserved by Bannatyne reveal the intricate rhetorical beauty of late medieval Catholic devotion. In contrast, mid-sixteenth-century reli-gious poetry is strikingly different, not only and obviously through its dif-ferent doctrinal purpose, but in form and style:

> All my hart ay this is my sang,   [always
>   With doubill myrth and ioy among,   [joy
> Sa blyith as byrd my God to fang,   [find, obtain, capture, acquire
>   Christ hes my hart ay.[8]   [has

This lyric comes from the collection of psalms, religious lyrics and Protestant satires known as *The Gude and Godlie Ballatis* (published in 1567 though many of its texts were composed several decades earlier; many draw on German sources and Lutheran verses) collected and composed by the Wedderburn brothers, James, John and Robert. 'Ane plane text', as the prologue states, their plainness and perspicacity is ironically a rhetorical art in itself, reflecting a new spiritual orientation in which the Word – *sola scriptura* – is the prime mediator between the worshipper and God. These lyrics were also devotional tools, sung to music. In addition to the often arrestingly direct incursions of satirical intent, the 'reworking' of these texts produces interesting aesthetic juxtapositions between their original secular 'trace' or imprint and their new devotional purpose. Their immediacy and directness are echoed in another hybrid devotional-literary practice: that of psalm translation. This vein of Protestant poetic purity, and its introspect-ive meditations, runs deep through the latter part of the sixteenth century (Alexander Scott, James VI, Alexander Montgomerie and William Mure of Rowallan all compose psalmic lyrics while Buchanan's Psalm translations were musically set by the French composer Jean Servin and dedicated to James VI).

Later Reformed poetry – or poetry doctrinally sympathetic to Protestant devotion – varies aesthetically and tonally. 'Of the Day Estivall' by Alexander Hume (*c.* 1557–1609) celebrates the rhythms of the created world, and of a single summer's day, which manifest God's grace: 'For ioy the birds with bouden [swollen] throts, / Agains his visage shein [lit. bright face, i.e. the sun], / Takes vp their kindelie musicke nots, / In woods and gardens grein.'[9] Hume's poetics of harmony recall medieval invocations of divinely infused nature; it is also part of his advocacy of the 'right vse of Poësie' and of his broader religiously motivated antagonism towards secular poetry.[10] Amongst the courtier poets of James's reign, John Stewart (c. 1545–c. 1605) composes a visionary allegory for the king in which the narrator's quest for spiritual 'trew felicitie', despite being armed with 'ane sourd … [sword] of the spreit' and his 'febill feit' 'schod' 'vith the gospell', fails to diminish the poetic (and political) anxiety of pleasing his king.[11] The religious poetry of Alexander Montgomerie (early 1550s–1598) is especially interesting, given the apparent intimacy – poetic and emotional – between himself ('maister-poete') and James, destroyed on his conversion to Catholicism. James's vision of a Christian poetics modelled on French Protestant poetry (fulfilled, for example, by Thomas Hudson's 1584 translation of Du Bartas's *Judith*) sits awkwardly with a work such as Montgomerie's *The Cherrie and the Slae* (first printed in 1597), and its beautifully orchestrated, yet opaque, visionary world in which the dreamer learns to taste the healing, 'merrie' consolations of the 'Cherrie', perhaps emblematic of the Catholic faith – 'Since for it onely thou but thirsts' – rather than the 'poysond SLAE' of Reformed faith.[12] This highlights the way in which literary articulations of devotion in the period are, if not deliberately polemical, highly charged. The popular allegory *Ane Godlie Dreame* (1603) by Elizabeth Melville (*fl.* 1599– 1631) demonstrates how her Calvinist faith confers poetic legitimacy and preacherly authority: it exhorts the necessity of salvation and the falsity of Catholic doctrine but still depicts a moving unity between God and dreamer which recalls pre-Reformation, feminised visions of Christ, and anticipates the intense spiritual communions narrated by later seventeenth-century evangelical women.[13]

William Drummond of Hawthornden (1585–1649) is arguably the finest religious poet of the period. *Flowres of Sion* (1616) is a sonnet sequence on a series of philosophical themes (such as mutability and mortality) which builds up towards the final consolation – a providential vision of divine goodness – through a succession of individual 'tableaux'. These include meditatively visceral portraits of Christ's Passion, which seem the poetic equivalent of the shadowed, sensuous flesh of European Baroque art.[14] Drummond's sacred, like his secular, sequence looks to Neoplatonic philosophy to unveil a vision of the promised heaven which 'owlie eyed' humanity cannot yet see, its beauty arrestingly apprehended through 'Signes that clearlie shine',[15] and the poet's own highly wrought language. Drummond's spiritual poetics are distinctive and, amongst Scottish religious writers, perhaps only the 'metaphysical' religious poetry of William Mure of Rowallan (1594–1657) approaches it in its figurative complexity:

> If Lines which Sphears in equall shares divyde,
> But once the Center, twice the Circle touch,
> Like slow-plac'd snails, why there still doe we crouch,
> Still crawle on earth, still grov'ling bide?[16]

Literature of the heart

In the European Renaissance, 'love words' constituted much poetic activity; the Scottish context is no different, and some of the most beautiful and striking poetry is erotic in nature and associated with the courts of Mary and James from the collection of love 'ballattis' found in the Bannatyne Manuscript to the individual lyrics and sonnet sequences of Jacobean poets. Yet a love poem is rarely all that it seems. A Bannatyne lyric may declare its desire simply – '[Y]e ar [th]e bontie bliss of all my baill [grief] / Bayt [both] lyfe and deth standis in to your hand'[17] – but it is impossible to assume the 'truthfulness' of any lyrically desiring voice. Scottish courtly art (as recognised of English Henrician and Elizabethan art) demands a realignment of conventional readerly bearings; the circulation of love poetry resembles a 'theatre' or 'game' of what one lyric calls 'amouris play and sport'. Performances of desire (in many instances, musical settings survive[18]), in a way as crafted as the masques known to have been performed at Mary's court.[19] In a period where dramatic activity was severely curtailed by Reformed legislation, desire and performance coalesce in the drama *Philotus*, an erotic farce with roots in Latin drama and the Italian *commedia erudita*, which Jamie Reid Baxter persuasively dates to Mary's reign rather than James's.[20] The play's comically Byzantine layering of sexual folly and misidentification may have appealed to a courtly culture sympathetic to Renaissance debates about *questioni d'amore*. In their preoccupation with conduct, 'service' and courtesy, the Bannatyne lyrics – and those of Alexander Scott (*c.* 1520–82/3) in particular – recall the medieval ideal of love familiarly known as 'courtly love' (*amour courtois* or *fin' amor*). These are often framed as miniaturised allegories in which personified reason and desire, body and soul, compete for autonomy within a lover. The precariousness of erotic desire is also explored in John Rolland's allegorical *The Court of Love*, printed in 1575 but written around 1560. Here, the late medieval aesthetic of *amour courtois* is invoked, ostensibly to result in the lover's fortunate expulsion from 'thir Ladeis and Court venereane' [the court of Venus],[21] but not without portraying love's mercurial power in deftly witty and graceful ways.

46

'Medievalism' endures in the Jacobean love poetry of the 1580s but in this decade the most popular Renaissance means of fashioning love-words – Petrarchism – takes root in Scottish courtly poetry, somewhat belatedly compared to European, and even English, modes. The *Rime sparse* of the Italian poet Petrarch (1304–74) bequeathed a legacy both of writing artfully about love, and of conceptualising it philosophically and spiritually. First associated with 'newness' (a rhetorical model which could develop the potential of vernacular languages), throughout the sixteenth century it became so ingrained an imitative model that dissent from, and parody of, the model became another popular form of response. In Scottish courtly culture, the creation of love poetry followed a rather different pattern from that in England. As R. D. S. Jack has demonstrated,[22] the recognisable Petrarchan love poetry, which only poets such as William Fowler and William Alexander compose in the 1580s and 90s, is sustained well into the seventeenth century in the love sequences of Drummond and others. Significantly, from the mid sixteenth century onwards, French models and sources – particularly Ronsard, Marot, Desportes, du Bellay – inspire and direct the work of writers such as Montgomerie and Stewart (although, to a degree, Italian literature is mediated through their use of earlier French Pléiade poets just as Stewart's translation of Ariosto's *Orlando Furioso* is indebted to French translations of the Italian romance).

There may be several reasons for the slightly different configuration of the influences of European erotic poetry. Firstly, in Mary Stewart – despite her reign's political turmoil – was embodied an artistic as well as political alliance with France; the Marian associations of adapting Pierre de Ronsard's poetry (a writer close to Mary) may have shaped the Catholic Montgomerie's preference for French over Italian erotic sources. Secondly, the legacy of the so-called Casket sonnets raised high the moral stakes of writing love poetry; these love poems ascribed to Mary were adduced as proof of her adultery and responsibility for Darnley's murder, and used in English trials as well as printed defamations of her.[23] Thirdly, James himself, on the evidence of the king's own poetry and his literary treatise, *The Reulis and Cautelis* (discussed below), was disinclined to make much intellectual or aesthetic room for love poetry. This may explain why at the Jacobean court the sonnet was strikingly used for a variety of thematic purposes beyond its primary association with love (the rhyme scheme of this fourteen-line lyric form, with its exigently disciplined poetic architecture, now associated with Edmund Spenser, was earlier used by James's poets as a distinctive vernacular model).[24] Virtuosically, Montgomerie's sonnets encompass moral meditations on fortune and death, spiritual laments, comic diatribes and trenchant political complaints, sonnet-flytings which prove John Rolland's warning that 'Ze ken [you know] the Court can nocht ay stabill stand.'[25]

This refusal to adhere to love poetry's generic and formal prescriptions is mirrored in Jacobean love poetry, renewing the genre's engagement with issues of sexual, political and moral desires. This is seen in the darkly named *Tarantula of Love* by William Fowler (1560/1–1612), where a Protestant sensibility wrestles with the Catholic apotheosis of Petrarch's sequence. In Montgomerie's lyrics love often fails to transcend or resist the materialism of death; William Alexander (1577–1640), in naming his beloved, Aurora, punningly evokes Petrarch's Laura but also creates a mythic web of allusion which embeds it within other Ovidian subtexts. The persistence of the erotic sonnet sequence (like that of romance) after the Union of 1603 is often used to suggest how early seventeenth-century Scottish literature is critically, as well as politically, untuned. But though it is difficult to impose coherent artistic direction on poets who all held disparate roles politically and culturally (Ayton, Craig, Murray, Mure, Hannay, Drummond, for example), that should not prevent recognition of the experimental nature of this erotic literature. *Caelia* by David Murray (1567–1629) self-reflexively confesses that his feminised 'love-sicke verse' contradicts literary ideals whilst still illustrating how writing about love means writing about literary history; citation, allusion and echo are stitched together in the fabric of an extraordinary sequence by Alexander Craig (*c.* 1567–1627). Addressed to eight different women (constituting eight different narratives with their own symbolic potential), it playfully fissures the idea of desire, and of the beloved as a stable, unitary figure.[26] The love lyrics of Robert Ayton (1570–1638) are infused by the fashion for anti-Platonism. As witty, ironic inversions of the idea that love is spiritually and morally transcendent, their ludic grace does not always diminish a darker sense that desire, as well as identity and meaning itself, is a fragile illusion: 'Methinkes I turn a childe again / And of my shadow am a chaseing.'[27] Similarly, in Drummond's *Poems* (1616), his beloved exists both *in vive* and *in morte*, like Petrarch's Laura; although Christianised Neoplatonic philosophy offers a higher and enduring world in which she lives on, this is undercut by the narrator's closing perception in which the world still remains contingent and imperfect. Although post-Union love poetry is culturally and linguistically unmoored from its earlier courtly context, this confers a new kind of freedom and 'experimentalism' on writers. Love's poetic traditions, as well as the nation's political contours, are challengingly redrawn and remapped in this period. Significantly, Anna Hume (*fl.*1644) will return to Petrarch mid-century to produce a translation of his *Trionfi* (as William Fowler had done) which reimagines and reinterprets Laura; Petrarch has an enduring afterlife in Scotland.[28]

Imagining words

In recent years, there has been some resistance to the idea of a coherent Scottish Jacobean Renaissance, or more particularly to the existence of the 'Castalian band': named after the mythological stream Castalia, an emblem of poetic inspiration, this is used to refer to the group of poets intimately associated with, and respondent to, the king's literary will in the 1580s and 90s. Whilst this may unfairly 'centralise' the idea of literary production in the period, it still usefully captures the extraordinary and deliberate ways in which James fashioned both himself and the art around him. Renaissance sovereigns invariably sculpted their own mythology (in this James was not unusual), but there was a particularly pressing necessity for James to establish authority in the early 1580s as a young king emerging from two decades of civil war and political instability after Mary's deposition. James's first printed text, *The Essayes of a Prentise in the Divine Arte of Poesie* (1584), in which the *Reulis and Cautelis* appeared, is best considered a kind of symbolic 'legislation' in which poetic creativity mirrors political creativity.[29] James's English reign has garnered much attention in terms of the symbolic myth-making – the panoply of insignia, emblems, processions – which he used to consolidate his governance after the death of the Virgin Queen, but this myth-making is at work too in his Scottish reign. Significantly, after the mid-century religious extirpation of drama, James is sympathetic to performance, granting English player companies a licence to perform; the erotic drama *Pamphilus speakand of lufe*, by John Burel, based on a twelfth-century Latin *comoedia* and elegantly composed in 'ballad royal' verse, stems from this period.[30] As the self-appointed incarnation of Apollo, the god of music and poetry, James composes sonnets which solicit the powers of mythological deities to seal his literary coronation, while those on the Danish astronomer Tycho Brahe reflect this preoccupation with order and creation, 'subtle and celestiall sweete accord'.[31] Poetic composition shows a king's command of the faculty of imagination, though throughout all his writings (even in his political treatise, the *Basilikon Doron* (1599), and in his treatise against witchcraft and the occult, the *Daemonologie* (1597), the capacity of language to betray and deceive, as well as to coerce and inspire, preoccupied James.

This blend of assertion and anxiety runs through *The Reulis and Cautelis*. James (disingenuously) denies any borrowing from a well-established tradition of sixteenth-century rhetorical manuals, offering it instead as a template for his own courtly revolution: 'lyke as the tyme is changeit sensyne [since then], sa is the ordour of Poesie changeit … as for thame that hes written in it of late, there hes neuer ane of thame written in our language'.[32]

His prescriptions range from the conceptual (the importance of 'Invention' and of desirable verse genres) to the ideological (the need to avoid overtly political subjects) and the precisely technical (syllabic measurement; the metrical means to ensure 'flowing' verse, vitally correspondent with the 'musique' which underpins so much lyric composition in this period).[33] This is reflected in the strikingly intricate and intensely wrought form and rhetoric of Jacobean court poetry. This mirrors broader Renaissance notions of *copia* (verbal abundance), but this ideal is also put to playful, subversive use in the survival of the flyting genre: *The Flyting betwixt Montgomery and Polwart* conjoins vituperative slang, demonic conjurations and comic riotousness to make the poem a differently virtuosic kind of verbal and sensory assault from that of courtly *préciosité*. This quintessentially Mannerist notion that style alone (the more artful and ingenious the better) makes for a beautiful or pleasurable textual artifact is in part peculiar to Jacobean courtly poetry in terms of Scottish literary history, but it can also be seen in the highly ornamented romance of *Clariodus*; as R. D. S. Jack has shown, the rhetorical tradition is a fundamental but often misunderstood part of Scottish poetic history, and in the early to mid seventeenth century it flourishes again both through the endurance of a romance tradition, and in Sir Thomas Urquhart's translation of Rabelais in 1653. In this way – as well as through the wealth of translations which Jacobean poets produced – Scottish Renaissance poetry is bridged with a European imaginative sensibility. Throughout the 1580s and 90s it retains its vernacular identity, all the while transmuting the emotional and political impulses of the courtly environment into a rich, dynamic culture; inevitably, though, it was short-lived.

Transformations

With the Union of the Crowns in 1603, and the absorption of king and court within London, there could be no artistically unified centre within Scotland. The pressures of Anglicization (seen as early as the previous mid-century) were now more or less absolute: the preface to Alexander's closet classical dramas, *The Monarchike Tragedies*, justifies the use of English for its 'elegance and perfection' while the Scottish poet at the new court was termed a 'Scoto-Brittanicus'. Yet one means of resisting an uncompromisingly elegiac reading of early seventeenth-century Scottish literature (which tends to ignore the specificity of work produced) is to register that poetry finds renewed political purpose.[34] It still performs a public, ceremonial function (as on the death of James's son, Henry) but, along with the profusion of pamphlets and treatises which debated the state of the new Union, it becomes a subtle, skilfully manipulated means of quiet dissent. The entwining of myth and classicism in Craig's poetry, for example, produces encoded but nevertheless sharp political complaint; England's 'glorius day' dawns on James's ascension yet

> we are but *Cymmerian* slaues with gloomy clouds ou'rcled.
> Rich neighbour nation then, from thy complaining cease:
> Not thou, but we should sigh, & so to our complaints giue place.
> Our Garland lacks the Rose, our chatton tins the stone,   [the circle or
>   band of a ring in which the stone is held; lacks]
> Our Volier wants the *Philomel*, we left allace alone.   [birdcage]
> What art thou *Scotland* then?[35]

Simeon Graham, in a poem ostensibly praising 'great *Iames*', evokes memories of 'the *Castalean* spring' and, in both an exculpatory and defensive move, points out that 'Kings are sometime forc'd / To yeeld consent with vnconsenting hart.'[36] *Forth Feasting*, a river pastoral written on the occasion of the king's only return 'to the North' in 1617, reveals Drummond as an adroit political poet. It provides 'panegyricke' – praise for a king whose 'Raigne' brings multiple 'Wonders' – but also, through the feminised, erotic topography of the contemporary landscape, makes the Forth's lament express Scotland's betrayal and neglect, 'jelous' of the king's devotion to a richer but meretricious rival: 'O love these Bounds, whereof Thy royall Stemme [ancestry/lineage] / More than an hundreth wore a Diademe.'[37] In such political complaint, the use of pastoral portrays the post-Union world as fallen, that of the pre-Union idyllic and 'golden'; the myth of seventeenth-century Scotland's 'broken culture' was partly woven by contemporary poets themselves.

This, of course, is a partial story. David Parkinson has recently used the pastoral writing of the Presbyterian Samuel Rutherford (*c.* 1600–61) to argue persuasively for the thematic and stylistic diversity of a seventeenth-century literary culture which 'broadens, gaining readers and writers across the political, social, regional, and religious landscape'.[38] The Neo-Latin tradition in Scottish poetry, of which Buchanan in the previous century had been a leading European exemplar, was consolidated. The publication of the *Delitiae poetarum Scotorum* (Amsterdam, 1637) by the Aberdeenshire writer Arthur Johnston (*c.* 1569–1641) was a prodigious gathering of over forty Scottish Latin poets from the previous six decades. A 'national' poetic assemblage in line with other European Neo-Latin anthologies of the period, it demonstrates the extraordinary versatility of Renaissance Latinity (a tradition which throughout Europe had coexisted with vernacular poetry), and of individual poets (such as Ayton) who composed in both languages. This

Neo-Latin tradition – with its roots in north-east, Episcopalian culture, and its embrace of erotic, elegiac, political, dedicatory, scientific, mythological and religious subjects – enjoyed republication and interest a century later, but it is only recently that Robert Crawford's translations and versions of Johnston's own poems have opened up its linguistic and artistic vitality to a broader readership.[39]

The period covered by this chapter is in a privileged position to unearth and challenge some of the preconceptions and myths which beset Scottish literature. This overview has hopefully helped to cast the richness and diversity of sixteenth- and seventeenth-century Scottish literature in a sharper light or, to use one of James's artistic ideals, more 'vivelie' [brightly, clearly].

Notes

1 See William Gillies, 'Gaelic: The Classical Tradition', in R. D. S. Jack (ed.), *The History of Scottish Literature* (Aberdeen University Press, 1988), vol. 1, pp. 245–61.

2 See Hamish Henderson, 'The Ballad and Popular Tradition to 1660', in Jack (ed.), *History of Scottish Literature*, pp. 263–84.

3 See Priscilla Bawcutt, 'Manuscript Miscellanies in Scotland from the Fifteenth to the Seventeenth Century', in Sally Mapstone (ed.), *Older Scots Literature* (Edinburgh: John Donald, 2005), pp. 189–210; Sebastiaan J. Verweij, '"The inlegebill scribling of my impromt pen": The Production and Circulation of Literary Miscellany Manuscripts in Jacobean Scotland, *c.* 1580–*c.* 1630', unpublished Ph.D. thesis, University of Glasgow (2008).

4 Lyndsay's best-known work, the drama *Ane Satyre of the Thrie Estaitis*, first performed in 1540, was not printed until 1602 but his satirical, comic and political poetry was popularly printed throughout the second half of the century.

5 See David McRoberts, 'Material Destruction Caused by the Scottish Reformation', *Innes Review*, 10 (1959), 126–72.

6 Bill Findlay, *History of Scottish Theatre* (Edinburgh: Polygon, 1998), p. 27.

7 See Crawford Gribben and David George Mullan (eds.), *Literature and the Scottish Reformation* (Farnham: Ashgate, 2009); cf. Margo Todd, *The Culture of Protestantism in Early Modern Scotland* (New Haven: Yale University Press, 2002).

8 A. F. Mitchell (ed.), *Gude and Godlie Ballatis* Scottish Text Society (Edinburgh, 1897), p. 139, lines 1–4.

9 Alexander Lawson (ed.), *The Poems of Alexander Hume*, ?*1557–1609*, Scottish Text Society (Edinburgh: William Blackwood and Sons, 1902), p. 26, lines 37–40.

10 See Gerard Carruthers, 'Form and Substance in the Poetry of the Castalian "Band"', *Scottish Literary Journal*, 26 (1999), 7–17; Deirdre Serjeantson, 'English Bards and Scotch Poetics: Scotland's Literary Influence and Sixteenth-Century English Religious Verse', in Gribben and Mullan (eds.), *Literature and the Scottish Reformation*, pp. 178–9.

11 Thomas Crockett (ed.), *Poems of John Stewart of Baldynneis*, Scottish Text Society (Edinburgh, 1913), p. 225.

12 David J. Parkinson (ed.), *Alexander Montgomerie: Poems*, Scottish Text Society, 2 vols. (Edinburgh, 2000), vol. I, p. 213, line 483; p. 222, line 612; quotations from the 1597 printing.

13 See Deanna Delmar Evans, 'Holy Terror, Love Divine: The Passionate Voice in Elizabeth Melille's *Ane Godlie Dreame*', in Sarah M. Dunnigan, C. Marie Harker and Evelyn S. Newlyn (eds.), *Woman and the Feminine in Medieval and Early Modern Scottish Writing* (Basingstoke: Palgrave Macmillan, 2004), pp. 153–61.

14 On the Baroque dimensions of Drummond's poetry, see David J. Atkinson's essay, 'William Drummond as a Baroque Poet', *Studies in Scottish Literature*, 26 (1991), 394–409.

15 Robert H. MacDonald (ed.), *William Drummond of Hawthornden: Poems and Prose* (Edinburgh: Scottish Academic Press, 1976), pp. 126, 122.

16 William Tough (ed.), *The Works of Sir William Mure of Rowallan*, Scottish Text Society, 2 vols. (Edinburgh, 1898), vol. I, lines 1–4; see R. D. S. Jack, 'Scottish Sonneteer and Welsh Metaphysical: A Study of the Religious Poetry of Sir William Mure and Henry Vaughan', *Studies in Scottish Literature*, 3 (1965–6), 240–7.

17 W. Tod Ritchie (ed.), *The Bannatyne Manuscript Writtin in Tyme of Pest 1568*, Scottish Text Society, 4 vols. (Edinburgh: W. Blackwood, 1928–34), vol. III, p. 269, lines 17–20 (anon.).

18 For example, the music for the lyric 'O lusty May' (fol. 229v) survives in manuscript and printed song books (e.g. John Forbes, *Cantus, Songs and Fancies* [Aberdeen, 1662]).

19 See Findlay, *History of Scottish Theatre*; Sarah Carpenter, 'Performing Diplomacies: The 1560s Court Entertainments of Mary, Queen of Scots', *Scottish Historical Review*, 82:2 (2003), 194–225.

20 Jamie Reid Baxter, '"Philotus": The Transmission of a Delectable Treatise', in Theo van Heijnsbergen and Nicola Royan (eds.), *Literature, Letters and the Canonical in Early Modern Scotland* (East Linton: Tuckwell Press, 2002), pp. 52–68.

21 Walter Gregor (ed.), *Ane Treatise Callit the Court of Venus Deuidit into Four Buikis Newlie Compylit be Iohne Rolland in Dalkeith, 1575*, Scottish Text Society (Edinburgh, 1884), line 733.

22 See R. D. S. Jack's classic study, *The Italian Influence on Scottish Literature* (Edinburgh University Press, 1972) and most recently 'Petrarch and the Scottish Sonnet', in Martin McLaughlin and Letizia Panizza with Peter Hainsworth (eds.), *Petrarch in Britain: Interpreters, Imitators, and Translators over 700 Years* (Oxford University Press/British Academy, 2007), pp. 259–73.

23 See Sarah M. Dunnigan, *Eros and Poetry at the Courts of Mary, Queen of Scots and James VI* (Basingstoke: Palgrave Macmillan, 2002).

24 See Katherine McClune, 'The Scottish Sonnet, James VI, and John Stewart of Baldynneis', in Nicola Royan (ed.), *Scottish Poetry from Barbour to Drummond* (Amsterdam: Rodopi, 2007), pp. 165–80.

25 Gregor (ed.), *Ane Treatise*, line 18.

26 See Josephine A. Roberts, '"Contraries by contraries": The Artistry of Alexander Craig's Sonets', *Studies in Scottish Literature*, 21 (1986), 119–34.

27 Charles B. Gullane (ed.), *The English and Latin Poems of Sir Robert Ayton*, Scottish Text Society (Edinburgh: William Blackwood and Sons, 1955–6), p. 189, lines 7–8.

28 See Sarah M. Dunnigan, 'Daughterly Desires: Representing and Reimagining the Feminine in Anna Hume's *Triumphs*', in Dunnigan, Harker and Newlyn (eds.), *Woman and the Feminine*, pp. 120–35.

29 There is a considerable literature on James's poetry: see most recently, Daniel Fischlin and Mark Fortier (eds.), *Royal Subjects: Essays on the Writings of James VI and I* (Detroit: Wayne State University Press, 2002); Jane Rickard, *Authorship and Authority: The Writings of James VI and I* (Manchester University Press, 2007).

30 Jamie Reid Baxter, 'Politics, Passion and Poetry in the Circle of James VI: John Burel and His Surviving Works', in L. A. J. R. Houwen, A. A. MacDonald and S. L. Mapstone (eds.), *A Palace in the Wild: Essays on Vernacular Culture and Humanism in Late-Medieval and Renaissance Scotland* (Leuven: Peeters, 2000), pp. 199–248.

31 James Craigie (ed.), *The Poems of James VI of Scotland*, Scottish Text Society (Edinburgh: William Blackwood and Sons, 1955–8), p. 101, line 12.

32 *Ibid.*, p. 67.

33 See R. D. S. Jack, 'Music, Poetry, and Performance at the Court of James VI', *John Donne Journal: Studies in the Age of Donne*, 25 (2006), 37–63; Helena Shire, *Song, Dance, and Poetry of the Court of Scotland under King James VI* (Cambridge University Press, 1969).

34 See, for example, Michael R. G. Spiller 'The Scottish Court and the Scottish Sonnet at the Union of the Crowns', in Sally Mapstone and Juliette Wood (eds.), *The Rose and the Thistle: Essays on the Culture of Late Medieval and Renaissance Scotland* (East Linton: Tuckwell Press, 1998), pp. 101–15; Gerard Carruthers and Sarah Dunnigan, '"A reconfused chaos now": Scottish Poetry and Nation from the Medieval Period to the Eighteenth Century', *Edinburgh Review*, 100 (1999), 81–94; Morna Fleming, 'The Translation of James VI to the Throne of England in 1603', in van Heijnsbergen and Royan (eds.), *Literature, Letters and the Canonical*, pp. 90–110; Sandra Bell, '"No Scot, No English Now": Literary and Cultural Responses to James VI and I's Policies on Union', *Renaissance Forum: An Electronic Journal of Early Modern Literary and Historical Studies*, 7:1–2 (2004), www.hull.ac.uk/renforum/v7/bell.htm.

35 David Laing (ed.), *Poeticall Essayes of Alexander Craige, of Rose-Craig, 1604–1631* (Glasgow, 1873), p. 19.

36 Robert Jameson (ed.), *The Anatomie of Humors and the Passionate Sparke of a Relenting Minde by Simion Grahame* [reprints of the Edinburgh editions of 1609 and 1604] (Edinburgh, 1830), stanzas 1, 30, 24 (n.p.).

37 MacDonald (ed.), *William Drummond*, p. 87, lines 399–400.

38 David Parkinson, 'Rutherford's Landscapes', in Sarah Carpenter and Sarah M. Dunnigan (eds.), *'Joyous Sweit Imaginatioun': Essays on Scottish Literature in Honour of R. D. S. Jack* (Amsterdam: Rodopi, 2007), p. 178.

39 See Robert Crawford, *Apollos of the North: Selected Poems of George Buchanan and Arthur Johnston with English Versions* (Edinburgh: Polygon,

2006); John MacQueen, 'From Rome to Ruddiman: The Scoto-Latin Tradition', in Thomas Owen Clancy and Murray Pittock (eds.), *The Edinburgh History of Scottish Literature*, vol. i, *From Columba to the Union (until 1707)* (Edinburgh University Press, 2007), pp. 184–208.

Guide to further reading

Cummings, Brian and James Simpson (eds.), *Cultural Reformations: Medieval and Renaissance in Literary History* (Oxford University Press, 2010)

Durkan, John, 'Cultural Background in Sixteenth-Century Scotland', *Innes Review*, 10 (1959), 382–439

Jack, R. D. S., *The Italian Influence on Scottish Literature* (Edinburgh University Press, 1972)

Jack, R. D. S. (ed.), *The History of Scottish Literature*, vol. i, *Origins to 1660 (Mediaeval and Renaissance)* (Aberdeen University Press, 1988)

MacDonald, A. A., Michael Lynch and Ian B. Cowan (eds.), *The Renaissance in Scotland: Studies in Literature, Religion, History, and Culture Offered to John Durkan* (Leiden: Brill, 1994)

van Heijnsbergen, Theo, 'Paradigms Lost: Perceptions of the Cultural History of Sixteenth-Century Scotland', in Alasdair A. MacDonald and Michael W. Twomey (eds.), *Schooling and Society: The Ordering and Reordering of Knowledge in the Western Middle Ages* (Leuven: Peeters, 2004), pp. 197–211

4

LEITH DAVIS

The Aftermath of Union

In his now classic *The Paradox of Scottish Culture: The Eighteenth-Century Experience* (1964), David Daiches divides Scottish writers after the Union into two camps, arguing that 'Those poets who did not emigrate to England and write in English in an English tradition either wrote in Scotland in English for an English audience or turned to a regional vernacular poetry in a spirit of sociological condescension, patriotic feeling, or antiquarian revival.'[1] Influenced by the notion of a 'Caledonian Antisyzygy' proposed in G. Gregory Smith's *Scottish Literature: Character and Influence* as well as T. S. Eliot's account of 'The Metaphysical Poets', Daiches also suggests that writers after the Union suffered from a 'dissociation of sensibility' caused by thinking in one language (Scots) and writing in another (English, the language of power).[2] Daiches's assessment was initially important in helping to raise awareness of some of the socio-political factors influencing eighteenth-century Scottish literature and has proved extremely influential over the years as critics have grappled with its implications and revised it accordingly.[3] In the *Grammar of Empire*, for example, Janet Sorensen comments that this assessment of a Scottish 'split [schiz] mind [phrene]' pathologises Scottish literature by positing a central, organic national identity against which Scottish national identity appears always already flawed.[4] More recently, in *Scottish and Irish Romanticism*, Murray Pittock characterises post-Union Scottish writing not in terms of a lack or a splitting but in terms of doubleness: 'Scottish doubleness was a cultural language, both participative in the British public sphere and withdrawn from it.'[5]

Such critical discussion indicates the important role that Scotland's relationship with England plays in the history of Scottish literature. However, as the work of Robert Crawford and Gerard Carruthers suggests, it is also important to keep in mind the multiple influences on Scottish writers after the Union. In *Scotland's Books*, for example, Crawford discusses the ways in which individual writers have historically responded to Scotland's 'centuries-old multilingual inheritance'.[6] In a similar vein, Carruthers comments on the multifaceted 'Scottish poetic compass' at the beginning of the eighteenth century.[7] This chapter considers literary production in Scotland in the wake of the 1707 Union, acknowledging the unique circumstances of writers in Scotland, many of whom were galvanised by the political events that culminated in the transfer of political power from a Scottish to a British parliament and by the material and cultural effects of Union. At the same time, it attempts to move away from binary descriptions of post-Union Scottish writing, focusing instead on the multiplicity of influences on Scottish writers after 1707. If there is a characteristic that unites the writers considered in this chapter, however, it is their awareness of the power of print. The Union took place at the same time that the marketplace for print was enjoying exponential growth, twelve years after the lapse of the Licensing Act and two years before the first copyright law.[8] Many of the Scottish writers who published after the Union were also engaged in aspects of the print marketplace – printing, bookselling, editing. Their collections, editions and original work suggest a profound concern with the business of books. Even those writers who were not directly involved in the print industry recognised the possibilities that the rapidly expanding print market – both in Scotland and in a united Britain – could offer.

The debate surrounding the proposed Union of Scotland and England prompted a flurry of pamphlets, many of which drew their particular animus from points raised in works circulating during the recent Darien debacle.[9] It also inspired a number of less ephemeral national literary projects. In 1706, for example, James Watson published the first volume of his *Choice Collection of Comic and Serious Scots Poems both Ancient and Modern*.[10] Watson was an Edinburgh printer who was editor of the first newspaper in Scotland, the *Edinburgh Gazette*, and had been prosecuted for printing a pamphlet by George Ridpath criticising William III for his actions regarding Darien, *The People of Scotland's Groans and Lamentable Complaints* (1700).[11] Watson's *Collection* is frequently credited with providing the raw material for the eighteenth-century vernacular revival. His preface 'To the Reader' draws attention to the unique linguistic aspects of his work, commenting that his *Choice Collection* is *'the first of its Nature which has been publish'd in our own Native Scots Dialect'*.[12] A number of poems included in the *Collection* do feature 'Scots *Dialect*'. The collection begins with 'Christ's Kirk on the Green', a poem in Scots that was, as Watson asserts, *'Composed (as was supposed) by King James the Fifth'* and that presents the 'dancing and disarray' of labouring-class life from the perspective of a sophisticated observer.[13] The *Choice Collection* also features other poems in Scots such as 'The Life and Death of the Piper of *Kilbarchan*', written in the Standard Habbie stanzaic form that would prove so influential on later poets like

Allan Ramsay and Robert Burns, as well as more complex works in Scots like Alexander Montgomerie's 'The Cherry and the Slae'.

Critical focus on Watson's claims for *'our own Native Scots Dialect'* has tended to obscure other aspects of the *Collection*, however, including its outward-looking gaze. For as well as drawing attention to the linguistic production of Scotland, the preface 'To the Reader' situates Watson's national project within a wider European context, noting that *'the frequency of Publishing Collections of Miscellaneous Poems in our Neighbouring Kingdoms and States, may, in a great measure, justify an Undertaking of this kind with* us'.[14] Watson alludes here to the miscellanies recently published in France and England.[15] It is furthermore significant that he chooses to publish in a genre that is by nature both diverse and diverting, the 'miscellany', for by doing so, he succeeds in reflecting a range of national interests in his *Collection*. Standard English, literary Scots, Scoto-Latin verse and oral culture are all represented, drawn from a number of media: manuscripts, broadsides and songs. The *Choice Collection* represents Scotland, like its *'Neighbouring Kingdoms and States'*, as a modern nation of readers who exercise their own taste.

Two years after the first volume of the *Choice Collection* appeared, Watson printed the first volume of another national project: the *Lives and Characters of the Most Eminent Writers of the Scots Nation* by George Mackenzie, a physician and a fellow of the Royal College of Physicians in Edinburgh. The *Lives and Characters* targets a more affluent readership than Watson's anthology. At a price of twenty shillings, a volume of the *Lives and Characters* sold at twenty times the price of a volume of the *Choice Collection*. Moreover, where Watson presents his material ahistorically, paying little attention to chronology, Mackenzie is concerned to establish an accurate chronological account of those of Scotland's 'Illustrious Predecessors, as have been Eminent, either for Piety, Valour, or Learning'.[16] What is apparent, however, is that Mackenzie is as much concerned with establishing the character of the nation as he is with chronicling the nation's characters. He notes that he deliberately chooses biography over history because biography is able to demonstrate better than history *'all the Ancient Customs and Virtues of the* People *or* Nation'.[17] In giving the example of Buchanan's 'Epithalamium' on Queen Mary in his preface, Mackenzie suggests the seamless connection he wants to draw between the subjects of his biographies and the Scottish nation: 'By perusing the *"following Sheets, the Reader will find how Just and True that* Beautiful Character *is, which our incomparable Poet,* Buchanan, *gives of the Ancient Scots"*.' In fact, the passage quoted has little to do with the life and character of Queen Mary and everything to do with elucidating the life and character of the 'Ancient'

Scots, as the poet praises their imperviousness to heat, cold and hunger, their bravery and loyalty, and, most importantly, their ability to keep intruders out of Scotland: '*The* Scots *alone their Ancient Rights Enjoy'd / And Liberty, for which they Noblely [sic] Dy'd.*'[18] As becomes clear in the reading of the *Lives and Characters*, each author stands as a palimpsest not only for the writers who have come before him, but for the nation's citizens in general. Where Watson's *Collection* served to imagine Scotland as an ahistorical collection of readers, Mackenzie is concerned to delineate a specific character for the nation that is consistent through historical time.

But the *Lives and Characters* also demonstrates its writers' outward-looking gaze, as like Watson, Mackenzie indicates his awareness of Scotland's relationship to literary projects that have occurred in other nations. He notes in his Preface that 'All the Wise Nations in the World, have … transmitted to their Posterity, the *Lives* and *Actions* of their Illustrious Predecessors', and although 'our Nation has produc'd as Great Men as any other Nation in the World, yet we have been so unjust to their Memories and to our Posterity, that hitherto there has not been made a Collection of their Lives'.[19] Mackenzie, like Watson, suggests that Scotland needs a specific genre of printed work in order to bring it up to the level of other nations. He proposes that his *Lives and Characters of the Most Eminent Writers of the Scots Nation* will constitute a 'Paper-Monument' to Scotland's 'mighty Heroes in Learning'.[20] *The Lives and Characters* also reaches beyond the borders of England to convey the historical relationships between Scots and the rest of Europe, as many of the individuals whom Mackenzie tracks spent much of their lives in and had an impact on the nations of '*Italy, France* and *Germany*'.[21]

The 1710 republication of *Virgil's Æneis, Translated into Scottish Verse, by the Famous Gawin Douglas Bishop of Dunkeld* suggests a similar desire to extend Scotland's affiliations with the rest of Europe. The printers of the 1710 *Æneis*, the former Episcopalian minister Andrew Symson and the Jacobite Robert Freebairn, were both scholars who had published works in Latin themselves. Editorial material for the volume was supplied by another Latinist, Thomas Ruddiman.[22] In choosing to reprint Douglas's sixteenth-century *Eneados*, the first complete translation of the Aeneid into vernacular language in the British Isles, Symson, Freebairn and Ruddiman were attempting not only to assert their Jacobite sympathies but also to connect Scottish writing with the classical tradition in Europe.[23]

John Corbett comments that Douglas's original translation was 'a work of Scottish nationalism written in a climate of hostility against England – yet it is written by a man whose family ties and personal loyalties linked him to the English royal family and English ecclesiastical influence'.[24] In the 1710 edition, however, Ruddiman reworks the politics associated with its original author. The biographical material about Douglas suggests that the charge of treason against him issued when he fled Scotland for England was an invention of 'his Enemies' in the Court Party in Scotland. In contrast, it notes how he worked with the French king Francis I to 'renew the Ancient League between the two Nations' and conveyed to Scotland 'the first Account of the great Promises and many Ceremonies of the *French* at the Confirmation of the League, with their Protestations for preserving and maintaining the Liberties of the Kingdom of *Scotland*, against all who would endeavor to impair them'.[25]

The original version of Douglas's translation also represents what Margaret Tudeau-Clayton regards as a marked 'ambivalence' towards Scots.[26] On the one hand, the poetic narrator announces that he set himself the task of making his translation 'brade and plane, / Kepand no sodroun, but oure awin langage'; on the other hand, he notes that he includes words from other languages when necessary: 'Sum bastard *Latyne, Frensch*, or *Ynglis* ois, / Quhare scant wes *Scottis*, I had nane uther chois.'[27] The 1710 edition reconceives the linguistic politics of the original, however, as Ruddiman suggests that the printer of the 1553 London edition was too influenced by the work of English poets to accurately represent Douglas's poem. The Preface argues that this earlier edition contains a 'Comma *about the middle of the each* Line ...; *which, without Doubt, was intended for a* Pause *or* Stop, *that so the Verse might run and sound more smoothly: But, tho somewhat like to this was us'd by the* Anglo-Saxon *Poets, yet it is not to be found in our* MS'.[28] The republication of the *Eneados* also serves as an opportunity to print a 'Dictionary to the Old Scottish Language' in order to explain 'the Difficult Words' and to illustrate the history of the Scots language. Ruddiman suggests the continuity between old Scots and contemporary Scots by acknowledging that he has turned for his source to the language still spoken in parts of Scotland today: '*There are many Words, which are to this Day used in some parts of* Scotland *by the* Common People, *and therefore we have distinguish'd them from the rest by a Capital* S. *subjoined to them.*' Not only does the glossary suggest a link between the poetry of the Scottish court and the 'Vulgar' of eighteenth-century Scotland, it also offers a striking subversion of the dominance of the English language and literature as Ruddiman notes, '*As Occasion offer'd, we have explained a great Number of* Scottish *Words*, Phrases *and* Proverbs, *which are not to be found in our Author; so that by the Help of the* Glossary *one may not only understand this* Translation *of* Virgil, *but be also very much assisted to Read with profit any other Book written in the same Language. Yea* Chaucer *and other* English *Writers about that time are rendred* [sic] *more plain and easy by it*' (3). A knowledge of 'Scottish *Words*', it would seem, can actually help readers decode the work of canonical 'English *writers*'. At the same time, Ruddiman indicates the uniqueness of Scots by suggesting that certain Scots words are untranslatable, even with a dictionary: Scots has '*very many* Words *and* Phrases *most* Significant *and* Emphatical; *which makes it hard, and almost impossible, to find* English *Words fit to express them in their full Force and genuine Meaning*' (3).

Ian Ross and Stephen Scobie note that with its text and glossary, the 1710 *Virgil's Æneis* remains 'one of the most influential works in the eighteenth-century vernacular revival'.[29] It was certainly influential on the work of another post-Union writer, Allan Ramsay. Ramsay chose the name 'Gawin Douglas' for his moniker in the Easy Club after the club switched from English to Scots names. One of Ramsay's earliest published works, a republication of 'Christ's Kirk on the Green', includes a quotation from the Preface to the *Eneados*.[30] Like his contemporaries, Ramsay was informed by a number of different influences. His work creatively hybridises Scots and English languages, Scottish and Augustan English literary forms, and includes antiquarian and contemporary references, rural and urban perspectives. Rather than just reprinting the text of 'Christ's Kirk on the Green', for example, Ramsay included with his reprinting a new canto that he wrote in a bawdy but urbane style of Scots similar to that of the original. By repackaging the original language of the poem, he suggests that 'Scottish *Words*' do not just belong to antiquarian collectors or to the 'Vulgar', as Ruddiman had implied in *Virgil's Æneis*, but constitute a vibrant contemporary literary language. Ramsay's new canto reanimates the original characters, bringing them together to settle their differences through fear of the knife-wielding 'Blythe Bess' as well as mutual enjoyment of drinking and dancing. The reconciliation of the characters in this and the previous version suggests Ramsay's interest in uniting the various political parties in the interest of the nation, a project which he hints at in another edition of the poem published the same year (this time featuring 'Three Canto's' [*sic*]), when he protests too much: 'I would intreat every News-Monger, not to offer to pump Politics from this Poem.'[31]

Ramsay republished 'Christ's Kirk on the Green' yet again in a collection printed by Ruddiman entitled *The Ever Green, Being a Collection of Scots Poems, Wrote by the Ingenious before 1600* (1724).[32] The pro-Jacobite Dedication to the duke of Hamilton and the Royal Company of Archers suggests the 'Politics' that can be 'pumped' from this collection, as does Ramsay's assertion that the poetry included in his collection reflects a 'Spirit of Freedom' from the time of the 'antient Heroes' of Scotland (iv). The poems, he writes, provide a way for the 'OLD BARDS' to convey their 'Love of Liberty' to the present generation. But like Watson, Freebairn and

Ruddiman, Ramsay was intimately involved in the market for print. Although he had started life in Edinburgh as a wig-maker, he soon made a name for himself as a bookseller. The *Ever Green* indicates his concern to appeal to the marketplace. Although Ramsay asserts that the *Ever Green* will serve as an antidote to the '*Fopery* [sic] *of admiring nothing but what is either new or foreign*' (iv), the Preface suggests that the appeal of the 'new' is also very much operative in the *Ever Green*; it just appears under a different guise. While Ramsay proudly announces that the work by the poets collected in his anthology is '*the Product of their own Country, not pilfered and spoiled in the Transportation from abroad*' (vii–viii), he also characterises that past as being as remote as any foreign nation: '*the* Manners *and* Customs *then in Vogue … will have all the Air and Charm of* Novelty; *and that seldom fails of exciting Attention and pleasing the Mind*' (ix). Moreover, he suggests, the verse forms themselves, being from '*Times that are Past*' (ix), will also '*appear new and amusing*' (x). Ramsay's 'Miscellany', like Watson's, is a product designed with the market in mind, as it includes both 'serious and comick' works, with a view to giving the readers a '*Diversity of Subjects*' from which to choose (viii). In addition to representing the poetry of the '*good old* Bards' (vii), Ramsay also included new work, including his own 'The Vision' and Elizabeth Wardlaw's 'distressed' ballad, 'Hardyknute', to which he added several stanzas of his own.[33]

As well as recreating the poetry of the past, Ramsay also reconfigures popular contemporary styles of poetry. His early satirical pamphlet *The Scriblers Lash'd* indicates his bookseller's sense as he identifies three kinds of poetry by 'the scribling [sic] Crew' that are meeting with popular success.[34] First on the list are works that 'attack the Fair' (5) and their fashions; such works, he suggests, 'Make printers presses groan with Nonsense' (6). Next Ramsay condemns writers who write 'Ballads', popular songs which 'Hawkers sing and cry' (12) and which 'waste / Our paper and debauch our Taste' (11). Finally, he condemns what he calls the worst of the 'rhiming Herd', those writers who write memorial poems: 'An honest Burgess cannot dy, / But they must weep in Elegy' (13). These popular forms of poetry, he asserts, are dulling the national taste. Although there still exist readers who are 'learn'd' and 'deserning', the 'Scriblers' are having a detrimental effect on the nation, as readers are unable to 'distinguish' good poetry from that which the 'Vulgar' enjoy:

> Hence Poets are accounted now
> In *Scotland*, a mean empty Crew:
> Whose Heads are craz'd, who spend their Time,
> In that poor wretched Trade of Rhime. (11–12)

In a number of his early works, however, Ramsay turns precisely to these popular genres, reinventing them to serve both 'Poets' and the national interest. '*Tartana, or the Plaid*', for example, begins ostensibly as a comment on the fashion of '*Caledonian* BEAUTIES',[35] but quickly changes into a condemnation of male fashion, specifically, the loss of the plaid, symbolic of Scotland's independent nationhood and martial glory. The narrator traces the 'antiquity' of the plaid to the time when Scotland defied Roman rule and 'Our own bold NATIVE PRINCE then fill'd the Throne / His PLAID array'd, magnificently shone' (10). Now, suggests Ramsay in a Miltonic echo, the situation is sadly different:

> O Heavens, how chang'd! How little looks their Race
> When Foreign *Chains*, with Foreign *Modes* take Place;
> When East and Western *Indies* must combine,
> To make th' effeminate in their Gew-gaws shine. (11)

In his *Scots Songs*, first published in 1718, then reworked into the *Tea-Table Miscellany* in 1724 and subsequent editions, Ramsay reconfigures the 'Ballads' that 'Hawkers sing and cry'. The volume draws upon popular folk songs such as 'The Last Time I Came O'er the Moor' and 'The Lass of Peatie's Mill', but, as Steve Newman argues, Ramsay writes lyrics to make them suitable for middle-class aspirations.[36] Ramsay also capitalises on the success of the third of his poetic bugbears with a series of elegies which, instead of mourning the death of an 'honest Burgess', focus on citizens of a much less elevated position: 'Elegy on Maggy Johnston, who died *Anno* 1711' and 'Elegy on Lucky Wood in the Canongate, May, 1717' celebrate the community achievements of two female publicans, while the 'Elegy on John Cowper Kirk-Treasurer's Man' mockingly speculates on the detrimental effect that the removal of Cowper will have on civic morality.[37]

Ramsay reprinted 'Tartana', 'Scots Songs', the elegies and also 'The Scriblers Lash'd' and 'Christ's Kirk on the Green' in his hefty collected *Poems* of 1720, along with numerous other works.[38] In the 1721 edition of this work printed by Ruddiman, the prefatory material serves to further complicate and recontextualise the contents. In his Preface to this volume, Ramsay acknowledges the classical affiliations of Scotland suggested by Ruddiman and others, as he includes a quotation from Dr Sewell that suggests that the '*Scotticisms*' in the volume 'become their Place as well as the *Doric* Dialect of Theocritus'.[39] The volume ends with 'five or six Imitations of *Horace*' (viii) and a self-consciously bookish 'Conclusion' that is 'After the Matter of Horace, ad librum suum'. In addition to drawing attention to the classical associations of his *Poems*, Ramsay sets out what appears to be his manifesto on his 'native Dialect':

[G]ood Imagery, just Similies [*sic*], and all Manner of ingenious Thoughts, in a well laid Design, disposed into Numbers, is Poetry ... good Poetry may be in any Language ... in [Scots], the Pronunciation is liquid and sonorous, and much fuller than the *English*, of which we are Masters, by being taught it in our Schools, and daily reading it; which being added to all our own native Words, of eminent Significancy, makes our Tongue by far the completest. (vi)

With its footnotes in standard English and its 'Glossary, or Explanation of the Scots Words Us'd by the Author', however, the 1721 *Poems* appears as interested in getting English consumers to become 'daily read[ers]' of Scots as in suggesting that Scottish readers are 'Masters' of English. Poems inserted after the Preface by three English writers praising Ramsay's rural subjects and Scots terms further suggest the dialogic nature of Ramsay's work. Written as a recantation for having at first dismissed the 'Beauties' of Scots, for example, C. Beckingham's 'To Mr. Allan Ramsay' admits that the author has been 'Too blindly partial to my native Tongue / Fond of the Smoothness of our *English* Song' (xvii), but has grown to relish the Scottish register through reading Ramsay's poetry.

In fact, much of Ramsay's work appears in the context of linguistic and textual dialogues with English works and English writers. 'Richy and Sandy: A Pastoral on the Death of Mr. Joseph Addison' (1720) addresses the loss of that icon of English culture and taste in a dialogue in Scots between two shepherds. It was included in Pope's 1720 edition of *Eloisa and Abelard*[40] and was also printed in London with an English translation by Josiah Burchett, an epistolary poem by Burchett, 'To Mr. Allan Ramsay on his Richy and Sandy' and Ramsay's poetic response to Burchett. *Patie and Roger: A Pastoral* (1720), which Ramsay would later expand into his comic opera, *The Gentle Shepherd*, also includes an introductory epistle to Burchett written in Standard Habbie in which Ramsay invites his Muse to 'skiff to the Bent away, / To try anes mair the Landart Lay, / *With a thy speed*, / Since BURCHET awns that thou can play / *Upon the Reed*'.[41] Burchett was a Secretary of the Admiralty who was intermittently a Whig MP and one of the Commissioners appointed to take subscriptions for the South Sea Company.[42] Ramsay's poem acknowledges that Burchett's reputation has spread, 'frae the North to Southren Line', and praises him for commanding '*Briton*'s Royal Fleet' as well as writing about it:

> These doughty Actions frae his Pen,
> Our Age, and these to come, shall ken,
> How stubborn Navies did contend
> > *Upon the Waves,*
> How free-born *Britons* faught like Men,
> > *Their Faes like Slaves.*[43]

Ramsay's work, then, commingles a number of options available to post-Union Scottish writers, hybridising classical, Scots, English and imperial interests.[44]

With its representation of British conquest of the seas and British liberty, Ramsay's poem to Burchett has remarkable similarities to the work of another post-Union Scottish writer who, with his Whig politics and Presbyterian upbringing, is often juxtaposed to the Jacobite Ramsay: James Thomson.[45] Unlike Ramsay, Thomson was classically educated, first at grammar school at Jedburgh, then at the College of Edinburgh. In 1725, Thomson left his divinity studies and Edinburgh behind, seeking greater opportunities in London and following his friend David Malloch, who had gone south two years earlier (at the same time Anglicising his name to Mallet).[46] In contemporary accounts of Scottish literature, Thomson is often ignored or criticised for abandoning his native land, but as Gerard Carruthers suggests, 'Thomson illuminates, negotiates and works fruitfully with the complex possibilities in the Scottish cultural and literary identity of his day.'[47] This complexity is evident in his first major publication, *Winter*, a religious meditation in blank verse on the relationship between the natural world and '*Providence*' that was published in 1726.[48] Thomson's educational background is evident in the Latinate expressions in *Winter*. In addition, the poem's premise that close contemplation of the natural world serves to bear 'the swelling Thought aloft to Heaven' suggests the influence of Thomson's Presbyterian upbringing, as well as his interests in natural history and Newtonian science, fostered at the College of Edinburgh:

> Lo! from the livid East, or piercing North,
> Thick clouds ascend, in whose capacious Womb,
> A vapoury Deluge lies, to Snow congeal'd:
> Heavy, they roll their fleecy World along;
> And the Sky saddens with th' impending Storm. (10)

Winter also hints at Thomson's poetic aspirations for himself and for the united nation of Britain. Solitude 'in the wild Depth of Winter' (11) offers not only poetic inspiration but also the opportunity to 'hold high Converse with the mighty Dead' (12), during which time the narrator views 'Great *Homer*', that '*Parent* of Song', walking 'Hand in Hand' with 'The *British Muse*' (12). Thomson would return to the idea of Britain as the new centre of poetic and political progress – and himself as the nation's spokesperson – in his poem *Liberty* (1735–7), as well as in the lyrics to 'Rule Britannia' from *Alfred: A Masque*, which he wrote with Mallet.

Although he was not directly involved in the print industry himself, Thomson, like his contemporaries who remained in Scotland, demonstrates a canny awareness of the possibilities that the expanding market for print could offer. As an outsider to the metropolitan centre, however, he relied on connections with other Scots and embedding himself firmly within a system of patronage. Mallet supplied him with a number of introductions, including to the influential poet Aaron Hill, and Thomson carefully chose the dedicatees of his works in order to advance his reputation among Whig politicians.[49] In addition, Thomson made a number of savvy publishing decisions. His letter of August 1726 to Mallet suggests his concern with marketing issues, as he notes that he is at work on 'a Panegyric on Brittain, which may perhaps contribute to make my Poem popular. The English People are not a little vain of Themselves, and their Country. Brittania, too, includes our native Country, Scotland.'[50] Capitalising on the success of *Winter*, he also published *Summer* (1727), *Spring* (1728) and *Autumn* (1730), then corrected and enlarged all four poems in the comprehensive *The Seasons* (1730);[51] each individual poem appeared in numerous editions both before and after their publication as a whole.[52] The case of Thomson illustrates another important aspect of post-Union Scottish writing: the success of a number of Scottish printers in London after the Union. Thomson sold limited rights for the first edition then a revised second edition of *Winter* to one Scottish publisher working in London, John Millan, and worked extensively with another, Andrew Millar, who specialised in the works of Scottish writers.[53]

The writers examined in this chapter suggest that Scottish writing after the Union is complicated and multi-faceted. While post-Union writers do indeed demonstrate what Daiches refers to as 'patriotic feeling' for Scotland, their means of demonstrating this feeling do not necessarily include a turn to 'regional vernacular poetry'. Mackenzie, for example, connects Scottish writing to a European background, while Ruddiman promotes a classical connection. Moreover, as the work of Ramsay and Thomson demonstrates, 'patriotic feeling' can be directed at both 'our native Country, Scotland', as well as Britain. Even those writers who do demonstrate an interest in 'vernacular poetry' (itself a term which needs revision, given the fact that many writers use a constructed form of Scots), employ it strategically. Watson tempers his Scots poetry with other kinds of verse, suggesting the multiplicity of choices of 'Scottish Poems', while Ramsay provides opportunities for his English readers to respond to the Scottish register. It is vital, then, to take account of the ambiguities involved in Scottish writing of the early eighteenth century and not to read post-Union writing simply through the lens of binaries, but to recognise the multiplicity of possibilities open to Scottish writers. It is also important to consider post-Union writing in the context of the changing landscape of print. The appearance of a number of projects to 'imagine the nation' in print, like those of Watson, Mackenzie and Ruddiman, as well as others like Patrick Abercromby's *The Martial Achievements of the Scots Nation*,[54] reflects the growth of the number of printers in Scotland after 1707, many of whom had Jacobite associations. At the same time, the success of Scottish printers in London also contributed to the number of works by Scots that found their way into print in the years after the Union.

Notes

1 David Daiches, *The Paradox of Scottish Culture: The Eighteenth-Century Experience* (London: Oxford University Press, 1964), p. 21.

2 *Ibid.*; G. Gregory Smith, *Scottish Literature: Character and Influence* (London: Macmillan, 1919), p. 4; T. S. Eliot, 'The Metaphysical Poets', in *Selected Essays* (New York: Harcourt Brace, 1950), p. 247.

3 See, for example, Kenneth Simpson, *The Protean Scot: The Crisis of Identity in Eighteenth-Century Scottish Literature* (Aberdeen University Press, 1988).

4 Janet Sorensen, *The Grammar of Empire* (Cambridge University Press, 2000), p. 6.

5 Murray Pittock, *Scottish and Irish Romanticism* (Oxford University Press, 2008), p. 87.

6 Robert Crawford, *Scotland's Books* (Oxford University Press, 2009), p. 13.

7 Carruthers identifies 'Scottish folk-poetry and ballads', a 'Scottish Latinist/ humanist intellectual heritage, Scots vernacular verse, Augustan verse in English ... and a mode of poetry, usually in English, which might be described as Calvinist pietism'. Gerard Carruthers, 'Eighteenth-Century Scottish Literary Identity', in Richard Terry (ed.), *James Thomson: Essays for the Tercentenary* (Liverpool University Press, 2000), p. 169.

8 See Rick Sher, Introduction to *The Enlightenment and the Book* (University of Chicago Press, 2006), pp. 1–42.

9 See Chris Whatley, *The Scots and the Union* (Edinburgh University Press, 2006) and Karin Bowie, *Scottish Public Opinion and the Anglo-Scottish Union, 1699–1707* (Woodbridge: Royal Historical Society, 2007).

10 James Watson, *A Choice Collection of Comic and Serious Scots Poems both Ancient and Modern. By Several Hands*, 3 vols. (Edinburgh: Printed for J. Watson, 1706). Subsequent volumes were published in 1709 and 1711.

11 See Leith Davis, 'Imagining the Miscellaneous Nation: James Watson's *Choice Collection of Comic and Serious Scots Poems*', *Eighteenth-Century Life* (in press).

12 Watson, *Choice Collection*, vol. 1, n.p.

13 *Ibid.*, p. 1. See Allan Maclaine, *The Christis Kirk Tradition: Scots Poems of Folk Festivity* (Aberdeen: Association for Scottish Literary Studies, 1996).

14 Watson, *Choice Collection*, vol. 1, n.p.

15 See, for example, *Recueil des plus belles pièces des poëtes françois, tant anciens que modernes, depuis Villon jusqu' à M. de Benserade*, 5 vols. (Paris: Barbin, 1692) and the English examples in Barbara Benedict, *Making the Modern*

Reader: Cultural Mediation in Early Modern Literary Anthologies (Princeton University Press, 1996).

16 George Mackenzie, *Proposals for Printing The Lives and Characters of the Most Eminent Writers of the Scots Nation* (Edinburgh, 1707), n.p.

17 George Mackenzie, *Lives and Characters of the Most Eminent Writers of the Scots Nation*, 3 vols. (Edinburgh: Printed for J. Watson, 1708–22), vol. I, p. 18.

18 *Ibid.*

19 *Ibid.*, vol. I, p. i.

20 *Ibid.*

21 *Ibid.*

22 The Ruddimans also began the *Caledonian Mercury* in 1720. See Douglas Duncan, *Thomas Ruddiman: A Study in the Scholarship of the Early Eighteenth Century* (Edinburgh and London: Oliver & Boyd, 1965).

23 See Murray G. H. Pittock, 'The *Aeneid* in the Age of Burlington: A Jacobite Document?', in Toby Barnard and Jane Clark (ed.), *Lord Burlington: Architecture, Art and Life* (London: Hambledon, 1995), pp. 231–49.

24 John Corbett, *Written in the Language of the Scottish Nation: A History of Literary Translation into Scots* (Clevedon, Avon: Multilingual Matters, 1999), p. 33.

25 Gawin Douglas, *Virgil's Æneis, Translated into Scottish verse* (Edinburgh, 1710), p. 8; further references will appear in the text.

26 Margaret Tudeau-Clayton, 'Richard Carew, William Shakespeare, and the Politics of Translating Virgil in Early Modern England and Scotland', *International Journal of the Classical Tradition*, 5:4 (Spring 1999), 507–27.

27 Douglas, *Virgil's Æneis*, p. 5.

28 *Ibid.*, Preface (n.p.).

29 Ian Ross and Stephen Scobie, 'Patriotic Publishing as a Response to the Union', in T. I. Rae (ed.), *The Union of 1707: Its Impact on Scotland* (Edinburgh: Blackie and Son, 1974), p. 107. See also Charles Jones, 'Phonology', in *The Edinburgh History of the Scots Language* (Edinburgh University Press, 1997), pp. 267–335.

30 *Christ's Kirk* [sic] *on the Green in Two Canto's* [sic] (Edinburgh, 1718), p. 6.

31 Advertisement, *Christ's-Kirk* [sic] *on the Green, in Three Cantos* (Edinburgh: Printed for the Author, 1718), n.p.

32 Allan Ramsay, *The Ever Green, Being a Collection of Scots Poems, Wrote by the Ingenious before 1600* (Edinburgh, 1724); further references will appear in the text.

33 See Mel Kersey, 'Ballads, Britishness and Hardyknute, 1719–1859', *Scottish Studies Review*, 5 (2005), 40–56.

34 Allan Ramsay, *The Scriblers Lash'd* (Edinburgh, 1718), p. 4; further references will appear in the text.

35 Allan Ramsay, *Tartana, or the Plaid* (Edinburgh, 1718), p. 7; further references will appear in the text.

36 Allan Ramsay, *Scots Songs* (Edinburgh: Printed for the Author, 1718); Steve Newman, 'The Scots Songs of Allan Ramsay: "Lyrick" Transformation, Popular Culture, and the Boundaries of the Scottish Enlightenment', *Modern Language Quarterly*, 63:3 (2002), 282.

37 Allan Ramsay, *Elegies on Maggy Johnston, John Cowper and Lucky Wood* (Edinburgh: Printed for the Author, 1718).

38 Allan Ramsay, *Poems* (Edinburgh: Printed for the Author, 1720).

39 Allan Ramsay, *Poems* (Edinburgh: T. Ruddiman, 1721), p. vii; further references will appear in the text.

40 Alexander Pope, *Eloisa to Abelard. Written by Mr. Pope* (London: Bernard Lintot, 1720), pp. 51–60.

41 Allan Ramsay, *Patie and Roger: A Pastoral* (Edinburgh, 1720), p. 1.

42 *A View of the Coasts, Countries and Islands within the Limits of the South-Sea-Company* (London, 1711), p. 213. Burchett was also a poet, having published *Strife and Envy, since the Fall of Man: A Poem, by Josiah Burchet, Esq;* (London, 1716).

43 Ramsay, *Patie and Roger*, p. 2. See Newman, 'Scots Songs' for more on *The Gentle Shepherd*. Burchett published *A Complete History of the Most Remarkable Transactions at Sea* in 1720, a revised and extended version of his earlier *Memoirs of Transactions at Sea during the War with France* (1703).

44 See also Murray Pittock, 'Allan Ramsay and the Decolonisation of Genre', in *Scottish and Irish Romanticism*, pp. 32–58.

45 See James Sambrook, *James Thomson 1700–1748: A Life* (Oxford: Clarendon Press, 1991), p. 7.

46 See Sandro Jung, *David Mallet, Anglo-Scot: Poetry, Patronage and Politics in the Age of Union* (Cranbury, NJ: Rosemont Publishing, 2008), p. 24.

47 Carruthers, 'Eighteenth-Century Scottish Literary Identity', p. 169.

48 James Thomson, *Winter* (London: J. Millan, 1726), p. 14; further references will appear in the text.

49 See Sambrook, *James Thomson*, ch. 3.

50 Quoted in Sambrook, *James Thomson*, p. 48.

51 *Proposals to Print The Seasons*.

52 Christine Gerrard, 'James Thomson, *The Seasons*', in Christine Gerrard (ed.), *A Companion to Eighteenth-Century Poetry* (Malden, MA: Blackwell, 2006), p. 197.

53 Sher, *Enlightenment and the Book*, pp. 275–94.

54 Patrick Abercromby, *The Martial Atchievements of the Scots Nation* (Edinburgh: Robert Freebairn, 1711).

Guide to further reading

Bowie, Karin, *Scottish Public Opinion and the Anglo-Scottish Union, 1699–1707* (Woodbridge: Royal Historical Society, 2007)

Carruthers, Gerard, 'James Thomson and Eighteenth-Century Scottish Literary Identity', in Richard Terry (ed.), *James Thomson: Essays for the Tercentenary* (Liverpool University Press, 2000), pp. 165–90

Daiches, David, *The Paradox of Scottish Culture: The Eighteenth-Century Experience* (London: Oxford University Press, 1964)

Crawford, Robert, *Scotland's Books* (Oxford University Press, 2009)

Davis, Leith, *Acts of Union: Scotland and the Literary Negotiation of the British Nation, 1707–1830* (Stanford University Press, 1997)

Jung, Sandro, *David Mallet, Anglo-Scot: Poetry, Patronage and Politics in the Age of Union* (Cranbury, NJ: Rosemont Publishing, 2008)

Pittock, Murray, *Scottish and Irish Romanticism* (Oxford University Press, 2008)

Sher, Richard B., *The Enlightenment and the Book: Scottish Authors and Their Publishers in Eighteenth-Century Britain, Ireland, and America* (University of Chicago Press, 2006)

Sorensen, Janet, *The Grammar of Empire* (Cambridge University Press, 2000)

5

NIGEL LEASK

Robert Burns

Robert Burns (1759–96) needs no introduction as Scotland's national poet, but he also has a good claim to be considered the most original British poet writing between Alexander Pope and William Blake. Developing the eighteenth-century tradition of Scots verse associated with Allan Ramsay and especially Robert Fergusson, Burns crafted the first modern vernacular style in British poetry, providing a resource for subsequent verse written in non-standard English, especially by 'peasant poets' like James Hogg, Robert Bloomfield and John Clare, as well as later American poets like Walt Whitman. More immediately, Burns was a vital influence on the British Romantics, especially Wordsworth, in championing the values of rural and peasant life, and (despite Burns's own debts to Pope, Gray and Shenstone) attacking the generalist aesthetics and poetic diction of much eighteenth-century Augustan poetry. Ironically though, while still enthusiastically celebrated in Scotland and globally at Burns Suppers on 25 January, Burns has been marginalised in English departments across the world, as a result of a mistaken view that his writing is linguistically incomprehensible, and of interest to Scottish readers only.[1]

Burns was born on 25 January 1759, in Alloway, near Ayr, where his father William Burnes (the poet later dropped the 'e' from his surname) was initially employed as head gardener, before embarking on an ill-starred career as a tenant farmer at nearby Mount Oliphant and, later, Lochlie, in central Ayrshire.[2] Robert described boyhood life on the farm as 'the cheerless gloom of a hermit with the unceasing moil of a galley-slave', and laboured at the plough to save his father the cost of hiring additional labour.[3] Later, at the time of William Burnes's death in 1784 (precipitated by a stressful litigation with the landlord of Lochlie), Robert took the joint lease of the farm of Mossgiel, near Mauchline, with his brother Gilbert. It was here that most of the poems published in his first Kilmarnock volume of 1786 were written, at a time when his farming career looked untenable, and his personal and amorous affairs had reached a crisis. Burns accordingly made arrangements to travel to Jamaica to work on a slave plantation as a 'book-keeper' or 'negro driver'.[4] The success of the Kilmarnock poems, dedicated to his friend and landlord the Mauchline lawyer Gavin Hamilton, led to the abandonment of this desperate scheme, and an invitation to Edinburgh, where in 1787 he oversaw a second edition of his poetry from the press of William Creech, the major publisher of the Scottish Enlightenment.

The following year, after playing the literary lion in the drawing rooms of the Scottish capital, and touring the Borders, Highlands and north-east of Scotland, Burns signed the lease of Ellisland farm near Dumfries. Here he settled with his newly-wed bride Jean Armour (already mother of several of his children), but once again he found the farm to be a 'ruinous bargain', hopes of improvement stymied by the impossible conditions facing many Scottish tenant farmers in these years.[5] Making the most of the patronage opportunities afforded by his meteoric success as a poet, Burns had trained as an Excise officer in the hope of securing a stable income, and unsuccessfully sought to combine farming with an Excise career between 1788 and 1791. He finally abandoned farming for full-time Excise employment in 1791, and moved with his growing family into Dumfries, where he died prematurely in 1796 at the age of thirty-seven.

Given that Burns was a farmer, and never a professional poet, it's hardly surprising that his poetry is profoundly marked by his agricultural vocation and personae, in addressing the human and social consequences of the revolutionary transformation of Scottish rural life during the decades of agricultural improvement. Like other Scottish tenants of the Enlightenment era, he was well educated in the literature and techniques of agricultural improvement. But despite the myth of his natural genius fostered by Burns himself, and furthered by Henry Mackenzie's influential description of the poet as a 'Heaven-taught ploughman', the poet's education extended further than this. Although he never attended college, he did have some schooling in and around Ayr, and in 1765 his father hired the eighteen-year-old John Murdoch to tutor his sons in English and French literature, arousing Robert's appetite for the fashionable cult of sensibility promulgated by Rousseau, Richardson, Sterne and Mackenzie.[6]

Burns's cultural location in the environs of the forward-looking eighteenth-century town of Ayr identifies him as a product of the 'Ayrshire Enlightenment'. Stimulated by the profits of American and Caribbean trade (the product of African chattel slavery) and the civic energies of its enlightened burghers and improving gentry, Ayr boasted a grammar school, bookshops, coffeehouses and taverns, as well as a subscription library supplied by William Creech: in contrast to much of south-west Scotland with its strongly orthodox and Covenanting traditions, it was also a bastion of

Moderate Presbyterianism.[7] Complementing (rather than controverting) the influence of Enlightenment ideas, Burns nurtured an enthusiasm for the rich popular culture of rural south-west Scotland later evoked in poems like 'Halloween', 'Address to the Deil' and 'Tam o' Shanter', a passion also manifest in his song collecting. He later acknowledged the influence of a maid of his mother's 'remarkable for her ignorance, credulity and superstition' on his boyhood imagination, who possessed 'the largest collection in the county of tales and songs concerning devils, ghosts, fairies, brownies, witches, apparitions, cantraips, giants, inchanted towers, dragons, and other trumpery'.[8] The combination of enthusiasm and ironic distance in this account perfectly illustrates Burns's complex attitude to popular culture.

Moving as a teenager to the more conservative inland parishes of Tarbolton and Mauchline, Burns quickly found himself in conflict with the puritanical 'Auld Licht' faction who dominated the kirk, especially in Mauchline. In 1780 he founded (with his brother Gilbert) the Tarbolton Bachelor's Club: although essentially an artisan conversation and debating club for young unmarried men, 'practising enlightenment' in this libertarian sense also entailed spirited resistance to the moral and sexual control of the Revd William Auld and the Mauchline Kirk Session, the 'houghmagandie pack'. Burns's amours with Elizabeth Paton, his future wife Jean Armour and Mary Campbell ('Highland Mary') earned him the reputation as 'a Country Libertine', in the words of the critic John Logan,[9] inspiring poems like 'The Fornicator' and 'A Poet's Welcome to his Love-Begotten Daughter'. The homosocial club milieu was also the seedbed for Burns's vernacular verse epistles to associates like David Sillar and John Rankine, praising the values of male fellowship and sexual enjoyment over worldly prudence, as well as anti-clerical 'kirk satires' like 'The Holy Tulzie' and 'Holy Willie's Prayer'. These were circulated (like the epistles) in manuscript around Tarbolton and Mauchline parishes to the fury of the orthodox faithful. Much of this verse remained unpublished during the poet's lifetime, forming part of what Gerard Carruthers calls Burns's 'reserved canon'.[10]

In 1781 Burns joined Tarbolton's Freemasonic Lodge, being elected Depute Master in 1874. Masonry offered Burns another institutionalised haven from the forces of orthodox conformity, as well as the opportunity to mix on an equal footing with members of the middle and upper classes, affording him access to an extensive patronage network to which his success as a poet was indebted. Masonic networks were largely responsible for his transition from a local to a national poet and his triumphant reception in Edinburgh. An important indicator of his turn to poetry is the *Commonplace Book* which he began in April 1783, at the very nadir of his family's farming fortunes: 'It may be some entertainment to a curious observer of human-nature', Burns wrote, 'to see how a ploughman thinks and feels under the pressure of Love, Ambition, Anxiety, Grief, etc.'[11] Burns's 'curious observer' here acknowledges the influence of Adam Smith's theory of the 'internal spectator' as formulated in the *Theory of Moral Sentiments*, a work quoted later in the *Commonplace Book*, revealing a formidable intellectual hinterland; it also shows that his poetic ambitions aimed for a wider readership than that afforded by his rural social network. Burns's local identity as an Ayrshire 'bardie' (the diminutive form parodied the gran-diose claims of the Ossianic Bard) proved just as important as the pastoral persona of the 'Heaven-taught ploughman' in constructing his poetic fame, establishing the romantic localism later mined by Wordsworth, Scott, Clare, Hogg and many other writers of the Romantic age.[12]

Although many of Burns's poems and songs were written in English (some-times with a 'sprinkling' of Scots diction), the hallmark feature of his verse was its artful use of the 'Scottish dialect', as well as its frequent eschewal of polite Augustan couplets in favour of sixteenth- and seventeenth-cen-tury Scots verse forms like the 'Christ's Kirk', 'Cherry and Slae' and espe-cially 'standard habbie'. Many of Burns's most famous poems (such as 'To a Mouse' and 'Holy Willie's Prayer') employ the six-line 'habbie' stanza:[13] although previously employed by earlier poets in the Scottish vernacular revival as a vehicle for comedy and satire, the form was deployed by Burns in a more sentimental and serious manner. Burns breathed new life into the 'broken and mutilated' Scots vernacular tradition by engaging it with rural modernity and social change; as Thomas Campbell noted, 'Burns has given the *elixir vitae* to his dialect.'[14] Unfortunately, his consummate success often seems to have deterred skilled followers, and poetry written in Scots was easily subsumed into the 'Kailyard' idiom, the nostalgic parochialism of much nineteenth-century Scottish pastoral.

Poems in the Kilmarnock and Edinburgh volumes

On 31 July 1786, John Wilson of Kilmarnock completed a run of 612 cop-ies of a handsome 240-page octavo volume entitled *Poems Chiefly in the Scottish Dialect, by Robert Burns*, selling for the modest price of three shil-lings. Surviving copies of Burns's flier circulated to subscribers reveal that he had originally intended to publish poems *exclusively*, rather than 'chiefly', in the 'Scottish Dialect', but in the event the book was linguistically a mixed bag, from the full Scots of 'Halloween' and 'The Auld Farmer's New-Year Morning Salutation' to the neo-Augustan 'graveyard' style of English poems like 'Despondency, an Ode' and 'To Ruin'. Evident here is the influence of English poets like Pope, Thomson, Gray, Goldsmith, Young and Shenstone, as well as the Scottish precursors mentioned above, from Montgomerie and Sempill to Ramsay and Fergusson. The poetry ranges over an extensive linguistic gamut, from anglo-latinic macaronics and the rhetoric of sensibility, to homely Scots proverbs and Ayrshire agricultural idiolect. 'Kilmarnock' contains forty-four poems, including four songs, as well as a short preface and a glossary by the poet: unconventionally, the dedication to Gavin Hamilton is buried more than half-way through the volume, and burlesques the normal conventions of dedication and patronage. Although he was assiduous in seeing his book through the press, Burns could afford to be cavalier because he published by subscription, building on the existing local reputation of his poems that had circulated in manuscript. The Kilmarnock volume was a runaway success, being avidly sought after by readers from all social backgrounds, from Edinburgh as well as Ayrshire and the southwest of Scotland; a month after publication only thirteen copies remained unsold.

Burns's Preface and poems skilfully construct the persona of the 'Simple Bard, unbroken by rules of Art', together with a partially submerged autobiographical narrative to match, loosely based on the contemporary crisis afflicting his own life, but disclaiming any literary influences other than the poetry of Ramsay and Fergusson. The Preface's 'anti-pastoral' claim to be 'unacquainted' with 'Theocrites and Virgil' underpins the ploughman persona of many of the poems that follow: ironically, this claim to literary *ignorance* underwrites the poet's pastoral realism, his authentic portrayal of the world of his 'rustic compeers' in 'his and their native language'. The fact that this was an authorial fiction is suggested by Dr Robert Anderson, recalling a conversation with the poet in 1787:

> It was, I know, part of the machinery, as he called it, of his poetical character to pass for an illiterate ploughman who wrote from pure inspiration. When I pointed out some evident traces of poetical inspiration in his verses, privately, he readily acknowledged his obligations and even admitted the advantages he enjoyed in poetical composition from the *copia verborum*, the command of phraseology, which the knowledge and use of the English and Scottish dialects afforded him; but in company he did not suffer his pretensions to pure inspiration to be challenged, and it was seldom done where he might be supposed to affect the success of the subscription for his Poems.[15]

Allowing the pastoral mask to slip for a moment (not without expressing a concern for his subscription list), Burns here underlines the fact that, rather than struggling with an 'impoverished' or 'restricted' idiom, the Scottish poet who commands both 'the English and Scottish dialects' in fact enjoys a peculiar advantage over others limited to standard English poetic diction alone. The literary self-consciousness concealed by Burns's pastoral persona is evident in 'The Twa Dogs', the poem that opens the Kilmarnock volume, which was partly inspired by a translation of Cervantes's *El coloquio de los perros* (1613); other significant literary intertexts are Anna Barbauld's 'The Mouse's Petition' (1773) for 'To a Mouse', and 'The Lousiad' (1786) of John Wolcot (Peter Pindar) for 'To a Louse'.

'The Twa Dogs' takes the form of a pastoral eclogue between the humble collie 'Luath' and the aristocratic Newfoundland 'Caesar', favourably comparing the hard life of the poor to the *otium* of the rich. (A darker view of the social inequality of eighteenth-century Scottish society, unrelieved by the comic tone of 'The Twa Dogs', is presented later in the volume in the 'dirge' 'Man was Made to Mourn', based on an old broadside ballad.) 'The Twa Dogs' is followed by two 'whisky' poems entitled 'Scotch Drink' and 'The Author's Earnest Cry and Prayer' concerned with popular politics and the Scottish whisky industry. Burns's brilliance in employing demotic language to comment on high politics is further revealed in his breathtaking *lese-majestie* in 'A Dream' (a satire responding to Poet Laureate Joseph Warton's 'Birthday Ode' to George III), in which the 'humble bardie' offers some homely advice to the unpopular monarch. By contrast, the customary superstitions of the rural poor are the subject of 'The Holy Fair' and 'Halloween', although the headnote to the latter poem undermines the 'Heaven-taught' persona of the Preface by promising 'entertainment to a philosophic mind ... among the more unenlightened in our own' age (73). Squarely within the pastoral tradition, this reveals an incongruity between the demotic rural language and address of the poems themselves, and the sophisticated, urban reader.

This cluster of largely Scots poems on whisky, popular traditions and farming (especially the two 'Poor Maillie' poems and the 'Auld Farmer's ... Salutation to his Auld Mare Maggie') occupy much of the first half of the collection, a prelude to its 'dark centre', dominated by English lyrics in the fashionable 'graveyard manner' concerned with unrequited love, despondency and ruin. Although 'The Vision' has been attacked by modern critics for its uncharacteristically georgic tone and its shift from Scots into Augustan English after the first eight habbie stanzas, in fact it is the most ambitious poem in the Kilmarnock volume (62). The despondent poet's resolution to abandon poetry and dedicate his energies to farming is interrupted by the apparition of his local muse Coila (representing the Ayrshire district of Kyle, but partly based on the supernatural sylphs of Pope's *Rape of the Lock*), upon whose green mantle is depicted a topographic image of her native district. After resolving his vocational doubts and delivering a panegyric to the civic virtue of Ayrshire's improving gentry, Coila consecrates Burns as Ayrshire's 'rustic bard' by crowning him with a holly wreath. Rather than aspiring to emulate Thomson, Shenstone or Gray, she urges him to acknowledge his humble station as a *pastoral* genius;

> 'I taught thy manners-painting strains,
> The *loves*, the *ways*, of simple swains,
> Till now, o'er all my wide domains,
> Thy fame extends;
> And some, the pride of *Coila's* plains,
> Become thy friends.' (62, lines 241–6)

'The Vision', a pitch for patronage among 'the pride of Coila's plains', is deliberately held back to tenth place in the Kilmarnock volume: its 'polite' georgic tone is perhaps intended to mitigate the raucous vernacular satire on George III in 'A Dream' that immediately precedes it.

If 'The Vision' is the most 'georgic' of all the poems published in the Kilmarnock volume, 'The Cotter's Saturday Night' is the most conventionally 'pastoral', even if it prefers a realistic view of the harshness of peasant life to the enamelled platitudes of neoclassical pastoral tradition. The long Spenserian stanza and the pentameter line (adapted from Fergusson's pastoral masterpiece 'The Farmer's Ingle') permit the descriptive depth and extension requisite for such domestic scene-painting; the frequent switching from Scots to English diction creates an effect of intense localism, punctuated by philosophic reflection and moralising sentiment. The Covenanting zeal of the old cotter's call to worship '*And let us worship GOD!*' (line 108) (which, Burns told Gilbert, was the poem's original inspiration, vol. III, p. 1111) and the 'artless singing' of the psalm tunes 'Dundee', 'Martyrs', and 'Elgin', as well as the Bible readings, represent Presbyterian family worship in a very different light from that of the kirk satires. The poem's uncharacteristic piety, alongside its Scottish patriotism ('O SCOTIA! my dear, my native soil!', line 172), suggests why it became the most popular and widely imitated of all Burns's poems in the Victorian era. Yet the poem also communicates a radical spirit which complicated its subsequent appropriation by Tory propagandists;

> And *certes*, in fair Virtue's heavenly road,
> The *Cottage* leaves the *Palace* far behind:
> What is a lordling's pomp? a cumbrous load,
> Disguising oft the *wretch* of human kind,
> Studied in arts of Hell, in wickedness refin'd! (72, lines 168–71)

Notable, however, is the poem's failure to acknowledge that the cotters whose exemplary virtues it hymns were on the verge of extinction, as they were cleared from the rural lowlands by the juggernaut of improvement. The theme of dispossession is displaced on to the poem that immediately follows 'The Cotter' in the running order of Kilmarnock, Burns's most famous lyric, 'To a Mouse': 'Now thou's turned out, for a' thy trouble, / But house or hald, / To thole the Winter's *sleety dribble*, / An' *cranreuch* cauld!' (lines 33–6). Although the poet/ploughman is himself the agent of destruction (it is after all his plough that has 'turned up her nest'), his sentimental identification with the mouse's homelessness chimes with his own predicament of imminent ruin and exile, a fate that runs like a thread through all the poems in the Kilmarnock volume: 'An *forward*, tho' I canna see, / I *guess* an' *fear*!' (lines 47–8).

The poems in the second half of Kilmarnock feature a concentration of the verse epistles, representing Burns's consummate skill in deploying the traditional forms of the 'habbie' or 'Cherry and Slae' stanzas while creating a sense of informal epistolary 'conversation' in Scots. His major poetic model (as acknowledged at lines 13–18 of 'Epistle to Willie Simson') was the published epistolary exchange of 1719 between Allan Ramsay and Lieutenant William Hamilton of Gilbertfield. Although Burns did address epistles to his social superiors (Gavin Hamilton, Andrew Aiken, Robert Graham, Hugh Parker), those published here specifically address men of his own class, friends from the Tarbolton Bachelor's Club and the Court of Equity, 'the hairum-scairum, ram-stam boys' at loggerheads with the Mauchline Kirk Session ('Epistle to James Smith', line 165), fellow Ayrshire 'bardies' like James Smith, William Simson, Davie Sillar, John Lapraik and John Rankine. Struggling tenant farmers, linen-drapers, grocers, school-teachers, postmasters, these men were the nascent *petit bourgeoisie* of rural Ayrshire, educated in the aspirational ideology of improvement but, like the Burnses, father and sons, victims of the booms and busts of the new capitalist economy and landlord intransigence. In addition to mining the *carpe diem* theme and praising the compensatory pleasures of friendship, the epistles follow Horatian convention by meditating on the art of poetry or (more colloquially) 'crambo'. In the first 'Epistle to Lapraik', for example, Burns follows Ramsay in disingenuously identifying himself as 'nae *Poet*, in a sense, / But just a *Rhymer* like by chance' (57, lines 49–50). He criticises the pride of 'your Critic-folk' (line 55) and the 'jargon o' [their] Schools' (line 61) before making his famous appeal 'Gie me ae spark o' Nature's fire, That 's a' the learning I desire' (lines 73–4). (Like the Preface's disavowal of literary learning, this profession of 'untaught' genius alludes to both Sterne and Pope.) The later poems in the collection pick up the submerged autobiographical theme again, with 'On a Scotch Bard Gone to the West Indies', 'From Thee Eliza I Must Go' and 'The Farewell': the poet emerges as a type of Virgil's dispossessed shepherd Meliboeus in the *First Eclogue*, unjustly forced to leave his farm and travel into exile. Taking up the rear is 'A Bard's Epitaph', in which a 'posthumous' Burns runs over his personal failings, concluding with the unconvincing moral 'know, prudent, cautious, *self-controul* / Is Wisdom's root' (lines 29–30).

In contrast to the egalitarian credentials of Kilmarnock, the Edinburgh edition published the following year was prefaced by a fulsome dedication to the aristocratic members of the Caledonian Hunt: its copious subscription list included the names of over 1,500 of Scotland's great and good, pledged to receive a total of 2,876 copies at five shillings apiece. The most significant additions were 'Death and Dr Hornbook', a humorous satire on medical quackery, the celebrated 'Address to a Haggis' and the mixed-register 'The Brigs of Ayr' in which Burns debated the losses and gains of improvement in a flyting dialogue between the town's old and new bridges. Also published here for the first time are early songs like 'When Guildford Guid', 'Green Grow the Rashes' and 'John Barleycorn', displaying a precocious talent in the medium of song art. The low point, however, is the feeble 'Address to Edinburgh' (135), an exercise in the kind of poetry that the Edinburgh literati might have preferred Burns to have written. Burns had taken pains to play down religious satire in the Kilmarnock edition of 1786 for fear of the 'holy artillery' of the Kirk Session in the Ayrshire heartland of orthodoxy. But throwing caution to the winds as he prepared the Edinburgh edition, he added 'The Ordination', 'The Calf' and 'Address to the Unco Guid', giving a much stronger flavour of anti-orthodox satire to the volume as a whole, and playing well with the Moderate churchmen of the Edinburgh Enlightenment.

Poems and songs of the Dumfries period

Much of Burns's poetry written in the period after 1788, often composed in the strained poetic diction of 'Address to Edinburgh', eulogises aristocratic or polite patrons, and is largely concerned with the themes of patronage and Scottish county politics. There's also a body of work inspired by the Highland tour of 1787, the best of which is probably 'The Humble Petition of Bruar Water, to the Noble Duke of Athole'. Absent from many of these polite, Anglicised efforts is the demotic energy that radiates from the songs Burns had begun to produce for Johnson's *Scots Musical Museum* in 1788, or 'Tam o' Shanter: A Tale' (321), written in 1790 and added to the Edinburgh edition in 1793. It's no surprise that Burns's narrative masterpiece focuses on the illicit pleasures of alcohol, sexuality, popular music and dancing, defiantly 'counterposed' to the disciplinary demands of his new occupational concerns as an Excise officer, that is, a gauger and tax-collector for the British state. In a sense Tam o' Shanter's near-escape from hellish retribution at the hands of Cuttie Sark anticipates the fate of the radicalised poet in the darkening political climate of the 1790s.

'Tam o' Shanter' is also a product of an enthusiasm for popular anti-quarianism shared by Burns's Dumfriesshire circle: especially his neighbour Robert Riddell of Glenriddell and his friend Captain Francis Grose, the 'British Antiquarian', who commissioned the poet to furnish a description of the superstitions attached to Kirkalloway in his Ayrshire birthplace for his *Antiquities of Scotland* (1789–91). (In the event, the 226-line poem first appeared in book form as a long footnote to Grose's rather spare text in the second volume of this work.)[16]

Central to what Carole McGuirk calls 'Tam o' Shanter's' 'elusive mean-ing'[17] is the pattern of structural contrasts dividing hedonistic pleasure (Tam's enjoyment of the Ayr tavern and the dancing witches) from self-regulation, upheld at one level by the narrator's use of English or light Scots diction (most famously exemplified by lines 59–66, 'But pleasures are like poppies spread') compared to the fuller Scots of the main narrative, and of course Tam's sole illocution, 'Weel done Cutty Sark!' Burns's only attempt at narrative verse, the poem's carefully modulated octosyllabic couplets, con-trolled variations in tempo and deft pace perhaps express a sense of the poet/exciseman's new professional mobility in these years, a mobility shared with his addressee, the 'peregrinating' Captain Grose.

Tam's outburst at line 189 brings the poem to its climax by breaking the erotic enchantment, as well as the observer's detachment from the diabol-ical spectacle, but in doing so summons the vindictive powers of darkness. Surrendering his silent invisibility, the watching Tam is instantaneously 'con-taminated' through his identification with the anarchic and orgiastic pow-ers gathered within the ruined kirk. Tam's admiration for the half-naked dancing Nannie connects him with Burns's fascination with what Murray Pittock calls the 'hidden Scotland' of 'music, song and dance',[18] as well as with Grose's fixation with the satanic, the popular, the curious, in contrast to the judicious distance of the Enlightenment historian. Like Burns's own dangerous involvement in the singing of the revolutionary anthem 'Ça ira' in the Theatre Royal, Dumfries, in 1792, which nearly cost him his Excise post, Tam has much to lose from his heedless act of self-exposure. Both his wife Kate's threatened prophecy that he will be 'found deep drown'd in Doon; / Or catch'd wi' warlocks in the mirk, / By Alloway's auld, haunted kirk' (lines 30–2) and the demands of poetic justice require that he be punished for his transgression. As the narrator thunders in the lines that immediately follow, 'Ah, *Tam*! ah, *Tam*! thou'll get thy fairin! / In hell they'll roast thee like a herrin! / In vain thy Kate awaits thy comin! / Kate soon will be a woefu' woman!' (lines 201–4).

Despite the threats, however, Tam gets off scot-free. Unfortunately, his mare Maggie, who has saved him from the furious witches by leaping across the bridge, isn't so lucky. Tam's near-emasculation at the hands of the witches is suffered instead by his mare, who loses her tail; it's a misogynistic conclusion to a misogynistic poem, even if Maggie is a mare not a woman. Although ostensibly a cautionary tale for tavern hedonists, Burns's poem lodges a protest against the abuse of supernatural terror in the enforcement of conventional morality, a familiar theme to readers of the kirk satires: it's entirely appropriate (especially considering the pun) that this much-loved poem should have become Scotland's 'national tale'.

Burns and song

Although contact with Robert Riddell's antiquarian network undoubtedly stimulated Burns's interest in popular song (he was formidably well read in the copious eighteenth-century literature on Scottish song), he was already very much 'inside' the tradition.[19] His mother, Agnes, was an accomplished singer, and he claimed that his earliest poetic composition, addressed to his first love, Nelly Kilpatrick, was a song 'O Once I Loved a Bonnie Lass'.[20] Although a scattering of songs appeared at the end of the 1786 and 1787 volumes, Burns's outstanding early achievement in this department was his 'Scots Cantata', 'Love and Liberty', otherwise known as 'The Jolly Beggars', the longest and most significant work in Burns's reserved canon (84). This was allegedly inspired by the poet's late-night encounter with a group of beggars or 'randie, gangrel bodies' in Poosie Nancy's tavern in Mauchline (lines 7–8). The cantata's very full scene-setting (and rudimentary plot) is carried by the *recitativo*, the Scots idiom of which contrasts with the lyrical content of English and Anglo-Scots songs, set to a combination of Scottish and English melodies, performed by each of the *dramatis personae* in turn.

Allan Cunningham seems to have been the first commentator to have described Burns's 'Love and Liberty' as 'a sort of Beggar's Saturday Night',[21] celebrating the desperate hedonism of the 'undeserving poor', but in stark contrast to the pious virtues of 'honest poverty' addressed in 'The Cotter's Saturday Night', which was intriguingly written about the same time, in the autumn of 1785.[22] The young poet here shows off a precocious skill in matching newly minted lyrics to traditional Scottish and English melodies. Eight 'swaggering' songs are performed (in order of precedence) by the 'Son of Mars', the 'Martial Chuck', the 'Merry Andrew', the 'Highlandman's widow', the 'Pigmy Scraper' and the 'Sturdy Caird' (Tinker), the whole concluding with two songs by the 'Bard of no regard'. The final song sounds a note of Blakean antinomianism: 'A fig for those by law protected! / LIBERTY'S a glorious feast! / Courts for Cowards were erected, / Churches built to please the PRIEST' (lines 254–7). We've already noted that *carpe diem* was an abiding theme of Burns's poetry and song, and there's no doubt that the cantata's 'glorious feast' powerfully transformed the eighteenth-century genre of 'beggar pastoral' that it inherited from both the literary and popular traditions. It remained unpublished until 1799, when it appeared as an unauthorised chapbook.

The majority of the *c.* 373 Scottish songs that Burns composed or adapted from tradition were the work of the Dumfries period, as the poetic *afflatus* of the Mauchline years began to wane. Burns is unquestionably the outstanding songwriter of the Romantic period, and for many critics, his achievements as a songwriter outshine those of the poet, transforming traditional Scottish song from a popular into a national art-form, as well as broadcasting his fame world-wide, to a greater extent than the verse. Many of the songs were contributed to Johnson's *Scots Musical Museum* (1787–1803) (Burns also played an editorial role in this collection) and, after 1792, George Thomson's more exclusive *Select Collection of Original Scottish Airs* (1793–1846). In the spirit of patriotism, the poet refused to accept any payment for his work. Burns's songs stand apart from his poetry to the extent that their verbal art is intimately wedded to traditional melody; 'until I am complete master of a tune, in my own singing, (such as it is) I never can compose for it'.[23] Despite the currency of such 'English' pastoral songs, Burns preferred a more robust idiom and what he called a 'sprinkling of 'our native tongue' to achieve the sought-after effect of 'naivete, [or] a pastoral simplicity'.[24] Although the pastoral tone dominates, Burns's songs address a wide range of subjects, from the occupational, the political (both Jacobite and Jacobin), the bacchanalian, to (above all) songs concerned with sex, love, courtship and marriage, especially the question of 'tocher' or dowry. Donald Low suggests that nearly one half of all Burns's songs are concerned with love in one or other of its manifestations.[25] Burns's radical songs, though fewer in number, exploit the anonymity of the genre to evade censorship in the anti-Jacobin climate of the early 1790s, while their well-known melodies served as vehicles for rapid transmission and public performance. Little wonder that his most famous song in this genre, 'Is there for Honest Poverty', quickly became an anthem for British radicalism: as Marilyn Butler writes, the final lines, 'It's comin yet for a' that, / That Man to Man the warld o'er, / Shall brothers be for a' that', are 'probably the closest rendering in English of the notorious Jacobin "Ca ira"'.[26]

Burns's premature death in the summer of 1796 (probably from rheumatic heart disease) was the occasion for much soul-searching by his friends and admirers, and for moral blame from his detractors. Lurid accounts of his decline into seedy dissipation in the Dumfries years flowed from the pens of George Thomson and Robert Heron shortly after the poet's death, and were broadcast in the popular press; an ineffectual defence by his friend Maria Riddell did little to redeem the situation.[27] English commentators, especially those of a radical stamp, blamed Scotland's detested 'Dundas despotism' for failing adequately to patronise the humbly born genius in their midst: the fact that Burns's Edinburgh edition had been dedicated to the Caledonian Hunt, the flower of the Scottish gentry and nobility, made his subsequent neglect at their hands seem all the more unpardonable. Most were in agreement that an Excise Commission was an insulting form of patronage, although there is little evidence that the poet would have concurred. Coleridge concluded his 1796 poem 'To a Friend who had Declared His Intention of Writing no more Poetry' by construing Burns as a martyr, and imagining a garland of 'rank hensbane' and deadly nightshade twined upon the 'illustrious Brow of Scotch Nobility'.[28]

The poetic achievements of Robert Burns shared the fate of Byron's poetry, and to a lesser extent the works of other Romantics, of being overshadowed by a popular fixation with the biographical narrative of a troubled, albeit inspirational, life. This was largely influenced by Dr James Currie's 1800 biography prefaced to his edition of Burns's *Works*, the main portal through which Burns reached the nineteenth-century reader, as well as the standard edition for Romantic writers.[29] As national poet, Burns's strengths seemed to mirror traits of Scottish frankness and democracy, but his weaknesses were taken to reflect her deep national insecurity as junior partner in the Victorian Empire. In the present era of postcolonialism and devolution, the time is ripe to reassess Burns as not only Scotland's greatest poet, but also a Romantic poet of European stature, in the same league as Blake, Wordsworth, Coleridge, Byron and Shelley. His unparalleled reinvention of Scottish idiom and identity offers a new orientation to the entire cultural geography of Romanticism in British Isles and beyond.

Notes

1 For a development of many of the arguments of this chapter, see my *Robert Burns and Pastoral: Poetry and Improvement in Late Eighteenth-Century Scotland* (Oxford University Press, 2010).

2 For the most up-to-date biography, see Robert Crawford, *The Bard: Robert Burns, a Biography* (London: Jonathan Cape, 2009).

3 J. De Lancey Ferguson and G. Ross Roy (eds.), *The Letters of Robert Burns*, 2nd edn, 2 vols. (Oxford: Clarendon Press, 1985), vol. I, p. 137.

4 On Burns's problematic attitudes to slavery, see Gerard Carruthers, 'Robert Burns and Slavery', in Johnny Rodger and Gerard Carruthers (eds.), *Fickle Man: Robert Burns in the 21st Century* (Dingwall: Sandstone Press, 2009), pp. 163–75, and Nigel Leask, 'Burns and the Politics of Abolition', in Gerard Carruthers (ed.), *The Edinburgh Companion to Robert Burns* (Edinburgh: Edinburgh University Press, 2009), pp. 47–60.

5 See Richard Hindle Fowler, *Robert Burns* (London: Routledge, 1988), pp. 114–56.

6 Liam McIlvanney, *Burns the Radical: Poetry and Politics in Late Eighteenth-Century Scotland* (East Linton: Tuckwell Press, 2002), pp. 38–66; Carol McGuirk, *Robert Burns and the Sentimental Era* (Athens, GA: University of Georgia Press, 1985).

7 John Strawhorn, 'Ayrshire and the Enlightenment', in Graham Cruikshank (ed.), *A Sense of Place: Studies in Scottish Local History* (Edinburgh: Scotland's Cultural Heritage, 1988), pp. 188–201; John Strawhorn (ed.), *Ayrshire at the Time of Burns* ([Ayr]: Ayrshire Archaeological and Natural History Society, 1959).

8 Ferguson and Roy (eds.), *Letters*, vol. I, p. 135.

9 Donald Low (ed.), *Robert Burns: The Critical Heritage* (London: Routledge & Kegan Paul, 1974), p. 7.

10 Gerard Carruthers, *Robert Burns*, Writers and Their Work (Tavistock, Devon: Northcote House, 2006), p. 3.

11 *Robert Burns' Common Place Book*, ed. Raymond Lamont Brown (Wakefield: S. R. Publishers Ltd, 1969), p. 1.

12 See Robert Crawford, *Devolving English Literature* (Edinburgh University Press, 2000), p. 93.

13 See Douglas Dunn, '"A very Scottish kind of dash": Burns' Native Metric', in Robert Crawford (ed.), *Robert Burns and Cultural Authority* (Edinburgh: Polygon, 1997), pp. 58–85.

14 Quoted in John Gibson Lockhart, *Life of Robert Burns* (London: Dent, 1959), p. 227.

15 Quoted in James Kinsley, *The Poems and Songs of Robert Burns* (Oxford: Clarendon Press, 1968), vol. III, pp. 1537–8; further references will appear in the text.

16 It was published twice in the newspapers prior to this.

17 Carol McGuirk (ed.), *Robert Burns: Selected Poems* (London: Penguin, 1993), pp. 265–6.

18 Murray Pittock, *Scottish and Irish Romanticism* (Oxford University Press, 2008), p. 163.

19 Thomas Crawford, *Burns: A Study of the Poems and Songs* (1960; repr. Edinburgh: Canongate Academic, 1994), p. 258.

20 Ferguson and Roy (eds.), *Letters*, vol. I, p. 137.

21 Low (ed.), *Robert Burns*, p. 407.

22 See McGuirk (ed.), *Selected Poems*, p. 220.

23 Ferguson and Roy (eds.), *Letters*, vol. II, p. 242.

24 *Ibid.*, pp. 149, 181.

25 Donald Low, '"My Tocher's the Jewel": Love and Money in the Songs of Burns', in Kenneth Simpson (ed.), *Burns Now* (Edinburgh: Canongate, 1994), pp. 117–28.

26 Marilyn Butler, 'Burns and Politics', in Crawford (ed.), *Robert Burns and Cultural Authority*, p. 102.

27 See Low (ed.), *Robert Burns*, pp. 99–101, 101–7, 117–30.

28 Samuel Taylor Coleridge, *Poetical Works*, ed. J. C. C. Mays (Princeton University Press, 2001), vol. I, p. 271, lines 34–7.

29 Robert Thornton, *James Currie: The Entire Stranger and Robert Burns* (Edinburgh: Oliver & Boyd, 1963); see also Nigel Leask, 'The Shadow Line: James Currie's Robert Burns and British Romanticism', in Claire Lamont and Michael Rossington (eds.), *Romanticism's Debatable Lands* (Basingstoke: Palgrave Macmillan, 2007), pp. 64–79.

Guide to further reading

Carruthers, Gerard, *Robert Burns* (Tavistock: Northcote House, 2006)

Carruthers, Gerard (ed.), *The Edinburgh Companion to Robert Burns* (Edinburgh University Press, 2009)

Crawford, Robert (ed.), *Robert Burns and Cultural Authority* (Edinburgh: Polygon, 1997)

Crawford, Thomas, *Burns: A Study of the Poems and Songs* (1960; repr. Edinburgh: Canongate, 1994)

Leask, Nigel, *'His Hero's Story': Currie's Burns, Moore's Byron, and the Problem of Romantic Biography*, The Byron Foundation Lecture 2006 (Nottingham: Centre for the Study of Byron and Romanticism, 2007)

  Robert Burns and Pastoral: Poetry and Improvement in Late Eighteenth-Century Scotland (Oxford University Press, 2010)

McGuirk, Carol, *Robert Burns and the Sentimental Era* (Athens, GA: University of Georgia Press, 1985)

McIlvanney, Liam, *Burns the Radical: Poetry and Politics in Late Eighteenth-Century Scotland* (East Linton: Tuckwell Press, 2002)

Pittock, Murray, *Scottish and Irish Romanticism* (Oxford University Press, 2008)

Stafford, Fiona, 'Burns and Romantic Writing', in Carruthers (ed.), *Edinburgh Companion to Burns*, pp. 97–109.

6

MURRAY PITTOCK

Enlightenment, Romanticism and the Scottish Canon: Cosmopolites or Narrow Nationalists?

The concept of a 'Scottish literature' by its very phrasing invokes a claim to be a national literature. A collection such as the present one accepts the existence of a 'Scottish' literature in these terms: distinct in important respects from any other literature, and having within it qualities which express, reflect or relate to a set of experiences which are sufficiently widely shared and expressive of certain collectivities of culture, institutions or banal quotidian association that we have come to call 'national'. What the validity or otherwise of this term is is a different matter, which I have explored elsewhere.[1] The chapter which follows is instead aimed at teasing out a question of periodicity and aesthetic in this national literary history: the extent to which 'Scottish' literature partakes of European and Western literary movements which are normally taken as transcending national boundaries, and the extent to which the Scottish case inflects these in distinctive ways in the Romantic period.

In the context of the long eighteenth century, this is an important question, because – in recent years in particular – Scotland has been seen as having a key role in the European Enlightenment. The Scottish Enlightenment has been treated as a key intellectual powerhouse, not least in the United States, where books such as Arthur Herman's *How the Scots Invented the Modern World: The True Story of How Western Europe's Poorest Nation Created Our World and Everything in It* (2004) present an extravagantly maximalist case for a national Enlightenment promoting the universal values of modern rationality while serving as the creative engine-room for the disciplines of modern thought and the achievements of modern technology. Closer to home, Alexander Broadie's *Cambridge Companion to the Scottish Enlightenment* (2003) is currently the best-selling Cambridge Companion, and was published in Mandarin in 2010. The Scottish Enlightenment has a long and unquestioned national reach.

Until recently, there has been more doubt about the existence of a Scottish national Romanticism, which seems on the surface strange, since in the nineteenth century the importance of Macpherson, Burns, Scott, *Blackwood's* and the *Edinburgh Review* was widely understood and acknowledged. The reasons for this neglect have been explored in an explosion of recent literature. Katie Trumpener's *Bardic Nationalism* (1997) was an avatar for a large number of more recent studies, including Leith Davis, Ian Duncan and Janet Sorensen's *Scotland and the Borders of Romanticism* (2004), David Duff and Catherine Jones's *Scotland, Ireland and the Romantic Aesthetic* (2007), Ian Duncan's *Scott's Shadow* (2007) and my own *Scottish and Irish Romanticism* (2008). These works in their turn are supported by a range of new author-focused studies, such as Robert Crawford's *The Bard* (2009) and Andrew Lincoln's *Walter Scott and Modernity* (2007), together with the major textual editions which now dominate the landscape of Scottish Romantic scholarship: the Edinburgh Edition of the Waverley Novels, the Stirling–South Carolina Research Edition of the Works of James Hogg, the Oxford Collected Burns and the Yale Edition of the Private Papers of James Boswell.

Given the enduring and now dominant strength of the national *Scottish* Enlightenment, one of the key questions has been the nature of the relationship between that Enlightenment and Scottish Romanticism. In a number of respects the two movements may seem at odds. The Enlightenment, in Scotland perhaps more than anywhere else, foregrounded the application of reason to knowledge in a context of material improvement. In the context of the stadial models of society posited by its leading theorists such as Adam Smith, William Robertson and Dugald Stewart, this trend in Enlightenment thinking reinforced and to a degree created what was to become known as Whig history: the idea of history as a progress towards ever more perfect forms of liberty and society, what might be called a teleology of civility. The teleology of civility provided, through historical and sociological stadialism, a universal model for human progress through different kinds of society. In his 1762 *Lectures on Jurisprudence*, Adam Smith had posited a four-stage theory of society, beginning with nomadic hunter-gatherers, progressing through shepherding pastoralists to settled agriculturalists, and having its apotheosis in a realm of national and international commerce and exchange: the expanding mercantile universe of the first age of Empire. At any given time in history, some societies might be at one stage and some at another, and the stages were universalisable across the globe: so it was legitimate to read the Scottish Highlands of 1750 in terms of contemporary Native American or Afghan societies (as Scott did in an 1816 article in the *Quarterly Review*), and likewise legitimate to consider English commercial society as the apogee towards which humanity was struggling. In Scott's *Rob Roy* (1818), for example, the French commercial house of Dubourg (located in an absolute monarchy with strong feudal/agricultural aspects) is presented as less skilful and developed than the cutting-edge business of Osbaldistone and Tresham in a more commercially minded London. Enlightenment ideas of sympathy and association likewise supported this stadial model: sympathy was developed by civility and promoted by mutual understanding (which implied commonality of language); the association of ideas was a process guaranteed to be more refined by a more enriching environment and a more civil society, which in its turn might breed more sophisticated levels of sympathy. Henry Mackenzie's *The Man of Feeling* (1771) demonstrated that sensitivity was heightened by the associations made possible within a refined environment, while Mary Shelley's *Frankenstein* (1818) showed that association of ideas alone might breed a monster, if that monster was deprived of human society and its refinements: not least the refinements of sympathy and society promised by the presence of women.

Many of the core ideas associated with Romanticism seem to run counter to this. The universalisability of Enlightenment ideas was challenged by Johann Gottfried von Herder, who stressed the cultural particularity of national literatures and their traditions, and thus laid one of the keystones of Romantic nationalism. In contrast to Enlightenment notions of stadial and social progress, Romanticism reinscribed the importance of the primitive and isolated person, the figure of genius touched by what Wordsworth called 'the self-sufficing power of solitude', whose insights, acquired apart from the bustle of cities and commercial modernity, aligned him (it was usually a him) with the autochthonous and authentic, beyond the reach of urban 'refinements' and their numerous, distracting and shallow associations of news, gossip and daily interchange. Associationism itself was linked by Coleridge in *Biographia Litteraria* (1817) with the inferior power of Fancy, in contradistinction to the creative power of the Imagination.

Yet things are not perhaps so clear cut as they appear. Although Herder believed that Enlightenment 'system-building leads to a premature closure of inquiry',[2] his strong linkage of morality to sentiment clearly derived from the world of Hutcheson, Hume and Smith, while his passionate commitment to the individuated nation, true to the *Geist* of its *genius loci*, was moderated by his Smithian confidence in the power of trade to '*unify* human beings, not divide them' (407). Herder's statements of the importance of an individuated language as the expression of personal and national cognition and perception seem at odds with Enlightenment universalism, but at the same time he is reliant on Enlightenment notions of sympathy to moderate chauvinism ('the Latvian does not want to enter into heaven as soon as there are Germans there' (383)) and imperialism ('"Rule, Britannia, rule the waves" – many people believe that with this slogan there is given to them … the nations, and the riches of the world' (385)) in the cause of self-respect. Where he does diverge from the Enlightenment, it is often in an Enlightenment cause. Herder's view is that much Enlightenment thought is a concealed 'measuring of all peoples *by the measure of us Europeans*' (386). His view here was to an extent justified by contemporary events: for example, the French Revolutionary use of '*esclavage*' in the context of metropolitan politics while being less willing to adopt it in the discourse of colonial exploitation – in Robespierre's words, '*Périssent les colonies*'.[3] As an alternative to this slippery and dishonest use of Enlightenment ideas in one's own interest, Herder strives towards a more acceptable mutual language of self-respect, for 'the negro has as much right to consider the white man a degenerate, a born albino freak, as when the white man considers him a beast' (394–5). In addition, as a philosopher of history and a philosopher of language, as well as in his strongly empiricist theories of cognition, Herder was an intellectual scion of the Enlightenment, concerned with interrogating its major theoretical positions as much in the cause of finessing them as destroying them (vii); he was also deeply involved in Scottish literature, being an enthusiast for Macpherson and translating Burns. Herder's work inspired Goethe on a number of counts, not least in his famous poem on the erl-king (after Herder's 'Erlkoenig's Tochter') which Scott, himself influenced strongly by German Romanticism, translated.

In these things, Herder as a great champion of Romantic nationalism (as Scott was later to be seen in Continental Europe) was in tune with the wider intellectual developments of his own day. As Joep Leerssen has argued, the Romantic moment really arrives when 'antiquarianism founders in the rise of historicism'.[4] The historicist moment was in these terms not just an Enlightenment, but also a Romantic one. How could the medievalism some Romantics came to glorify be identified as a stage in human history to valorise, unless it had been identified as such a stage first by historiography? How could the primitive be exhibited as an ideal except in terms of the modelling which allowed it to be recognised as 'primitive'?[5]

Macpherson's Ossian poetry communicated the glories of ancient Scotland by speaking the teleological language of Enlightened civility, as is immediately apparent when one compares the visceral violence of Homeric primary epic or even Iain Lom's Gaelic poetry of Montrose's wars with the discreetly veiled allusions to bloodshed in Macpherson's heavily edited *Fingal* (1761), itself perhaps drawing on the bolder and more violent portrayal of the Gaidhealtachd's present and future suffering in Alasdair MacMhaighstir Alasdair's *Birlinn Clann Raghnaill*. Similarly, Robert Burns presented himself and was accepted on the European stage (particularly in Germany), as both the voice of an undisturbed autochthonous community and the advanced spokesman of a radical and progressive poetry. This double account of Burns is present in the earliest versions of his genius, such as the poem 'Oran Ussaig' in *The Bee* for 27 April 1791, which portrays him both as a 'heav'n-born poet ... soaring sweetly on the muse's wing' and the ploughman poet of 'old Coila's rustic scenes' far below.[6] James Hogg too presented his sophisticated analysis of genre and form in the guise of various bucolic personae, the rootedness of experience exposing the pretensions of abstraction. A separate public sphere in Scotland provided both the institutional infrastructure for the achievements of the Enlightenment and the success of the Romantic periodicals. Within this national public sphere, literature inflected genre in order to reflect in hybrid form both the variety of language and register in Scottish literature (across English and Scots, and in MacMhaighstir Alasdair's case across Gaelic too) and to present a basis for the celebration of a taxonomy of glory, the organised memoralisation of the Scottish past, present also in the British Empire in a growing diaspora which celebrated that past and was to erect statues to mark it throughout the nineteenth century. These were the conditions for a national literature and national Romanticism, and they acted in ways which to an extent relied on the findings of the Enlightenment, to an extent interrogated them and in part also rejected them. But they were not innocent of them.

When Scott borrowed aspects of Byron's 'Song of the Albanian Highlanders' in *Childe Harold* (1813) for Rory Dall's song in chapter 22 of *Waverley* (1814), both writers were utilising an Enlightenment model which encouraged the drawing of parallels between mountain peoples in one place and those of another, estimated as both were to be at the same stage of society; they were also drawing both on Jacobite and older Scottish patriot historiographical models which saw the mountaineer as a friend to liberty, itself to be a strongly marked Romantic theme, *Rauberromantik*, 'bandit romanticism'. Place was important, not just paradigm. Likewise, if as Maureen McLane argues, Mungo Park in Africa saw 'a song, or the idea of a song', as an 'index of time spent in another place – whether that place is the Borders' past or travelling another African country',[7] the Romantic collecting of ballads by Herder or Scott became a measure of the nature of society and time in the place from which it was collected. What Pascale Casanova calls 'the Herder effect' cuts both ways[8]: particularity of the 'other place' may be one subject to Enlightened enquiry as much as Romantic valorisation, and this of course may be the same process, which explains why Blair and other Edinburgh Enlightenment figures welcomed Macpherson's Ossian poetry. Thus when Scott in *Rob Roy* writes that 'the effect of music arises ... from association, and sounds which might jar the nerves of a Londoner or Parisian, bring back to the Highlander his lofty mountain, wild lake, and the deeds of his fathers',[9] he endorses both the structure of Enlightenment's universal argument, and the deep particularity of its appeal to those from what he wishes to present to his own readers as a Romantic environment. In stadial terms, Scott has compared the Highlanders in general and Rob Roy in particular to Native Americans and Arabs in his introduction: he has also carefully set up two non-historical sources of information about his hero, 'popular recollection' and the 'fictitious' and 'pretended' chapbook, *The Highland Rogue*. Scott is thus both challenging Enlightenment historiography as the sole source of accurate information, and also reversing expectations with regard to the reliability of the alternative sources by criticising the print record as against the popular oral one, an issue to which the main narrative will return in the shape of Diana Vernon's critique of historiography's winners' bias, discussed below. It is not the only occasion on which Scott uses this approach – the quicksands of history in *The Bride of Lammermoor* is another example of a master-metaphor which seems to provide closure while in fact challenging it – but its use in *Rob Roy* is particularly sophisticated. The print record can be biased and erroneous, the oral, with both 'good report and bad report', is more balanced (Scott's contemporaries and successors, notably Hogg in *Confessions* and John Buchan in *Witch Wood*, explore this question too). Orality contests history and transcends fiction: such is the idea lingering at the edges of Scott's Introduction. Similarly, he notes the idleness of Highlanders without law and magistracy in the Introduction, while in the early chapters of the book Rob Roy's ceaseless activity is obvious, and his intercession delivers Frank Osbaldistone from the threat posed by the pettifogging legalism and self-indulgent idleness of the local English magistrate. Justice and law, key parts of the teleology of civility, simply do not work in the narrative as advertised in the Introduction, whose premises are being interrogated throughout.

Far from 'the Scottish Enlightenment' being 'Romanticism's antithesis', the Enlightenment and Romanticism are inextricably intertwined in Scottish Romanticism. Not only does associationism arguably give rise to an 'imaginary network' of 'national sympathy', located in the performance of its singers rather than its published texts,[10] but Scottish Romantic writers are also engaged in a prolonged argument about the validity and definition of Enlightenment terms and claims, when they are not simply writing in the shadow of their historiographical values. This approach renders them often more socially engaged with these very questions, and thus less autonomously in pursuit of a Romantic aesthetic than some of their English contemporaries. To the extent that Scottish Enlightenment historiography was concerned with nation-building, national myth and the conversion of Whig party history into the apparently studied detachment of rational enquiry, it was a fit subject for both Romantic interest and Romantic contestation. Nationality was at the core of Enlightenment historiography in Scotland, since so much of it was a justificatory praxis for the teleological absorption of an older Scottish into a newer British society. It was thus a fit subject for Romantic engagement; moreover, its use of rhetorical strategy especially enabled that engagement, which itself – as under Napoleon – valorised a 'National Historicism'.[11] For example, William Robertson's 'emotional allegiance to the enduring virtues of Scottish culture, such as its martial spirit of independence and self-reliance', allowed a space for sentiment and the imaginative play on feeling it aroused without any implication of political relevance. In his portrayal of Mary, Queen of Scots 'as a sentimental heroine rather than as a fully responsible political agent ... Robertson laid the ground for the subsequent reinvention of Jacobitism, by Sir Walter Scott and others, as an aesthetic attitude only'.[12]

Yet Robertson's statute of limitations for the imagination, intending to confine it to the limits of sentiment, was not shared by all Enlightenment authors. Dugald Stewart, who taught Scott at Edinburgh University and was himself a friend of the United Irishman William Drennan, was a radical thinker as well as a stadial historian, and thought that 'there is very little danger that men should err on the side of rebellion without a just cause'.[13] Stewart was a stadialist, but believed that 'education and social reform' were necessary for progress,[14] and dryly remarked of Robertson's *History of Scotland* that 'such is the effect of that provincial situation to which Scotland is now reduced, that the transactions of former ages are apt to convey to ourselves exaggerated conceptions of barbarism'.[15] Adam Ferguson, whose *Essay on the History of Civil Society* (1767) was also important for Scott, 'clearly saw both losses and gains in historical change' with 'a tension between material and moral advance'. Ferguson also thought (with Herder) that historical regression was possible, with 'highly developed societies ... in near and clear danger of retreating into barbarian despotism'. Ferguson is closer to Rousseau's interest in the primitive than some other Scottish Enlightenment writers, and in his emphasis on the 'Influence of Climate and Situation' shows the Enlightenment interest in particular conditions as much as in universal claims.[16]

Particular circumstances also led to the intertwining of Enlightened and Romantic ideas and practice in Scotland. If Scottish Highlanders were often identified as Native Americans at a stadially 'inferior' juncture of history, the rehabilitation of Highland soldiers in the British Army in the Seven Years War could lead Henry Mackenzie in *The Man of the World* to present the Indians as emblematic of 'honesty, truth, and savage nobleness of soul' who quote Ossian: idealised Scots-American primitives. And there were those who acted out this role, such as John Norton, the Mohawk chief, who sang Scots songs (that Herderian marker of nationality) and translated *The Lady of the Lake* into Mohawk.[17] Herder's own criticism of the destruction of 'the cultures of indigenous peoples, such as ... the American Indians', was entirely compatible with this strain of Enlightenment thought in Scotland, even if, as Luke Gibbons argues, 'the Enlightenment, in its dominant American and French forms ... set its face firmly against "first peoples" or vernacular cultures'.[18]

To understand the nature of Scottish Romanticism as a nationally inflected Romanticism thus requires an appreciation of its particular as well as general engagements with the social questions raised by the enormously powerful intellectual environment of its own country in the Enlightenment. In the rest of this chapter, I am going to examine the kind of social debate with the Enlightenment had by Scotland's Romantic authors by discussing a key text of perhaps the most significant writer of that era: Walter Scott's *Rob Roy* (1817).

Scott's *Rob Roy*, like a number of his other Scottish novels, features a central character who is colourless and to that degree an apparently transparent guide to the more 'exotic' world which forms the principal subject of the text, a world whose exoticism is revealed by transforming landscape through historical memorialisation to reveal a hitherto unsuspected rich sedimentation of associations, a geological literature. As Cairns Craig puts it, Scott 'draws on historical memories to generate associations that will make the landscape aesthetically interesting but thereby *adds* to the associational resources of the landscape, increasing its potential for future aesthetic experience'.[19] The guide Scott chooses in *Rob Roy*, however, unusually reveals this in a direct first-person narrative, ostensibly revealing thereby a 'Frankness' which in reality unveils its own limitations, which are those of the Enlightenment vision unmodified by experience of the lore of places and their special qualities. Frank Osbaldistone, despite some reference to his poetry, is not primarily of a romantic disposition, his head full of tales of chivalry (unlike his predecessor Waverley, whose education has been disorganised), but a man who has enjoyed an Enlightenment education: he is in his own words 'a citizen of the world, and my inclination led me into all scenes where my knowledge of mankind could be enlarged' (92). Later it is the villain Rashleigh who endorses this view, calling Frank 'a man of the world' as an apparent compliment but real sneer, so it is a judgement we are meant to interrogate (169). Frank's job is on the surface that of the science of man: to recite 'incidents which befell me among a people singularly primitive in their government and manners' (65), those who belong to an antecedent stage of society, unlike his father, who although 'an ambitious conqueror' realises his 'acquisitions' not through the wasteful feudal language of war, but rather that of commerce, which 'connects nation with nation, relieves the wants, and contributes to the wealth of all' (68, 75). Yet, as Jane Millgate has noted, Osbaldistone has no reflection, no hindsight, even though he is writing some fifty years after the events in the narrative take place. The transparency of his narrative record is illusory: at odds with the plot, inadequate in its analysis, it is clear that the 'science of man' cannot stand apart from society and say anything worth the saying: 'frankness alone is not enough'.[20]

Although, like Waverley, Frank Osbaldistone is interested in literature, it is not that of medieval romance, but a poetry of modernity; like that of his contemporary James Thomson (1700–48; we presume Frank to have been born around 1693–5), Frank's verse mixes up England and Britain (78), an elision of which he will shortly be disabused. The story which follows is an education – not for those patronised by Frank, who sits in judgement on the products of a particular *genius loci* with the aloofness of the cosmopolitan – but for Frank himself.

Frank is far more arrogant than Waverley or Morton in Scott's contemporary fictions; more arrogant indeed than Guy Mannering. This pridefulness manifests itself through his confidence in his Enlightenment education (the story is set in 1715, but both the *mentalités* of the main protagonists and some of the social detail (e.g. Nicol Jarvie's West Indian interests) belong to a period some fifty to seventy years later: unusually in Scott, *Rob Roy* is significantly – not just partially – set in a period different from that in which the action ostensibly occurs).

Young Osbaldistone is confident of the theories he has been taught to the point of ridiculousness: he explains, for example, that highwaymen might be gentleman because their occupation dates from before 'the division of labour' (89), referring to Smith's *Wealth of Nations* (1776). When he first meets Rob Roy, Frank's first interest is to 'dispute' with this 'coarse' figure, 'confiding in my knowledge of the world, extended as it was by my residence abroad, and in the stores with which a tolerable education had possessed my mind'. Unfortunately, Rob immediately turns out to be 'much better acquainted than I was myself with the present state of France' (97): the provincial is more of a citizen of the world than the self-proclaimed cosmopolitan. Frank learns nothing, though: when Rob risks his life to facilitate young Osbaldistone's meeting with Owen in the Glasgow Tolbooth, Frank thinks of him as one of the 'half-goblin half-human beings, distinguished ... for courage, cunning, ferocity, the length of their arms, and the squareness of their shoulders' (273). Rob Roy, the expert on contemporary France, who saved Frank before Justice Inglewood with 'a slight ironical smile' as he presented himself as 'a man of peace and quietness' (141–2), is now simply a 'shaggy' Highlander, less than human (237, 273); later he has 'the limbs of a redcoloured Highland bull' (374), swims like an otter and is likened by Frank to deer (381, 394). This identification has already been made by Helen MacGregor (358): but in her mouth it signifies not the animal nature of her people, but the fact they have been treated as animals, just as their king has been. Denham's *Cooper's Hill* introduced the comparison of the Stuart king to the deer to anglophone literature (as a symbol of sovereignty in Gaelic literature it is much older), and King James shares with the MacGregors, whose race is royal, the indignity of being hunted and regarded as less than fully human. Helen MacGregor calls her people 'your hewers of wood and drawers of water' (359), thus implicitly likening their lot to that of black slaves, such as those that are employed, for instance, on Bailie Nicol Jarvie's plantation. The original reference in the Old Testament comes in reference to aliens in Deuteronomy 29:11: Helen is clearly saying that the Scottish Highlander is not being treated as a fellow subject of Great Britain, but as an internal alien kept for slave labour, the victim of oppression.

The crowning irony of a text which ironises its narrator at many points is that it is provincial Rob, not cosmopolitan Frank, who is the artful shapeshifter, and can accommodate himself to all shapes, places and seasons. Unlike the Enlightenment theorist, the Romantic man of action can discern the differing requirements of differing locations, and act accordingly to be accepted in each. At Aberfoyle, Frank remarks, '"Rob Roy?" said I, in some surprise; "I know no such person"' (333), but not long afterwards he is made aware that the man he knows as Mr Campbell has a liminal identity as well as liminal language (English, Scots, Gaelic and presumably French), and can cross and recross borders with the ease of a true cosmopolite, even while remaining a detested and outlawed 'provincial'. Barring the coldness and wetness of the Trossachs, Rob is what Aravamudan identifies as a 'Tropicopolitan': 'the colonized subject who exists ... as a fictive construct of colonial typology' while in fact acting as a 'resident ... agent of resistance'.[21] His is 'a mind, neither to be daunted, nor surprised' (388). When he says to Frank, 'Speak out, sir, and do not Maister or Campbell me – my foot is on my native heath, and my name is Mac-Gregor!' (391), he reveals the *genius loci* of all identity and the provisionality of the universalist claims of Enlightenment cosmopolitanism: this is a moment where Rob reveals the essential link of 'the heather ... I have trod upon when living, must bloom ower me when I am dead' (407).

Frank begins to understand a little at last, and the language he uses concerning Rob changes. Instead of an animal, Rob is now the 'Sultan of Delhi' (394), alien, colonial (at least by the high Enlightenment era, if not 1715), but majestic, impressive and civilized. He is no longer to be found in the 'hospitable wigwam' of Aberfoyle (394), but is transformed from a West to an East Indian, from a tribal leader to a potentate. When Rob displays his sporran with its hidden pistol, from which he takes the money to pay his debt to Jarvie, Frank compares him to another hero of many wiles and disguises – Odysseus, a name charged with the high generic associations of epic (398). Frank also corrects his initial description of the Highlanders from 'savage' to 'rude' (410), and notices for the first time that Helen MacGregor (though still 'a she-bear' in her terrifying power) has 'the manners of a princess ... the tone and style of a court ... Nor was there the least tincture of vulgarity, which we naturally attach to the Lowland Scottish' (411). Rob Roy himself is naturalised as an honorary English hero: 'the Robin Hood of Scotland' (452), a man who of course – like Rob – stood up for the rights of an absent king and his own title, as Scott shows us in *Ivanhoe* (1819). Yet even now, Frank does not appreciate how cosmopolitan Rob in fact is, how truly a citizen of the world: in offering to try and find his sons employment in foreign (British) service, and thus to export the political problem of the Highlands (404), Rob answers that 'French or Spanish service' would be the right option: in truly foreign armies, not just imperial ones, and moreover those who might fight to restore the Stuarts and Scottish independence – Rob stresses nationality in citing this option (407). The citizen of the Trossachs remains a citizen of the world, as Frank is not.

Frank Osbaldistone has on the surface, in travelling north, travelled back from stage four of Smithian society (commercial) through stage three (the feudal squires of Northumberland), to stage two bordering on stage one (pastoralists in the Highlands with nomadic hunter properties, hence the 'wigwam' reference). But the progress north as a regress backward is disrupted. Rob Roy is one agent of that disruption: he is instrumental in clearing debts in the commercial world (significantly, he is the only character to settle in gold, not in paper credit, and he indeed burns Jarvie's discharge of the debt), he is more cosmopolitan than the Osbaldistone heir, and at the end he delivers Diana Vernon's father in a daring raid in Northumberland. While the chasing of dishonoured paper contracts is central to the modern dimension of the novel, the fact that 'men allow Rob keeps his word', despite Owen's sneer that 'this is a very singular contract of assurance' (303), turns out to be true. It is Rob who can be trusted: and in this, he challenges the superiority of paper contract over word of honour, mercantile bill over gold. Indeed, the Mississippi bubble in France in 1720 and the failure of the Ayr land bank in 1769 were but two examples within the novel's chronotope which challenged Smithian stadialism and the ascendancy of commercialism. Is 'credit a decent honest man', as Jarvie protests (297): the novel hardly bears this out. As Ian Duncan puts it, the 'primitive Highlander is also the archetype of economic man' (xxvi). But Nicol Jarvie also challenges this stadialism: just as commercial as Osbaldistone and Tresham, he is nonetheless bound by kinship, ancestry and shared history to Rob Roy, and indeed sympathises with his position and that of his wife (302): Jarvie, despite being a magistrate, is even prepared to overlook Morris's murder (420). Both Jarvie and Rob are Scotsmen, and share that solidarity of time, place and locale against 'southron and stranger' (299): yet even at the end of the book, when Frank revalues the 'Highlander', he still feels bound to point up the 'vulgarity' of 'the Lowland Scottish' in comparison (411), whom he had begun by thinking much closer to the standard set by English civility than the bestial Gaelic-speakers on their frontiers. Even as the book ends, Frank reveals himself in some ways as foolish as ever.

Jarvie shows that even when Frank is faced with a cosmopolitan encounter, if it comes from a different quarter from one he is familiar with, he cannot recognise it properly. Bailie Nicol Jarvie, like Frank's own father, pursues commercial opportunities and acquisitions: but whereas Osbaldistone has opened himself to potentially crippling risk by domestic investment in 'large speculations concerning oak-woods, the property of Highland proprietors' (95), Jarvie is a global mercantile capitalist with tea from China and coffee 'from a snug plantation of his own ... in the island of Jamaica' (282–3). His association with slavery is clear, but he understands his business, which Frank's father at one level does not: the 'Highland proprietors' are shorter of ready cash than he imagines, and the 'oak-woods' are hidden indicators of Stuart loyalty, just as they are at the family home of 'Osbaldistone Hall ... peeping out from a Druidical grove of huge oaks' (100). Frank's father (who has abandoned his family roots, unlike Jarvie) is less interested in local circumstance, culture and politics than he should have been, and this renders him vulnerable to Rashleigh. Frank, too, is less aware of these things: Jarvie is an alternative father figure, who, like Osbaldistone senior, subscribes to Smithian stadialism ('Honour is a homicide and a bloodspiller ... but Credit is a decent honest man' (297)), but Frank – like Owen – misjudges him as coarse and crude. Yet it is Jarvie who rescues Frank from the depredations of Andrew Fairservice's manipulative greed, and Jarvie too who understands the balance between Enlightenment and Romantic value, between commercial interest and 'bluid' kinship and 'langsyne' association (270).

Arguably Frank's greatest folly, however, and one of the most deeply interesting aspects of *Rob Roy*, is the challenge posed to Enlightenment ideas of civility by Diana Vernon, and that on the grounds of its concealed gender politics, which echo the political agenda of the 'unnatural women' of the 1745 and 1798 Risings – Vernon is of course a Jacobite. On the one hand, Frank is charmed by her because she – as Andrew Lincoln argues – resists being incorporated into a polite and commercial modernity where women, when they are not actually reified as objects of marital exchange, are treated as secondary and ornamental. Frank is seduced by her frankness: he has the name, she the reality of the quality, being

> [t]otally devoid of the circumlocutions, shadings, softenings, and periphrasis, which usually accompany explanations betwixt persons of different sexes in the higher orders of society. (181)

Yet, while falling in love with a woman who challenges every feature of his education, its prejudices remain: he concludes that Diana's 'setting at naught and despising the forms and ceremonial limits which are drawn round females in modern society' is due to the bad influence of Rashleigh (189). She, in other words, only appears to be free of the conventions of patriarchy while in reality being its victim: she can have no fundamentally independent existence. In his relations with Diana, Frank repeatedly seeks to identify another man, actual or imaginary, who is in real control of her, and whom he can challenge for that control. In doing this, he even spies on her: in fearing the influence over Diana of a Catholic priest, Frank acts in a way which Protestant prejudice alleged characterised Catholicism – the act of secret surveillance (cf. Charlotte Brontë's sectarian use of this theme in *Villette*). If Frank acts the Catholic, though, Diana, who *is* a Catholic, responds like a Protestant might be expected to, with manly directness, and 'I felt the childishness of my own conduct, and the superior manliness of Miss Vernon's' (210). Once again, Frank's education and expectations are shown as partial, prejudiced and often the reverse of reality.

Moreover, Miss Vernon is not simply constructed through the male gaze, but speaks in her own right. She is under no illusion regarding the gendered politeness of civility and its effect on women: 'I would be shut up in a madhouse, if I did half the things that I have a mind to ... I am a girl ... born one of their Helots' (149). She ironises male expectation, saying 'she is ignorant of what the Spectator calls the softer graces of the sex', thus indicating that – far from being an ignoramus – she knows the *Spectator* and has decided to resist its advice (113). 'Science and history' are her favourite topics: she can neither sew nor cook, but can ride and fire a gun. Diana is also a critic of history as an ostensibly neutral subject of Enlightened enquiry. Her ancestor, Sir Richard Vernon, killed at the Battle of Shrewsbury (1402) on behalf of Yorkist Plantagenet legitimists (this is the Jacobite parallel) and Owain Glyn Dwr's rights in Wales (the Scottish one), has been 'slandered by a sad fellow called Will Shakespeare, whose Lancastrian partialities, and a certain knack at embodying them, has turned history upside down, or rather inside out' (154–5). Diana's use of the Battle of Shrewsbury in an implicitly Jacobite context seems close to the Herderian suspicion that history might be cyclical, and her critique reaches far beyond this: History is not neutral enquiry, but a combination of a *parti pris* and the quality of the rhetoric that sustains it. This is a devastating critique of the intellectual integrity of one of Diana's favourite subjects, and of one of the central claims of Enlightenment historiography to be part of the 'science of man'. This is seen again in Diana's advancing the case of the 'Abbess of Wilton', dismissed from her senior clerical office by the apostate earl of Pembroke on no pretext but that of raw male power, which in its very enunciation condemns an entire sex to the private sphere of domestic employment: 'Go spin you jade, go spin' (461 n.). When Frank adds 'a kiss to the half-crown' with Jarvie's servant Mattie (279), he begins the equation of commercial with imperial power that is destined to turn marriage into a marketable commodity and presents women as in the last resort tradeable assets. Marriage to Diana may be the novel's reward to Frank, but like many of Scott's endings, it is huddled up almost arbitrarily at the end of the narrative, with many of Diana's questions to modernity unanswered: like that national Union, seldom far from Scott's thoughts, it is a personal union which leaves much unresolved, not least the status of the 'junior partner', reflected in the imperceptiveness of the 'Frank' but unobservant and prejudiced 'senior' one.

Just as Diana is a 'helot', so Helen MacGregor is a 'hewer of wood and drawer of water'. The two are parallel: Helen and Diana are alike, both initially seen in man's dress (101, 349) and behave more like men than women. Both alike describe the attempt to subdue them (politically or sexually) in colonial terms: for Diana, 'compliments' 'serve fine gentlemen who travel the country, instead of the toys, beads, and bracelets, which navigators carry to propitiate the savage inhabitants of newly discovered lands' (112). Diana too occupies, like Helen, a 'theatre of colonial resistance' (xxvii), but one based on gender not ethno-cultural background. The commercial world is shown to be inadequate to the ethical challenges set before it: Frank is a 'grumbling shopkeeper' as he spies on Diana Vernon, hoping to gain advantage through the deceit and cowardice of espionage (217); although Frank's father supposedly knows 'the country, and the lawless character' of the Highlands (418), the limits of his information almost ruin him, and above all, Morris's petty calculations end in disaster, with his murder metaphoricised in brutally commercial terms: 'the unit of that life for which he had pleaded so strongly, was for ever withdrawn from the sum of human existence' (365). Behind commerce lurks utility, and the individual is dispensable in such a realm.

Rob Roy then advances both a stadialist schema and interrogates it; places commerce at the acme of human society and shows it being redeemed by the 'primitive'; advances Enlightenment universalist claims of aspiration towards politeness and civility and shows them as inadequate in judging the fidelity of Jarvie, the trustworthiness of Rob or the place of women in society in general. The cosmopolitan citizenry of the world is shown to be better accomplished by the mobile and oppressed (a foretaste perhaps of the disproportionate role played by Scots in the British Empire) than by the rooted and prejudiced; commerce is linked to exploitation and enslavement; the ownership of historical and religious narratives is challenged; and sympathy is demonstrably not to be equated with civility. The rough and opinionated Jarvie is more sympathetic than the smooth MacVittie, while Rob Roy/Ruadh, the red man of blood, is nonetheless 'le brigand au grand coeur', the big-hearted outlaw whose very sympathetic generosity (an Enlightenment virtue) is a better guarantor of integrity than a mere subscription to the commercial system ever can be. What is wrong and what is right about Enlightenment thinking are again entwined in a single personality, the title of the book, though one who is neither its narrator nor its main subject, a man both marginal and crucial to the action.[22]

Unlike some of Scott's other novels, the characters who represent the past are not treated sentimentally: perhaps that is easier in Rob's case, for despite his apparent Jacobitism, he does not really represent a political threat – he never contradicts Jarvie's outspoken Presbyterian Unionism, for example. For whatever reason Scott's narrative embraces, but his plot and characters question, Robertson's historiography and Smith's stadialism, as well as Smith's model of sympathy in his *Theory of Moral Sentiments*, first published in 1759, and substantially altered during its progress towards a sixth edition in 1790, which 'valorized the virtues of assimilation', associating refined sentiment with greater literacy and better expression and in its concept of the impartial spectator invoking 'the disinterested rationality of the sciences'. Primitiveness and provincialism were expressed in a different language or a different dialect: if the 'rules of justice may be compared to the rules of grammar', as Smith argued in *Moral Sentiments*,[23] then perhaps those with whom we do not share a language cannot obtain our sympathy (because they cannot be understood) and do not deserve our justice either. The limitations of such a position are clearly shown by the disinterestedness of Rob Roy, the outlaw of differing registers, tongues and characters who risks his life for Frank, Owen and Vernon and who repays his debts in gold not paper: like Robin Hood, he is the social bandit who challenges Smith's hidden alignment of sympathy with power and conformity.

If Scott interrogates Smith and Robertson by setting Frank's narrative and the plot and characters which contest its 'frankness' at odds, he does not altogether throw the Enlightenment models aside. An interrogation of the universal on behalf of the Herderian *genius loci Rob Roy* may be, but it is not a blanket condemnation of Enlightenment modelling of human experience into stadial or other forms. Yet in creating his own national tale as a Romantic and patriotic act, Scott reinscribes the potency of some of the core values he allows to be challenged. Smith – as in Edgeworth's *Ennui*, where he is also interrogated – will never go away, even if he can be contradicted; and for Scott unlike Edgeworth, the great figures of the Scottish Enlightenment are his own as a Scot as they never can be for an Irishwoman, part of the very national tale that lays them open to question.[24]

Notes

1 See Murray Pittock, 'What is a National Culture?', *Scotland in Europe*, special issue of *Litteraria Pragensia*, 19:38 (2009), 30–47.

2 Johann Gottfried von Herder, *Philosophical Writings*, trans. and ed. Michael N. Foster (Cambridge University Press, 2002), p. x; further references will appear in the text.

3 For the limited use of *'esclavage'* in the French Revolutionary era, see Srinivas Aravamudan, *Tropicopolitans* (Durham, NC, and London: Duke University Press, 1999), p. 306.

4 Joep Leerssen, unpublished address to Wales-Ireland Symposium, Cardiff, 23 October 2008.

5 See Murray Pittock (ed.), *The Reception of Sir Walter Scott in Europe* (London: Continuum, 2007), and Murray Pittock, *Scottish and Irish Romanticism* (Oxford University Press, 2008), ch. 1. For Romantic medievalism, see Michael Alexander, *Medievalism* (New Haven: Yale University Press, 2007), and Alice Chandler, 'Sir Walter Scott and the Medieval Revival', *Nineteenth-Century Fiction*, 19:4 (1965), 315–32.

6 'Oran Ussaig – To R. Burns', *The Bee*, 27 April 1791, 317–18.

7 Maureen McLane, *Balladeering, Minstrelsy and the Making of British Romantic Poetry* (Cambridge University Press, 2008), p. 101.

8 Pascale Canova, quoted in Ian Duncan, 'Introduction', *Romancing Scotland*, special issue of *Modern Language Quarterly*, 70:4 (2009), 403–13.

9 Sir Walter Scott, *Rob Roy*, ed. Ian Duncan (Oxford University Press, 1998), pp. 5, 20, 25, 37, 51; further references will appear in the text. The Magnum version is referred to because of the importance of Scott's notes in defining his own interpretative parameters of the text: for example, he glosses Frank's statement that Aberfoyle is 'hardly … much improved at the present day' that he can 'assure the reader, whose curiosity may lead him to visit the scenes of these romantic adventures, that the Clachan of Aberfoil now affords a very comfortable little inn' (344, 464). Scott is to an extent – though 1817 is later than 1770, it must be acknowledged – setting up his own narrator as unreliable and to a degree prejudiced.

10 Duncan, 'Introduction', 405, 409.

11 For 'National Historicism', see Joep Leerssen, *National Thought in Europe: A Cultural History* (Amsterdam University Press, 2006), pp. 119ff.

12 Murray Pittock, 'Historiography', in Alexander Broadie (ed.), *The Cambridge Companion to the Scottish Enlightenment* (Cambridge University Press, 2003), pp. 258–79; Karen O'Brien, 'Historical Writing', in David Womersley (ed.), *A Companion to Literature from Milton to Blake* (Oxford: Blackwell, 2000), pp. 530–1.

13 *The Collected Works of Dugald Stewart*, ed. Sir William Hamilton (1854–8; repr. Bristol: Toemmes, 1994), vol. I, p. xiii.

14 Michael Brown, 'Dugald Stewart and the Problem of Teaching Politics in the 1790s', *Journal of Irish and Scottish Studies*, 1:1 (2007), 87–126, 103.

15 Dugald Stewart, Introduction to William Robertson, *The History of Scotland*, 2 vols. (London: Jones, 1827), vol. I, pp. xviii, 1.

16 Adam Ferguson, *An Essay on the History of Civil Society*, ed. Fania Ozberger (Cambridge University Press, 1995), pp. xx, 106; Pittock, 'Historiography', pp. 274–5.

17 Tim Fulford, *Romantic Indians* (Oxford University Press, 2006), pp. 4, 7–9, 102–3.

18 George G. Iggers and Q. Edward Wang with Supriye Mukherjee, *A Global History of Modern Historiography* (Harlow: Longman, 2008), p. 32; Luke Gibbons, *Edmund Burke and Ireland* (Cambridge University Press, 2003), p. 232.

19 Cairns Craig, *Associationism and the Literary Imagination* (Edinburgh: Edinburgh University Press, 2007), p. 117.

20 Jane Millgate, *Walter Scott: The Making of the Novelist* (University of Chicago Press, 1987), pp. 148–9.

21 Aravamudan, *Tropicopolitans*, p. 4.

22 See Eric Hobsbawm, *Bandits*, 3rd edn (1969; London: Abacus, 2007), p. 159.

23 Adam Smith, *Theory of Moral Sentiments*, ed. D. D. Raphael and A. L. Macfie (1976; Oxford: Clarendon Press, 1979), p. 175.

24 Thomas P. Miller, *The Formation of College English* (University of Pittsburgh Press, 1997), pp. 190–1, 200–1; Gibbons, *Edmund Burke*, p. 84. For Edgeworth, see Pittock, *Scottish and Irish Romanticism*, ch. 7; for Burns, see Murray Pittock, '"Nibbling at Adam Smith": A Mouse's Sma' Request and the Limits of Social Justice', in Johnny Rodger and Gerard Carruthers (eds.), *Fickle Man: Robert Burns in the 21st Century* (Dingwall: Sandstone Press, 2009), pp. 161–73.

Guide to further reading

Broadie, Alexander (ed.), *The Cambridge Companion to the Scottish Enlightenment* (Cambridge University Press, 2003)

Craig, Cairns, *Associationism and the Literary Imagination* (Edinburgh University Press, 2007)

Duncan, Ian, *Scott's Shadow: The Novel in Romantic Edinburgh* (Princeton University Press, 2007)

Lincoln, Andrew, *Walter Scott and Modernity* (Edinburgh University Press, 2007)

Pittock, Murray, *Scottish and Irish Romanticism* (2008; Oxford University Press, 2011)

Sorensen, Janet *The Grammar of Empire in Eighteenth-Century British Writing* (Cambridge University Press, 2000)

7

IAN DUNCAN

Scott and the Historical Novel: A Scottish Rise of the Novel

Walter Scott was the major novelist of the nineteenth century. 'During the Romantic period, the "Author of Waverley" sold more novels than all the other novelists of the time put together'; a generation later he was still, 'by several orders of magnitude, the author whose works had sold the largest number of copies in the English-speaking world.'[1] This popularity was accompanied by a commensurate critical prestige. The Victorians revered Scott as at once the last of the classics and the first of the moderns – the wizard who reanimated the ancient genres of ballad, epic and romance for an industrial-age reading public. His reputation stood if anything still higher outside Britain: from Russia to Italy, Ontario to Bengal, the historical novel exemplified the modernising national literary form of the novel as such.[2] Scott's fiction supplied a template for the epic ambitions of the next great medium of nation-making narrative, in the cinema of D. W. Griffith, and *Waverley*, *Rob Roy*, *Ivanhoe* and the rest continue to shape the fables of our postmodern global mass culture.[3]

Scott's achievement was comprehensively sidelined by the aesthetic revolutions of modernism, consolidated in Anglo-American criticism by works such as F. R. Leavis's *The Great Tradition* (1948) and Ian Watt's *The Rise of the Novel* (1957), which installed academic canons of moral and formal realism inhospitable to Scott's practice. Twentieth-century taste made the Waverley Novels the literary equivalent of a Victorian municipal monument – dilapidated, unsightly, impeding the flow of traffic. The lip-service paid to Scott's stature in the global history of the novel gave his reputation a lopsided cast: the once universally influential Great Unread, a tail without the comet. Recent decades have seen a refurbishing of that reputation, if so far confined to the academy, sustained by the new Edinburgh Edition of the Waverley Novels, a general reorientation of critical inquiry towards historicist approaches and (not least) a strong resurgence of the historical novel itself across the reading publics and credential-granting institutions of world literature.

Scott's standing in the Scottish tradition suffered a comparable decline, but for different reasons. The nationalist movement of the 1920s–30s, the so-called Scottish Renaissance, cast him as the impresario of a Tory Unionist internal colonialism, whose spellbinding substitutions of romance for real history transformed Scotland into a tartan-swathed, retro-Jacobite theme park. This view of Scott's achievement prevailed in Scottish Studies until recently, and it still has some currency. It was framed by the diagnosis of a larger national-cultural pathology: Gregory Smith's 'Caledonian Antisyzygy' or 'zigzag of contradictions', first articulated a hundred years earlier by John Gibson Lockhart in his Tory Romantic anatomy of post-Enlightenment Scotland, *Peter's Letters to His Kinsfolk* (1819), a major document in the early canonisation of Scott. Lockhart pioneers the analysis of a modern Scottish tradition fissured by social, linguistic and psychological antagonisms (between popular and elite, Scots and English, feeling and thinking), reckoned against a putatively organic English standard.[4] In Lockhart's account Scott wields historical romance to redeem the national culture from its post-Union bondage to Presbyterian and Enlightenment ideologies. Even as it reverses this evaluation, debunking Romantic cultural nationalism as false consciousness, the modern critique perpetuates the key strategy of Lockhart's apotheosis of the Wizard of the North: his obliteration of the intellectual roots of Scott's art in the sceptical empiricism of the Scottish Enlightenment. A recovery of those roots may go far towards recovering the critical and philosophical force of Scott's historical fiction.

Scott's literary career as ballad editor, national minstrel and 'Author of Waverley' prospered in – as it came to govern – the brilliant cultural ascendancy of Edinburgh in the first three decades of the nineteenth century. Between 1802 (the year of the founding of the *Edinburgh Review* as well as *Minstrelsy of the Scottish Border*) and 1832 (the year of Scott's death and the first Reform Bill), Edinburgh more than held its own against London and Paris as a capital of 'international literary space'. Achievements in the human and natural sciences had made Scotland a centre of the eighteenth-century Enlightenment; after 1800 Edinburgh (eclipsing the other Lowland cities) played a leading role in the expansion of print production and formal innovation that constituted the literary field of British Romanticism. Here the booksellers' genres that would dominate the nineteenth-century public sphere acquired their definitive forms and associations: periodicals, including the quarterly review (the *Edinburgh*), monthly miscellany (*Blackwood's Edinburgh Magazine*, 1817) and weekly magazine (*Chambers's Edinburgh Journal*, 1832); popular poetry, including the national ballad-anthology and ballad-based metrical romance; and prose fiction, including the historical novel, magazine tale and fictitious local memoir. Practising nearly all of these, Scott defined the parameters of two of them, the metrical romance and historical novel. With the latter he set the main trends in nineteenth-century fiction publishing, including the standardisation of format for first publication (three post-octavo volumes, a guinea and a half the set).[5] The unprecedented print-runs of new titles (10,000 copies of *Rob Roy*, 1818) were followed by reissues in different formats, culminating in the publishing innovation of Scott's last years, the appearance of his collected novels in a uniform inexpensive edition, the so-called 'Magnum Opus', corrected with new introductions and notes (1829–33), which set the pattern for author's editions for the next hundred years.[6]

Scott's success stimulated a national literary boom in which rivals as well as imitators flourished. The proportion of Scottish fiction titles published in Great Britain increased threefold in the decade following the appearance of *Waverley* in 1814, reaching 15 per cent in the peak years 1822–5.[7] This Scottish rise of the novel was complicit with the rise of the Edinburgh periodicals: the *Edinburgh Review* belonged to Scott's publisher, Archibald Constable, while William Blackwood, Constable's chief rival in the post-war decade, became the main broker of Scottish fiction in the Romantic period, much of it published in *Blackwood's Magazine.* Scott was an early contributor to the *Edinburgh Review*, which founded the post-Enlightenment phase of Scottish culture on its renovation of the liberal intellectual projects of Enlightenment in the industrialising print market. Turning from poetry to prose fiction, Scott drew on the tropes of 'literary authority' established by the *Edinburgh Review* to dignify the novel, hitherto deprecated by critics as a sentimental, feminine genre: reclaiming authorship as a professional (rather than aristocratic-dilettantish or merely commercial) occupation, and investing romance with the gravity of the Enlightenment human sciences, foremost among which was history. This elevation of the novel's status recoded it as a properly masculine genre.[8] The outstanding titles among the few novels published in Scotland before Scott's ascendancy were by women, domestic adaptations of the Irish national tale: Elizabeth Hamilton's *Cottagers of Glenburnie* (1808), Mary Brunton's *Discipline* (1814), Christian Johnstone's *Clan-Albin* (1815). Generally, however, what was widely recognised as a feminine tradition of moral and domestic fiction did not thrive in Edinburgh as well as it did elsewhere in the British Isles. Only one notable practitioner, Susan Ferrier, emerged after *Waverley*, while the most versatile of the Scottish women authors, Johnstone, eventually forsook the novel for periodical genres.

Scott's rivals included claimants on alternative versions of national historical fiction, bearing alternative visions of Scotland and its history. The best of them – James Hogg, John Galt, Ferrier, Lockhart, John Wilson – were published by Blackwood, who established a distinctive profile of regionally based, comic or sentimental or sensational Scottish fiction. *Blackwood's Magazine*, founded as a Tory counterblast to Constable's Whig periodicals, made itself into the leading forum for experiment and innovation in prose genres by the 1820s, not just in Scotland but throughout the English-speaking world, influencing Dickens, Poe and the Brontës. The magazine's miscellaneous format (scrambling together fiction and non-fiction) incubated the modern short story as well as more volatile forms of anecdote, sketch, serial and satirical symposium (the famous 'Noctes Ambrosianae'). *Blackwood's* provided especially fertile soil for the satirical mock-autobiography, which would blossom into one of the outstanding rival forms of Scottish historical fiction in the work of Galt. In the early 1820s Galt and Hogg emerged as the most original of the authors who challenged Scott's dominant form of the historical novel. The last section of this chapter will consider that challenge and Scott's response to it.

'The classical form of the historical novel'

Scott founded 'the classical form of the historical novel' unassisted by literary precursors, according to Georg Lukács, since it was the onset of new historical conditions – the opening of vistas of mass experience and popular consciousness through the French Revolution and Napoleonic Wars – that made the new form of representation possible.[9] Recent scholarship has challenged Lukács's account of Scott's originality by bringing to light the novelistic innovations that preceded *Waverley* but were then overshadowed by its author's world-wide media triumph. These include Jacobin and Anti-Jacobin novels which harnessed the political debates of the 1790s to explore the relations between private and public life in an age of revolution, and Irish 'National Tales' by Maria Edgeworth, Sydney Owenson and Charles Robert Maturin, which brought those debates to bear on the ideologically charged categories of nation and empire. Edgeworth's tales test the theories of social and economic progress developed in Scottish Enlightenment philosophical history; Owenson's *Wild Irish Girl* models the Unionist fable developed in *Waverley*, in which a young gentleman from the imperial metropolis ventures out to the Celtic hinterland and learns sympathy for its peoples through falling in love with an indigenous heiress.[10] More recently, Richard Maxwell has revised (rather than debunked) Lukács's claim by reconsidering Scott's pivotal role in the long European genealogy of historical fiction, which turns upon a Franco-Scottish axis.[11] A comprehensive reckoning with Scott's antecedents enhances the account of his originality, far from diminishing it.

Where an earlier French tradition (Prévost, Mme de Lafayette) built the emergent historical novel around the tension between a fictitious story of private lives and the public record of historical events, Scott's novels decisively integrate the two. They do so not just by juxtaposing private and public destinies but by representing the 'inundation' of ordinary life by the tides of economic and social change that subtend historical events: the decay of feudalism, the break-up of traditional cultures and the long-durational onset of modernisation. If the French Revolution and ensuing world war revealed modernity in the mode of crisis – a cataclysmic political mobilisation of nations and peoples – the discourses of economic, social and anthropological history developed in the Scottish Enlightenment 'science of man' provided a philosophical framework for understanding that crisis. Scott's novels render the whole of human life – social forms, institutions, manners, morals, psychology, 'culture' – as historically saturated, evolving and interconnected. This historical field includes the common people as well as the court and gentry. Scott was the first European novelist to represent not just the middle ranks but the labouring poor as leading their own lives, in something like their own terms, with their own outlooks and languages. His most ambitious novels, like *The Heart of Mid-Lothian* (1818), represent the dynamic extensions (and folds and rifts) of an entire society across national space and historical time. Scott bequeathed to nineteenth-century fiction a vivid heteroglossia of languages, styles and discourses, including popular speech, as the formal medium of this representation. Especially in his great series of novels of the making of modern Scotland, Scott disclosed the past as 'the prehistory of the present', in Lukács's phrase, 'giving life to those historical, social, and human forces which, in the course of a long evolution, have made our present-day life what it is and as we experience it'.[12] The reader's world too is revealed to be part of the continuum of history, a product of the story the novel tells.

History enfolds all of human life, including our own lives; the past is historical because the present is. At the same time, Scott narrates a historical dialectic in which modern conditions make possible an ambiguous intellectual deliverance within the flow of history. Perhaps the most famous invention of the Scottish Enlightenment was the idea of a civil society separate from the state (and thus from politics) – the distinctive habitat of the modern middle-class citizen. Civil society allows its subjects a cognitive detachment from the contending fanaticisms (dynastic, ethnic, sectarian) of the pre-modern past, which they are able to reflect upon through the print media of history and historical fiction. Scott's fiction projects the idea of civil society as the horizon of our present act of reading: it affords the historical conditions for our reading, and our reading (in turn) reconstitutes civil society as a liberal domain of ongoing reflection, conversation and enjoyment. The story the historical novel tells is also, then, a story of the rise of the novel, of its material and psychological conditions and its reading practices. By virtue of its sympathetic reanimation of the past, which is more vivid than history by itself can provide, and which yet maintains a crucial aesthetic distance (since we know it is a fiction), the historical novel presents itself as the exemplary literary form of modernity.

Scott installs these innovations in his first novel *Waverley; or, 'Tis Sixty Years Since*, where they inform the story of a 'moderate' protagonist, Scott's notoriously blank or mediocre hero, caught between rival allegiances in a civil war; paradoxically, Waverley's passivity guarantees his survival, and his emergence as the typical denizen of modern life. After Shakespeare (who supplies the title-page epigraph), Scott made civil war the key topic of the historical novel; departing from Shakespeare, he made the losing side the repository of human interest and feeling, given an objective, anthropological solidity. History becomes visible in the catastrophic breach of common life, in this case the 1745 Jacobite rising, the last armed conflict on British soil and the last attempt of the exiled Stuart dynasty to regain the throne. The rising's failure confirms the anachronistic character of the old regime and its organic base of support, the Highland clans, sacrificed in the irreversible drive of modernisation. Edward Waverley, a callow English officer, travels north to the Highlands, the last remaining haunt of patriarchal clans. Following the plan of Enlightenment philosophical history, which locates a particular society at a developmental stage in the universal progress towards modernity, Scott makes this a journey back in time, recasting ethnological difference as historical anteriority. *Waverley* renders clearly the imperial logic that rewrites Highland society as archaic, already superseded, doomed to pass, as the condition of its fascination for the modern reader. The Highlanders that befriend Waverley are executed for treason while he survives and prospers: once Jacobitism and the clans are destroyed as political and social realities, civil society can reclaim them as a form of aesthetic and sentimental capital. Empire renews itself ideologically by digesting primitive virtues of courage and loyalty.[13]

Rather than simply administering this agenda, however, *Waverley* makes it available for critical scrutiny, by opening a distance between ourselves and the naive protagonist. In the novel's final scene the happy survivors contemplate 'a large and spirited painting', sketched in Edinburgh after the rebellion and finished in London, which depicts Waverley posing in Highland dress beside the executed Jacobite chieftain and the clan. Framed within its representation, the novel exhibits the spurious 'invention of tradition' with which Scott has often been charged by modern critics. But the alert reader recognises the painting's sentimental purification of Waverley's adventure, at odds with Scott's persistently ironical narration of it in the preceding volumes. The painting mirrors the story we have been reading – published in Edinburgh and London – even as the story invites us to reflect on that representation and its historical conditions, including the conditions of our reading. Only a reader as oblivious as Waverley himself can acquiesce in its nostalgia, or mistake it for the narrative that frames it.

Waverley narrates the eventual triumph of an aesthetic attention to the world, threatened by an unacknowledged historical reality but finally absorbing it for a recognisably liberal form of consciousness. In the early chapters Waverley cultivates a 'feminine', narcissistic sensibility that secures itself by framing his experience with romantic tropes and images. As the tale unfolds, his narcissism enjoys a rich and complex expansion, ironised against his ignorance of the historical reality of the scenes he visits. Waverley's role as romantic reader endows our own act of reading with a critical reflexivity that his cognition, embedded within the story, lacks – until the failure of the rising brings a chastened self-awareness: 'He felt himself entitled to say firmly, though perhaps with a sigh, that the romance of his life was ended, and that its real history had now commenced.' Despite this narratorial summary, Scott's novel does not trace anything as straightforward as a progress from (archaic, immature) 'romance' to (modern, manly) 'real history'. An occult work of plotting rescues the hero from the consequences of his involvement in rebellion and rewards his romantic inattention with bride, estate and family honour, in an elaborately fictitious set of restorations – crowned by that painting that commemorates the romance of his life rather than its real history.[14]

The history contained in *Waverley* includes more than the chronicle of the 1745 rising or the antiquarian data of Scottish life sixty years since. It also includes the novel's own genealogy and function in modern culture, in Scotland and in the wider world of Great Britain and Europe in 1814, which Scott represents in an internal allegory of the rise of the novel as modern national form. The dialectical progression from romance – the narrative of pre-modern cultures – through history yields a third, synthetic term, the combination of romance and history that *Waverley* itself instantiates. Scott's historical novel, the material medium of our work of reading, constitutes the vantage point of modernity, reflexively producing the plot of its own production. With his final entry into private life and civil society, the hero blends into the time and space of our reading, as the novel has hinted he will do all along. The difference between Waverley's mystified, reactionary or primitivist investment in romance and the reader's sophisticated, critical investment in the work of fiction lies in the recognition of defeat and loss that falls between the historical experience and its representation. Our knowledge of the violence that has brought us here (the sacrifice of the wild world of the clans) makes for a melancholy as well as a comic resolution, with which Scott fixes a characteristically modern structure of feeling.

The historical novel thus absorbs history into the cognitive work of fiction, in a dynamic theorised by the Enlightenment philosopher David Hume. Hume's argument (in his *Treatise of Human Nature*, 1739) dissolves the metaphysical foundations of reality and covers the resulting void with a sentimental commitment to 'common life', everyday social intercourse, intermittently recognised as an imaginary construction of reality ratified by custom – in other words, as a fiction. *Waverley*, in these terms, narrates not only the emergence of modern civil society through the final conquest of an ancient regime (and the sentimental and literary analogues of this progress) but a Humean dialectic of Enlightenment, in the movement from metaphysical illusion through melancholy disenchantment to an at once sentimental and ironical reattachment to common life. Reflexively insistent on their fictional status, Scott's novels activate scepticism rather than belief as the subjective cast of their reader's (although not necessarily their protagonists') relation to history, which includes, in the logic of metafictional reflection, the reader's own historical situation. Following Hume, Scott makes fiction the performative technique of a liberal ideology – one that stakes its modernity on the claim of having superseded primitive modes of ideological identification (superstition and fanaticism) through a capacity to stand back and reflect on its own historical conditions.[15] Double consciousness, not false consciousness, is the novel's gift to its reader.

Scott, Hogg and Galt

Some commentators have assumed that Scott kept on repeating, or at best ringing variations on, a singular aesthetic and ideological formula. Instead, the later novels vary the 'classical form' established in *Waverley*, sometimes radically, as they depart from the dialectic of national formation to explore other thematic possibilities, some of which are played out in a more remote past or in an imperial arena (as in the Crusader romances *Ivanhoe* (1820) and *The Talisman* (1825)). *Guy Mannering* (1815) and *The Antiquary* (1816) followed *Waverley* to make up a trilogy of Scottish historical novels set in 1745, the 1770s and the mid 1790s, respectively. The novels differentiate these stages of the recent past through striking shifts of form and style. *Guy Mannering* activates a pre-novelistic romance tradition for its fable of imperial expansion and domestic modernisation after the Seven Years War, in a plot that extends across a generation and between Scotland and India.

The Antiquary, in an allusive meditation on the sources and contexts of its author's work, invokes and then suspends a more than usually complicated plot to create a kind of meta-Waverley Novel in which nothing happens – or rather, sensational events (manslaughter, infanticide, incest, a discovery of buried treasure, a French invasion, the defeat of a Roman invasion, the writing of an epic poem) turn out not to have happened: as though the dense narrative accretion of non-eventfulness will ward off the era's great historical event, revolution, from national life. Here Scott's insistence on his work's fictional character, even as he loads every rift with historical and antiquarian detail, exuberantly realises the logic of a Humean 'moderate skepticism' at the service of things as they are. Scott's next full-length novel, *Old Mortality* (1816), undertakes his most intense exploration of the abyss of civil war, tracking the radicalisation of a regional insurrection towards the apocalyptic horizon of revolution. After a series of gripping plot twists, the final chapter flashes forward to the present day, where the dressmaker Miss Martha Buskbody, connoisseur of 'the whole stock of three circulating libraries in Gandercleuch and the next two market towns', persuades the editor to wrap up his story according to the usual conventions. This conclusion, an effervescent display of Scott's 'Romantic postmodernity',[16] erects a defensive barrier between the late seventeenth-century escalation of rival fanaticisms and our pacified present, balancing the opening chapter's evocation of once-furious militants quietly decomposing in a country churchyard.

It was with *Old Mortality* that Scott's Humean fictionalisation of national history became controversial. His treatment of radical Presbyterianism, the source of a Scottish tradition of popular democratic politics, proved more divisive than his treatment of counter-revolutionary Jacobitism. Dissenting reviewers refuted the novel's claim on a principled Whig Moderatism struggling to be born between revolutionary and royalist extremes as the ideology of modern civil society. They especially objected to Scott's depiction of the Covenanters, champions of Scotland's civil and religious liberties, as murderous zealots. Rival Covenanter historical fictions challenged Scott's. Both Hogg's *The Brownie of Bodsbeck* (1818) and Galt's *Ringan Gilhaize* (1823) undo the equation of the Covenanters with an archetypal revolutionary fanaticism, Hogg by stressing the natural piety of rural communities, Galt by distinguishing between the heroic epoch of the Scottish Reformation and its traumatised terrorist remnant. More striking is their formal challenge to the assumptions and procedures of Scott's historical novel.[17] *The Brownie of Bodsbeck* defies the retrospective, rationalising logic of Enlightenment, realised in a unified complex plot and an abstract English narration, for a simulation of irregular oral recitation in which local actors tell their stories in their own words. *Ringan Gilhaize* fuses memory and history into a single narration through which Ringan transmits the life stories of his grandfather, his father and himself, and with them the ideological legacy of the Reformation. Ringan's narration renounces Humean fictionality for a story that rests on the strong term of belief, faith: keystone of an agency that undergoes a tragic declension from revolutionary collectivism to solitary psychotic obsession.

Tales of My Landlord, to which *Old Mortality* belongs, sets the agenda for the characteristically 'Blackwoodian' fiction which flourished in the early 1820s. Scott described his work as a set of 'Tales, illustrative of ancient Scottish manners, and of the Traditions of their Respective Districts'; the most original of the Blackwood authors would make regional tradition and the tale (before the novel) the preferred media for their versions of historical fiction. Hogg founded his tales – collected in *The Brownie of Bodsbeck*, *Winter Evening Tales* (1820), *The Shepherd's Calendar* (1829) and *Altrive Tales* (1832) – on the popular traditions of the Scottish Borders, while Galt conceived of a series of 'Tales of the West' set in Ayrshire and Glasgow, a world socially and culturally distinct from Edinburgh. Hogg and Galt gave the miscellany-based form of the tale its richest contemporary development, the first-person fictional memoir embedded in local patterns of experience and discourse. Their characteristic work (radically divergent in other respects) promoted vernacular Scots to the main narrative language, in contrast to Scott's framing of Scots speech within a general literary English.

Galt took care to distinguish his experiments in historical fiction from Scott's, characterising *Annals of the Parish* (1821) and *The Provost* (1822) as 'theoretical histories of society' rather than 'novels or romances'.[18] Galt's imaginary autobiographies of a rural minister and a small-town politician renounce the Scott model of plot-intensive romance for an alternative fictional development of Enlightenment philosophical history: an annalistic, anecdotal narration of historical change as it unfolds in the micro-political domain of provincial society. Galt forges a fictional medium that registers the vibrations between local, everyday life and the emergent political economy of world empire, between objective processes of social change and the jolts and nuances of subjective experience, with unprecedented sensitivity.[19] While these works exhibit the virtue Galt claimed as his 'originality', his most ambitious works are essays in the three-volume historical novel associated with Scott. His best novels, *Ringan Gilhaize* and *The Entail* (1823), join in a strenuous and subtle debate with the early series of Scott's *Tales of My Landlord*. In *The Entail*, his masterpiece, Galt recasts his rival's most formidable work, *The Heart of Mid-Lothian*. Like Scott's novel, Galt's combines a family chronicle with a legal crux that lays open a general moral crisis in eighteenth-century Scottish society, with its indomitable anti-heroine, the Leddy Grippy, a parodic counterpart to Scott's Jeanie Deans.

Galt challenges the Humean dialectic at work in the Waverley Novels with a strong development of one of its terms, empirical social history, and a refusal of the other, antiquarian romance. Hogg, in contrast, affirms vernacular principles of storytelling against an Enlightenment cultural teleology. His tales experiment with a range of forms and styles, appropriate to their periodical matrix. The novella-length picaresque autobiography 'Renowned Adventures of Basil Lee' (in *Winter Evening Tales*) reproduces its miscellaneous origins as an internal formal principle, dispatching its feckless protagonist through pastoral misadventures in the Borders, anti-heroic exploits in the American War of Independence, ghost-hunting on the Isle of Lewis and the Edinburgh marriage market. In the 1820s Hogg, like Galt, moved from the short forms of the tale to take on the prestigious and profitable multi-volume historical novel defined by Scott. *The Three Perils of Man: War, Women and Witchcraft* (1821), a medieval 'Border Romance', rebuts Scott's masterful antiquarian fictions (*Ivanhoe, The Monastery*) with a savagely comic performance of a proto-postmodern magic realism. Far from fading into an anthropological anteriority marked 'superstition', wizards and demons occupy the same narrative dimension as historical barons and peasants. *The Three Perils of Woman: Love, Leasing and Jealousy* (1823), arranged into narrative 'Circles' which trace a chronological retrogression from the present back to 1745, rehearses the literary-historical development of domestic national tale to historical romance (the trajectory of *Waverley*) as a cultural and psychological collapse rather than a progress. The final chapters, set in the ravaged Highlands after Culloden, are by turns ludicrous and harrowing.

The historical novel at its limits

Nor did Scott stand aloof from these rival developments in Scottish fiction. In 1824, following a series of romances with various 'Gothic' settings (and a problematic experiment in the 'feminine' novel of contemporary domestic manners, *Saint Ronan's Well*), Scott reclaimed his signature form of Scottish historical novel with one of his finest works, *Redgauntlet; A Tale of the Eighteenth Century*. The historical retrospect of *Redgauntlet* comprises a virtual anthology of eighteenth-century genres – letters, journal, folktale, popular song, Gothic novel, family chronicle, law case, criminal autobiography, stage comedy – as well as of themes and motifs from the Scottish Waverley novels, as Scott rewrites the plot of Jacobite rebellion enmeshed with family romance that he had developed in *Waverley* and *Rob Roy*.[20] In the summer of 1765 a final attempt at Jacobite insurrection falls apart into anticlimax and non-event, a failure to re-enter history which is confirmed in the plot's historiographic status as Scott's own fictional invention. (No such twenty-years-after return of Charles Edward Stewart took place.) *Redgauntlet* reaffirms – with scintillating virtuosity – the aesthetic of Romantic scepticism inaugurated ten years earlier in *Waverley*. This reaffirmation, mediated through the novel's insistent formal miscellaneity, rebuts the aesthetic and ideological challenge offered by Galt in *Ringan Gilhaize*. (Scott burlesques *Ringan Gilhaize* in the inset story of the Redgauntlet family curse; Galt returned the compliment with a burlesque of this episode, in a chapter called 'Redgauntlet', in his next novel, *Rothelan* (1824).)

Hogg's sardonic and terrifying masterpiece *The Private Memoirs and Confessions of a Justified Sinner*, published the same month as *Redgauntlet* (June 1824), has also been read as a reply to Galt's fable of terrorist declension of the Covenant, as well as a critical deconstruction of the Scott historical novel.[21] Hogg splits his tale between the contending forms of imaginary memoir, its subjective horizon intensified into psychopathic delirium, and fictitious history, presented by an 'enlightened' (but baffled) modern editor. Far from resolving into a 'moderate' synthesis, antinomies and antagonisms swarm disastrously across the text, in a virulent formal as well as thematic proliferation. Like *Redgauntlet*, *Confessions of a Justified Sinner* reflects upon its status as a 'tale of the eighteenth century' ten years after *Waverley*. Where *Redgauntlet* reaffirms the Humean model of historical romance and its ideological medium, the liberal breathing-space of civil society, *Confessions of a Justified Sinner* opens a metaphysical abyss – a suicide's grave – that swallows not only its wretched protagonist but the author (since the 'James Hogg' who appears in the final pages cannot be the person who wrote this book) and the reader too. Hogg's novel proved too fiendish and perverse for post-Enlightenment Edinburgh, and it would not find a public until after the literary revolutions of modernism. The dark star of *Confessions of a Justified Sinner* rose even as Scott's was setting.

If *The Private Memoirs and Confessions of a Justified Sinner* marks one limit of Scottish Romantic historical fiction, Scott's second-to-last novel *Count Robert of Paris* (1831) marks another. Mangled as it went to press by Scott's executors and unpublished in its original form until 2006, *Count Robert* is an arrestingly bizarre performance. Set in late eleventh-century Constantinople – about as far from eighteenth-century Scotland as Scott could get – the story features Byzantine Greeks, Turks, Normans, Varangians, Africans, Scythians, a homicidally irascible warrior-princess, a seditious philosopher nicknamed 'the Elephant', a real elephant, a tiger, a mechanical lion and an eight-foot-tall orangutan who understands Anglo-Saxon. Cultural differences lapse into racial differences, while the boundaries between race and species, and between human and non-human species, warp and blur. In his prefaces to *Waverley* and *Ivanhoe*, Scott had defended a universal human nature as the philosophical ground of historical fiction: 'It is from the great book of Nature, the same through a thousand editions, whether of black letter or wire-wove and hot-pressed, that I have venturously essayed to read a chapter to the public.'[22] *Count Robert of Paris*, more a work of anthropological science fiction than a historical novel, subjects this principle – the cornerstone of the Enlightenment 'science of man' – to sustained critical erosion. Scott's Edinburgh was a key site for the British reception of advanced scientific thought from the Continent, including the work of Jean-Baptiste Lamarck, whose challenge to the fixity of species, including the human species, stirred up a notable controversy in the early 1830s.[23] Even in his last years, ailing and distracted, Scott kept his fiction open to the intellectual currents of the age: including those that were breaking up the historical novel's philosophical foundation.

Notes

1   William St Clair, *The Reading Nation in the Romantic Period* (Cambridge University Press, 2004), pp. 221, 245–6, 418–20; for Scott's Victorian reputation, see Philip Waller, *Writers, Readers and Reputations: Literary Life in Britain, 1870–1918* (Oxford University Press, 2006), pp. 177–82.

2   See, e.g., Murray Pittock (ed.), *The Reception of Sir Walter Scott in Europe* (London: Continuum, 2006).

3   See James Chandler, 'The Historical Novel Goes to Hollywood: Scott, Griffith and the Film Epic Today', in Robert Lang (ed.), *The Birth of a Nation: D. W. Griffith, Director* (New Brunswick, NJ: Rutgers University Press, 1994), pp. 225–49.

4   For the 'Antisyzygy', see Margery Palmer McCulloch (ed.), *Modernism and Nationalism: Literature and Society in Scotland, 1918–1939* (Glasgow: Association for Scottish Literary Studies, 2004), pp. 6–7; Tom Nairn, *The Break-up of Britain: Crisis and Neo-Nationalism* (London: Verso, 1981), pp. 118–23; Cairns Craig, *Out of History: Narrative Paradigms in Scottish and British Culture* (Edinburgh: Polygon, 1996), pp. 82–118. On *Peter's Letters*, see Ian Duncan, *Scott's Shadow: The Novel in Romantic Edinburgh* (Princeton University Press, 2007), pp. 59–69.

5   See Peter Garside, James Raven and Rainer Schöwerling, *The English Novel 1770–1829*, vol. II, *A Bibliographical Survey of Prose Fiction Published in the British Isles, 1800–1829* (Oxford University Press, 2000), p. 15.

6   See Jane Millgate, *Scott's Last Edition: A Study in Publishing History* (Edinburgh University Press, 1987).

7   Garside, Raven and Schöwerling, *English Novel*, p. 76.

8   See Ina Ferris, *The Achievement of Literary Authority: Gender, History, and the Waverley Novels* (Ithaca, NY: Cornell University Press, 1991), pp. 19–59.

9 Georg Lukács, *The Historical Novel*, trans. H. and S. Mitchell (Lincoln: University of Nebraska Press, 1983), pp. 23–5.

10 See Katie Trumpener, *Bardic Nationalism: The Romantic Novel and the British Empire* (Princeton University Press, 1997), pp. 128–57.

11 Richard Maxwell, *The Historical Novel in Europe, 1650–1950* (Cambridge: Cambridge University Press, 2009).

12 Lukács, *Historical Novel*, p. 53.

13 See Saree Makdisi, *Romantic Imperialism: Universal Empire and the Culture of Modernity* (Cambridge University Press, 1998), pp. 70–99; James Buzard, *Disorienting Fiction: The Autoethnographic Work of Nineteenth-Century British Novels* (Princeton University Press, 2005), pp. 81–98.

14 Ian Duncan, *Modern Romance and Transformations of the Novel: The Gothic, Scott, Dickens* (Cambridge University Press, 1992), pp. 79–105; Yoon Sun Lee, *Nationalism and Irony: Burke, Scott, Carlyle* (New York: Oxford University Press, 2004), pp. 19–24.

15 For a fuller discussion, see Duncan, *Scott's Shadow*, pp. 119–38.

16 See Jerome McGann, 'Walter Scott's Romantic Postmodernity', in Leith Davis, Ian Duncan and Janet Sorensen (eds.), *Scotland and the Borders of Romanticism* (Cambridge University Press, 2004), pp. 113–29.

17 See Ferris, *Achievement of Literary Authority*, pp. 161–94.

18 John Galt, *Autobiography*, 2 vols. (London: Cochrane & McCrone, 1833), vol. II, pp. 219–20.

19 For a full account, see Trumpener, *Bardic Nationalism*, pp. 153–6.

20 See Leah Price, *The Anthology and the Rise of the Novel: From Richardson to George Eliot* (Cambridge University Press, 2000), pp. 54–65.

21 Douglas Mack, '"The rage of fanaticism in former days": James Hogg's *Confessions of a Justified Sinner* and the Controversy over *Old Mortality*', in Ian Campbell (ed.), *Nineteenth-Century Scottish Fiction: Critical Essays* (Manchester: Carcanet, 1979), pp. 37–50; Gary Kelly, *English Fiction of the Romantic Period 1789–1830* (London: Longman, 1989), pp. 260–73.

22 Sir Walter Scott, *Waverley*, ed. Peter Garside (Edinburgh University Press, 2006), p. 6.

23 See James A. Secord, 'Edinburgh Lamarckians: Robert Jameson and Robert E. Grant', *Journal of the History of Biology*, 24:1 (1991), 1–18.

Guide to further reading

Duncan, Ian, *Scott's Shadow: The Novel in Romantic Edinburgh* (Princeton University Press, 2007)

Ferris, Ina, *The Achievement of Literary Authority: Gender, History, and the Waverley Novels* (Ithaca, NY: Cornell University Press, 1991)

Lincoln, Andrew, *Walter Scott and Modernity* (Edinburgh University Press, 2006)

Maxwell, Richard, *The Historical Novel in Europe, 1650–1950* (Cambridge University Press, 2009)

Robertson, Fiona, *Legitimate Histories: Scott, Gothic and the Authority of Fiction* (Oxford: Clarendon Press, 1995)

Trumpener, Katie, *Bardic Nationalism: The Romantic Novel and the British Empire* (Princeton University Press, 1997)

8

PETER MACKAY

The Gaelic Tradition

The introduction to Alexander MacDonald's 1751 *Aiseirigh na Seann Chànain Albannaich* [The Resurrection of the Old Scottish Language], the first secular publication in vernacular Scottish Gaelic, engages in celebration, advertisement and rapprochement. Coming only five years after the Battle of Culloden, the introduction carefully makes the case (in English) for Gaelic literature to be understood both in terms of classical and historical precedents, and as a part of the fabric of Scottish cultural life. MacDonald presents his collection of poems as entertainment for those who can read Gaelic, and a possible encouragement for those who cannot to learn; this may happen, he argues, if readers can be brought to see that Gaelic

> might possibly contain in its bosom the charms of poetry and rhetoric, those two great sources of pleasure and persuasion, to which all other languages have owed their gradual advancement, and, in these improving times, their last polish and refinement.[1]

MacDonald also proposes a future anthology, a

> collection of poems of the same sort, in all kinds of poetry that have been in use amongst the most cultivated nations, from those of the earliest composition to modern times; their antiquity either proved by historical accounts, or ascertained by the best tradition; with a translation into ENGLISH verse, and critical observations on the nature of such writings, to render the work useful to those who do not understand the GALIC [*sic*] language.[2]

MacDonald's language is that of the Scottish Enlightenment: the association of 'rhetoric' with 'advancement' and 'polish and refinement'; the emphasis on the 'cultivated nations'. In using such language, MacDonald is engaging with the dominant forms of contemporary cultural discourse within Scotland, in part to advertise the merits of Gaelic literature, and in part to highlight the 'Scottishness' of that literature. These are repeated concerns of the Introduction: the title, as Ronald Black comments, stresses the language's

'Scottishness' rather than its 'Gaelicness' or 'Celticness';[3] the audience for the proposed anthology of Gaelic verse is imagined as including

> the inhabitants of the lowlands of Scotland, who have always shared with them [the Gaels] the honour of every gallant action, and are now first invited to a participation of their reputation for arts, if that too shall be found, on an impartial scrutiny, to be justly claimed by them.[4]

MacDonald – complacently, given his well-known Jacobite connections – presents his ambition as being 'to approve himself a lover of his country, and an inoffensive man'.[5]

MacDonald's is a precarious balancing act, on the threshold between different cultures, languages and political environments: the English and Gaelic languages; Highland and Lowland culture; the political worlds of pre-Culloden Jacobitism and post-Culloden Enlightenment Edinburgh; and the Presbyterian, Episcopalian and Catholic branches of Christianity (at different parts of his life MacDonald subscribed to each of these denominations, although such allegiances appear to have been subordinate to political considerations). His attempt to celebrate Gaelic literature (and sell his own book) was exceedingly difficult in these circumstances; his solution to emphasise the antiquity and, more importantly, the international nature of that literature, by reintegrating it into the history of European culture. MacDonald's first tack is to proclaim the antiquity and wealth of Gaelic's Celtic origins:

> the CELTIC nation, of which [Gaelic speakers] are a small, but precious remain, once diffused itself over a great part of the globe. From its bosom have issued the conquerors of Rome, the planters of Gaul, Britain, Ireland; still found subsisting in this last, in Wales, in some parts of Spain, and along the coast of France; once great and flourishing in Asia; and peculiarly distinguished, in having one of the holy epistles of the great Apostle of the Gentiles addressed to them. A people so extensive and numerous could not fail of having made considerable improvements amongst them, though many of their monuments are lost, and the greatest monument of all, the language, entirely neglected.[6]

His second argument is to emphasise the extent to which Gaelic was formed through its encounters with other civilisations, cultures and climates over this long history:

> It would be agreeable, to trace the progress of their [the Celts'] genius as far as it is now possible to discover it, through all its modifications and changes; to observe what different tinctures, as one may say, it has received, from the many different climates, people and customs, through which, as so many strainers, it has passed.[7]

That is, although Gaelic literature is based on an original 'genius', it is also a product of meetings with other languages and cultures. It is, like MacDonald himself, liminal and flexible, constantly changing to cope with new contexts and new demands; and the introduction to the *Aiseirigh* (and the 'manifesto' poem 'Moladh an Ùghdair don t-Seann Chànain Ghàidhlig' which immediately follows it) is part of the process by which MacDonald attempts to reconfigure Gaelic literature to the altered political landscape of contemporary Scotland.

The version of Gaelic literature suggested by MacDonald's Introduction is supported by his poetry. MacDonald draws on previous Gaelic models and metrics, but also innovates, most famously introducing the structures of the *Ceol Mòr* (the 'floor' and 'variation' found in pipe music) into his epic *Birlinn Chlann Raghnaill* [The Galley of Clanranald]. However, he also adopts poetic structures, tropes and ideas from other literatures. His reworking of James Thomson's *The Seasons* in 'Oran an t-samhraidh' [The Song of Summer] and 'Oran a' gheamhraidh' [The Song of Winter] has been well documented; as Ronald Black notes, the loan words used in 'Oran a' gheamhraidh' are taken from Thomson's poems.[8] (MacDonald is – despite his claims for the autonomy of Gaelic in 'Moladh an Ùghdair don t-Seann Chànain Ghàidhlig' – free with the use of loan words from Scots and English.) His 1751 collection also includes three translations of poems by the seventeenth-century earl of Montrose,[9] and some passages from Allan Ramsay, whose *Tea-Time Miscellany* MacDonald would have known (Ramsay is most likely the 'Ailean Bàrd' mentioned in MacDonald's 'Mìomholadh Mòraig' [The Dispraise of Morag])[10]; MacDonald also set his songs to extant Lowland airs (there are ten such airs named in the *Aiseirigh*).[11] Other tropes he introduced included references to the Greek and Roman gods: this was very much in tune with his aggrandisement of Gaelic literature.

MacDonald's *Aiseirigh* is one of the bases of modern Gaelic written literature and his formulation of the relationships between Gaelic and other cultures informs how much later Gaelic literature can be understood. He stresses the interaction of Gaelic literature and that of the 'cultivated nations' – there is no Gaelic isolationism in MacDonald – but he does so knowing that such interaction comes in many different forms: translation, borrowing, adoption, competition. The 'Gaelic Tradition' – if such a thing exists – that the *Aiseirigh* inaugurates is not simply a canon of texts and figures, but is a tradition of cultural negotiation, flexibility and relocation, with the aim of survival and – at least for MacDonald – 'refinement' or 'cultivation'.

Among these forms of interaction, translation is central. Although MacDonald's was the first secular book in Gaelic, there had long been religious publications, with translations of religious material – bibles, catechisms and moral texts – prominent. The popularity of religious material has been a constant throughout the history of Gaelic publishing: John Bunyan's *Pilgrim's Progress*, for example – translated into Gaelic as *Cuairt an eilthirich* – was reprinted fourteen times between 1812 and 1953. There is a case to be made that the most important poet in printed Gaelic during the eighteenth century was not MacDonald, but the religious poet Dugald Buchanan. Buchanan's *Laoidhe Spioradail* [Hymns] was published in 1767 (as was the first translation of the New Testament into Gaelic, the publication of which he oversaw); by 1946 they had been reprinted forty-three times.[12] These hymns were also heavily indebted to translation, and English-language precursors; as Donald Meek has argued, Buchanan was a follower of Bunyan, Isaac Watts – three of his eight extant poems are influenced by Watts's *Horae Lyricae* (1706) – and Robert Blair as well as James Thomson and Edward Young.[13]

Buchanan's collection – like MacDonald's[14] – was published in Edinburgh; this was also the case for Duncan Bàn MacIntyre's 1768 *Orain Ghaidhealach* [Gaelic Songs]. That Edinburgh was the original publishing centre for Gaelic literature (though quickly followed by Glasgow and Perth) is remarkable given the relatively low standing of the Gaelic language in the city and the association of Gaelic with Highland 'barbarism' and the Jacobite cause. However, it is testament to both the multiplicity of 'Edinburgh' in the mid eighteenth century and to the swift acceptance and appropriation of Gaelic literature by the Scottish Enlightenment. Buchanan was different from MacDonald, however, in that he was writing after the greatest Gaelic (and Scottish – and crucially Scottish Enlightenment) literary phenomenon of the eighteenth century: the publication by James Macpherson of *Fragments of Ancient Poetry Collected in the Highlands of Scotland* in 1760 and of *Fingal* (1761), *Temora* (1763) and *The Works of Ossian* (1765). Macpherson's Ossianic 'translations' caused a sea-change in how Gaelic poetry was viewed within Scotland and Europe as a whole. The championing of Ossian by Enlightenment figures such as Hugh Blair and Adam Ferguson, and the publicity created by the controversy about the veracity of Ossian and his poems, helped create a new audience and so new publication possibilities for Gaelic literature; this was a far greater audience than Alexander MacDonald had aspired to in the Introduction to the *Aiseirigh*, in which he tentatively appealed only to 'the inhabitants of the lowlands of Scotland'.[15] Gaelic writers from then on would have at least one eye – often both – on this new metropolitan audience.

Macpherson's Ossian was also important in that it offered a putative origin and antiquity to Gaelic literature that went further back than anything in Scots or English (or, the tendentious argument went, Irish); as a result it gave Gaelic literature a grandeur and import that was important given the contemporary reality of political disintegration and cultural attenuation.

Criticism of Ossian's inauthenticity or falseness rarely came from within the Gaelic speaking population, who were able to identify songs that lay behind Macpherson's translations (and, anyway, his manipulation of the texts was far from uncommon in editorial practice of the time). Instead, Macpherson's translations allowed for a notion of tradition as something that was neither true nor false, but could be applied and modified as necessary for different cultural contexts,[16] and laid a basis for a Gaelic literature that was, by necessity, the result of a passing between languages (most commonly Gaelic and English).

The possibilities that this new interest afforded Gaelic writers and Gaelic literary entrepreneurs are visible from Dugald Buchanan's attempts to gain support for a project to publish Gaelic dictionaries (as a follow-up to the translation of the New Testament into Gaelic). Donald Meek has shown how Buchanan used distinctly Ossianic terms – 'tender Passion' and 'sublime Sentiment' – in a letter seeking help from Sir James Clerk of Penicuik, one of the leading figures in the Scottish Enlightenment.[17] The publication of collections – and especially anthologies – was also encouraged by the Ossianic phenomenon, as Ossianic material was often contained within these anthologies; the growing taste for Gaelic collections can be seen by the fact that Duncan Bàn MacIntyre and then Kenneth MacKenzie were able to raise subscriptions to pay for their collections of poems (an ingenious response to the problem of how to pay for poetry following the collapse of traditional systems of patronage). A late eighteenth- and nineteenth-century craze for anthologies of Gaelic song and poetry arose in part because of the growth of an urban audience for that poetry as Gaelic literature found a place and audience in the drawing-rooms and clubs of Edinburgh and London (the Highland Society of London, for example, was created in 1778).[18] The Gaelic song that was desired for urban consumption was heavily influenced by Macpherson's work, and especially the 'overwrought melancholy' that Macpherson had introduced to his Ossianic material.[19]

More generally for Gaelic writers, Macpherson's 'Ossian' also established a poetic mode or sensibility which dovetailed with broader 'Romantic' tendencies, but also could be seen to have some degree of indigenous rooting: the nostalgia, gloom and abstract nouns which characterise much nineteenth-century verse could be seen as reappropriation of the motifs and mood of Macpherson back into Gaelic literature. Macpherson can then – somewhat ironically – be seen as one of the main *external* influences on Gaelic literature, as well as one of the main 'exporters' of Gaelic verse. Macpherson was far from the only 'external' influence in this period, however. His creation of a Gaelic, Homeric 'epic' (almost a necessary creation of the self-styled 'Athens of the North'[20]) was followed by the translation of the first eight books of a real Homeric epic, the *Iliad*, into Gaelic by Ewen MacLachlan (1773–1822). MacLachlan, a Scottish Gaelic scholar-poet prolific at the turn of the century, played his own role in the Ossianic controversy: between 1811 and 1812 MacLachlan prepared a report for the Highland Society of Scotland into the Gaelic manuscripts that lay behind 'translations', and found in Macpherson's favour.[21] The following year (and probably as a result of his work for the Highland Society), MacLachlan prepared transcriptions of the sixteenth-century manuscript Book of the Dean of Lismore;[22] like MacDonald and Buchanan before him, MacLachlan was also interested in the compiling of dictionaries or vocabularies, contributing to what would be the Highland Society's *Dictionarium Scoto-Celticum*. This attentiveness to Gaelic and earlier Gaelic texts combined in MacLachlan with a passion for other languages and other literary models, both classical and modern. Following MacDonald's lead, he became the first Gaelic poet to write poems to each of the four seasons in the mode of James Thomson;[23] he also oversaw publication of versions of the *Odyssey* and the *Iliad* in the original with Latin translations.

MacLachlan's own, partial, translation of the *Iliad* into Gaelic was finished by 1816 (though it was not published until 1937).[24] This translation is very loose, beginning:

> Aithris, a bhan-dia nam fonn!
> Fearg mhic Pheleuis nan glonn àigh,
> Fearg mhillteach a chiùrr a' Ghréig
> Le beud nan deich mile cràdh,
> Fearg a sguab a dh'ifrinn duinn
> Mìltean làn-ghàisgeach romh 'n am,
> An cuirp rùisgt' aig coin mar phronn,
> 'S aig uil-ealtainn nam fiadh-bheann.[25]
> [Tell, goddess of melodies! / The anger of the son of Peleus of the glorious deeds, / The destructive anger that put Greece / harmfully into ten thousand pains, / The anger that swept to hell / Thousands of heroes before their time, / Their naked bodies a dinner for dogs, / and for every flock in the deerhills.]

There are significant ways in which this eschews the precision of the Greek original: Achilles is not mentioned by name in line 2; the 'Achaens' become 'Greece' in line 3; 'Orcus' becomes 'hell'.[26] Two elements, on the other hand, have been introduced: the epithet 'nan glonn àigh' [of the glorious deeds]; and the association of the birds of prey with the 'fiadh-bheann' [the deerhills]. These are ways of connecting the epic with the Highlands of Scotland and with the Ossianic texts popular at the time: 'Oscar nam mór glonn' [mighty Oscar] was a common descriptor for Ossian's son.[27] The desire to

reduce the distance between his readership and the poem is obvious from
the summary of the first book, which begins

> Anns an t-sean aimsir bha a' Ghréig uile ... air a roinn 'na dùthchannaibh, 's i
> fo fhlaitheachd cheanna-feodhna, coltach ri Gaidhealachd na h-Albann romh
> bliadhna a' chomhuich, 1745.[28]

> [In olden times all of Greece ... was separated into regions, controlled by
> aristocratic chieftains, like the Highlands of Scotland before the year of the
> [defeat/dispute], 1745.]

This suggests once more the aspirational Scottish Enlightenment association
of the Highlands with ancient Greece; what is of crucial importance, however,
is that MacLachlan identifies ancient Greece with the ancient Highlands; he
carefully separates Highland life into pre- and post-1745, to distinguish a
modern, progressive, Enlightened – and yet still Highland – perspective.

This is a perspective which is generally lacking in nineteenth-century
Gaelic literature, however. The nineteenth century, more than any other,
tends to be dismissed as a period of retrenchment, with over-dependence
on imported (English) literary models and the collapse of cultural vitality
and confidence (following the collapse of the traditional social systems, and
associated with patterns of poverty, clearance and emigration);[29] it also saw
the absorption or assumption of Highland/Gaelic culture into a mainstream
British identity. The tension between absorption and assimilation on the
one hand and dissent and rebellion on the other characterises much of nineteenth-century verse.

The assimilation of Gaelic culture into mainstream British identity is
most obvious from the post-Romantic (and post-Ossian) versions of that
culture portrayed in the Balmoralism of Walter Scott and, later, Queen
Victoria.[30] These were almost historical pastiche, in much the same way
that the appointments of John MacCodrum and Allan MacDougall 'as poets
to, respectively, Sir James MacDonald of Sleat and Alexander Ranaldson
MacDonell of Glengarry' were 'conscious exercise[s] in antiquarianism,
stimulated by the Ossianic controversy'.[31] Such Balmoralism/Highlandism
met a Celticism derived from Matthew Arnold's 'On the Study of Celtic
Literature',[32] and can be identified in much of the poetry from the second
half of the nineteenth century, especially the work of Neil MacLeod and
Henry Whyte. Whyte's 'Fuadach nan Gaidheal' [The Dispersal of the Gaels]
is an extreme case in point. The Gaelic begins:

> Gura mise tha tùrsach,
> A' caoidh cor na dùthcha,
> 'S na seann daoine cùiseil
> Bha cliùiteach is treun ...[33]

Donald Meek provides a literal translation as follows:

> I lament with great sadness
> the plight of my country,
> and the thrifty old people
> who were famous and brave ...[34]

Whyte, however, translated the poem himself, and his English translation works within what Donald Meek identifies as 'a quite different conceptual frame'[35]:

> I mourn for the Highlands,
> Now drear and forsaken,
> The land of my fathers,
> The gallant and brave ...[36]

The sentiment is similar in the two versions, the details – 'Highlands' / 'my country', 'land of my fathers' / 'thrifty old people' – quite different; Whyte's translation is an obvious example of the poet adjusting his own Gaelic song to the expectations of a metropolitan audience accustomed to set tropes and images of the Highlands of Scotland.

Whyte's Gaelic text presents one of the most common features of nineteenth-century Gaelic verse: a quasi-Wordsworthian 'egotistical sublime'. The focus in his poems (as with those of Neil MacLeod) tends to be on the emotions and feelings of a first-person narrator rather than on any imagined external world (as was the case in Duncan Bàn MacIntyre's 'Moladh Beinn Dobhrain' [In praise of Beinn Dorain], for example). Donald Meek notes:

> The eighteenth-century poets were often at their best when describing a natural scene, or the seasons, or portraying a battle. They could, on occasion, give vent to their emotions, as in the great songs of grief which followed Culloden. William Ross, for example, did so memorably, and some of his verse appears to anticipate the romantic inclination which came on stream after 1800. Our nineteenth-century poets, on the other hand, are much more concerned to tell us how it *feels* to see a deserted landscape, where there was a once lively community; how it *feels* to be in an emigrant context, far from home; how it *feels* to be on a steam train or ship [and so on].[37]

Sentiment in such verse quickly gives way to sentimentality, and an overpowering sense (and frequent descriptions) of 'cianalas' [nostalgia/homesickness/longing] characterises much of the more conservative and formulaic nineteenth-century verse. One pattern is particularly common in such verse: eulogy of the landscape; celebration of the (now absent) population; lament for the present/encouragement to improve the situation. This is the structure, for example, of Neil MacLeod's 'Fàilte don Eilean Sgitheanach'

[Salute to the Isle of Skye] and 'An Gleann san robh mi Og' [The Glen where I was Young].[38] 'Nuair a bha mi Og' [When I was Young] by Mary Macpherson [Màiri Mhòr nan Oran] follows a similar pattern; however, the difference between the quality of Macpherson and MacLeod's verse is the emotional depth. There is, for example, descriptive precision and eroticism to Macpherson's 'cianalas' (and her evocations of freedom) that outstrips anything in MacLeod:

> Nuair bha mi gòrach a' siubhal mòintich,
>   'S am fraoch a' stròiceadh mo chòta bàn,
> Feadh thoman còinnich gun snàthainn a bhrògan,
>   'S an eigh na còsan air lochan tàimh
> [When I was heedless traversing moorland, / and the heather tearing my white petticoat / through the mossy tuffets, with no thread of footwear, / and ice in pockets on stagnant lochs.][39]

Macpherson was the most high profile of the poets engaged in the land struggle, the main counter-cultural movement of the century. The political role Macpherson adopted was in some ways a continuity of the panegyric tradition that had survived into the previous century, with her (adopted) role being to encourage or comment on political change; she had a social and political role within her own community in much the same way as the eighteenth-century Sutherland satirist Rob Donn Mackay, and with this communal role was less focused on an urban anglophone audience than some of her contemporaries. Such political purpose – allied with an antiquarian bent – is also seen in the second of the most lauded nineteenth-century poets, William Livingstone, whose 'Fios chun a' Bhàird' ['A Message for the Poet'] serves not only to highlight the political changes in the Highlands but also to restate the traditional role of the poet as the mouthpiece and broadcaster of his or her community.[40]

Much Gaelic verse from the nineteenth century was also wedded to the other sweeping socio-cultural changes, such as religious revivals (and schisms) and large-scale emigration from the Highlands. In terms of the latter, there is a case to be made that the most interesting Gaelic literature of the nineteenth century was not written in Scotland, but in the emigrant community in America (a rare instance of Gaelic literature crossing linguistic and cultural frontiers without first being translated into English). John MacLean, 'Bàrd Tighearna Cholla' [The Bard to the Laird of Coll], is the most famous of the emigrant poets. In 'Oran do dh' Ameireaga' [A Song to America][41] and 'Craobhsgaoileadh an t-Soisgeil san Tìr seo' [The Propagation of the Gospel in this Country], he evokes first the difficulties and culture shocks of his first winter in Nova Scotia and then the developing

sense of belonging; the later song is a statement of progress and the development of the New World going hand in hand with the spread of the Gospel.

Both of these songs engage with and develop extant genres: anti-emigration
literature; and (largely) Puritan literature describing the Christian improvement of the New World. In both cases, however, what we find is the Gaelic
language and patterns of Gaelic literature being adapted to new social
and cultural contexts. This is most painfully apparent in 'Oran do dh'
Ameireaga', as MacLean states (a common refrain) how he feels his Gaelic
to be insufficient:

> Chan fhaigh mi innse dhuibh ann am Gàidhlig,
> Cha dean mo nàdur a chur air dòigh
> Gach fios a b' àill leam thoirt do na càirdean
> San tìr a dh' fhàg mi, rinn m' àrach òg.
> [My Gaelic fails me when I try to tell you, / nor can my nature arrange in
> form, / all I'd wish conveyed to my relations / in the land I left, where I
> was once a boy.]⁴²

However, what the song also shows is the poet's attempt to fit his own
experience (and his own language) to the new circumstances. A cobbler by
trade, MacLean is precise about the footwear he discovers:

> Is ge math an triùbhsair cha dean i feum
> Gun stocainn dhùbailt sa mhocais chlùdaich
> Bhios air a dùnadh gu dlùth le èill;
> B' e am fasan ùr dhuin a cosg le fionntach
> Mar chaidh a rùsgadh den bhrùid an-dè.
> [and though the trouser's good it will not suffice / without a double
> stocking in a ragged moccasin / tight-closed with thongs around the foot: /
> it was our new fashion to wear it hairy, / as skinned yesterday from the
> brute.]⁴³

The slipping into Gaelic of the 'mocais' [moccasin] shows the process by
which Gaelic found its footing in the New World.

It was not only Gaelic verse, however, that developed on the western side
of the Atlantic. The nineteenth century saw the burgeoning for the first time
of a secular Gaelic prose, largely based around newspapers and journals,
with a wide range of types of text: journalism, editorials, testimonials of
emigrants, letters, advertisements and short stories. The most important
figure in early Gaelic periodical publishing was Norman MacLeod who,
writing as 'Caraid nan Gaidheal' [The Friend of the Gaels], edited the first
two Gaelic periodicals, *An Teachdaire Gàelach* [*The Courier of the Gaels*]
(1829–31) and *Cuairtear nan Gleann* [*The Tourist of the Glens*] (1840–3);⁴⁴
however, there was also a periodical published in Canada at the end of

the century. *Mac Talla* (1892–1904), edited by Jonathan G. MacKinnon in Sydney, Cape Breton, is an example of the strength of the Gaelic-speaking community (and Gaelic publishing) in Canada.

By the start of the twentieth century, Gaelic literature had witnessed centuries of engagement with other languages, literatures and cultures, through many different routes: translation; literary competition; religious movements; emigration; imperial conquest. There had also been a growth in prose writing (although the first Gaelic novels would not appear until the twentieth century). These are the historical contexts in which the literature of the last century has to be understood. The continued importance of 'Celticism/Highlandism' can be seen, for example, in the various anthologies of Marjorie Kennedy-Fraser and the Revd Kenneth MacLeod. In many ways, these and other 'Celtic Twilight' texts used similar techniques to Macpherson's 'Ossian' as extant Gaelic texts were adapted to suit the cultural mores of Edinburgh, Glasgow and London. Similarly, the adoption of English poetic patterns continued in the work of John Munro (one of the Gaelic First World War poets); his use of free verse in his poems 'Ar Gaisgich a Thuit sna Blàir' [Our Heroes who Fell in Battle], 'Air sgàth nan sonn' [For the Sake of the Warriors] and 'Ar Tìr' [Our Land] is remarkable, given that almost all other verse of the time still had strict, singable, rhythms.[45]

Munro was the immediate predecessor of the poets Sorley MacLean and George Campbell Hay, whose emergence in the 1930s heralded what was almost immediately claimed as a Gaelic Renaissance (to dovetail with Hugh MacDiarmid's Scottish Renaissance). The internationalism of their poetry can be seen to draw on the trends of Gaelic literature over the previous two and a half centuries. MacLean claims in an introduction to his long polemic poem 'An Cuilithionn' [The Cuillin], for example, that he envisaged it as 'radiating from Skye and the West Highlands to the whole of Europe';[46] this is repeating on a thematic and structural level the scope and reach for Gaelic literature that was unexpectedly achieved by Macpherson's work (and which was beyond the dreams of MacDonald in the Introduction to his *Aiseirigh*). Similarly, the central trope of much of Hay's polylingual work is of crossing cultural boundaries, whether they be the linguistic boundaries of Scots, Gaelic and English or the parallels that he drew between the Highlands of Scotland and North Africa in his Second World War poems 'Bisearta', 'Atman' and the unfinished *Mòchtar is Dùghall* [Môkhtar and Dougal].[47] Meanwhile, *Gairm*, the journal which ran for fifty years from 1952 under the stewardship of Derick Thomson, shared the tendency of the nineteenth-century journals towards the multi-generic and extra-literary. Thomson's own repeated gestures in his criticism towards placing Gaelic literature within multiple international contexts also suggest a desire to change the tendency which sees Gaelic literature as interacting primarily with English literature. A practical development of this has been seen in recent years in the publishing of parallel texts in Gaelic and Irish (in the cases of the poetry collections published by Coiscéim in Dublin[48]) and Gaelic and German,[49] as a counterbalance to Gaelic and English parallel texts (which had become the common way of publishing Gaelic poetry since the 1970s). These publications suggest sensitivity to the place of Gaelic literature as one literature among many, with the need to position and negotiate the literature between and across languages; as we have seen, however, this has been a central, 'traditional' crutch of Gaelic literature from the earliest Gaelic publications onwards.

Notes

1 Alexander MacDonald [Alastair Mac-Dhonuill], *Aiseirigh na Seann Chànain Albannaich* (Edinburgh, 1751), p. v. As in this instance, the translations throughout this chapter are my own unless otherwise indicated.

2 *Ibid.*, pp. v–vi.

3 See Ronald Black, 'Sharing the Honour: Mac Mhaighstir Alastair and the Lowlands', in Christopher MacLachlan (ed.), *Crossing the Highland Line* (Glasgow: Association for Scottish Literary Studies, 2009), pp. 45–57.

4 MacDonald, *Aiseirigh*, p. vi.

5 *Ibid.*, p. viii. Derick Thomson's comment that 'hopes of a further rising probably persisted into the early 1750s, and may well have been an important part of the motivation for the 1751 publication of his [MacDonald's] poems', is instructive here; see Derick Thomson (ed.), *Alasdair Mac Mhaighstir Alasdair: Selected Poems* (Edinburgh: Scottish Gaelic Texts Society, 1996), p. 12.

6 MacDonald, *Aiseirigh*, pp. vi–vii.

7 *Ibid.*, p. vii.

8 Black, 'Sharing the Honour', pp. 53–4.

9 See Thomson (ed.), *Alasdair Mac Mhaighstir Alasdair*, p. 12.

10 See Black, 'Sharing the Honour', pp. 48–9.

11 Thomson (ed.), *Alasdair Mac Mhaighstir Alasdair*, p. 7.

12 See Mary Ferguson and Ann Matheson, *Scottish Gaelic Union Catalogue: A List of Books Printed in Scottish Gaelic from 1567 to 1973* (Edinburgh: National Library of Scotland, 1984). In comparison, MacDonald's *Poems*, first printed in 1802, were reprinted nine times by 1924, while Duncan Bàn MacIntyre's *Orain Ghàidhealach* was reprinted seventeen times between 1768 and 1952.

13 Donald E. Meek, 'Evangelicalism, Ossianism and the Enlightenment: The Many Masks of Dugald Buchanan', in MacLachlan (ed.), *Crossing the Highland Line*, pp. 97–112.

14 Tradition has it that MacDonald's book was burnt as seditious by the hangman at Edinburgh's Mercat cross. See Hugh Cheape, 'Gaelic Genesis', *Scottish Book Collector*, 7:9 (2004), 15–23.

15 MacDonald, *Aiseirigh*, p. vi.

16 See Michael Gardiner's discussion of Cairns Craig and Alasdair MacIntyre in Gardiner, *The Cultural Roots of British Devolution* (Edinburgh University Press, 2004), p. 80.

17 See Donald E. Meek, 'The Sublime Gael: The Impact of MacPherson's *Ossian* on Literary Creativity and Cultural Perception in Gaelic Scotland', in Howard Gaskill (ed.), *The Reception of Ossian in Europe* (London: Thoemmes Continuum, 2004), pp. 40–66.

18 Anthologies of note include Ronald MacDonald's *Comh-Chruinneachidh Òrannaigh Gàidhealach* (1776) (Ronald was the son of Alexander MacDonald); John Brown's *Rannaibh Nuadh do'n t'Sean Éididh Eachdoil Ghàelich* (1786); John MacKenzie's *Sàr Obair nam Bard Gaelach* (1841); Archibald Sinclair's *An t-Oranaiche* (1879); and Henry Whyte's *Celtic Lyre* (1898). There are many more, as can be seen from the *Scottish Gaelic Union Catalogue*. These anthologies reflect not only the commodification of Gaelic literature, but also the steady development of a printed canon of songs. See also Donald Meek (ed.), *Caran an t-Saoghal: An Anthology of Nineteenth-Century Gaelic Verse* (Edinburgh: Birlinn, 2003), pp. xix–xx.

19 J. S. Smart, *James Macpherson: An Episode in Literature* (London: D. Nutt, 1905), p. 75, quoted in Kenneth Simpson, 'The Place of Macpherson's Ossian in Scottish Literature', in MacLachlan (ed.), *Crossing the Highland Line*, pp. 113–122.

20 That this argument has become the orthodoxy is shown by the way in which it is sketched out in Simpson, 'Place of MacPherson's Ossian', p. 113; the argument is most fully developed in Fiona Stafford's seminal *The Sublime Savage* (Edinburgh University Press, 1988).

21 See John MacDonald, *Ewen MacLachlan's Gaelic Verse* (Inverness: Carruthers, 1987), p. ix.

22 *Ibid.*

23 See Ronald Black (ed.), *An Lasair: Anthology of 18th Century Scottish Gaelic Verse* (Edinburgh: Birlinn, 2001), p. 518: '[MacLachlan's] greatest claim to literary fame probably lies in his poems to the seasons. Mac Mhaighstir Alastair made songs to both summer and winter, Donnchadh Bàn and William Ross to summer only, Rob Donn and Dugald Buchanan to winter only, but MacLachlan – and yes, it is all rather revealing of the respective temperaments of these six major figures – MacLachlan made songs to spring, summer, autumn and winter.'

24 See MacDonald, *Ewen MacLachlan's Gaelic Verse*, p. xii, and Meek (ed.), *Caran an t-Saoghail*, p. 481.

25 MacDonald, *Ewen MacLachlan's Gaelic Verse*, p. 3.

26 See the Greek text and interlineal translation in Sidney G. Hamilton and Thomas Clark's *The Iliad of Homer* (New York: David McKay, 1888) republished by the University of Michigan in 2009: www.ellopos.net/elpenor/greek-texts/interlinear-iliad.asp?homer=1.

27 See the entry for 'glonn' in Edward Dwelly, *Illustrated Gaelic–English Dictionary* (Edinburgh: Birlinn, 2008).

28 MacDonald, *Ewen MacLachlan's Gaelic Verse*, p. 1. This is my own translation: I take 'chomhuich' to be 'comhaich' – defeat/dispute; a possible alternative is 'cuthach' – madness.

29 The work of Donald Meek critiques this dismissive view of nineteenth-century literature, in particular identifying forms of verse which continued from the eighteenth into the nineteenth century, such as the panegyric, satire and humorous verse. See Meek (ed.), *Caran an t-Saoghal*, pp. xxxv–vi, and Donald Meek (ed.), *Tuath is Tighearna* (Edinburgh: Scottish Gaelic Texts Society, 1995), p. 16.

30 'Balmoralism' was itself a modulation of the figure of the 'Highland Laddie', which predated 1745. See Domhnall Uilleam Stiùbhart, 'Highland Rogues and the Roots of Highland Romanticism', in MacLachlan (ed.), *Crossing the Highland Line*, pp. 161–194: 'Although, with some notable exceptions, scholars have been content to situate the foundations of Highland romanticism in the later eighteenth century, in the wake of the Jacobite risings and Macpherson's *Ossian*, this is clearly not the case. The construction in the late seventeenth century of the figure of the Highland Laddie, that potent amalgam of heroism, proto-Romanticism and hard and soft primitivism melded together, was a fundamental step towards the construction of a gendered image for the Scottish Gael/Highlander which would prove highly resilient until the present day. For contemporaries, however, this literary figure represented a reworking of older heroic values, in an increasingly post-heroic age.'

31 Black (ed.), *An Lasair*, pp. x–xi; Black contrasts this phenomenon to the poets who still had the bardic designation 'Aos-Dàna' at the beginning of the eighteenth century.

32 'Celticism'/'Highlandism' are, though not identical, extremely similar phenomena; indeed Arnold's 'Celticism' developed from 'Highlandism' to some extent: it was not a phenomenon without precedent, but rather a continuation of themes and motifs that had passed back and forth between the Celtic languages and English from (at least) the work of James Thomson onwards. See Gerard Carruthers, '"Poured out extensive, and of watery wealth": Scotland in Thomson's *The Seasons*', in MacLachlan (ed.), *Crossing the Highland Line*, pp. 21–30: 'Matthew Arnold's invention of "Celtic Literature" with its special ability in portraying nature has several critics see Thomson in the light of this "Celtic" made manifest, obviously enough, in the natural description of *The Seasons*. There is a big irony, however, in the fact, as Derick Thomson and others have shown, Duncan Ban MacIntyre, Alexander MacDonald and Dugald Buchanan … owe a debt to Thomson's method of didactic interaction with the natural environment.'

33 Meek (ed.), *Caran an t-Saoghal*, p. 384.

34 *Ibid.*, p. 469.

35 *Ibid.*

36 *Ibid.*, p. 385.

37 *Ibid.*, p. xxvii.

38 *Ibid.*, pp. 16–19, 54–63.

39 *Ibid.*, pp. 20–1 (Meek's translation).

40 *Ibid.*, pp. 42–9. For more on Livingston, see Donald Meek, 'The World of William Livingston' and 'Making History: William Livingston and the Creation of "Blar Shunadail"', and Christopher Whyte, 'William Livingston's "Na Lochlannaich an Ìle"', all in J. Derrick McClure, John M. Kirk and Margaret Storrie (eds.), *A*

Land that Lies Westward: Language and Culture in Islay and Argyll (Edinburgh: Birlinn, 2009), pp. 123–48; 173–96; 149–72.

41 This song is also commonly known as 'A' Choille Ghruamach' [The Gloomy Wood].

42 Meek (ed.), *Caran an t-Saoghal*, pp. 70–1 (Meek's translation).

43 *Ibid.*, pp. 66–7 (Meek's translation). 'Clùdach' here can mean 'filled with rags', as well as 'ragged': I am grateful to Iain S. Macpherson for this suggestion.

44 Excerpts from both of these are available (in Gaelic only) in Richard Cox (ed.), *Ri Linn nan Linntean: Taghadh de Rosg Gàidhlig* (Ceann Drochaid: Clann Tuirc, 2005).

45 Ronald Black (ed.), *An Tuil: Anthology of 20th Century Scottish Gaelic Verse* (Edinburgh: Birlinn, 1999), pp. 214–19; see also Peter Mackay, 'John Munro – Clach air a' Chàrn', *Zed20*, 23 (Spring 2008), 24–6.

46 Sorley MacLean, 'An Cuilithionn' [Introduction and Part I], *Chapman*, 50–1 (10:1–2) (Summer 1987), 158.

47 See Black (ed.), *An Tuil*, pp. 774, 348–79, and George Campbell Hay, *Collected Poems and Songs of George Campbell Hay*, ed. Michel Byrne, 2 vols. (Edinburgh University Press, 2000), vol. I, pp. 105–77.

48 Coiscéim have published collections in Gaelic by Christopher Whyte, Myles Campbell and Meg Bateman with *en face* Irish translations; they also publish *An Guth* [The Voice], an annual anthology of Irish and Scottish Gaelic poetry (either with translations or glosses across the languages), edited by Rody Gorman, which was been in existence since 2004.

49 See Mìcheal Klevenhaus and Joan NicDhòmhnaill (eds.), *Der Schädel von Damien Hirst / An claigeann aig Damien Hirst* [The Skull of Damien Hirst] (Llandysul: Gomer Press, 2009). This collection of short stories was published in 2008 in Gaelic under the Ùr-Sgeul imprint.

Guide to further reading

Black, Ronald (ed.), *An Lasair: Anthology of 18th Century Scottish Gaelic Verse* (Edinburgh: Birlinn, 2001)

  An Tuil: Anthology of 20th Century Scottish Gaelic Verse (Edinburgh: Birlinn, 1999)

MacLachlan, Christopher (ed.), *Crossing the Highland Line* (Glasgow: Association for Scottish Literary Studies, 2009)

Meek, Donald (ed.), *Caran an t-Saoghal: An Anthology of Nineteenth-Century Gaelic Verse* (Edinburgh: Birlinn, 2003)

Thomson, Derick (ed.), *Alasdair Mac Mhaighstir Alasdair: Selected Poems* (Edinburgh: Scottish Gaelic Texts Society, 1996)

9

DAVID PUNTER

Scottish Gothic

So it was that Janet saw the male figure as it emerged from deep blackness into lesser blackness. The Moon had granted her wish, had brought her happiness. Crazed and joyful she careered down the stairs and flung herself passionately at the dark figure. There was a dreadful cry of outrage and disgust; she heard a voice hiss, 'You filthy wee whore', but she did not feel the knife as it stabbed again and again and again. Only a great langour seemed to draw her downwards, slowly falling as Orpheus cried out for her, falling towards the roar of the waters of Avernus.

Jim wiped his rabbit-skinning knife on his trouser leg. He had come in to turn off the music and the lights and so he turned them off. Then he went into the outer darkness. For a long time the castle was silent.

The wild winds of dawn beat about Auchnasaugh, moaning through the treetops and rattling the windowpanes. At last they retreated northwards, bearing with them Janet's spirit, far north of love or grief, until their withdrawing was no more than the sigh of the sea in a shell.[1]

This is the bleak conclusion to Elspeth Barker's 1991 novel *O Caledonia*, but it can serve also as an oblique introduction to nineteenth-century Scottish Gothic. The shadowy, doom-laden figure; the shades of darkness and blackness; the sudden stab of violence, perhaps especially against women; the blank prosaism of the rabbit-skinning knife and the trouser leg when contrasted with the classical references in the previous sentence; the setting of the castle; the omnipresence of a fearsome and dominating natural world; the specific symbolisms of both 'the north' and 'the sea': all of these are features which we can find in the best-known writers of nineteenth-century Scottish Gothic, and in particular in works by Walter Scott, James Hogg, Margaret Oliphant and Robert Louis Stevenson, which will be my focus of attention in this chapter.

But already we need to mention a problem, namely, whether – or rather, in what sense – there is such an animal as 'Scottish Gothic'. A number of the themes I have mentioned above, it could be argued, could be found in any work of Gothic fiction – Matthew Lewis's monasteries and convents are full of shades and shadows within which lurk mysterious robbers and assassins; Ann Radcliffe's persecuted heroines, although never treated as brutally as

Barker's Janet, pass their lives in towering castles which are the topographical embodiment of villainy and fear. And this is a problem which a number of critics, including, for example, Ian Duncan and Fiona Robertson, have addressed in some detail;[2] here I would only want to say that there are particular inflections in Scottish Gothic – and here I am speaking of 'Gothic' written by Scottish writers rather than of the exoticised Scottish settings beloved of many English writers of Gothic from Radcliffe onwards – which serve to distinguish, if not a genre, then a generic practice which we might fairly regard as typical of, in the Deleuzian sense, a 'minor literature'.[3]

One can also suggest that Scottish Gothic will inevitably be different from – if never separate from – English Gothic because of the central importance of Gothic's dealings with history. It has been said that Gothic is overall a distorted way of dealing with history; this is partly true, but it needs also to be remembered that history, in its official form, is written by the victors; what may appear from the dominant perspective to be distortion will be from another angle, to quote Rory Watson's phrase, 'true history written on the walls'.[4] In fact the resonances of this phrase are seemingly endless: the walls of the castle? of the asylum? of the stairwell, the close? And if the castle, then is the true history written on the outside, where we might expect a daylight world of historical explanation to dominate, or on the inside, where the denizens of a 'subjected' world might be expected to have access to, and to promulgate, if given the opportunity and the voice, a different kind of truth? A kind of truth, perhaps, to which Scott alludes when in the guise of narrator, at a crucial point in his 1819 novel *The Bride of Lammermoor*, he says:

> By many readers this may be deemed overstrained, romantic, and composed by the wild imagination of an author, desirous of gratifying the popular appetite for the horrible; but those who are read in the private family history of Scotland during the period in which the scene is laid, will readily discover, through the disguise of borrowed names and added incidents, the leading particulars of AN OWER TRUE TALE.[5]

'An ower true tale': this telling 'lapse into the vernacular', as a dominant discourse might describe it, tells its own story, a story of how 'other' truths of history strive to make themselves felt through the fabric of the official version. The notion of the 'private family history', again, refers us to the crucial question of what is the 'private' and what the 'public': all of this is set in particular motion in *The Bride of Lammermoor* because the novel itself claims to be – and is, in part – a reworking of older sources, specifically the marriage of Janet Dalrymple (another, earlier Janet) to David Dunbar of Baldoon in 1669. Yet, as many critics have attested, this is not a simple matter of setting a 'true' historical account against one which is fictionalised; rather, Scott's process works in reverse. Throughout the novel we are invited to compare uncertainties: there is no 'original' version, rather it is a question of a matching of different partialities, the production of a palimpsest of interwoven histories, none of which, perhaps, will survive the falling of the wall on which they have been written.

The central concerns of *The Bride of Lammermoor* may be simply described – as can the concerns of much early Gothic – in terms of the relations between an older, feudal order represented by the family and name of Ravenswood and a newer, more modernising tendency held, if rather shakily, in the family of the Ashtons. The attempt to surpass this ancient yet enduring rift is doomed not merely, as we might expect, to failure but also to result in an extremity of violence as Lucy Ashton passes from a state of victimhood to the status of murderer. It needs to be said at this point that the novel has frequently been regarded as an oddity among Scott's works, either positively – in the depth of its passions, in the sureness with which it relates its text to previous, especially Shakespearian, contexts, in its tragic content and trajectory – or negatively – in its curious construction, in its blend of overt symmetry and problematic abruptness, even in its presumed mode of creation. For many years the intriguingly Gothic myth held sway that Scott, who was certainly ill while he wrote it, was in fact in a state of hallucination: James Ballantyne famously claimed that when he (Scott) read the published version, 'he did not recollect one single incident, character, or conversation it contained!',[6] and J. G. Lockhart claimed that most of the novel was dictated to amanuenses while Scott was dazed with pain. More recent criticism tends to discount these accounts as inflated, but it is nonetheless of interest that the novel which may be regarded as Scott's most Gothic seems to require a kind of severance from his overall *oeuvre*, while in fact it would seem that it strikes most directly at the heart of many of his concerns: with the specific Scottish history of the period around the Act of Union of 1707, with the complex role of the Scottish aristocracy, especially as a land-owning class, and with the ever-present possibility of faltering on the winding path towards modernity. Gothic is, above all, not modern (even though it has now become, in a different sense, contemporary): it may seem a wild generalisation, but if we were to search for an antonym to Gothic, it would be not realism but modernity.

Modernity occupies a different discursive and practical space in different realms: we might characterise this difference in terms of 'exporting' cultures and 'importing' ones, cultures which have the neo-imperial power to export their own version and to make it 'take' in subaltern cultures, and ones which receive the modern message and then need to adopt a variety of strategies of adaptation, resistance or indeed destruction.[7] Simple accommodation between the two rules is not possible and, in *The Bride of Lammermoor*, it is Blind Alice – blind, of course, according to the logic of a long classical legacy on the question of the meaning and location of the visionary – who, although she expresses it in a personal way, nevertheless speaks the political 'truth' of Scottish Gothic when she admonishes the Master (a term deployed with some irony throughout the text) of Ravenswood:

> if you are indeed a gentleman and your father's son – you will make it a motive for flying from her presence. Her passion will die like a lamp, for want of that the flame should feed upon; but, if you remain here, her destruction, or yours, or that of both, will be the inevitable consequence of her misplaced attachment. I tell you this secret unwillingly, but it could not have been hid long from your own observation; and it is better you learn it from mine.[8]

The attraction, it would seem, lies in the past, in the possibility of a smooth return to the ancient order; what Alice knows, what her blindness permits her, is the understanding that such a thing is not possible, that the paths of the past have bifurcated. What she also seems to know, or to suggest, is that in some way this knowledge is 'secret', but of course this too is the subject of a certain irony: the enmity between old and new, the problem of how to secure Scotland's own past against invasion – at least cultural if not military, but in Scott the military option is never far away – these matters are far from secret. But there is a gap, and it is this gap which Alice is addressing: what might be seen as brutally obvious on the wider political scene may nevertheless be consciously or unconsciously occulted as 'private' stories of passion, love, attachment are played out on a 'private' stage. But in fact there is no private stage, there is no special shelter from history under which romance may flourish. Many of the characters in *The Bride of Lammermoor* self-consciously take on roles, in what one may presume to be an attempt to break free from conditioning political and cultural circumstance, but these attempts to preserve a realm of separation, of secrecy, are always doomed to failure. In any case, the relation between Gothic and secrecy is a complex one. Certainly one aspect of the Gothic is to do with secrets – the monastery, the dungeon, the labyrinth – but another is to do with ostentatious display, with grandeur, with a reconstruction of the past in order to impress its magnificence on the present. In the Scottish context, perhaps this is seen to best advantage not directly in literature but in architecture.

Scott, of course, is famous for what is sometimes termed a 'revival' of the baronial style at Abbotsford; but in truth the 'Scottish baronial' is a far more deeply embedded phenomenon which has frequently been referred to as the 'national architectural style', and which endured from the early nineteenth to the early twentieth centuries. The crucial features are no doubt familiar, from prominent buildings as various as Balmoral and Tynninghame to less dramatic landmarks such as Greenock Sheriff Court and what is now the Scandic Hotel on Edinburgh's Royal Mile. Castellations, turrets, uneven roof lines and stepped gables, lancet windows – all of these were supposedly derived from the long tradition of medieval fortified manor houses and farms, many of which survive in one form or another to this day across the Scottish countryside, but were in fact the mark of a curious and multiple hybridity, owing something indeed to this vernacular Scottish source but something also to the traditional English medieval castle, and something too, albeit occluded, to a wider European architectural tradition. One could therefore refer to Scottish baronial as a 'minor architecture', not of course in the sense that its most significant works were minor – anything but – but in so far as the attempt to create a 'pure' style inevitably became enmeshed in an ongoing negotiation between the 'native' and the 'imperial'. Nevertheless, such buildings played a powerful part in 're-minding' Scotland of its past, even as it was, inevitably, remaking that past, involved in the constant process, at the cultural level, of turning past defeats into former glories, subjugations into victories, internal divisions into the substance of enduring national solidarity, a process still at work with the utmost visibility in such a recent film as *Braveheart* (1995).

Nevertheless, the memory of past humiliation cannot in the end be avoided, at the historical or the psychological level. James Hogg's apparently endlessly echoic novel *The Private Memoirs and Confessions of a Justified Sinner* (1824) is most frequently regarded as Gothic because it emblematically deals with the topic of the double, and it is of course true that the double is one of the most frequent topics of the Gothic, and has been frequently construed according to the classic formulation of Freud, which is (as we might expect) double: namely that the double reminds us of the possibility of enduring life, in so far as we can, as it were, place our subjectivity outside ourselves and be assured that we will survive death and destruction, while at the same time reminding us of death itself in so far as our double always threatens to replace us and to render our self unnecessary to the future proceedings of the world.[9] The *Confessions*, of course, provide material for this reading par excellence: is Gil-Martin, the demon who apparently haunts the protagonist, Robert Wringhim, an objective entity with supernatural powers, or the product of Wringhim's own internal convulsions, caused by a rigidly Calvinist upbringing perhaps coupled with envy of an accomplished and socially confident brother? Famously, the text declines fully to resolve this question, partly through a series of dubious paratextual manoeuvres not dissimilar to those Scott invokes to preclude himself from responsibility for the narrative of *The Bride of Lammermoor*. But it is possible also to look at the *Confessions* in other ways: particularly in terms of the relation between public and private accounts which, I am suggesting, is at the heart of Scottish Gothic, and in terms of the ways in which past humiliation at the hands of a dominating force – and perhaps especially one which is perceived as somehow *effortlessly* dominating – can be handled and what residues it might leave within the individual and/or cultural psyche.

The *Confessions* is a book about humiliation. We might consider the tennis scene, which concerns Robert's brother George, whom Robert has identified as a reprobate, and which is told, like many other events in the text, twice, once from the perspective of the *soi-disant* editor, and a second (doubled) time from the perspective of Robert. In the first account, we hear that

> George, in flying backward to gain the point at which the ball was going to light, came inadvertently so rudely in contact with this obstreperous interloper [Robert], that he not only overthrew him, but also got a grievous fall over his legs; and, as he arose, the other made a spurn at him with his foot, which, if it had hit its aim, would undoubtedly have finished the course of the young laird of Dalcastle and Balgrennan. George, being irritated beyond measure ... struck the assailant with his racket, rather slightly, but so that his mouth and nose gushed out blood.[10]

Robert then proceeds, according to this version, to run around the court, 'impeding every one who attempted to make at the ball' (24), while gushing blood from every orifice (including, strangely, his toes). Robert's own version is, as we may imagine, rather different. Fired with righteous indignation at the 'sin' represented by the game of tennis (being played, interestingly, by 'a number of young noblemen and gentlemen'), says he,

> Yes, I went boldly up and struck him with my foot, and meant to have given him a more severe blow than it was my fortune to inflict. It had, however, the effect of rousing up his corrupt nature to quarrelling and strife, instead of taking the chastisement of the Lord in humility and meekness. He ran furiously against me in the choler that is always inspired by the wicked one; but I overthrew him, by reason of impeding the natural and rapid progress of his unholy feet, running to destruction. (148–9)

The passage continues; but the principal point is that these different versions of a 'minor' incident also constitute (re)writings of history and the attempt to expunge the story of a humiliation; or, even more, to replace it by an alternative version. One way in which this 'replacement' of history is managed is through the replacement of one language by another; in this case a language which purports to deliver an objective account of events by one which seeks intrinsically to explain the course of action through a version of Calvinist biblical exegesis, within which the possibilities of free will are subsumed under the heading of fate or, perhaps better, at least in this context, a certain fatalism.

The writings of Scott and Hogg, and the omnipresence of the Scottish baronial style, all contribute to what we might be now beginning to adumbrate as 'Scottish Gothic': what is central is history, usually political but sometimes psychological. The crucial question behind these rewritings and revisions is whether it is possible to assert a historical field which is in some sense free from the traces of conquest and assimilation. Yet to say this is to portray the Scotland of the earlier part of the nineteenth century as beleaguered (I return below to the notion of the 'beleaguered' in the context of Oliphant), whereas, of course, this was not at all the case; or rather, even to seek the notion of a 'whole Scotland' in this way is to travesty its internal differences, the complexity of a nation where the extreme distinctions between rural and urban life, shadowing and sometimes matching precisely the differences between feudal trace and modern trajectory, are written starkly. And within this nexus, Edinburgh was of course one of the great literary cities of the British Isles, and among its most powerful organs was *Blackwood's Magazine*.

Blackwood's was founded in 1817 (originally as the *Edinburgh Monthly Magazine*) and was designed to promote a 'new Tory-ism', as opposed to the domination of the Whig-supporting *Edinburgh Review* and the old-fashioned stuffiness of the *Quarterly Review*. There are many things to be said about *Blackwood's* and its cultural role throughout the nineteenth century, but for our purposes here the main point is that, alongside poetry, political and cultural commentary and polemic, it also published a considerable number of Gothic stories; it was an influence on Dickens and the Brontë sisters, and perhaps more importantly, from a Gothic point of view, Poe took the journal's obsession seriously enough to refer to it in such tales as 'Loss of Breath' (1835), subtitled 'A Tale neither in nor out of "Blackwood"'. This raises interesting questions. It is true that, in any kind of final analysis, Gothic has often been seen as a conservative form. It raises ghosts and terrors, but either it allays our fears of their presence through what has been referred to as the 'explained supernatural', or it refers them to a spiritual realm (the 'unexplained supernatural'). Although it has been argued – rightly – that the European Gothic endured its birth pangs during the upheaval of the French Revolution, it has never been suggested that Gothic might figure as a revolutionary cultural agent in its own right, but rather as a complex refractor of social and cultural anxieties.

It would perhaps be going too far to suggest that the Gothic – or horror – strand in *Blackwood's*, prominent though it was, can be aligned with a political programme, but the possibility remains. For if the Gothic sets out to shock an otherwise complacent middle class, then arguably this is what *Blackwood's*, relying as it did on a spiky, controversial, even choleric 'persona', set out to do too. Here, then, and in a specifically Scottish context, one might see horror as not merely a plaything, a realm conveniently outside the mainstream of fictional representations, but as one element in a carefully constructed repertoire of affront. But it is also true that very rarely are *Blackwood's* Gothic stories set in Scotland; rather, they follow the dominant English practice of locating superstition and terror in southern Europe. In a collection of *Blackwood's* ghost tales published in 1969 (by, naturally, the Blackwood publishing house in Edinburgh),[11] none of the thirteen tales has a clearly Scottish environment, preferring settings ranging from Brittany and Malta through the Caribbean to New Zealand (an inverse Scotland, as has sometimes been claimed) with one exception, which is not in fact a story at all but rather a discursive essay by Andrew Lang, called 'Ghosts before the Law' (1894), which revisits Scott's 1831 extraordinary essay of the same name. The reader might reasonably suspect that Lang – here at least – lacks Scott's wit and is thus drawn into a set of ludicrous attempts to discriminate between which testimonies of a ghost might be admissible in a court of law and which not, but the most interesting moment occurs when, discussing a much earlier case of 1754 concerning the murder of one Sergeant Arthur Davis by Duncan Terig or Clerk and Alexander Bane Macdonald in Glenconie and the subsequent reappearance of the sergeant's ghost, we hear the judge enquiring of the chief witness what language the ghost used when addressing him:

> [H]e answered: 'As good Gaelic as he had ever heard in Lochaber'. 'Pretty well', said [the accuseds'] counsel ... 'for the ghost of an English sergeant'. The repartee was probably conclusive with the jury, for they acquitted the prisoners, in the face of the other incriminating evidence.[12]

A clearer example of nationalist sentiment could hardly be required; but Lang feels impelled to point out that the jury's opinion was 'illogical', since 'modern students of ghosts, of course, would not have been staggered by the ghost's command of Gaelic; they would explain it as a convenient hallucinatory impression, made by the ghost on the mind of the "percipient"'.[13] Without going into detail about the complexity of this account, or about the cultural rivalry at stake, it is certainly worth pointing out that Lang is, here at any rate, assuming, with whatever degree of irony, a type of 'reality' for the ghost, and it is these sorts of assumptions, albeit in a 'removed', exoticised context, that many *Blackwood's* stories make.

One of the major authors whose work *Blackwood's* published in the late nineteenth century was Margaret Oliphant. Among her most significant works is a short novel called *A Beleaguered City* (1900), which essentially concerns the return of the dead in a small walled city in France – although some commentators have called attention to the issue of why it is set there rather than in Scotland, generally concluding that it was a practical matter, for the story relies on the separation occasioned by total fortification, and such sites are difficult to find in Britain. The return of these dead has the effect of pushing the living inhabitants out, for a time, from their own city. It would surely not to be difficult to find here a further metaphor for questions of location, domination, supremacy, subjugation. 'You love these dead tyrants', says one character to another, 'Yes … you love them best. You will go to – the majority, to the strongest. Do not speak to me! Because your God is on their side, you will forsake us too.'[14] Who, however, are the dead tyrants? Are they, perhaps, ghosts of a previous order within Scotland which cannot be laid to rest, or are they instead ghosts of those who have exercised, and perhaps still continue to exercise, domination over the land?

> Why should it be a matter of wonder that the dead should come back? the wonder is that they do not. Ah! that is the wonder. How can one go away who loves you, and never return, nor speak, nor send any message – that is the miracle: not that the heavens should bend down and the gates of Paradise roll back, and those who have left us return.

It would be fair to say that *A Beleaguered City* is a tale of mourning and melancholia: to put it in perhaps more familiar Scottish terms, it is a lamentation for all the glory that has been and simultaneously a reminder that the past is never far away. 'It is a longing all your life after – it is a looking – for what never comes.'[15] This line is not from *A Beleaguered City*, but from 'The Library Window', a story Oliphant published in *Blackwood's* in 1896 which concerns a number of Gothic themes: a beckoning ghost, the sapping of life from the living, perhaps even a double, although the question of the double, as I hope to show below in relation to Stevenson's *Dr Jekyll and Mr Hyde*, may not be as simple as it appears even in Freud's account, and might be better referred to here under the heading of a term well known to Scottish Gothic, the 'second sight'.

The tale is set in a thinly disguised St Andrews; it may well refer to a famous anecdote about Scott, derived from Lockhart. At all events, it deals in a revenant, something which comes back from the past, and in the shallowness, even fickleness, of contemporary life when it falls under the influence of a past which has been untamed and even, perhaps, uninterpreted. Yet again, we may take this, as in so much Gothic, at a social or psychological level; or, better, to be constructing and inhabiting a realm in which the social and the psychological are inextricable. What the heroine appears to experience is a longing to be reunited with the revenant, the spectre; yet she is also sporadically aware that such a reunion would be simultaneously a draining, an obliteration, that all prospect of a trajectory towards full adulthood, towards what Jung refers to as 'individualisation', would be prohibited by the tug back to the dreamless past which the figure – whatever its status in 'reality' – represents. 'The Library Window', then, represents a pull back from the present, a wish to be reunited, a derogation from modernity – it is, obviously, crucial that the window be in a library, conceived as the repository of the past, as the summation of previous knowledge which is nevertheless in some sense sequestered away from the present, so that its heritage can survive untarnished even though the very function of the window in the story is to render the reader increasingly uncertain as to what can and cannot be seen – within the notional 'library', but also between the inside and the outside, between the public and the private account, within the very 'walls' which serve to protect consciousness while at the same time preventing a potentially damaging understanding of the outside world, a world filled with a dominating, 'foreign' power against which there is no strength to stand.

In 1896, Robert Louis Stevenson had been dead for two years, although *The Strange Case of Dr Jekyll and Mr Hyde* would, as it happens, be reprinted that same year; it had originally been published in 1886, and in many ways it is the novel most closely associated with the Scottish Gothic of the late nineteenth century. Here again, however, definitional problems assail us. In what sense might we consider *Jekyll and Hyde* to be 'Scottish Gothic'? Stevenson, it is true, was Scottish; but *Jekyll and Hyde* has most usually been considered and contextualised within a range of *fin-de-siècle* British fictions, including, for example, Bram Stoker's *Dracula* (1897) and Oscar Wilde's *The Picture of Dorian Gray* (1891). Furthermore, it is set in London and has, apparently, little contentual bearing on Scotland. Finally, it has most normally been interpreted in terms of the double, and while, as we have seen with the *Confessions of a Justified Sinner*, the double is an all too present figuration in Scottish fiction, it is in no sense unique thereto. However, many of the classic assumptions about the double hinge, in the end, on an untenable assumption: namely, an assumption of symmetry. The double, it is supposed, is *exactly* like oneself; this is the very function, after all, of the mirror image. Yet this is not the story which the literature of the double tells. One of the cardinal examples is Joseph Conrad's *The Secret Sharer* (1912) (Conrad's *Heart of Darkness* (1899), of course, was first published in *Blackwood's*), and here we read that the strange arrival on the youthful captain's ship

> was not a bit like me, really; yet, as we stood leaning over my bed-place, whispering side by side, with our dark heads together and our backs to the door, anybody bold enough to open it stealthily would have been treated to the uncanny sight of a double captain busy talking in whispers with his other self.[16]

Jekyll and Hyde are, as is obvious from the whole drift of the text, as little alike as it might be possible to be – emotionally, behaviourally and physically. They are not in any sense doubles, even though it might be possible that Hyde is, in essence, a split-off part of Jekyll. Jekyll, until the denouement, remains dominant at all times: it is he who has control over the medical potion which grants Hyde life, it is he who has indeed invented the entire process whereby Hyde can have his temporary being. Above all, although it may seem a very simple point, Hyde is smaller than Jekyll:

> My Hyde was pale and dwarfish, he gave an impression of deformity without any nameable malformation, he had a displeasing smile, he had borne himself to the lawyer with a sort of murderous mixture of timidity and boldness, and he spoke with a husky, whispering, and somewhat broken voice.[17]

I suggest that what we have here is a fantasised English view of an equally fantasised Scot. Dwarfishness has been so frequently attributed to the Scottish and the Welsh that it is a standard feature of satire. The 'displeasing smile' is more interesting and can be referred back to Homi Bhabha's fascinating account of the relations between the imperialists and the 'natives' in British India, where he coins the concept of 'sly civility',[18] and this would also be relevant to the next phrase, for why, after all, should a mixture of timidity and boldness be termed 'murderous' unless there is a fear here of the possibility of violent insurrection? And the question of Hyde's voice can suitably take us back to where we started with Scott's 'ower true tale': whoever or whatever Hyde is, he does not speak, as do Jekyll and the character called Utterson (the clue is in the name) the 'Queen's English'.

Even more, we may fairly see Hyde as the barbarian (and for a further commentary on the relation between the 'barbarian' and Scottish culture, the best source is Iain Banks's *The Bridge* (1986)). If London is the site of metropolitan stability and courtesy, Hyde comes from elsewhere – from the margin, perhaps, into the centre – to remind the world of authority (represented most fully by Sir Danvers Carew, referred to in an odd and revealing phrase as an 'aged and beautiful gentleman'[19]) that there is a realm away from the capital where civilisation's writ does not entirely run and from which there may always be further incursions into territories regarded as entirely protected by their cultural and political power. Of course this is not the full story of Hyde: but it is the story of an asymmetry, of a relationship which is predicated on a situation in which one entity has life only by permission of the other and where he grows eventually tired of this dependence. It may be that *Jekyll and Hyde* furnishes an account of a kind of revolution in the psyche whereby material which has appeared firmly repressed – Jekyll, after all, is the epitome of civilisation but at the same the very embodiment, as he himself says, of hypocrisy – breaks out and assails boundaries which have hitherto held to be unbreachable (like the walls of the castle); but it may also be that within the story there is a refracted, partly transmuted account of what might result from an asymmetric exercise of power and what terrible transfigurations might occur if the operations of cultural repression and national stereotyping which are always concomitant with imperial or colonial domination were eventually, if also in the end impotently, to be challenged.

In conclusion, it is worth reiterating that Scottish Gothic, naturally, takes many forms, but it also suggests an underlying question. The question can be put most simply by asking which of the two terms, 'Scottish' or 'Gothic', is the dominant one? Is Scottish Gothic a subgenre within Gothic writing; or is it a mode of Scottish literature? The answer, of course, is that it is necessarily both; yet this answer will never be clear unless it also takes into account issues of power, and it is these issues of power – whether considered directly within a set of national contexts or in the displaced forms so frequently displayed in Gothic – which constantly recur within the field. The relations between England and Scotland are ones of continuing historical asymmetry; and it is this asymmetry which Scottish Gothic so often portrays, deploying as it does so a range of motifs – apparently often to do with the supernatural but also readable in terms of a political arena – which gain a new and different vitality from their attachment to an ongoing cultural situation which is made afresh with each new attempt to depict a different, and differentiated, perspective on Scottish history.

Notes

1 Elspeth Barker, *O Caledonia* (London: Hamish Hamilton, 1991), pp. 151–2.
2 See Ian Duncan, 'Walter Scott, James Hogg and Scottish Gothic', in David Punter (ed.), *A Companion to the Gothic* (Oxford: Blackwell, 2000), pp. 70–80; Fiona Robertson, *Legitimate Histories: Scott, Gothic and the Authorities of Fiction* (Oxford: Clarendon Press, 1994).

3 See Gilles Deleuze and Félix Guattari, *Kafka: Toward a Minor Literature*, trans. Dana Polan (Minneapolis: University of Minnesota Press, 1986).

4 See Rory Watson, *True History on the Walls* (Loanhead: M. Macdonald, 1976).

5 Sir Walter Scott, *The Bride of Lammermoor*, ed. Fiona Robertson (Oxford University Press, 1991), p. 340.

6 See J. G. Lockhart, *Memoirs of the Life of Sir Walter Scott*, 2nd edn, 10 vols. (Edinburgh: Robert Caddell, 1839), vol. VI, p. 89.

7 See David Punter, *Modernity* (London: Palgrave Macmillan, 2007).

8 Scott, *Bride of Lammermoor*, p. 203.

9 See Sigmund Freud, 'The "Uncanny"' (1919), in James Strachey *et al.* (eds.), *The Standard Edition of the Complete Psychological Works of Sigmund Freud*, 24 vols. (London: Penguin, 1953–74), vol. XVII, pp. 234–7.

10 James Hogg, *The Private Memoirs and Confessions of a Justified Sinner*, ed. John Carey (Oxford University Press, 1981), p. 23; further references will appear in the text.

11 *Ghost Tales from 'Blackwood'* (Edinburgh: William Blackwood, 1969).

12 Andrew Lang, 'Ghosts before the Law', *ibid.*, p. 70.

13 *Ibid.*

14 This, like later references, comes from the unpaginated version of Oliphant, *A Beleaguered City*, at www.gutenberg.org/files/11521/11521-8.txt.

15 This comes from the unpaginated version of Oliphant, 'The Library Window', at www.gaslight.mtroyal.ca/libraryw.htm.

16 Joseph Conrad, 'The Secret Sharer', in *'Typhoon' and Other Tales*, ed. Cedric Watts (Oxford University Press, 1986), p. 257.

17 Robert Louis Stevenson, *The Strange Case of Dr Jekyll and Mr Hyde*, ed. Katherine Linehan (New York: W. W. Norton, 2003), p. 17.

18 See Homi Bhabha, 'Sly Civility' (1985), in *The Location of Culture* (London: Routledge, 1994), pp. 93–101.

19 Stevenson, *Strange Case*, p. 21.

Guide to further reading

Duncan, Ian, 'Walter Scott, James Hogg and Scottish Gothic', in David Punter (ed.), *A Companion to the Gothic* (Oxford: Blackwell, 2000), pp. 70–80

Gardiner, Michael and Graeme Macdonald (eds.), *Scottish Literature and Postcolonial Literature: Comparative Texts and Critical Perspectives* (Edinburgh University Press, 2011)

Germana, Monica, 'Contemporary Scottish Gothic', special issue of *Gothic Studies* (special 'Scottish' issue), Vol.13 No.2 (2011).

Punter, David, 'Scottish and Irish Gothic', in Jerrold E. Hogle (ed.), *The Cambridge Companion to Gothic Fiction* (Cambridge University Press, 2002), pp. 105–23

Robertson, Fiona, *Legitimate Histories: Scott, Gothic and the Authorities of Fiction* (Oxford: Clarendon Press, 1994)

10

ANDREW NASH

Victorian Scottish Literature

The Victorian period in Scottish literature has long been viewed with embarrassment if not disdain. 'The less said about the two generations after Scott the better', remarked Kurt Wittig in 1955.[1] David Craig, writing in 1961, agreed: 'from 1825 to 1880 there is next to nothing worth attention'.[2] Scottish Victorianism was backward-looking and parochial. The spirit of Burns, shorn of all its radicalism, hung over popular poetry anthologies such as *Whistle-Binkie*, first published in the 1830s and reissued with new material throughout the century. In fiction, the dominant traditions were historical romance, typified by Robert Louis Stevenson, and nostalgic rural idylls epitomised by the so-called Kailyard fiction of J. M. Barrie and Ian Maclaren. The overwhelming image was of a rural, provincial culture, escaping into a pre-industrial past. In an influential book of 1951, the novelist George Blake complained that the 'representative writers during the nineteenth century had hardly a single word to say about the revolution that was so dramatically overtaking' them.[3] Instead, the printing presses across the nation were flooded with books of reminiscences, typified by E. B. Ramsay's *Reminiscences of Scottish Life and Character* (1857), which celebrated and lamented what Archibald Geikie termed 'the gradual decline of national peculiarities'.[4] The ascent of Victoria, it seemed, signalled the descent of Scottish culture.

This interpretation did not die easily. As late as 1988 a history of nineteenth-century Scottish literature opened with an essay which identified the late 1830s as 'one of the most obvious and drastic turning points in the literary history of Scotland' in which there was 'a loss of cohesion and self-confidence, a decline which lasted about 50 years'.[5] If the death of Walter Scott in 1832 signalled the end of an era of sustained cultural achievement, the departure of Thomas Carlyle for London in 1834 pointed to the death of the environment which had supported it. To Tom Nairn, 'intellectual emigration' in the nineteenth century emptied the country of its literary talent and left only a 'rootless vacuum ... a great "absence"'.[6] Recent scholarship, however, has proved this conclusion to be drastically oversimplified. Research into the popular press has revealed a flourishing urban tradition of vernacular prose fiction.[7] The vital role of Scots such as Andrew Lang and J. G. Frazer in the revival of mythology and social anthropology has also been uncovered, while research into the activities of Patrick Geddes, who in 1895 wrote of a 'Scots Renascence', has sharpened our awareness of the Scottish dimension of the Celtic Twilight. As T. M. Devine argues, the record of achievement 'hardly suggests that Scottish culture was in crisis'.[8] With new literary histories and a comprehensive history of the book, fuller contexts have been established for understanding the period.[9] This chapter will trace some of the ways that Scottish writers responded to major cultural and intellectual issues, such as the crisis of faith and the impact of materialism and mechanisation, arguing that a distinctive quality of Scottish Victorianism is its preoccupation with the imaginative apprehension of reality.

If Scottish novelists can be accused of failing to respond directly to the major social issues of the day, it is all the more significant that non-fictional prose writers developed some of the most penetrating of Victorian ideas. Samuel Smiles's doctrine of 'self-help', espoused in his best-selling work of 1859, has its roots in the democratic principles of the author's Scottish education. One of the defining ideals of mid-Victorian society, underpinning works such as Dickens's *Great Expectations* (1861), Smiles's doctrine is illustrated in the career of the self-taught stonemason Hugh Miller, whose autobiography, *My Schools and Schoolmasters* (1854), was written with the aim of 'rousing the humbler classes to the important work of self-culture and self-government'.[10] Miller's writings on geology and evolution exemplify the tension between science and religion in the period. His outspoken involvement in religious debates led to him becoming editor of the influential newspaper *The Witness*, where portions of his first scientific work, *The Old Red Sandstone* (1841), appeared. Though at the forefront of geological investigation, Miller never lost his faith, and his *In the Footprints of the Creator* (1849) was an attempt to reconcile evolutionary science with Genesis.

Miller described his autobiography as 'a sort of educational treatise, thrown into the narrative form'. Passages, such as the account of a description of Leith – 'a cold, dingy, ragged town, but so strongly relieved against the pale smoky grey of the background, that it seemed another little city of Zoar, entire in front of the burning' – are as significant for their style as much as their content.[11] The novelistic qualities of Miller's writing prompt us to consider why certain writers were reluctant to embrace fictional forms. The central figure here is Thomas Carlyle. In his essay 'Biography' (1832), Carlyle observed that fiction 'partakes, more than we suspect, of the nature of lying'.[12] This concern, which owes much to the influence of Calvinism on Scottish life and literature, is a feature of the Scottish novel from James Hogg through J. M. Barrie to modern writers such as Muriel Spark and John Burnside. Carlyle's early attempts at fiction were unsuccessful and he quickly abandoned the form. Nevertheless, his one full-length work of fiction, *Sartor Resartus* (1833–4), articulates the central tenets of his philosophy. Eccentric and experimental, its style owes much to eighteenth-century writers, especially Sterne and Swift. The ironic narrative form places it securely in a Scottish tradition, however. An 'Editor' presents and critically examines a work by a German writer, Diogenes Teufelsdrockh, on the 'Philosophy of Clothes'. As in Hogg's *Confessions of a Justified Sinner* (1824), the fictional editor's attempts to understand the book he presents are part of the fabric of the text, suggesting that *Sartor Resartus* is in some measure about the experience of reading and interpretation.

Though he spent more than half his life in London, Carlyle's temperament and intellect were conditioned by his Scottish upbringing. Rebelling against the discipline and piety of his Calvinist boyhood, his strongly religious sense of life found its sustenance in German Romantic literature, which offered him a faith in a transcendent spiritual order that was needed to replace the discredited forms of Christianity. Carlyle's faith in this order was nevertheless combined with 'an emphatic insistence that it was only through its reflections in this world that it could be discerned, and only by activity in this world – by practical work – that its demands could be met'.[13] This compulsion to see the world in two dimensions can be seen as a defining characteristic of Scottish Victorianism. In *Sartor Resartus* it is articulated through the use of clothes – a 'Visible' manifestation of the 'Invisible' – as a metaphor for human structures. Like clothes, human structures can, and must, be refashioned over time. Teufelsdrockh observes how, throughout history, Man has been haunted by spectral structures:

> [O]ne age, he is hagridden, bewitched; the next priestridden, befooled; in all ages bedevilled. And now the Genius of Mechanism smothers him worse than any nightmare did, till the Soul is nigh choked out of him, and only a kind of Digestive Mechanic life remains.[14]

The task was to fashion new structures to challenge the smothering power of mechanism. Teufelsdrockh calls on the 'Poet and inspired Maker; who, Prometheus-like, can shape new symbols' (170).

The idea of symbols is developed through Carlyle's concept of 'Natural Supernaturalism'. Symbols are the visible, or natural, manifestation of the invisible, or supernatural. Teufelsdrockh asserts: 'In the symbol proper … there is some embodyment or revelation of the Infinite; the Infinite is made to blend itself with the Finite, to stand visible, and, as it were attainable, there' (166). Works of Art can be symbols but for Teufelsdrockh, and Carlyle, the noblest and most 'divine' form of Art is not fiction or poetry but 'the Lives of heroic, god-inspired Men'. It is such men who must fashion the new symbols and the new human structures of the world. Here lies the germ of Carlyle's ideas on heroism, and work and duty. As Teufelsdrockh moves from 'The Everlasting No' to 'The Everlasting Yea', he advocates the importance of duty and self-knowledge:

> The Situation that has not its Duty; its Ideal, was never yet occupied by man … Fool! the ideal is in thyself, the Impediment too is in thyself: thy Condition is but the stuff thy art to shape that same ideal out of. (149)

Shaping new ideals for an age in crisis was Carlyle's life work.

Carlyle's faith in the primacy of the unconscious – the central theme of the essay 'Characteristics' (1831) – and his emphasis on symbols link him with George MacDonald, another Scottish writer who rejected the Calvinism of his youth and embraced German Romanticism. MacDonald would have agreed with Teufelsdrockh's claim that 'Fantasy' was 'the organ of the God-like' (165). It is in his contributions to the literature of fantasy, notably *Phantastes* (1858) and *Lilith* (1895), along with his fairy stories and children's books that MacDonald is best known, but he also wrote 'realist' novels, chiefly set in Scotland, which are valuable not least for the energetic use of the north-east vernacular. Among the best are *Alec Forbes of Howglen* (1865) and *Robert Falconer* (1868). Both take the hero from boyhood through university to manhood. Whereas Alec's experiences are those of fall and rebirth, Robert becomes a Christ figure, ministering to the poor and destitute of London in scenes that are as uncompromising as anything in Dickens. Though marred by intrusive preaching, this realist fable reveals much that is distinctive about the author's Scottish Victorianism.

MacDonald's eccentric theological views prevented him from succeeding in the church and so literature became his pulpit. The attack on narrowly dogmatic forms of Christianity finds its expression in *Robert Falconer* in the hero's questioning and gradual rejection of Calvinist doctrine. In one boyhood scene, he announces his plan for emptying Hell of sinners. In an outspoken rejection of his grandmother's Calvinism, he imagines himself rising in Heaven and announcing to the brethren:

> We're a' here by grace and no by merit [and] I call upo' ilk ane o' ye 'at has a frien' or a neeber down yonner, to rise up an' taste nor bite nor sup mair till we gang up a'thegither to the fut o' the throne, and pray the Lord to lat's gang and du as the Maister did afore's, and beir their griefs.[15]

Linked to this is the treatment of music in the novel. The Calvinist suspicion of the workings of the imagination, which led Carlyle to reject fiction altogether, had the opposite effect on MacDonald. For him, the freeplay of the imagination was essential for the apprehension of God. In 'The Fantastic Imagination', he writes: 'man may, if he pleases, invent a little world of his own, with its own laws; for there is that in him which delights in calling up new forms – which is the nearest, perhaps, he can come to creation'.[16] To Robert Falconer's grandmother, such attempts to usurp the creative energy of God would be blasphemous, and this is dramatised when the old lady burns the boy's violin, which functions as a symbol of the boy's imaginative freedom as well as his only link with his lost father. The instrument contains 'a story in its hollow breast', and Robert's creative and spiritual energies are nurtured by his nocturnal trips to a disused thread-factory – symbolic of the sterility of the mechanical world – where he unlocks the mysteries of music.

Throughout MacDonald's work, books and music are the means of accessing a different realm of existence. In *Lilith*, an enigmatic, deeply symbolic work where the different dimensions of the dream world are figured through recurring images of doors, mirrors and thresholds, the movement into fantasy takes place in a library. Thresholds have a symbolic function in *Robert Falconer* as well. A mysterious locked door leads to a neighbouring house where Robert discovers the angelic Mary St John (MacDonald's heroines are generally variations on a theme). The sexual implications seem obvious, except that Robert is an asexual symbol of religious purity. The entrance to the room is an opening onto 'infinite beauty' (160). Shortly after Robert discovers this 'Gate of Paradise', the entrance is walled up but the symbol returns in the second volume when another mysterious door leads him to discover the unknown magnificence of a church organ.

It is not incidental that the childhood scenes in MacDonald's novels are often the most striking. 'Children *will* see things as God sees them' (373), observes Robert. In *David Elginbrod* (1863), MacDonald asserts: '[t]here is a childhood into which we have to grow, just as there is a childhood which we must leave behind'.[17] This Wordsworthian faith in childhood as the root of divinity and morality explains MacDonald's comment that his fairy stories were written not for the child but for the 'childlike'. The *Bildungsroman* was the natural mode for him to articulate his belief in the necessity of moral and religious growth. The fantasy works are underpinned by the same idea. *Phantastes* could be read as a fantasy *Bildungsroman*, charting the growth to maturity and responsibility of a young man who inherits his father's estate. It is a 'Faerie Romance for men and women', as the subtitle has it, because Anodos becomes an adult through his experiences in fairy land. On his return he vows to 'translate the experience of my travels there into common life'.[18]

At twenty-one, Anodos is the same age as the eponymous heroine of *Adela Cathcart* (1864), an early work which fuses the realist and fantastic modes in a way that accentuates MacDonald's emphasis on the importance of stories and the imagination for fully embracing the real world. Bedridden, Adela is told stories in an effort to lift her from her ennui and return her to reality. One of these, 'The Light Princess', is explicitly concerned with the movement from 'lightness' – the princess in the story has no gravity – to maturity, in physical, spiritual and sexual senses. The princess's gravity is restored by the willing sacrifice of a prince with whom she shares nocturnal swimming adventures. As in most of his fairy tales, MacDonald's symbolism in this story seems to invite psychosexual readings and his expressive freedom in this area sets him apart from his Victorian contemporaries. John Ruskin questioned the morality of the swimming scenes, which led MacDonald mischievously to incorporate his prudish criticisms in the published text.

Like Carlyle, MacDonald's writing can be seen as a response to materialism and mechanisation. Born in Huntly, in rural Aberdeenshire, his time spent time living in Aberdeen and Manchester engendered the dual city/country perspective that characterises much of his work. In *Sir Gibbie* (1879), the Christ-child hero is a dumb, motherless waif who patrols the streets and grubs in the gutters of Aberdeen. As in S. R. Crockett's variation on the gamin genre, *Cleg Kelly* (1896), the action shifts from the city to the country, and Gibbie, like Dickens's Oliver Twist, turns out to be a landed gentleman. MacDonald's response to urban industrialism is more immediate in 'A Manchester Poem', one of his few significant efforts in verse:

> Slave engines utter again their ugly growl,
> And soon the iron bands and blocks of stone
> That prison them to their task, will strain and quiver
> Until the city tremble.[19]

That such lines could be penned by an author of fairy stories and fantasies is symptomatic of how Scottish writers addressed contemporary urban life more directly in poetry than they did in fiction. Although vernacular Scots poetry was dominated by weak imitations of Burns, some voices stand out for their sharp-eyed attention to the contemporary world. In 'Oor Location', the anti-temperance poet Janet Hamilton conceived the industrial town as the harbinger of a demon form – alcohol – that hung 'Like a millstone roun' the neck / O' the strugglin', toilin' masses.' Forthright and didactic, Hamilton's poem uses Scots to considerable aural effect: 'A hunner funnels bleezin', reekin', / Coal an' ironstane charrin', smeekin'.'[20] In sharp contrast,

Alexander Smith's 'Glasgow' (1871) finds a 'sacredness of love and death' in the 'noise and smoky breath' of the city. Smith's imagery – 'A sunbeam like an angel's sword / Shivers upon a spire' – has an incongruously positive embrace of death and fear: 'O wondrous sight! O stream of dread! / O long, dark river of the dead!'[21]

The most significant poets of urban life, however, are James Thomson and John Davidson, whose work anticipates developments in twentieth-century poetry. Thomson's long poem *The City of Dreadful Night* (1874) owes much to Dante and was a source for T. S. Eliot's *The Waste Land*. An insomniac speaker wanders through a nameless city whose inhabitants are trapped in a world of 'dead faith, dead love, dead hope'.[22] Possessing 'a soul too outworn for wondering', the speaker follows strangers to different parts of the city and hears 'bodiless voices in my waking dream'. Those who dwell in this nocturnal city are in 'Limbo' (42), attracted to Hell – 'That positive eternity of pain, / Instead of this insufferable inane' (40) – but unable to escape the phantasmagorical nightmare. Thomson's poem of despair captures the birth of the modern sensibility in its emphatic rejection of the Victorian quest to confirm an anthropocentric universe:

> Man might know one thing were his sight less dim;
> That it [the world] whirls not to suit his pretty whim,
> That it is quite indifferent to him. (45)

Christian images of salvation prove illusory. In section XIV, the speaker follows others into a cathedral, where a voice from a pulpit speaks to those 'battling in black floods without an ark!'. The only 'tidings of great joy', however, is the realisation that 'There is no God; no Fiend with names divine / Made us and tortures us ... This little Life is all we must endure' (56).

Thomson's pessimism and longing for oblivion was shared by Davidson, whose increasingly nihilistic outlook drove him to suicide. Brought up in the town of Greenock, the images of Davidson's youth were industrial. In 'A Ballad in Blank Verse of the Making of a Poet', he portrays his native place as

> this grey town
> That pipes the morning up before the lark
> With shrieking steam, and from a hundred stalks
> Lacquers the sooty sky[23]

Davidson's most famous poem, the dramatic monologue 'Thirty Bob a Week', rages against the ordinariness of the everyday life of an urban office clerk, travelling to work on the London underground – 'like a mole

I journey in the dark' – and coming home to 'Three rooms about the size of travelling trunks.'[24] Davidson's imagery attracted T. S. Eliot, who wrote of the poem's 'complete fitness of content and idiom'.[25] Colloquial in its language – 'rummiest', 'squelch', 'double-seated bike' – the musical rhythms and frequent internal rhymes accentuate the emotions of enduring monotony: 'And we cough, my wife and I, to dislocate a sigh, / When the noisy little kids are in their bunks.' Determined to 'face the music, sir', the speaker refuses to blame 'luck' or 'chance' for his position in life and the poem ends on a note of fatalism, as those who survive on thirty bob a week 'fall, face forward, fighting, on the deck'.

Thomson and Davidson, displaced Scots and unbelievers alike, represent figures of despair who were unable to find a solution to the Victorian crisis of faith. That crisis, which underpins the work of all of the writers discussed so far, has an extra dimension in the Scottish context. The Disruption in the Church of Scotland in 1843, in which over 450 ministers broke away to form the Free Church of Scotland, was a momentous event in society. In the absence of a parliament, the church had been 'the great unifying institution of the Scottish nation'.[26] The Disruption turned on the issues of patronage and the relationship between church and state, and provided novelists with the opportunity to explore, from a distinctively Scottish angle, that characteristically Victorian theme of the relationship between self and society. The finest fictional treatment comes in William Alexander's *Johnny Gibb of Gushetneuk* (1871). With a sophisticated, uncompromising use of the Aberdeenshire dialect, Alexander, in the manner of Walter Scott, portrays how circumstances drive his central character to become an active participant in history:

> [T]he question before which they had succumbed was a question of great principles, in relation to which he, Johnny Gibb, was a mere entity of only the smallest dimensions, and not once to be named as a power in the case at all. In short, he was Johnny Gibb of Gushetneuk, as he had been for the last thirty and odd years; an inconsiderable person, speaking and acting as the impulse moved him, in accordance with what he believed at the time to be right.[27]

The events of the Disruption are mirrored by the portrayal of rural farm life. The absentee laird's influence in church affairs is juxtaposed with his control over the land and, subsequently, the life of this small community. Johnny is a tenant farmer whose livelihood comes under threat by the impending termination of his lease and the introduction of capitalist methods of farming. Alexander's critique of materialism lies in his portrayal of Johnny and his farmer class as a touchstone for moral integrity. He has earned a comfortable living 'by dint of honest industry' but remains unaffected, furnishing his house and clothing himself simply.[28] He stands for a communitarian ideal of living and working which Alexander shows to be fading away.

The same theme is treated in a more idealised way in Ian Maclaren's *The Days of Auld Langsyne* (1895). Maclaren's sketches of rural Perthshire, which sold prodigiously in the 1890s, illustrate the continued legacy of the Disruption to Scottish fiction. For all its contrived sentimentality, Maclaren's work is an important index to contemporary religious debates at the end of the century. The Disruption also forms the backdrop of Margaret Oliphant's first novel, *Passages in the Life of Mrs Margaret Maitland* (1849), as well as *A Son of the Soil* (1865), which also engages with the religious debates that permeated England. Apart from Stevenson, Oliphant is the major Victorian Scottish novelist. Author of 125 books and innumerable periodical articles and reviews, her most popular works were the 'Chronicles of Carlingford' series set in a provincial English town. In addition to biographies and works of history, she also wrote supernatural tales and an autobiography which, in its newly unexpurgated form, is arguably her masterpiece. Along with Jane Carlyle's voluminous letters, it is a reminder of how Scottish women writers in particular cultivated the art of life-writing.

Oliphant's psychological realism and her close engagement with social and intellectual concerns of the period place her among the best of Victorian novelists. Although she opposed female suffrage and vociferously attacked the New Woman of the 1890s, her fiction offers an acute examination of women's roles in society. *Hester* (1883), set in the 1860s but subtitled 'A Story of Contemporary Life', presents two strong-willed, independent-minded women: the elderly Catherine Vernon, jilted in her youth, who has risen to power as the head of a family bank, and the temperamental Hester, just fourteen at the beginning of the novel. Hester, whose appetite for 'a world more serious, more large' is aroused to the point where she asks 'Why was not she a man?', would like to follow Catherine and do '[s]omething of one's own free will ... Something voluntary, even dangerous.'[29] But Oliphant paints an ambivalent picture of the gains and losses of achievement in the public sphere. Catherine is vulnerable and lonely in spite of her position as head of the family and centre of local society, and Hester's fate at the end of the novel is left provocatively open. The lives of the two women are dramatised against the backdrop of the role of money and finance in Victorian society. Like Dickens and Trollope, Oliphant explores the impact on human relationships and moral actions of a society built on capital investment. The financial crises of the 1820s and 1860s, with their reckless stock speculation and runs on the banks, are paralleled with the gambling and speculation that pervades all human behaviour.

Oliphant left her native country at the age of ten, and her portrayals of Scotland were more the product of memory and imagination than observation. Nevertheless, she had a historian's eye for detail. *Kirsteen* (1890) is set during the Napoleonic Wars and shares the retrospective view of the immediate past that characterises novels such as *Vanity Fair* and *Middlemarch*; the story ends in the Edinburgh of the 1850s, in 'times which are not ancient history' but a recognisable contemporary world.[30] It also engages with two characteristically Scottish-Victorian themes outlined earlier in this chapter: Carlylean work and duty and Smilesian self-help. Kirsteen, the daughter of a Highland laird, defies her tyrannical father and journeys to London to escape an enforced marriage. With her business acumen she quickly rises in the dressmaking trade, becoming a partner in a flourishing firm. Her success enables her, at the end of the novel, to shore up her family's finances and begin to restore its decaying estate. As in *Hester*, Oliphant presents an able woman preserving and restoring a family fortune which has been wasted or neglected by men. Whereas Catherine remains a lonely spinster, Kirsteen's story has a romantic love plot. She is separated from her sweetheart, Ronald, early in the novel when he leaves for India to serve in the army. He dies on the battlefield clutching a bloodstained handkerchief which Kirsteen later enshrines in a casket after taking from it 'like a sacrament, his dying lips'. The religious imagery might be seen as cloying, but Kirsteen's devotion to work and duty forestall sentimentality: 'thus life was over for Kirsteen; and life began'.[31] Like the eponymous heroine of *Margaret Maitland*, she refuses the path of marriage but Oliphant lays bare the cost of Kirsteen's renunciation of love as well as celebrating her determined achievements in work and business.

As a historical novel, *Kirsteen* illustrates the continued legacy of Scott, a legacy that was energised by Robert Louis Stevenson's transformation of the romance genre in *Kidnapped* (1886). Together with another Scot, Andrew Lang, Stevenson was the major figure in the theorisation and revival of the romance in the 1880s which inspired the early works of Arthur Conan Doyle and John Buchan, and facilitated the success of S. R. Crockett. One of the best-selling authors of the 1890s, Crockett's finest novel, *The Raiders* (1894), is a characteristically *fin-de-siècle* work which transforms the author's native Galloway landscape into a historical adventure world on the edge of abyss. Too easily consigned to the Kailyard, a context which does little justice to the author's range, Crockett's work is nevertheless marred by his exploitation of the contemporary vogue for Scotland as an exotic region. That vogue reached its height in the work of William Black, whose immensely popular Highland romances explore, through love stories, the collision of rural simplicities and metropolitan (generally English) fashions.

The Highland settings are chiefly exploited for picturesque descriptions, such as the following:

> Sunset in the wild Loch Scavaig. Far up amid the shoulders and peaks of Garsven there were flashes of flame and the glow of the western skies, with her and there a beam of ruddy light touching the summits of the mountains in the east.[32]

This was an age of expanding literary tourism, and Black's proficiency for scene-painting explains in part his considerable readership.

The two major novelists at the turn of the new century, however, are J. M. Barrie and George Douglas Brown. Barrie soon abandoned fiction for drama, and Brown lived long enough to complete only one successful novel. Sharply contrasting, they nevertheless show how late Victorian Scottish writers were grappling with modern literary themes. Barrie's early fiction, *Auld Licht Idylls* (1888) and *A Window in Thrums* (1889), created a vogue for rural, 'Kailyard' idylls. It was against the static, idealised world depicted in this fiction that Brown wrote *The House with the Green Shutters* (1901), which sets its human drama against social and economic change and portrays the collapse of community values. John Gourlay, a goods-carrier, has risen to pre-eminence in the town of Barbie through 'brute force of character'.[33] In this mercantile age, the ministers and schoolmaster, who carry authority and respect in Kailyard fiction, are distant or pernicious influences on a community whose dominant values are competition and self-interest. The church, as a physical landmark, is conspicuously absent in the novel, whilst the railway is a constant reminder of change and modernity. As early as the second chapter, the gossiping locals are predicting that 'if the railway came hereway ... Gourlay would go down' (46). Not 'quick enough to jump at the new way of doing', he is outmanoeuvred by a more commercially astute rival, who, like Donald Farfrae in Hardy's *The Mayor of Casterbridge* (1886), is better able to adapt to the changing technological environment.

Brown's novel is preoccupied with the relationship between character and environment, exploring this through the fall of Gourlay and the failure of his artistic son. Sensitive where his father is brutal, John's capacity for imagination is a curse. The cynical schoolmaster correctly identifies the boy's weakness: 'a sensory perceptiveness in gross excess of his intellectuality' (142). Sent away to college, John descends into drink but manages to win an essay prize. Brown's treatment of art and imagination recalls Carlyle in its insistence that the imagination must be related to the external world. John's imagination is vivid but, as the Professor who awards the prize detects, displays 'too nervous a sense of the external world' (162). The Professor distinguishes between different types of imagination, judging the highest form to be 'both creative and consecrative ... merging in diviner thought, it irradi-ates the world'. Young Gourlay's essay has no such Carlylean power: 'His mind, finding no solace in work, was left to prey upon itself' (147).

It is this concern with the function of the imagination that links Brown's novel with Barrie's *Sentimental Tommy* (1896) and *Tommy and Grizel* (1900). In these works, Barrie widened the concerns of his earlier fiction to portray characters whose imaginative apprehension of the world collides with reality. Both novels are studies in self-consciousness and the artistic instinct. Tommy is sentimental because he invents emotion and immerses himself in his fantasies so completely that he loses the boundary between reality and pretence. Whereas in the first novel fantasy is seen as the legitim-ate domain of childhood, in the sequel Barrie explores the destructive effects Tommy's fantasies have on others, especially Grizel, the woman who loves him. Though admiring, Barrie is essentially critical of his artist-hero, and Grizel's observation on Tommy's art echoes the criticisms of John Gourlay's Professor: 'If writing makes you live in such an unreal world it must do you harm.'[34]

The most strikingly modern aspect of Barrie's novel, however, is its treat-ment of gender. Barrie was alert to contemporary debates on sexuality,[35] and *Tommy and Grizel* has been acclaimed by a modern theorist as 'an extra-ordinary, and an unjustly forgotten, book', foundational in its treatment of male 'homosocial panic'.[36] Tommy's sentimentality prevents him from experiencing genuine desire, since the only women he can fall in love with are those of his own imagination. A psychological compulsion to desire, however, leads him to pretend to fall in love with Grizel, with fatal con-sequences. Barrie's representation of tortured masculinity had a powerful influence on the young D. H. Lawrence, who included references to *Tommy and Grizel* in his novel *The Lost Girl* (1920). In the links it makes between the relationship between internal and external reality and the formation of modern gender identities and sensibilities, Barrie's mature fiction takes one of the characteristic themes of Scottish Victorianism into the cultural and intellectual concerns of the twentieth century.

Notes

1 Kurt Wittig, *The Scottish Tradition in Literature* (Edinburgh: Oliver & Boyd, 1958), p. 254.

2 David Craig, *Scottish Literature and the Scottish People: 1680–1830* (London: Chatto & Windus, 1961), p. 273.

3 George Blake, *Barrie and the Kailyard School* (London: Arthur Barker, 1951), p. 9.

4 Archibald Geikie, *Scottish Reminiscences* (Glasgow: Maclehose, 1904), p. 7.

5 Paul Scott, 'The Last Purely Scotch Age', in Douglas Gifford (ed.), *The History of Scottish Literature*, vol. III, *Nineteenth Century* (Aberdeen University Press, 1988), pp. 13–22.

6 Tom Nairn, *The Break-Up of Britain* (1977; London: Verso, 1981), pp. 156–7.

7 William Donaldson, *Popular Literature in Victorian Scotland* (Aberdeen University Press, 1988).

8 T. M. Devine, *The Scottish Nation 1700–2000* (London: Allen Lane, 1999), p. 298.

9 See Ian Brown, Thomas Owen Clancy, Susan Manning and Murray Pittock (eds.), *The Edinburgh History of Scottish Literature*, 3 vols. (Edinburgh University Press, 2007); Robert Crawford, *Scotland's Books* (London: Penguin, 2007), ch. 9; Bill Bell (gen. ed.), *The Edinburgh History of the Book in Scotland*, 4 vols. (Edinburgh University Press, 2007–).

10 Hugh Miller, *My Schools and Schoolmasters; or, The Story of My Education* (Edinburgh: Constable, 1859), p. xi.

11 *Ibid.*, p. 305.

12 Thomas Carlyle, *Works*, Centenary Edition, ed. H. D. Traill, 30 vols. (London: Chapman & Hall, 1896–9), vol. XXVIII, p. 49.

13 A. L. Le Quesne, *Carlyle* (Oxford University Press, 1982), p. 11.

14 Thomas Carlyle, *Sartor Resartus*, ed. Kerry McSweeney and Peter Sabor (Oxford University Press, 1987), p. 167; further references will appear in the text.

15 George MacDonald, *Robert Falconer* (1868; London: Cassell, 1927), p. 82; further references will appear in the text.

16 George MacDonald, *The Complete Fairy Tales*, ed. U. C. Knoepflmacher (New York: Penguin, 2000), p. 6.

17 George MacDonald, *David Elginbrod* (1863; London: Hurst & Blackett, n.d.), p. 29.

18 George MacDonald, *Phantastes* (1858; London: Chatto & Windus, 1894), p. 279.

19 George MacDonald, *Works of Fancy and Imagination*, 10 vols. (London: Alexander Strahan, 1871), vol. III, p. 201.

20 *The New Penguin Book of Scottish Verse*, ed. Robert Crawford and Mick Imlah (London: Penguin, 2000), pp. 342–3.

21 *Ibid.*, pp. 351–4.

22 James Thomson, *The City of Dreadful Night*, ed. Edwin Morgan (Edinburgh: Canongate, 1993), p. 33; further references will appear in the text.

23 John Davidson, *Ballads and Songs* (London: John Lane, 1894), p. 8.

24 *Ibid.*, pp. 91–7.

25 T. S. Eliot, Preface to *John Davidson: A Selection of His Poems*, ed. Maurice Lindsay (London: Hutchinson, 1961), p. xi.

26 Olive and Sydney Checkland, *Industry and Ethos: Scotland, 1832–1914*, 2nd edn (Edinburgh University Press, 1989), p. 122.

27 William Alexander, *Johnny Gibb of Gushetneuk* (1871; East Linton: Tuckwell, 1995), pp. 162–3.

28 *Ibid.*, p. 20.

29 Margaret Oliphant, *Hester* (1883; London: Macmillan, 1884), pp. 82, 330.

30 Margaret Oliphant, *Kirsteen* (1890; London: Macmillan, 1891), p. 362.

31 *Ibid.*, p. 256.

32 William Black, *A Daughter of Heth* (1871; London: Sampson Low, 1892), p. 163.

33 George Douglas Brown, *The House with the Green Shutters*, ed. Dorothy Macmillan (1901; Harmondsworth: Penguin, 1985), p. 44; further references will appear in the text.

34 J. M. Barrie, *Tommy and Grizel* (London: Cassell, 1900), p. 101.

35 See Andrew Nash, 'J. M. Barrie and the Third Sex', in Sarah Carpenter and Sarah Dunnigan (eds.), *'Joyous Sweit Imaginatioun': Essays on Scottish Literature in Honour of Professor R. D. S. Jack* (Amsterdam and New York: Rodopi, 2007), pp. 229–40.

36 Eve Kosofosky Sedgwick, *Epistemology of the Closet* (1990; London: Penguin, 1991), p. 198.

Guide to further reading

Bell, Bill (ed.), *The Edinburgh History of the Book in Scotland*, vol. III, *Ambition and Industry 1800–1880* (Edinburgh University Press, 2007)

Crawford, Robert, *Scotland's Books* (London: Penguin, 2007), ch. 9

Donaldson, William, *Popular Literature in Victorian Scotland* (Aberdeen University Press, 1988)

Jay, Elisabeth, *Mrs Oliphant: 'A Fiction to Herself'* (Oxford: Clarendon Press, 1995)

Jessop, Ralph, *Carlyle and Scottish Thought* (Basingstoke: Macmillan, 1997)

Nash, Andrew, *Kailyard and Scottish Literature* (Amsterdam and New York: Rodopi, 2007)

PENNY FIELDING

Robert Louis Stevenson

Summing up his friend's career to date in 1886, Henry James wrote of Robert Louis Stevenson: 'Each of his books is an independent effort – a window opened to a different view.'[1] In its simplest sense, this remark recalls the experimental, adaptable attitude that Stevenson took to literary forms in a market that afforded authors new freedoms.[2] At the start of his writing career in the 1870s, the book trade was still dominated by the standard, three-volume novel, looming large in the view of any young writer beginning a literary career. As Stevenson himself put it, 'the fact of the existence of the modern English novel is not to be denied; materially, with its three volumes, leaded type, and gilded lettering, it is easily distinguishable from other forms of literature'.[3] But throughout Stevenson's life, sales of the three-volume novel, the medium of Charles Dickens and George Eliot, began to fall and the 'other forms of literature' to take their place. With the increasing popularity and widening distribution of magazines, shorter fictions and serial publication drove the development of literature, and new literary modes began to emerge to satisfy new readerships. Not yet quite solidified into the genres we would now recognise, these modes blended with each other as authors felt unconstrained by the demands of the realist novel. *Strange Case of Dr Jekyll and Mr Hyde* (1886), for example, could be described as an early example of many genres: the detective work of Mr. Utterson (or 'Mr. Seek' as he calls himself[4]), Henry Jekyll's mysterious chemical experiment and the monster that is Hyde are all potent models for, respectively, the detective story, science fiction and horror, yet the novel cannot be said to correspond precisely to any one of these genres.

The most common term used to encompass these non-realist modes was 'romance', a word which had a variety of meanings. 'Romance' had a general application to all works that were not very likely to take place in everyday life, or that defied the known laws of physics, but the term also had more specific resonances.[5] Stevenson engaged in an exchange of essays with Henry James in *Longman's Magazine* in 1884 in which they debated the relative capacities of realism and romance to deal with life. James's view of realism characterises the novelist as a kind of subtle 'historian' of impressions, someone who is finely tuned to psychological nuances and complexities of human actions, and who observes them carefully in order to record them in fiction. For James, the finest authors are able 'to guess the unseen from the seen, to trace the implication of things, to judge the whole piece by the pattern, the condition of feeling life, in general, so completely that you are well on your way to knowing any particular corner of it – this cluster of gifts may almost be said to constitute experience'.[6]

The key word here, for Stevenson, James and many of their contemporaries, is 'experience'. Like James, Stevenson thinks that experience constitutes 'the condition of feeling life'. But, unlike his friend, he does not believe that the novelist can take a careful impression of everything that drifts into what James calls a 'huge spider-web ... suspended in the chamber of consciousness' and then commit it in retrospect to a novel.[7] For Stevenson, replying to James in his essay 'A Humble Remonstrance', life cannot be contained within a novel: it is too 'monstrous, infinite, illogical, abrupt'.[8] The key relation is not that of the author committing his or her impressions to the novel, but that between the text and the reader. In an earlier essay for *Longman's* in 1882, Stevenson had written that when we read romance, 'Something happens as we desire to have it happen to ourselves ... then we plunge into the tale in our own person and bathe in fresh experience; and then, and then only, do we say we have been reading a romance.'[9] 'Romance', in this sense, is a condition of reading rather than of authorship. It calls upon immediate experience; rather than sensitively feeling out the whole from the parts (as in the Jamesian model), the reader encounters one part after another, as 'something happens' in a continuous present. This was most striking to Stevenson's first readers, who praised the apparent artlessness of the narratives, and the clear, direct, bodily experience of reading them. Of *Kidnapped* (1886), for example, an early reviewer commented: 'The scenes are flashed not only upon the mental vision, but upon the actual senses of the reader',[10] and this novel is memorable for its rendition of the sensory world of the characters. Its narrator, David Balfour, draws attention to the need for writing to be immediate, offering his own account as something more directly felt even than fiction itself: 'By what I have read in books, I think few that have held a pen were ever really wearied, or they would write of it more strongly ... I did not think of myself, but just of each fresh step which I was sure would be my last, with despair.'[11]

Interestingly, it is not energy, or activity, the staples of adventure, that David singles out here, but tiredness. Books, it is implied, have a responsibility to convey pain as well as pleasure, and Henry James, who admired

Kidnapped, called Stevenson 'an observer who not only loves life, but does not shrink from the responsibilities of recommending it'.[12] This is perhaps an ambiguous remark: on the one hand it signals that Stevenson was not ashamed of the populist connotations of the pure enjoyment of the novel of adventure. But, on the other hand, Stevenson's willingness to 'recommend life' is also tinged with a sense of loss. James himself was to devote an entire novel, *The Ambassadors* (1903), to the responsibilities of recommending life, in the person of Lambert Strether, whose famous injunction 'Live all you can; it's a mistake not to' echoes throughout a novel that explores the *cost* of living all one can, both to oneself and to others.[13] Many of Stevenson's works trace this cost, as the most daring and adventurous actions can exert a heavy price: for David Balfour, excitement is shaded with 'despair'; in the short story 'The Bottle Imp' (1891), living out one's desires carries the risk of damnation; Henry Jekyll's experiments lead to his suicide; Jim Hawkins's adventures bring him treasure at the expense of nightmares.

The question of 'life' and how it might be lived in fiction comes into focus in the 1880s in the movement generally known as aestheticism. From around 1860, the study of the aesthetic has one foot in art and another in psychology; instead of being a question for metaphysical philosophy, aesthetics could now be traced in the cognitive reactions of individuals to fine art, music and literature. Herbert Spencer's *Principles of Psychology* (1855) defined the aesthetic experience as one which exceeds the ordinary or bodily needs of the organism for sustaining life. The individual experiences these impulses as pleasure for its own sake rather than for biological needs, and these impulses, or impressions, were aesthetic ones, coming under the category of art. In human development, such impulses are first expressed in the form of play, as children channel their emotional impulses into imitative aesthetic forms. An interest in the imaginative capacities of children is part of a wider field of aesthetics and psychology. For Stevenson, play was the earliest form of literary experience, and seamlessly connected to reading fiction in later life. In a famous phrase he comments: 'Fiction is to the grown man what play is to the child.' Reading generates a superfluity of pleasure that is immediate and based on impressions, as is life, but, unlike life, this pleasure is not tied to the need for survival: 'there are lights in which we are willing to contemplate even the idea of our own death'.[14] As they pass into the realm of the aesthetic, the impressions that constitute experience can enact darker imaginative forms as they are no longer tied to biological need. To think of Stevenson as a writer for and about children is to acknowledge, as he did, the direct connection between the child's imagination and the more complex aesthetic responses of the adult. Even in the apparently simple *Child's Garden of Verses* (1885), it can be hard to tell whether the speaking voice is that of a child playing at adult roles, or an adult imaginatively recreating childhood.

'Romance', then, is a term that looks in two directions and joins two apparently differing concepts. On the one hand it names the kind of narrative that deals with 'the problems of the body and of the practical intelligence, in clean, open-air adventure',[15] while on the other it draws the reader into a world of impressions, and we enter the 'kaleidoscopic dance of images, incapable of sleep or of continuous thought', the world of aestheticism and Walter Pater's famous conclusion that 'art comes to you proposing frankly to give nothing but the highest quality to your moments as they pass, and simply for those moments' sake'.[16] Stevenson's interest in experience, the impulses and impressions that it comprises, and its ethical and imaginative responsibilities and costs, connects him both to the immediacy of the adventure novel and to the reflective qualities of aestheticism.

The sense in which Stevenson was a 'Scottish author' is harder to pin down, as his sense of location is always fluid and complex. Much of his writing is inflected with the global consciousness of modernity in which huge distances compete with the rapidity of modern communication technologies like the telegraph. 'But now, all the round world is known, we put girdles round the earth in the manner of Puck', commented the poet Lionel Johnson in a review of Stevenson.[17] The spaces between where one is and where one might be, where one was, and where others are now, become relative and hard to measure objectively. One of Stevenson's finest poems is a meditation on this kind of haunted, global spatiality. In 'The Tropics Vanish', he thinks about his present location in the Gilbert Islands in the Pacific (the modern Kiribati) in relation to distant Edinburgh on the other side of the world, the city where his dead ancestors lie in their 'grated cell'. The poem dizzily changes its spatial focus, from the graves in Edinburgh, to the expanse of continental oceans, bigger even than ordinary oceans, and to the tiny figure of the child, almost imperceptible on his 'lampless isle':

> The artificers,
> One after one, here in this grated cell,
> Where the rain erases, and the rust consumes,
> Fell upon lasting silence. Continents
> And continental oceans intervene;
> A sea uncharted, on a lampless isle,
> Environs and confines their wandering child:
> In vain.[18]

The poem emphasises both vast global distances and their relativity in the imagination, the colon after 'wandering child', and the way Stevenson (who

always exerts a very fine control of rhyme, rhythm and structure) delays
'in vain' with a line break, enact in verse the way Stevenson both was and
was not confined by his geographical environment. At the end of this poem,
Edinburgh, where Stevenson was born in 1850, is described as a 'city of the
dead', a place of absence rather than a living home. And much of his early
writing is about travelling away from Scotland – to France (*An Inland Voyage*
(1878), *Travels with a Donkey* (1879)) and America (*The Amateur Emigrant*
(published in 1895 after his death), *The Silverado Squatters* (1884)). Even
in his early set of pen-portraits, *Edinburgh: Picturesque Notes* (1879), the
sense of being in his home city evokes the ghostly absences of emigration.
Describing the slum clearances in Edinburgh's Old Town, Stevenson puts
himself in the place of Scots all over the world, linked not by a shared cultural identity, but by the absence of a geographical home: 'And all over the
world, in London, in Canada, in New Zealand, fancy what a multitude of
people could exclaim with truth: "The house that I was born in fell last
night!"'[19] Stevenson imagines a diasporic Scotland, united only in its shared
loss of a home. In the stories that remain wholly in Scotland, it is a place
touched with madness and doubled identities. In 'The Merry Men' (1882),
Charles Darnaway visits his Uncle Gordon and cousin Mary who live on a
tidal island off the West Coast. Soon he begins to suspect that Gordon is in
the grip of alcoholism and religious mania, and has murdered the survivor
of a wrecked ship. In the short story 'Thrawn Janet' (1881), the sober Revd
Soulis has to rethink his rational view of the world when the devil possesses
his housekeeper.

By far the most dominant author in nineteenth-century Scotland – and
one of the most widely read novelists in Britain, Europe and America – was
Walter Scott (1771–1832), and, although he at times claimed that Scott was
an untidy, even a careless author, Stevenson also hugely admired him and
wrote with the assumption that anyone attempting historical fiction in the
nineteenth century was writing in Scott's shadow. Scott's novels are composed on a large canvas, plotting the shape and movement of history itself –
how societies change in political and economic terms, and how ideologies
shape and are in turn shaped by these movements. The historical novel not
only measures the difference between past and present, but also represents
the experience of the individual subject in the flux of history. *Kidnapped* is
perhaps Stevenson's most Scott-like novel: David Balfour follows the literary footsteps of the heroes of Scott's *Waverley* (1814) and *Rob Roy* (1817)
as he journeys through Highland Scotland, witnessing the depopulation
of the land and the clashes between Jacobite and Hanoverian concepts of
the nation. Stevenson uses the experiential focal point of David to draw a
complex picture of a Scotland caught up in change and in interacting or

competing social and political systems. As Julia Reid points out, the novel undermines a powerful Victorian iconography of tartanry as it 'undercuts the myth of "Highlandism", whereby all Scots could claim a tartan heritage'.[20] Despite his friendship with the Jacobite Alan Breck Stewart, David's journey is through scenes of discontinuity, disjunction and the failure to understand. The novel is filled with different languages. Alan speaks Gaelic and can read French; in a scene at an inn David competes with the innkeeper in French and Latin; David finds it hard to tell if the boatman who rescues him is speaking English or a Gaelic that 'might have been Greek and Hebrew for me' (89). Communication is an act of translation dependent on social circumstances (Alan insists on English, rather than Gaelic, being spoken in David's presence as an act of hospitality). David speaks Scots but narrates in a very Anglicised form. He overhears an English soldier speaking what he calls 'the right English' (131), and then remarks on the man's localised speech patterns. The novel suggests that there is no 'right' language, and that some things evade language altogether: David is inflicted with a 'dreadful sense of illness, which we have no name for either in Scotch or English' (88). Scotland is not a homogenous place, nor even a place where different languages coexist, but a locus where speakers must constantly adjust or translate language according to circumstance.

In *The Master of Ballantrae* (1889), history seems to have become altogether cast loose from the tradition of the historical novel represented by Scott in which the forces of history can be read through the experiences of the individual. In this novel Stevenson represents a history that swirls almost chaotically around its characters and even its readers. The historical theorist Nicola Chiaromonte offers a view of history that he reads through a number of nineteenth- and twentieth-century novels. He argues that the idea of history as a collective experience, one that allows the subject to measure their own experiences against a common understanding of the meaning and shape of events, is a myth: 'The myth is about man and history. It tells us that history is a mirage, that when a man experiences a historical event, the event itself, instead of taking on majestic proportions, disappears, and something else appears in its place: the utterly ironical detail.'[21] Chiaromonte means that although we can *understand* history as shaped by causes, decisions and historical processes, we cannot *experience* it as such. If we were to look around for the historical event in which we are participating, we would not be able to see the event in itself, but just random, even unconnected details, which are 'ironic' because they distance us from the meaning of history. Chiaromonte thinks this is particularly true of war, which can only be experienced as something 'absurd',[22] and this is a helpful way of thinking about *The Master of Ballantrae*.

The novel traces the temporal and geographical contours of eighteenth-century British history, especially two historically significant conflicts: the Jacobite Rising of 1745–6 and the Seven Years War between France and Great Britain, a global struggle for colonial domination which ranged over India and North America as well as Europe. The reader experiences the Jacobite rebellion not as an encounter between two political forces of history, but as an awkward situation for the Durie family that can only be managed by the toss of a coin to decide which brother joins which faction. The characters take part in something we recognise as history, but their participation in it seems almost random. 'The Master's Wanderings', as the narrator Mackellar calls much of his narrative, seem similarly arbitrary: James Durie leaves Scotland, returns twice, visits North America (also twice) and turns up in India. Of course we could use recognisable patterns of history to explain what he is doing there. James is (probably) an agent for the British Army, then fighting the French over territory in India and North America during the Seven Years War. Historical figures are mentioned (Robert Clive in India, Henry Clinton, governor of New York) but rather as off-stage figures than the motors of historical destinies. Clive is someone whose presence obstructs James's shady business dealings; Clinton appears in the novel to arbitrate between the Durie brothers (on Henry's side) rather than to direct the course of the war.[23] We don't experience these 'real' figures as the determiners of historical 'events' whose causes, effects and contours we can witness from outside. Instead of delineating characters who demonstrate historical process, Stevenson makes it clear that 'history' is something we construct after the fact.

This is true not only of historical novels, but of contemporary ones as well. *The Dynamiter* (1885), which Stevenson wrote with his wife, Fanny van der Grift Stevenson, draws attention to the very recent events of the Irish nationalist bombing campaigns in London in the 1880s, which had been much reported in the press. Yet what was a popular and often-told narrative in the newspapers becomes in the Stevensons' novel a series of absurd experiences that can barely be organised into a coherent narrative. The plot (or rather plots: there are so many of them that any narrative sequence is undermined) follows the experiences of its three well-meaning but somewhat feckless heroes as they are manipulated by the inventive fictions of the Fenian Clara Luxmore. The reader gradually realises that events narrated several chapters ago in the plot are virtually simultaneous in the story. The Stevensons render these events incredible and absurd, splitting them up into fragmentary moments glimpsed in various times and from various angles. The terrorists themselves seek a narrative to give their actions a clear political reading. They consider blowing up a statue of Shakespeare as a representative of British hegemony, but the dynamite is accidently detonated as the bomber reaches for a newspaper to read about the latest bombing attempt: 'When the smoke cleared away the stall was seen much shattered, and the stall-keeper running forth in terror from the ruins; but of the Irish patriot or the Gladstone bag no adequate remains were to be found.'[24] Contemporary politics leaves no markers behind it to allow historical narratives to be constructed (William Ewart Gladstone, after whom the bag is named, was prime minister at the time of the volume's publication, and deeply concerned with 'The Ireland Question'). The Stevensons set their novel in London, together with Paris the metropolitan epitome of the modern city. A place of phantasmagorical speed, change and illusion, the city is almost cinematic: one of the characters describes a London square spinning round like a thaumatrope, a Victorian toy in which a two-sided picture is spun on a string to make a moving image.

As fiction moved away from the three-volume novel, it was no longer incumbent upon authors to write to a certain length or within a pattern of chapters. *The Dynamiter* has three additional stories narrated during the course of (what we later recognise as) the terrorism plot. An early reviewer called the novel a 'wanton profusion of a spendthrift whose resources seem inexhaustible',[25] and Stevenson categorised this and other stories as 'New Arabian Nights' (1882), alluding to the narrative structure in which stories can proliferate within a frame, without the frame ever (necessarily) coming to an end. Stevenson was mythologised as 'Tusitala', 'the teller of tales' (Tusitala was the name given to Stevenson by the Samoans; usually translated as 'storyteller', it literally means 'writer of stories'). Yet he is surprisingly reluctant to supply his readers with clearly shaped plot structures in which everything leads to a crucial event that is subsequently explained and laid to rest. Both *Dr Jekyll and Mr Hyde* and *The Master of Ballantrae* are composed of fragments, partial narratives, reports, interpellations and, in the case of *Ballantrae*, missing parts that an 'editor' has removed. Stevenson even resisted numbering the chapters, as if suggesting that they need not follow one logical sequence.[26] Neither story ends with a clear conclusion that explains the past: Jekyll's supposed 'full statement' of his case censors the details of his early life and refuses to explain how his transformation into Hyde is brought about. *Ballantrae* ends with the impromptu tombstone Mackellar has erected over graves of the brothers inscribed with puzzling and inconclusive summaries of their lives that don't seem to correspond very accurately with the events we have witnessed.

Neither does Stevenson correspond very closely with the kind of adventure stories that were appearing to satisfy a new market of youthful male readers. The traditional boys' island adventure unites Imperial Christian ethics and positivist science to put together a myth of the fitness of its young, white, male heroes to rule any place or people they happen upon. The youthful trio of Jack, Ralph and Peterkin, heroes of R. M. Ballantyne's *The Coral Island* (1857), find their island providentially supplied with everything they need: 'we seem to have everything ready prepared to our hands in this wonderful island – lemonade ready bottled in nuts, and loaf-bread growing on the trees!'.[27] Simply by observing their island, they can work out and profit from its natural systems. But where everything seems almost divinely provided on the Coral Island, Stevenson's *Treasure Island* (1883) is a place of unpredictability, chance and unforeseen consequences. Where the Coral Island boys learn through experimentation, Jim is rash and impulsive. His island is not Edenic, but a 'damp, feverish, unhealthy spot',[28] where, instead of food presenting itself in Westernised form (coconuts as bottles of lemonade), Jim encounters the strange sight of the castaway Ben Gunn begging for cheese. *The Coral Island* ends with its youthful heroes sailing off optimistically from their 'beautiful, bright' island, with the missionary and Christianised 'natives' waving and cheering from the shore. *Treasure Island* ends with Jim forcefully asserting that he could not be dragged back to 'that accursed island' (191), and that his dreams are haunted by the sound of the surf and the cry of the parrot. The last words of Stevenson's story – 'Pieces of eight' – turn the treasure-hunting narrative into an absurd parody: the notorious pirate, Captain Flint, the antihero of boys' adventure stories, here turns into the disembodied voice of the parrot. Where 'Bloody Bill', the most prominent pirate in *Coral Island*, dies with an outbreak of Christian repentance, no such considerations trouble the pirates of *Treasure Island*. The thoroughly modern Long John Silver has a bank account and political aspirations, imagining a time '[w]hen I'm in Parlyment, and riding in my coach' (61). A complex study of power, Silver is charismatic and duplicitous, a dubious role model for Jim, who finds his company more stimulating than that of the official forces of social order, the squire (Trelawney), the doctor (Livesey) and the captain (Smollett). Stevenson was to repeat this unravelling of the island Romance throughout his career. In the brilliant story 'The Merry Men', treasure-hunting turns into wrecking, madness and murder. In *The Master of Ballantrae*, what is buried and dug up is not treasure, but a body preserved in hideously suspended animation. In *The Ebb-Tide* (1894), the motif of three heroic boys washed up onto Ballantyne's Coral Island has become the degenerate trio of beachcombers (washed up in another sense).

In 1889 the Stevensons decided to settle permanently in Samoa, and Louis turned his literary attention to the islands of the South Pacific. Stevenson's Pacific is one constructed out of fraud. The South Seas were proving popular as a site for evidence for the new science of anthropology, premised on the idea that by observing the customs and rituals of supposedly 'primitive' peoples, general truths about human behaviour through history and across the globe could be ascertained. Stevenson rejects this idea. What we see in the Pacific of Stevenson's fiction is, in the words of Roslyn Jolly, imperialism in the shape of a 'powerful ideological presence in the form of symbols, discourses and institutions of the British Empire which are invoked, mimicked and manipulated by the traders in pursuit of power and profit'.[29] In 'The Beach of Falesà' (1892), the none-too-bright trader John Wiltshire tries to negotiate a living amid competing and confusing social rituals and sign-systems. Western concepts of trade come up against Polynesian systems of taboo, and missionaries vie with each other for influence. Wiltshire's increasingly pathetic assertions of authority on the grounds that he is a white man and backed up by Queen Victoria are no match for his cannier rival Case, who exploits the differences in social conventions to manipulate everybody, controlling the market in Western goods, conducting fraudulent marriage ceremonies and forging 'island curiosities' which he both exports as authentic native artifacts and uses to frighten the islanders. The readers of the story are not exempt from this as Stevenson manipulates their expectations. The first chapter, headed 'A South Seas Bridal', seems to promise an anthropological account of a 'native' kinship system, such as those described in, for example, John F. McLennan's *Primitive Marriage* (1865). What readers discover is Wiltshire's phoney and miscegenistic 'marriage' to the islander Uma.

In *The Ebb-Tide*, the Western heroes of adventure tradition have degenerated as far as they can go – barely surviving as beachcombers. Their desperate get-rich-quick plan to steal a shipload of champagne is already a fraud – they discover that the ship is an insurance scam and the champagne bottles (indicative of Western decadence) are filled with water. With only grimly ironic links to the adventure tradition, *The Ebb-Tide* predicts the collapse of Pacific society with its dispiriting opening sentence: 'Throughout the island world of the Pacific, scattered men of many European races and from almost every grade of society carry activity and disseminate disease.'[30] Activity, the mode of the adventure romance, is now equated with disease. Unlike 'The Beach of Falesà', where the Polynesians are one of a number of entangled social groups, the islanders barely appear in *The Ebb-Tide*, as if metaphorically wiped out by the European disease of the opening sentence (as well as literally suffering from an epidemic of influenza). The only figure to prosper here is the slaver and pearl trader Attwater, an even greater example of Western depravity than Huish, Herrick and Davis (although at the other end of the economic spectrum), who governs his island illegally through brutal violence and pure will.

At the end of his career (although he must have wondered if every novel would be his last), Stevenson returned imaginatively to Scotland. *Weir of Hermiston*, left unfinished at his death in 1894, looks back not only at Stevenson's former home, but also returns to that debate he started with Henry James about the functions and capacities of literature. The first part of the novel is set in the Edinburgh legal establishment of the early nineteenth century. The sensitive Archie Weir (like Stevenson, a legal student) challenges his father, the domineering Lord Hermiston, over the execution of Duncan Jopp, a pathetic criminal who barely understands what is happening to him. In the confrontation between father and son, Stevenson interrogates some of the questions that had, throughout his career, confronted him as a writer: style, ethics, Calvinism, the choice of literature as a profession. To Archie, his father resembles the God of Calvinism who demands obedience without reason, explanation or mediation. There is no point in Archie trying to influence his father's judgement of him because, as in Calvinist doctrine, Archie is *already* judged. During their agonising interview, Archie realises that his father is not available for persuasion, or even discussion, but must be understood to be right.

Later, Archie talks to his father's more sympathetic friend, Lord Glenalmond. But Glenalmond can only advise him to avoid taking ethical decisions, writing poetry and provoking arguments with his father. Glenalmond counsels: 'you will find some of these expressions rise on you like a remorse. They are merely literary and decorative; they do not aptly express your thought, nor is your thought clearly apprehended.'[31] The idea that Archie's language is 'merely literary and decorative' recalls Stevenson's own fears that becoming a poet was not quite the career that his family, three generations of engineers, expected of him. While they built lighthouses, he elected to 'play at home with paper like a child'.[32] But the phrase also touches on the Calvinist question of language: if the word of God alone can be the truth, then fiction becomes a delusion – an inauthentic and even sinful way of interpreting the world.[33] Not surprisingly, Adam Weir is contemptuous of all forms of artistic expression.

Banished by his father to the rural family property at Hermiston, Archie retreats to an older world in which it seems that violence – unlike the shocking death of Duncan Jopp – can be absorbed into stories and cultural practices. Feuds, vengeance, murder are not a violent intrusion into psychological modernity, as the hanging of Jopp is for Archie, but part of Border society. The housekeeper Kirstie can easily narrate for an appreciative audience the gory tale of the extra-legal execution of Dickieson, trampled to death by the Elliott clan. Fiction is not dismissed as a social affectation or, worse, a sin, but woven into social discourse: Dand Elliott, the youngest of the four black brothers, is an amateur poet who has acted as one of Walter Scott's informants for the *Minstrelsy of the Scottish Border* and is a drinking companion of James Hogg. He is a minor local celebrity who is 'made welcome for the sake of his gift through the farmhouses of several contiguous dales'.[34] Calvinism also plays an accepted part in local life: Gib Elliott is a weaver, baby-sitter for the rest of the family and part-time leader of 'God's Remnant', a small but enthusiastic Calvinist sect.

Weir exemplifies the way Stevenson's imagination works by the dismantling of antitheses. The novel does not deal in direct oppositions between city and country, modern and primitive. One of the Elliott brothers, Clem, is after all a wealthy manufacturer of 'ingenious mechanical improvements' in Glasgow who is expected to become a Bailie (a civic legal office in Scotland). Rather, the novel imagines a modern, sophisticated Scotland that is inseparable from its 'primitive' other. Clem's ruthlessness towards his family's enemies is a useful quality for a businessman in an expanding commercial city. Lord Hermiston is both a modern lawyer in Edinburgh and an 'aboriginal antique' of primitive force. Violence is socially contextual, understood through different forms of narrative, but it is as much a part of the urban, modern Scotland as the ape-like Hyde is part of modern, violent London. Throughout his career (and despite the best efforts of some of his critics), Stevenson refused to accept clear distinctions between realism and romance, serious fiction and adventure, ethics and aesthetics, Scotland and the world, modern and primitive. In his essay on style in literature, he refused to draw a line between fiction as artificial and as experience. Of literary 'artifices', he writes that 'if we had the power to trace them to their springs' we would discover 'indications of a delicacy of the sense finer than we conceive, and hints of ancient harmonies in nature'.[35] In the late nineteenth-century debate about the relation of 'art' to 'life', Stevenson offers one of the most complex – and often surprising – responses.

Notes

1 Paul Maixner (ed.), *Robert Louis Stevenson: The Critical Heritage* (London: Routledge, 1971), p. 293.

2 See Ian Duncan, 'Stevenson and Fiction', in Penny Fielding (ed.), *The Edinburgh Companion to Robert Louis Stevenson* (Edinburgh University Press, 2010), pp. 11–26.

3 Robert Louis Stevenson, 'A Humble Remonstrance', in Janet Adam Smith (ed.), *Henry James and Robert Louis Stevenson: A Record of Friendship and Criticism* (London: Rupert Hart-Davis, 1948), p. 87. All the exchanges between James and Stevenson are collected in this volume.

4 Robert Louis Stevenson, *Strange Case of Dr. Jekyll and Mr. Hyde*, ed. Richard Dury (Edinburgh University Press, 2004), p. 16.

5 For a helpful survey, see Anna Vaninskaya, 'The Late-Victorian Romance Revival: A Generic Excursus', *English Literature in Transition, 1880–1920*, 51:1 (2008), 57–79.

6 Henry James, 'The Art of Fiction', in Smith (ed.), *James and Stevenson*, p. 67.

7 *Ibid.*, p. 65.

8 Stevenson, 'Humble Remonstrance', p. 92.

9 Robert Louis Stevenson, 'A Gossip on Romance', in Glenda Norquay (ed.), *R L Stevenson on Fiction: An Anthology of Literary and Critical Essays* (Edinburgh University Press, 1999), p. 61.

10 Maixner (ed.), *Robert Louis Stevenson*, p. 243.

11 Robert Louis Stevenson, *Kidnapped* and *Catriona*, ed. Emma Letley (Oxford University Press, 1985), p. 145; further references will appear in the text.

12 Henry James, 'Robert Louis Stevenson', in Smith (ed.), *James and Stevenson*, p. 145.

13 Henry James, *The Ambassadors*, ed. Adrian Poole (London: Penguin, 2008), p. 176.

14 Stevenson, 'Gossip on Romance', p. 61

15 *Ibid.*, p. 54.

16 Walter Pater, *The Renaissance: Studies in Art and Poetry*, ed. Adam Phillips (Oxford University Press, 1998), p. 153.

17 Maixner (ed.), *Robert Louis Stevenson*, p. 418. In Shakespeare's *Midsummer Night's Dream*, Puck claims to be able to put a girdle round the earth in forty minutes.

18 Robert Louis Stevenson, *Collected Poems*, ed. Roger C. Lewis (Edinburgh University Press, 2003), p. 191.

19 Robert Louis Stevenson, *Ethical Studies; Edinburgh: Picturesque Notes*, Tusitala Edition (London: William Heinemann, 1924), p. 148.

20 Julia Reid, *Robert Louis Stevenson, Science, and the Fin de Siècle* (Basingstoke: Palgrave Macmillan, 2006), p. 126.

21 Nicola Chiaromonte, *The Paradox of History*, rev. edn (Philadelphia: University of Pennsylvania Press, 1985), p. 109.

22 *Ibid.*, p. 29.

23 Stevenson does, however, rearrange history a little in order to include Clinton. See Robert Louis Stevenson, *The Master of Ballantrae*, ed. Adrian Poole (London: Penguin, 1996), p. 236 n. 20; p. 243 n. 1.

24 Robert Louis Stevenson and Fanny van der Grift Stevenson, *The Dynamiter*, Tusitala Edition (London: William Heinemann, 1923), p. 201.

25 Maixner (ed.), *Robert Louis Stevenson*, p. 196

26 The first edition of *Ballantrae*, which was published in America, has no chapter numbers, but they appeared in the slightly later British edition.

27 J. M. Ballantyne, *The Coral Island*, ed. J. S. Braddon (Oxford University Press, 1990), p. 43.

28 Robert Louis Stevenson, *Treasure Island*, ed. Emma Letley (Oxford University Press, 1885), p. 104; further references will appear in the text.

29 Roslyn Jolly, 'Piracy, Slavery, and the Imagination of Empire in Stevenson's Pacific Fiction', *Victorian Literature and Culture*, 35:1 (2007), 157–73.

30 Robert Louis Stevenson, *South Sea Tales*, ed. Roslyn Jolly (Oxford University Press, 1996), p. 123.

31 Robert Louis Stevenson, *Weir of Hermiston*, ed. Paul Binding (London: Penguin, 1979), p. 72.

32 Stevenson, *Collected Poems*, p. 98.

33 For an extensive treatment of this idea, see Glenda Norquay, *Robert Louis Stevenson and Theories of Reading: The Reader as Vagabond* (Manchester: Manchester University Press, 2007).

34 Stevenson, *Weir*, p. 114.

35 Robert Louis Stevenson, 'On Some Technical Elements of Style in Literature', in Norquay (ed.), *R. L. Stevenson on Fiction*, p. 93.

Guide to further reading

Fielding, Penny (ed.), *The Edinburgh Companion to Robert Louis Stevenson* (Edinburgh University Press, 2010)

Jolly, Roslyn, 'Piracy, Slavery and the Imagination of Empire in Stevenson's Pacific Fiction', *Victorian Literature and Culture*, 35:1 (2007), 157–73

Norquay, Glenda, *Robert Louis Stevenson and Theories of Reading: The Reader as Vagabond* (Manchester University Press, 2007)

Reid, Julia, *Robert Louis Stevenson, Science, and the Fin de Siècle* (Basingstoke: Palgrave Macmillan, 2006)

Sandison, Alan, *Robert Louis Stevenson and the Appearance of Modernism: A Future Feeling* (London: Macmillan, 1996).

12

SCOTT LYALL

Hugh MacDiarmid and the Scottish Renaissance

Though commonly viewed as definitively rural and nationalist, the Scottish Literary Renaissance was actually begun in London by an émigré community of Burnsian Scots. The Vernacular Circle of the London Robert Burns Club, set up in 1920 to save the Doric from oblivion, boasted John Buchan and Violet Jacob as honorary members.[1] Christopher Murray Grieve ('Hugh MacDiarmid') was an initial sceptic, objecting in formalist tones that 'Mere patriotism is a Caliban's Guide to letters.'[2] In the early 1920s, Grieve thought any revival of the Scots vernacular could only invite cultural inferiorism and further marginalisation and was glad to be one of the movement's 'most indefatigably helpful enemies'.[3] Grieve disliked what he perceived as the Kailyard inflection in the Scots poems of Charles Murray (1864–1941), whose *Hamewith* (1900; 1909) was enormously popular, particularly in Murray's native north-east. Born in Alford, Aberdeenshire, Murray emigrated to South Africa in 1888 to manage a gold-mining company, rising to be Secretary of Public Works in the Transvaal. Murray's Doric poems are often infused with an exilic sentimentality for 'Scotland our Mither'. Character sketches of rural Aberdeenshire life, such as 'The Whistle' and 'Dockens Afore His Peers', link him tonally to William Alexander's *Johnny Gibb of Gushetneuk* (1871), but also to Lewis Grassic Gibbon's *Sunset Song* (1932). Grieve included Murray in his journal *Northern Numbers* (1920–2) but later turned on him, along with other established figures such as J. M. Barrie and Neil Munro, in the *Scottish Educational Journal*, accusing Murray and the Doric revival of exemplifying 'mental parochialism, a constitutional incomprehension and hatred of culture'.[4]

Contra Murray, Grieve sought a progressive hyper-modernism. *Annals of the Five Senses*, published in 1923 but substantially written during Grieve's tour of France and Salonika with the Royal Army Medical Corps, is marked by the First World War and is comparable to Edwin Muir's *We Moderns* (published in 1918 under the pseudonym Edward Moore) in its concern to express an emerging cultural *Geist*. Like its various narrators, *Annals*, with its somewhat artificial, self-conscious literary locution, is difficult to pin down. Combining early poetry and shorter fiction, it is a dilution of Grieve's plan to write a novel.⁵ But it is also his first bid to connect Scottish literature to European modernism. *Annals* displays the hectic breadth of Grieve's reading; its sometimes solipsistic interiority betrays the influence of Dostoevsky and Joyce, and has affinities with *Mauberley*-era Pound. Lifting its name from G. Gregory Smith's *Scottish Literature: Character and Influence* (1919), *Annals* demonstrates the contradictoriness central to the 'Caledonian Antisyzygy' proclaimed by Smith as the dialectical quintessence of Scottish writing. Grieve found in the antisyzygy a licence for a veritable multiplicity of selves.

It was no twist of the antisyzygy, however, that prompted Grieve's embrace of Scots, but a linguistic monograph by an ex-colonial civil servant. In 1922, after reading James Wilson's *Lowland Scotch as Spoken in the Lower Strathearn District of Perthshire* (1915), Grieve took on a new identity through which to write in a dialect he had recently scorned. What resulted was 'The Watergaw', first published in 1922 in the *Dunfermline Press*, and the text would install MacDiarmid at the forefront of the vernacular revival.

> Ae weet forenicht i' the yow-trummle
> I saw yon antrin thing,   [rare
> A watergaw wi' its chitterin' licht   [imperfect rainbow; shivering/trembling
> Ayont the on-ding;   [beyond; rain/snow fall
> An' I thocht o' the last wild look ye gied
> Afore ye deed!
>
> There was nae reek i' the laverock's hoose   [smoke; skylark
> That nicht – an' nane i' mine;
> But I hae thocht o' that foolish licht
> Ever sin' syne;   then
> An' I think that mebbe at last I ken
> What your look meant then.⁶

Translating 'The Watergaw' into Standard English is doomed in advance to render the poem utterly stilted. The first line, with help from *Chambers Scots Dictionary*, becomes: 'One wet evening (in the interval between twilight and bed-time) during a cold spell in early summer, around the time of sheep-shearing.' Indeed the difficulty of some of MacDiarmid's early Scots lyrics tempts the reductive act of interpretation *through* translation. When a gloss is required to read them, the meaning, metaphor and mood of their music may be lost. The untranslatability of 'The Watergaw' betokens the borders of cultural difference but also the liminal aura of its presiding theme: the mystery of life slipping into death. That inexpressible final fall into unconsciousness is expressed in Scots through the recollection and the linguistic re-collection of the racial unconscious. 'The Watergaw' is onto-logical, but no argument for God.

The pseudonymous MacDiarmid was born in the year of Joyce's *Ulysses* and T. S. Eliot's *The Waste Land*. Eliot's poem is cited – and sent up – in *A Drunk Man Looks at the Thistle* (1926), but Joyce was to be a more enduring influence. Grieve sought to link MacDiarmid's experimentalism in Scots to Joyce's revolutionary modernism and situate Scottish literature in an excitingly avant-garde European context.[7] In *The New Age* he endorsed 'Dadaism in France, Expressionismus in Germany and the possibilities of the *Zusammenballung* of speech with which James Joyce in English is experimenting so interestingly, and, on the whole, so successfully, and the implications of certain elements in recent Russian ego-futurism which seek to devise a language with audible and visual but no intellectual values'.[8] Grieve found improbable parallels between Joyce's method in *Ulysses* and John Jamieson's *Etymological Dictionary of the Scottish Language* (1808–9)[9]; MacDiarmid plundered archaisms from Jamieson for his modernist Scots lyrics. He wrote in 'Gairmscoile', '*It's soon', no' sense, that faddoms the herts o' men*',[10] but in fact he sought to instil lyrical Scots poetry with intellect and so destroy the heart/head, Scots/English duality that for MacDiarmid had plagued post-Enlightenment Scottish vernacular writers, not excepting Robert Burns. Edwin Muir, heavily influenced by Eliot, saw this as a crippling polarisation indicative of an irreparable dissociation of Scottish sensibility. Muir's refutation of the Scottish literary canon and the viability of writing in Scots in *Scott and Scotland* (1936) infuriated MacDiarmid and led to a permanent personal breach. In the 1920s, however, when Muir could still be counted part of the Scottish Renaissance movement, Grieve thought him 'incontestably in the first flight of contemporary critics of *welt-literatur*'.[11]

Muir matured to write a poetry informed by his Christian vision of a better, Edenic place. Orcadian by birth, he moved as a young man to Glasgow, but was disturbed by the poverty of the industrial city. 'The Labyrinth' has a figure lost and alienated in the modern maze who can only find escape through epiphanic moments of clarity. Muir began, however, by writing Scottish ballads. Grieve, often critical of the Doric revival, was keenly aware of – and surely eager to outdo – the Scots poetry of his contemporaries such as Muir, Violet Jacob (1863–1946), Marion Angus (1866–1946) and Lewis Spence (1874–1955). Author of the much-anthologised 'Tam i' the Kirk', the aristocratic Jacob was born in Montrose, and the town and surrounding area is the setting for much of her fiction and poetry, such as *Songs of Angus* (1915). Like Marion Angus, who was born in Aberdeen and raised in Arbroath, Jacob also wrote in English, but drew on the ballad tradition for her Scots poetry. MacDiarmid, too, would look back to the ballads in his Scots lyrics, even using the ballad form in the modernist *Drunk Man*. His imagistic 'Empty Vessel' is beautifully characteristic of a concern to meld the traditional and the contemporary, adapting the Scots ballad 'Jenny Nettles' and ingeniously relating that to the secular universe of modern Einsteinian physics:

I met ayont the cairney	[ruined building/heap of stones
A lass wi' tousie hair	[dishevelled/rough/shaggy
Singin' till a bairnie	[little child
That was nae langer there.	
Wunds wi' warlds to swing	[winds
Dinna sing sae sweet,	
The licht that bends ower a' thing	[light
Is less ta'en up wi'it.[12]	

Grieve rated the subtleties of Angus's poetry as finer than Jacob's work, pointing for evidence to Angus's 'Mary's Song', but he was particularly impressed by Lewis Spence's utilisation of the Doric, calling Spence in 1925 'the first Scot for five hundred years to write "pure poetry" in the vernacular'.[13] For all Grieve's scepticism regarding the continuity of the Scottish poetic tradition, it would have been impossible, as Colin Milton has pointed out, for MacDiarmid to write a modern vernacular poetry and build a Scottish Renaissance movement without the prior existence of a Scottish 'folk tradition' utilised by the late nineteenth-, early twentieth-century vernacular revival.[14] Grieve's contentious estimation of Scottish vernacular poetry, polemical rather than critical, was designed to upset the Burnsians and chimes with his slogan 'Not Burns – Dunbar!'[15] The early modern European Renaissance saw a move away from classical languages to national vernaculars. However, in Scotland the native vernacular played a distinct second fiddle to English. Wishing to retrieve the Scottish vernacular, MacDiarmid's modernist Scottish Renaissance would look to fifteenth- and sixteenth-century Scotland, valorising Robert Henryson, William Dunbar, Gavin Douglas and Sir David Lyndsay, Makars of the golden age before James VI took his court to London.

Grieve, always an activist, was especially dynamic in Montrose. He lived in the town for most of the 1920s and it became the epicentre of his efforts to establish a renaissance in Scottish cultural life. Whilst working as a full-time journalist for the *Montrose Review*, he also set up journals, such as *Scottish Chapbook* and *The Scottish Nation*, dedicated to art and politics. He became an independent town councillor in 1922 and was later appointed Justice of the Peace. He was intellectually engaged with the local community, delivering lectures on various challenging contemporary themes, from Lenin's politics to the theory of relativity.[16] Denis Saurat's 1924 article 'Le Groupe de la Renaissance Écossaise' corroborated the movement's European credentials even before MacDiarmid had published *Sangschaw* (1925) and *Penny Wheep* (1926), his first two collections of poetry. Both books exemplify MacDiarmid's creative methodology of resuscitating archaic words and usages from various Scottish regions and historical eras that he had found in Jamieson and Wilson. With Synthetic Scots, or what Tom Hubbard has termed 'reintegrated Scots', MacDiarmid sought a fusion of the disparate and often divided parts of Scotland into a unified cultural whole and of the Scottish linguistic past with the international modernist present.[17] Just as Gibbon's *Sunset Song*, like George Douglas Brown's *The House with the Green Shutters* (1901), uses 'Kailyard' conventions, settings and themes recognisable to the audience in order to unsettle and assail their expectations, so MacDiarmid's Scots poetry is set largely in rural locations that readers of Burns and the modern Doric revival would have found initially comforting and familiar.[18] But MacDiarmid's cabbage-patch contains thistles with beautiful flowers and sharp thorns. 'The Innumerable Christ' portrays Christ sympathetically whilst relativising the absolutes of Christian belief. 'The Eemis Stane' sees the world as a broken and indecipherable gravestone: what is the meaning of life on earth, the poem asks, when it inevitably terminates in death? Many of the poems of *Sangschaw* and *Penny Wheep* feature death with no afterlife, some broodingly, like 'The Watergaw' and 'The Eemis Stane', others, such as 'Tam', with bluntly amusing pragmatism. In his Scots lyrics MacDiarmid voids the Kailyard of Christian hope.

Critical orthodoxy has modernism as a metropolitan form practised by cosmopolitan artists in exile from their philistine provincial roots. Yet as the Irish critic Declan Kiberd points out, '[f]or all its emphasis on deracination ... modernism was a kind of village phenomenon'.[19] Scottish modernism was assertively local but resistant to parochialism. In Willa Muir's novel *Imagined Corners* (1931), Elizabeth flees her marriage and with the Europeanised Elise escapes to the Continent from the patriarchal limitations of Calderwick, a fictionalised Montrose. Born in Montrose to Shetland parents, Muir, aided by husband Edwin, was Kafka's chief English translator, but also translated other important German-language modernist novels such as Hermann Broch's *The Sleepwalkers*. Nan Shepherd (1893–1981) writes of the restrictions on female freedom in rural north-east Scotland in her novels *The Quarry Wood* (1928) and *The Weatherhouse* (1930). Shepherd is a noticeable absentee from Gibbon's 'Literary Lights', his 1934 essay on the principal Scottish Renaissance writers, but her portrayal of a strong female protagonist such as Martha Ironside, torn between individual development through education and commitment to community and personal ties, surely provided a template for the Chris Guthrie of *Sunset Song*. Gibbon also wrote under his own name, J. Leslie Mitchell. Mitchell's most accomplished novel is *Spartacus* (1933), but the greater literary achievement and alluring Scottish landscape of Gibbon's *A Scots Quair*, his Mearns trilogy, overshadows the diversity of an exciting *oeuvre* with distinctly postcolonial affinities that includes science fiction, biography, anthropology, short stories set in the Middle East and modernist *Bildungsroman*. A diffusionist who imagined a pre-civilisation cosmopolitan Golden Age, Mitchell shared with others of the Scottish Renaissance a mythic refusal of History's terms. He found creative stimulation in what may seem a rearguard action that has echoes in Muir's Eden, Neil M. Gunn's evocation of the ninth-century Celts in *Sun Circle* (1933) or MacDiarmid's pre-British Union, 'back-to-Dunbar' mantra. Naomi Mitchison also explores the past in her historical novels. The classical mythology of Mitchison's *The Corn King and the Spring Queen* (1931) learns from J. G. Frazer's *The Golden Bough*, a prominent source for Eliot's *Waste Land*, whilst *The Bull Calves* (1947), set post-Jacobite Rebellion in 1747, has as backdrop a divided Scotland where Highlanders are compared to the Red Indians ethnically cleansed by imperial Scots amongst others.

Creative emphasis on the past is related to the concern shared by many Scottish writers of the period regarding the contemporary and future state of the nation. This materialised most notably in *Scottish Scene*, co-authored by MacDiarmid and Gibbon, and Routledge's 'The Voice of Scotland' series.[20] Grieve's polemics often merged with his political positions. Along with Mackenzie, Gunn and R. B. Cunninghame Graham, Grieve was prominent in the National Party of Scotland (NPS), founded in 1928. His *Albyn: or Scotland and the Future* (1927) could read as a manifesto for the heavily culturalist NPS. MacDiarmid (the name has ancestry in Diarmuid from Ireland's Ossianic Cycle) was influenced by the Irish Literary Revival and like other Scottish Renaissance writers, such as Tom Macdonald ('Fionn Mac Colla') and Edwin Muir, he welcomed the idea of a more Catholic Scotland freed from the imagined delimitations of Calvinism. This had positive results, such as an emphasis on a revival of Gaelic and increasing receptivity later to the poetry of Sorley MacLean. However the downside was a deeply negative assessment of Scotland's post-Reformation past, captured in Edwin Muir's 'Scotland's Winter' and 'Scotland 1941' and his 1935 travelogue, *Scottish Journey*.

A national movement needs a national epic and MacDiarmid sought to provide it with *A Drunk Man Looks at the Thistle*. Unlike literary imperialism, such as Camoëns's *Os Lusiadas* or Spencer's *The Faerie Queene*, which glorifies as it recreates the national past, modernist epics like Pound's *Cantos* and Eliot's *Waste Land* imply modernity's fall from classical heights. *A Drunk Man* repositions this apparent decline in national terms, yet the poem's sheer imaginative gusto gives the lie to the Drunk Man's cultural pessimism. The poem issues a challenge to Scottish culture. At 2,685 lines it is intellectually demanding in length alone, and whilst the poem's vernacularity is not on the whole particularly dense, it is a bid by MacDiarmid to show that Scots can be deployed in poetry that is not solely lyrical and sentimental but modernist and difficult. *A Drunk Man* must be understood in its true satirical intent. MacDiarmid called his work a 'gallimaufry',[21] a term linked to the hash-like ragout concocted in cooking lots of different ingredients in the same pot. MacDiarmid's Braid Scots stew seeks to undermine powerful Scottish shibboleths, stereotypical markers of identity sold to the world as the essence of 'Scotland' through the industries in Burns and whisky. It achieves its affects by turning those markers into symbols having metaphysical implications far beyond their original national significance: the thistle, Scotland's emblem, signifies the mystery of life's meaning; whisky is Scotland's misprised spirit; and Burns is a Christ-like poet-prophet misrepresented by his own people. The Drunk Man is the antithesis of the canny Scot and wants to 'aye be whaur / Extremes meet', a stance that can be found in Nietzsche and Dostoevsky, as Kenneth Buthlay points out.[22] However, the phrase actually appears in 'Circe' from *Ulysses*: 'Jewgreek is greekjew. Extremes meet.'[23] *A Drunk Man*, like Joyce's 'Nighttown' dreamscape, releases the repressed sexual unconscious and the divided becomes whole. MacDiarmid's poem carves up Joycean stream of consciousness into quatrains, draws on Yeats's *A Vision*, translates Blok, cites Mallarmé and engages with Melville, Spengler and Freud. The international modernist allegiances of the poem and its Spinozan objective to see Scotland '*sub specie aeternitatis*', under the aspect of eternity, amplify the cultural, philosophical, political and moral ramifications of the Drunk Man's imperative that the Scots find themselves:

> And let the lesson be – to be yersel's,
> Ye needna fash gin it's to be ocht else.   take the trouble; if; anything
> To be yersel's – and to mak' that worth bein'.
> Nae harder job to mortals has been gi'en.[24]

A Drunk Man ends in a mystic Silence, but the poem is really MacDiarmid's epic endeavour to silence the Kailyard. With *To Circumjack Cencrastus*, an even lengthier work, MacDiarmid courts the Celtic Muse, claiming Yeats as his 'kingly cousin' and lauding Alasdair Mac Mhaighstir Alasdair, the

Scottish Gaelic poet whose 'The Birlinn of Clanranald' he would translate with assistance from Sorley MacLean.[25] Grieve explained in a letter to his former English teacher George Ogilvie that '*Cencrastus* is the fundamental serpent, the underlying unifying principle of the cosmos.'[26] Its ambitious scope and looser, tumbling form make for a less effectively controlled poem than *A Drunk Man*. Yet despite being written largely in idiomatic Scots-English, *Cencrastus* is the first poetic blast in MacDiarmid's campaign, integral to the Scottish Renaissance movement, to revive Gaelic as a key part of the national literary tradition. Later poems include 'Lament for the Great Music', 'Cornish Heroic Song for Valda Trevlyn' and *Dìreadh*, whilst MacDiarmid would anthologise several Gaelic poets in his 1940 *Golden Treasury of Scottish Poetry*. In his novels of Highland experience, Neil Gunn provides a prose complement to MacDiarmid's Celticism. Gunn's *Highland River* (1937) has thematic similarities to *Cencrastus*, though is more successful in its characterisation of the search for the source of a racially delineated spiritual understanding. In *The Silver Darlings* (1941), *Young Art and Old Hector* (1942) and *The Green Isle of the Great Deep* (1944), Gunn defends distinctive Highland communalism, an ethos attacked by the Highland Clearances he movingly depicts in *Butcher's Broom* (1934).

Gunn travelled to Munich and Bavaria in the late 1930s, and *Butcher's Broom* was translated into German and nominated for a German prize for its supposedly Nordic racial affinities.[27] MacDiarmid expressed early approval for Hitler's National Socialism in his essay 'The Caledonian Antisyzygy and the Gaelic Idea'.[28] Indeed in 1923, as editor of the *Scottish Nation*, enthused by what he heard of Mussolini's Italy, he called for a Scottish Fascism that would unite the disparate ideals of nationalism and socialism.[29] He was also an enthusiast for C. H. Douglas's Social Credit theory, advocated most strongly by Ezra Pound. MacDiarmid's radical, ostensibly contradictory positions could often be a liability to the political causes he espoused. In 1933 the NPS, a year before becoming the Scottish National Party, expelled Grieve for his part in allegedly promoting the development of a Scottish paramilitary organisation, although party leader John MacCormick was also disillusioned with Grieve's increasing communism. Grieve's politics were even considered a national security threatp and he was watched by the British Intelligence Services from 1931, when he published *First Hymn to Lenin*, until 1943.[30] *First Hymn* is a combative collection and yet is also MacDiarmid at his most abrasively intimate. 'At My Father's Grave' and 'Water of Life', amongst others, focus on his beginnings in Langholm; 'Charisma and My Relatives' is dedicated to his first wife's lover; while 'The Seamless Garment' acquaints Langholm mill-workers with Rilke and Lenin. Notoriously, the title poem, dedicated to D. S. Mirsky, who was to die in a Stalinist death-camp, includes an endorsement of revolutionary genocide:

> As necessary, and insignificant, as death
> Wi' a' its agonies in the cosmos still
> The Cheka's horrors are in their degree;
> And'll end suner! What maitters 't wha we kill
> To lessen that foulest murder that deprives
> Maist men o' real lives?[31]

W. N. Herbert has argued that the poet's 'economic, emotional, and literary powerlessness' can help explain, though not excuse, this propagandistic ruthlessness and his psychological need to belong to the communist movement.[32] This was certainly a period of personal unhappiness provoked by the failure of Grieve's first marriage leading to his eventual breakdown and hospitalisation.

Encouraged by poet Helen Cruickshank, Grieve moved to the Shetland island of Whalsay in 1933 with his second wife, Valda Trevlyn. The Angus-born Cruickshank's first collection, *Up the Noran Water*, was published in 1934. That same year Grieve joined the Communist Party. Despite such internationalist political affiliations, MacDiarmid's poetry just prior to his Shetland move had still retained a local inflection, although one far removed from the couthie tenor of the likes of Cruickshank's best-known poem 'Shy Geordie'. *Scots Unbound* (1932) follows on from where *First Hymn* left off in its use of water imagery to suggest the musical flow of language and humanity's evolutionary ebb. 'Water Music', concerning the rivers of Langholm, courses with some of the broadest Scots since the early lyrics and cites Joyce's Anna Livia Plurabelle. MacDiarmid was clearly keeping up with Joyce's 'Work in Progress', not to be published as *Finnegans Wake* till 1939, although Edwin Morgan, overturning canonical hierarchies, has suggested that Joyce's *Wake* may have been influenced by *A Drunk Man*.[33] Like *Finnegans Wake*, language and allusion are fundamental to 'Scots Unbound', which quotes from Rabelais, the New Testament and *King Lear* while the poet ponders the nature of his art, claiming 'English words are wide o' the mark / In a viese like this.'[34] However with *Stony Limits* (1934), MacDiarmid turned not only to English but to a dictionary-based scientific language as alien to readers as his experiments in Scots had been in the 1920s. The opening of 'On a Raised Beach' – 'All is lithogenesis – or lochia, / Carpolite fruit of the forbidden tree' – is a materialist's 'In the beginning …'.[35] Creation does not come through God's Word; rather, the word is with science as the explanatory principle of the earth's geological formation. The poem's first and last verse paragraphs are clotted with scientific terminology in a startling exploitation of the defamiliarisation tactics advocated by Russian Formalist Viktor Shklovsky:

> And art exists that one may recover the sensation of life; it exists to make one feel things, to make the stone *stony*. The purpose of art is to impart the sensation of things as they are perceived and not as they are known. The technique of art is to make objects 'unfamiliar', to make forms difficult, to increase the difficulty and length of perception because the process of perception is an aesthetic end in itself and must be prolonged. *Art is a way of experiencing the artfulness of an object: the object is not important.*[36]

In the unnervingly bleak Shetland landscape, of Scotland yet persistently foreign, Shklovsky's *ostranenie*, 'making strange', is a fitting tool of the poet's reinvention, his self-adjuration: 'I must get into this stone world now.'[37] That the Russian Formalists largely eschewed revolutionary politics is no matter; MacDiarmid's poet, spiritual atheist, is born again as the first man, a Marxist Adam.

> I look at these stones and know little about them,
> But I know their gates are open too,
> Always open, far longer open, than any bird's can be,
> That every one of them has had its gates wide open far longer
> Than all birds put together, let alone humanity,
> Though through them no man can see,
> No man nor anything more recently born than themselves
> And that is everything else on Earth.[38]

'On a Raised Beach' was MacDiarmid's greatest sustained poetic achievement since *A Drunk Man*. The poem is dedicated to James H. Whyte, editor of the *Modern Scot*, a culturally nationalist journal. Gibbon thought the *Modern Scot* pedalled 'literary Fascism'.[39] Grieve too would accuse Whyte of advancing a 'Fascistic line' after *Outlook*, of which Whyte was literary editor, published part of Muir's forthcoming *Scott and Scotland*.[40] Eric Linklater's *Magnus Merriman*, published in the same year as *Stony Limits*, skits the Scottish Renaissance and satirises MacDiarmid as Hugh Skene, a surname perhaps drawn from the scholar William Forbes Skene, author of *Celtic Scotland* (1876–80), but surely an ironical wink at MacDiarmid's Celtic schemes for Scotland. However in the 1930s, stirred by the Scottish revolutionary propagandist John Maclean, MacDiarmid in Shetland had already distanced himself from both the pessimism of High Modernism and the movement for a Scottish Renaissance.[41]

MacDiarmid's revolutionary politics found uneasy correspondence in his increasingly radical literary praxis. He would write three Hymns to Lenin and ultimately condone Stalinism, whilst seeking in *In Memoriam James Joyce* (1955) and *The Kind of Poetry I Want* (1961) a freedom of expression that challenges the laws of copyright and the ego rights of authorship. This 'found poetry' fails to acknowledge most of its diverse prose sources. Private property, at least in MacDiarmid's late poetry, has been abolished. Indeed if the concept of lateness in Marxist theory indicates the ideological survival of a form past its revolutionary sell-by date, then MacDiarmid's late poetry spells the end of traditional verse. Totalitarian politics was perhaps his pact with the devil in a Faustian drive to synthesise knowledge and enlarge consciousness: MacDiarmid, (post)modernist Renaissance Man. For MacDiarmid authorship was always a fiction. His late poetry, a poetry in theory, envisages Barthes's 'death of the author' and, elitism notwithstanding, shows affinities with the information superhighway of the internet communications revolution.

Substantially, MacDiarmid's poetry was written by the time he left Shetland in 1942, despite later publication dates attaching to the likes of *In Memoriam James Joyce*. MacDiarmid's plan for an epic *oeuvre*-poem, *Clann Albann*, was aborted; even the vast *In Memoriam James Joyce* was envisaged as part of the longer unpublished *Mature Art*. Publishing restrictions vetoed MacDiarmid's projects, rendering anachronistic his Spanish Civil War poem *The Battle Continues* (1957), yet the unrealisable nature of such gargantuan aims betrays the breadth of his uncompromising ambition. Whilst the centrality of language in Joyce's *Ulysses* and *Finnegans Wake* has invited structuralist and post-structuralist theorising, MacDiarmid's *In Memoriam James Joyce*, from *A Vision of World Language*, continues to await such exegesis.[42] Instead, MacDiarmid's late catalogue poems, frequently constructed from pillaged information rather than 'inspired', have given rise to academic source-hunting that is not entirely pertinent, since MacDiarmid recurrently advertises his own methodology.

> Poetry of such an integration as cannot be effected
> Until a new and conscious organisation of society
> Generates a new view
> Of the world as a whole
> As the integration of all the rich parts
> Uncovered by the separate disciplines.
> That is the poetry that I want.[43]

MacDiarmid's materialist late poetry seeks to synthesise art and science some time before C. P. Snow's 1959 lecture 'The Two Cultures and the Scientific Revolution' lamented the literati's ignorance of the sciences.[44]

The classically educated Norman MacCaig (1910–96) would write short, elegant poems in English shunning MacDiarmid's nationalist concerns:

> My only country
> is six feet high
> and whether I love it or not
> I'll die
> for its independence.[45]

However, while MacDiarmid was writing and publishing his late poetry in Synthetic English, early MacDiarmid was inspiring a 'Second Wave' of Scottish Renaissance poetry, most notably in the work of William Soutar (1898–1943), Robert Garioch Sutherland (1908–81) and Sydney Goodsir Smith (1915–75). Soutar's first collection in Scots, *Seeds in the Wind* (1933; 1943), was for children, followed by *Poems in Scots* (1935) and MacDiarmid's controversial edition of Soutar's *Collected Poems* (1948), but he is perhaps best remembered for his *Diaries of a Dying Man* (1954), which recounts his struggle with spondylitis. Garioch's Scots poetry was influenced by MacDiarmid's in its anti-Anglicization and philosophical themes, but also by Garioch's native Edinburgh and the city's laureate, Robert Fergusson. Goodsir Smith, born in New Zealand, was similarly stimulated by Edinburgh; his satirical novel set in the capital, *Carotid Cornucopius* (1947), MacDiarmid compared to Joyce's *Ulysses*.[46] His best work, the elegy sequence *Under the Eildon Tree* (1948; 1954), humorously connects the poet's persona to Burns and the lovers of classical myth. The progressive, boundless spirit of MacDiarmid's quest in poetry is arguably closer, however, to Edwin Morgan's planetary consciousness and W. S. Graham's self-conscious, quasi-Romantic commitment to the role of the marginalised poet than to the recapitulated Scots of the nationalistic 'Second Wave'.

In the 1972 author's note to his autobiography *Lucky Poet*, first published in 1943, MacDiarmid wrote, 'I do not claim to have originated the growing belief that English literature is petering out – but I certainly anticipated that it would.'[47] His work for a Scottish Renaissance has distinct postcolonial claims. Yet MacDiarmid is a problem for many contemporary theorists of Scottish culture. A photograph of an elderly Grieve stares out grimly from the front cover of *Beyond Scotland*, a book that repositions twentieth-century Scottish literature in a pluralist post-national framework.[48] Rather, though, than seeking anxiously to move beyond MacDiarmid and the Scottish Renaissance, we have perhaps not understood fully enough the meanings of this complex movement and MacDiarmid's deeply challenging poetic *oeuvre*.

Notes

1 See Margery Palmer McCulloch (ed.), *Modernism and Nationalism: Literature and Society in Scotland 1918–1939, Source Documents for the Scottish Renaissance* (Glasgow: Association for Scottish Literary Studies, 2004), p. 13.

2 C. M. Grieve, letter, *Aberdeen Free Press*, 27 January 1922; repr. in Alan Bold (ed.), *The Letters of Hugh MacDiarmid* (London: Hamish Hamilton, 1984), p. 754.

3 C. M. Grieve, 'Leaves from a London Diary', *Scots Pictorial* (1923); repr. in Angus Calder, Glen Murray and Alan Riach (eds.), *The Raucle Tongue: Hitherto Uncollected Prose*, volume I, *1911–1926* (Manchester: Carcanet, 1996), p. 45.

4 C. M. Grieve, letter, *Scottish Educational Journal* (24 July 1925); repr. in Hugh MacDiarmid, *Contemporary Scottish Studies*, ed. Alan Riach (Manchester: Carcanet, 1995), p. 43.

5 Alan Bold, *MacDiarmid: Christopher Murray Grieve: A Critical Biography* (London: John Murray, 1988), p. 101.

6 Hugh MacDiarmid, *Complete Poems*, vol. I, ed. Michael Grieve and Alan Riach (Manchester: Carcanet, 1993), p. 17.

7 The fifth plank of the 'Manifesto' of the Scottish Renaissance in Grieve's *Scottish Chapbook* is: 'To bring Scottish Literature into closer touch with current European tendencies in technique and ideation.'

8 C. M. Grieve, 'Mannigfaltig: Beyond Meaning', *New Age* (1924); repr. in Calder, Murray and Riach (eds.), *Raucle Tongue*, vol. I, p. 165.

9 C. M. Grieve, 'Causerie: A Theory of Scots Letters', *Scottish Chapbook*, 1:7 (February 1923), 182–4.

10 MacDiarmid, *Complete Poems*, vol. I, p. 74; emphasis in the original.

11 C. M. Grieve, 'Edwin Muir', *Scottish Educational Journal* (September 1925); repr. in MacDiarmid, *Contemporary Scottish Studies*, p. 93.

12 MacDiarmid, *Complete Poems*, vol. I, p. 66.

13 C. M. Grieve, 'The New Movement in Vernacular Poetry: Lewis Spence; Marion Angus', *Scottish Educational Journal* (November 1925); repr. in MacDiarmid, *Contemporary Scottish Studies*, p. 201.

14 Colin Milton, 'Modern Poetry in Scots before MacDiarmid', in Cairns Craig (ed.), *The History of Scottish Literature*, vol. IV, *Twentieth Century* (Aberdeen University Press, 1987), pp. 11–36.

15 C. M. Grieve, *Albyn: or Scotland and the Future* (1927); repr. in Hugh MacDiarmid, *Albyn: Shorter Books and Monographs*, ed. Alan Riach (Manchester: Carcanet, 1996), p. 14.

16 See Scott Lyall, *Hugh MacDiarmid's Poetry and Politics of Place: Imagining a Scottish Republic* (Edinburgh University Press, 2006), ch. 3, for an in-depth examination of MacDiarmid in Montrose.

17 Tom Hubbard, 'Reintegrated Scots: The Post-MacDiarmid Makars', in Craig (ed.), *History of Scottish Literature*, vol. IV, pp. 179–93.

18 Bold (ed.), *Letters*, p. 142.

19 Declan Kiberd, *Ulysses and Us: The Art of Everyday Living* (London: Faber, 2009), p. 22.

20 'The Voice of Scotland' series was edited initially by Grassic Gibbon, whose contribution was to be on Burns. When he died in 1935, MacDiarmid took

over as general editor. The books in the series are Neil M. Gunn, *Whisky and Scotland* (1935); Eric Linklater, *The Lion and the Unicorn* (1935); Victor MacClure, *Scotland's Inner Man* (1935); William Power, *Literature and Oatmeal* (1935); Compton Mackenzie, *Catholicism and Scotland* (1936); A. S. Neill, *Is Scotland Educated?* (1936); Edwin Muir, *Scott and Scotland* (1936); Willa Muir, *Mrs Grundy in Scotland* (1936). MacDiarmid's *Red Scotland: What Lenin Has Meant to Scotland* was suppressed.

21 Hugh MacDiarmid, 'Author's Note' (1926), *A Drunk Man Looks at the Thistle*, ed. Kenneth Buthlay (Glasgow: Association for Scottish Literary Studies, 1987), p. 196.

22 MacDiarmid, *Drunk Man*, p. 14; see editor's notes on p. 15.

23 James Joyce, *Ulysses*, Annotated Students' Edition by Declan Kiberd (Harmondsworth: Penguin, 1992), p. 622.

24 MacDiarmid, *Drunk Man*, pp. 108, 62.

25 MacDiarmid, *Complete Poems*, vol. 1, p. 185.

26 C. M. Grieve to George Ogilvie, 9 December 1926; repr. in Catherine Kerrigan (ed.), *The Hugh MacDiarmid–George Ogilvie Letters* (Aberdeen University Press, 1988), p. 125.

27 Alistair McCleery (ed.), *Landscape and Light: Essays by Neil M. Gunn* (Aberdeen University Press, 1987), pp. 12–14.

28 Hugh MacDiarmid, 'The Caledonian Antisyzygy and the Gaelic Idea', *Modern Scot* 2:2 (July 1931), 141–54, and *Modern Scot* 2:4 (January 1932), 333–7.

29 Hugh MacDiarmid, 'Plea for a Scottish Fascism', repr. in Hugh MacDiarmid, *Selected Prose*, ed. Alan Riach (Manchester: Carcanet, 1992), pp. 34–8; Hugh MacDiarmid, 'Programme for a Scottish Fascism', repr. in Calder, Murray and Riach (eds.), *Raucle Tongue*, vol. 1, pp. 82–7.

30 See Scott Lyall, '"The Man is a Menace": MacDiarmid and Military Intelligence', *Scottish Studies Review* 8:1 (2007), 37–52.

31 MacDiarmid, *Complete Poems*, vol. 1, p. 298.

32 W. N. Herbert, *To Circumjack MacDiarmid: The Poetry and Prose of Hugh MacDiarmid* (Oxford: Clarendon Press, 1992), p. 100.

33 Edwin Morgan, 'James Joyce and Hugh MacDiarmid', in *Crossing the Border: Essays on Scottish Literature* (Manchester: Carcanet, 1990), p. 169.

34 MacDiarmid, *Complete Poems*, vol. 1, pp. 169–87.

35 *Ibid.*, p. 422.

36 Viktor Shklovsky, 'Art as Technique' (1916); repr. in Julie Rivkin and Michael Ryan (eds.), *Literary Theory: An Anthology* (Oxford: Blackwell, 2004), pp. 17–23; emphasis in original.

37 MacDiarmid, *Complete Poems*, vol. 1, p. 426.

38 *Ibid.*, p. 423.

39 Lewis Grassic Gibbon, 'Literary Lights', in Lewis Grassic Gibbon and Hugh MacDiarmid, *Scottish Scene or The Intelligent Man's Guide to Albyn* (London: Jarrolds, 1934); repr. in Valentina Bold (ed.), *Smeddum: A Lewis Grassic Gibbon Anthology* (Edinburgh: Canongate, 2001), pp. 123–37.

40 C. M. Grieve to J. H. Whyte, 1 July 1936; repr. in Bold (ed.), *Letters*, p. 853.

41 Unsigned editorial, 'The Red Scotland Thesis: Forward to the John Maclean Line', *Voice of Scotland* (June/August 1938); repr. in Angus Calder, Glen Murray

and Alan Riach (eds.), *The Raucle Tongue: Hitherto Uncollected Prose*, volume III, *1937–1978* (Manchester: Carcanet, 1998), pp. 9–14.

42 Alan Riach's *Hugh MacDiarmid's Epic Poetry* (Edinburgh University Press, 1991) remains the only monograph dedicated to the late poetry.

43 Hugh MacDiarmid, 'The Kind of Poetry I Want' (1961), in *Complete Poems*, vol. II, ed. Michael Grieve and W. R. Aitken (Manchester: Carcanet, 1994), p. 1025.

44 C. P. Snow, *The Two Cultures* (1959; Cambridge University Press, 2009).

45 Norman MacCaig, 'Patriot', in *The Poems of Norman MacCaig*, ed. Ewen McCaig (Edinburgh: Polygon, 2005), p. 510.

46 Hugh MacDiarmid, 'Scottish Poetry, 1923–1953', *Lines Review* (January 1954); repr. in Calder, Murray and Riach (eds.), *Raucle Tongue*, vol. III, p. 320.

47 Hugh MacDiarmid, *Lucky Poet: A Self-Study in Literature and Political Ideas, being the Autobiography of Hugh MacDiarmid (Christopher Murray Grieve)*, ed. Alan Riach (Manchester: Carcanet, 1994), p. xii.

48 Gerard Carruthers, David Goldie and Alistair Renfrew (eds.), *Beyond Scotland: New Contexts for Twentieth-Century Scottish Literature* (Amsterdam and New York: Rodopi, 2004).

Guide to Further Reading

Herbert, W. N., *To Circumjack MacDiarmid: The Poetry and Prose of Hugh MacDiarmid* (Oxford: Clarendon Press, 1992)

Lyall, Scott, *Hugh MacDiarmid's Poetry and Politics of Place: Imagining a Scottish Republic* (Edinburgh University Press, 2006)

Lyall, Scott and Margery Palmer McCulloch (eds.), *The Edinburgh Companion to Hugh MacDiarmid* (Edinburgh University Press, 2011)

McCulloch, Margery Palmer, *Scottish Modernism and Its Contexts 1918–1959: Literature, National Identity and Cultural Exchange* (Edinburgh University Press, 2009)

McCulloch, Margery Palmer (ed.), *Modernism and Nationalism: Literature and Society in Scotland 1918–1939, Source Documents for the Scottish Renaissance* (Glasgow: Association for Scottish Literary Studies, 2004)

Riach, Alan, *Hugh MacDiarmid's Epic Poetry* (Edinburgh University Press, 1991)

13

DAVID GOLDIE

Popular Fiction: Detective Novels and Thrillers from Holmes to Rebus

Scottish writers have, at times, played a role in detective, adventure and thriller writing that is out of proportion to the size of the nation. Though Scotland played no significant part in the twentieth-century's so-called 'Golden Age' of crime fiction, which was dominated by English and American authors, its writers were influential in establishing the genre in the late nineteenth century and can, in the early twenty-first century, count among themselves some of its most popular global practitioners. This chapter may not be able to offer a satisfactory explanation of why this is the case – unfortunately, literary criticism is rarely as tidy as fictional detective work – but it will offer an account of the somewhat punctuated evolution of crime and thriller fiction in the Scottish context in the period that runs from Conan Doyle to so-called Tartan Noir.

Arthur Conan Doyle and Robert Louis Stevenson are Scottish writers who demand attention principally because of the impact their work had on a popular writing based on action and suspense, on psychological instability and the solving of puzzles. Conan Doyle's place in the history of detective fiction needs little elaboration. Though he took up a genre that had been established in the 1830s and 40s by Vidocq's *Mémoires*, the Newgate novels and Edgar Allan Poe's Dupin stories, and which had been experimented with variously by Charles Dickens, Wilkie Collins, Mary Elizabeth Braddon and, most successfully, by Émile Gaboriau, Conan Doyle established in the popular mind the type of the detective story in its modern form. In his Sherlock Holmes stories for the *Strand* magazine from 1891 and in novellas such as *A Study in Scarlet* (1887), *The Sign of Four* (1890) and *The Hound of the Baskervilles* (1902), Conan Doyle created a fiction that fed on the sensational elements of his predecessors' work, featuring luminescent hellhounds bounding out of moorland mist, diabolical master criminals and dark deeds in opium dens. But it kept that sensationalism tightly bound in satisfying plots that, through Holmes's reasoned application of observation, analysis and deduction, reduced the seemingly uncanny to the reassuringly explicable. He didn't so much invent the form, for most of the elements that are associated with Sherlock Holmes predated his creation – the use of a single detective figure to link disparate stories, his status as a 'consulting' amateur detective, the reliance on science and use of deduction, the personal eccentricity, the mastery of disguise, the use of a companion as an explicator and foil – but what Conan Doyle did was synthesise these elements by putting them under the control of a compelling, complex central character. The Holmes stories are primarily plot-driven, but their qualities of mystery and suspense are deepened by the fact that the detective figure is himself mysterious and contradictory. Holmes is a man who can at times seem self-absorbed to the point of autism and at others empathetic; he is a fundamentally rational being who loses himself in music and drugs, a model of punctilio and order who has deep connections with, and a dark understanding of, the criminal underworld. He solves crimes at a satisfyingly intellectual, forensic level, but he also understands the human passions that provoke them, the 'dark desires of apparently respectable people' that drive tales such as *The Hound of the Baskervilles*.[1]

Stevenson's fiction comes to a similar point, but arrives there from a different starting place, drawing as he does on the popular tradition of historical romance founded by Walter Scott as well as the darker dualisms of James Hogg's *Private Memoirs and Confessions of a Justified Sinner* (1824). The most obvious and celebrated example of this dualism in Stevenson's work comes in *The Strange Case of Dr Jekyll and Mr Hyde* (1886), a novella that bears many of the hallmarks of the emerging genre of detective fiction, not least a murder, a locked-room mystery, a closeted homosocial environment and a detective figure in the form of the lawyer Utterson. But *Jekyll and Hyde* is above all an exploration of an idea of divided identity that would manifest itself variously in the following few years in the psychology of Sigmund Freud, the anthropology of J. G. Frazer and the fiction of Bram Stoker and Joseph Conrad: the notion of an underlying atavism, an ungovernable appetitive instinct that lurks within and threatens to overthrow even the most civilized and rational modern mind. The contrast between the deformed, stunted Mr Hyde and urbane Dr Jekyll is, as the reader ultimately finds out, not that between blackmailer and victim as Utterson first believes, but is rather the internal division of one person – an idea that Conan Doyle would draw directly on in the Sherlock Holmes story 'The Man with the Twisted Lip' (1891) in which the deformed beggar Hugh Boone is revealed to be in fact the man he is suspected of murdering, the thoroughly respectable Neville St Clair. The articulation of this particular idea of division is new to Stevenson in *Dr Jekyll and Mr Hyde*, but as a structural principle it is common to many of his more straightforward historical adventures and is what generates much of their intrigue and their speculative content on national issues. In *Kidnapped* (1886) Stevenson follows the example of Scott's *Waverley* in using antipodal characters, David Balfour and Alan Breck, to embody the division between Lowland and Highland Scotland and to examine the terms on which reconciliation between the two can be effected in the wake of the failed Jacobite rebellions. In *The Master of Ballantrae* (1889), also set in the immediate post-Jacobite period, the division is that between two brothers. Again, an issue of the divided nature of the Scottish character is projected onto a contrasting pair of characters who embody, in the younger brother Henry, the dull virtues of domestic responsibility and commitment to duty and, in the elder, James, the attractive vices of fearlessness and impulsiveness.

It is tempting to put these two factors together and argue that there is something particular to the Scottish formation of Conan Doyle and Stevenson that is fundamental to their success as popular writers of suspense and detection: that the condition of Scottishness – its confused political status as a stateless nation, its geographical and cultural splitting between Highland and Lowland, its religious divisions – lends itself to the sense of doubleness, the duplicity on which crime and thriller fiction feed. Such a reading is bolstered by G. Gregory Smith's much-cited and subsequently influential diagnosis, in his *Scottish Literature: Character and Influence* (1919), of a Caledonian Antisyzygy at work in Scottish writing that marks out the national literature as fundamentally bipolar, oscillating between extremes of piety and irreverence, civilized urbanity and savage rusticity.

But this is to ignore some of the most salient facts of Conan Doyle's and Stevenson's fiction. It is possible to see Scottish precedents in the work of both, but it is also possible to insist too hard on these and so ignore the wider British and international contexts within which their work might more fruitfully be seen. Conan Doyle suggested that Sherlock Holmes was based on the Edinburgh doctor Joseph Bell, and it is arguable that Holmes's empiricism comes directly out of the principles of the Scottish Enlightenment. Similarly, Dr Henry Jekyll might rightly be seen as a successor to the notorious Deacon Brodie, and the novella in which he appears be interpreted as a kind of mind map of an Edinburgh split between its teeming, corrupt Old Town and rational, civilized New Town. The fact is, however, that the metropolis of *Jekyll and Hyde* is not Edinburgh but London, and its characters are recognisably English. This suggests either that Stevenson saw some quality in the divided Scottish mind that had wider application for his British and international readers or that what he was describing was a fundamental condition of modernity which had its local expression in Scottish and English culture and so was equally applicable to both. This latter reading arguably squares better with Stevenson's wider interests as primarily an international writer and his authorship of works, among them *Treasure Island* (1883), *The Black Arrow* (1883), the *South Sea Tales* (1893), *St Ives* (1897), that range widely across temporal and national boundaries. His literary antecedents, likewise, are international rather than peculiarly Scottish: his grounding in historical romance, for example, coming as much from Victor Hugo and the elder Dumas as it does from Walter Scott, whom he famously disparaged in his 'A Gossip on Romance' as 'a great romantic – an idle child'.[2]

Sherlock Holmes is similarly unmistakably, perhaps irredeemably, English, and his sleuthing activities are based almost wholly in London and the South of England, where Conan Doyle settled. Holmes's literary heritage is that mixture of American, English and French writing that formed the foundation of crime fiction and which might be seen in the vector that runs from Vidocq through Lecocq to Sherlock. The occasional irruption of something more exotic and international comes not from the North but from the East or, as in *A Study in Scarlet*, Mormon America (a theme perhaps picked up from the 'Story of the Destroying Angel' written by Stevenson with his American wife in *The Dynamiter*, 1885). By an interesting quirk, the Sherlock Holmes stories frequently alternated in the *Strand* magazine with a series that featured the Glasgow detective Dick Donovan – a figure who was rather more dogged and a little less inspirational than Holmes but, initially at least, his equal in popularity. Donovan's creator was an Englishman, J. E. Preston Muddock, who had only a limited acquaintance with Glasgow, having created Donovan during a four-year spell working for W. & D. C. Thomson in Dundee. This sometimes shows in the rather hazy geography of the stories' plots and their indeterminate dialogue. In his story 'The Pearl Necklace', for example, Muddock displays his mastery of the Glasgwegian vernacular by having one hardened Glasgow criminal mutter to another, rather unconvincingly, 'The blooming Sheeny (Jew) has got some of the swag.'[3] Donovan drew, as did Conan Doyle, on a tradition of indigenous popular Scottish crime writing that included the casebooks of two Edinburgh policemen, the real James McLevy (an Irishman whose memoirs were published in the 1850s and early 60s) and the fictional James McGovan (the creation of William Crawford Honeyman in the 1870s), but he wrote, like Conan Doyle, with an ear cocked to the London underworld and an eye on the British and the international market.[4] This strange conjunction meant that the two most popular fictional characters in the *Strand* magazine in the early 1890s were an English detective created by a Scotsman and a Scottish detective (albeit one whose provenance seems a little confused) created by an Englishman – an early sign perhaps, of the tendency of the genre of crime fiction to defy easy categorisation according to national boundaries.

Apart from occasional series, such as that following the exploits of 'Bobby Gibson, Footballer-Detective' in the *People's Journal* in the years before the First World War, the detective novel was rarely visible in Scottish writing for a long time after Conan Doyle. The suspenseful historical romance tradition continued by Stevenson, as well as by Conan Doyle in *Micah Clarke* (1889), *The White Company* (1891) and *Sir Nigel* (1906), was kept alive in Neil Munro's fiction, particularly in his *The New Road* (1914), and by John Buchan in novels such as *John Burnet of Barns* (1898) and *Witch Wood* (1927) and would find its way into the popular novels of Nigel Tranter and Dorothy Dunnett. Sensational crime cropped up in novels such as McArthur and Long's *No Mean City* (1935), but the main legacy of the detective novel was to be seen in the spy fictions that came into vogue with the First World War. The outstanding British writer associated with this new genre was John Buchan, whose *Thirty-Nine Steps* (1915) and *The Power House* (1916) launched the two principal figures, Richard Hannay and Edward Leithen, who would feature in several of the adventure books that Buchan would call his 'shockers'. Buchan was, like Conan Doyle and Stevenson before him and Alistair MacLean and Val McDermid after, a Scot by formation who found a home, a subject matter and an audience outside the country. His shockers are interesting not just for their suspenseful narratives but for the tension that exists in them between an optimistic will to civilize and unify and the nagging fear of a persisting instinct that destabilises this will. In *The Power House* Leithen's comfortable idea of what he calls the 'goodwill of civilisation' is challenged by the wealthy anarchist Andrew Lumsden who tells him, 'You think that a wall as solid as the earth separates civilisation from barbarism. I tell you the division is a thread, a sheet of glass. A touch here, a push there, and you bring back the reign of Saturn.'[5]

In the Hannay novels, the main unifying power against such saturnalias of barbarism, and in particular the barbarisms of continental Europe and Ireland, is that of Britishness and its associated Imperialism. Buchan conceives a British imperial identity that is notably wide-ranging and permissive. It refuses to discriminate within the white empire: Hannay is a South African expatriate Scot and he and his Boer confederate Peter Pienaar enjoy a relationship of total equality with the Ulsterman MacGillivray, Englishman Sir Walter Bullivant and, stretching the definition to its widest, the American Blenkiron. Class difference, likewise, causes little friction, as working–class Scots like Geordie Hamilton share common purpose with aristocrats such as Sandy Arbuthnot. It is, of course, a tendency of political thrillers to emphasise external difference where crime fiction explores internal conflict and contradiction, so it not surprising to find the wartime Hannay novels following this pattern and defining a virtuous Britishness threatened by devious foreign shape-shifters such as Graf Otto von Schwabing in *The Thirty-Nine Steps* and *Mr Standfast* (1919) and the denatured, sadistic Hilda Von Einem and Ulric Von Stumm – a brute with 'a perverted taste for soft delicate things' – in *Greenmantle* (1916).[6]

But there is also the threat from within. This is only hinted at in the early Hannay books, but it becomes an important factor in what is perhaps the most interesting novel in the series, *The Three Hostages* (1924), in which Hannay comes close to understanding the darker implications of the Unconscious of Freudian psychoanalysis. The theme is introduced by the novel's Dr Greenslade, and is expressed in his belief that the 'barriers between the conscious and the subconscious' that have always 'been pretty stiff in the average man' have broken down. 'The result is confusion', he tells Hannay, 'you can't any longer take the clear psychology of most civilised human beings for granted. Something is welling up from primeval depths to muddy it.'[7] This impacts not only on crime itself, but on the way it must be conceived: 'you can hardly take anything for granted and if you want detective stories that are not childish fantasy, you'll have to invent a new kind'.[8] *The Three Hostages* doesn't quite mark such a departure in fictional form, but it does offer a shift in Buchan's thinking – perhaps occasioned by the war and by his role in directing propaganda at the Ministry of Information – in which his characteristic focus on regulation and restraint moves from the physical to the psychological. In thrillers like *The Thirty-Nine Steps*, *Greenmantle* and *Mr Standfast*, control is exerted by force, by means of bodily constraint and imprisonment, or physical deception, through disguise and subterfuge. In the post-war novels this sense of control is challenged from within, from the sense that there lurk disruptive forces deep in the personality that may be unleashed by a range of stimuli: in *The Three Hostages* by hypnotism, in *The Dancing Floor* (1926) and *Witch Wood* by atavistic ritual and in *The Courts of the Morning* (1929) by drugs.

In Buchan's thriller fiction, then, the good man (for it is generally a man) is usually defined in his relation to a set of principles that largely align with the values of the British imperium – although the occasional good American and even good German do turn up from time to time. The villains who generate the novels' suspense are those like Andrew Lumley who threaten that British self from the outside by way of an anarchic internationalism or those like Dominick Medina in *The Three Hostages* who attempt to rot it from the inside by laying bare its hypocrisies and repressions. Both villains can pass as English gentlemen, and so can understand from the inside, so to speak, how vulnerable its values are to attack from without and within and direct their sinister campaigns accordingly. But what is never in question is that Scotland might be a source of that threat. Scottishness is not a condition of separation and internal division in Buchan's thrillers but a principle of integrity and a warrant of united effort.

The sense in which Scottish particularity is effaced by adventure fiction is reinforced in the work of Alistair MacLean, one of the most successful British authors of the third quarter of the twentieth century with sales of over 150 million copies of some twenty-six novels.[9] MacLean's personal journey took him from a Gaelic-speaking childhood near Inverness to tax exile in Switzerland, but apart from *When Eight Bells Toll* (1966), set in the Western Isles, his fiction concerns itself largely with wartime and Cold War adventure to which his Scottishness is incidental. Occasionally a Scot turns up in his work, such as the Clydeside engineer Casey Brown in *The Guns of Navarone* (1957), but this is only to augment multi-national casts of men, like Buchan's homosocial groups, engaged in saving the free world from political and criminal intrigue. Membership of these groups is more dependent on qualities of masculinity than nationality. The novels are well paced but formulaic, relying for their jeopardy, consistently from his first novel *HMS Ulysses* (1955), on simple treachery rather than the internal conflicts of individual characters, and for their lower-level tension by an undercurrent of mistrust on the part of NCO characters of their socially superior but morally suspect officers.

The period in which MacLean was writing went unmarked by any significant Scottish crime writing. The only partial exception came in the form of two short novels by Muriel Spark that, rather characteristically, turned the genre on its head. *The Driver's Seat* (1970) has its victim, the enigmatic Lise, plot her own death at the hands of an unwilling murderer – turning the book from a potential whodunnit into what Lise herself alludes to as a 'whydunnit in q-sharp major'.[10] *Not to Disturb* (1971), meanwhile, twists a scenario reminiscent of a locked-room country-house murder mystery into a farcical comedy of below-stairs attitudes, as the servants of Baron and Baroness Klopstock plan the ways they will cash in on the murders they anticipate are about to happen in the library.

It is not until the surprisingly late date of 1977 that Scottish literature got, in the publication of William McIlvanney's *Laidlaw*, its first truly modern detective. Laidlaw is particularly modern for the understanding he brings that the detective's primary job is not to separate out the lawless in order to isolate, stigmatise and punish them for their transgressions, but rather to understand the complex workings of personality and environment that might make a criminal of anyone: as he puts it, 'we share in everyone else or forgo ourselves'.[11] Laidlaw tells his children frightening stories but then defuses the terror by showing how even potentially terrifying situations can have banal explanations. This is to educate them, as he tells his son, that 'there *are* no monsters', and that instead 'there's only people'.[12] This sense of criminality, and even murder, as activities which are not so much the product of savagery, or a denial of the human, as unfortunate but fundamental consequences of what it is actually to be human is what drives Laidlaw. His habit of submerging himself in the city in order to solve his cases may be seen partly as an affectation and partly a simple trope of the detective genre, reminiscent perhaps of Sherlock Holmes's forays into the underworld or his going native on the moor and inhabiting its mystery in *The Hound of the Baskervilles*, but it is also a statement of his empathy for and his refusal to place himself above the criminals and the victims of their crimes.

Laidlaw is a novel that operates through a series of binarisms that are familiar to the fiction of the west of Scotland – male versus female, individual versus family, Catholic versus Protestant, heterosexual versus homosexual, urban versus rural, housing scheme versus tenement – as well as that most pertinent of dualisms in detective fiction, that of the law and the outlaw. But once he has set up these binarisms, McIlvanney attempts throughout the three novels that feature Laidlaw to dissolve rather than exploit them. In *Laidlaw*, for example, the father of the victim, for whom we might normally expect to feel sympathy, is a criminal and a domestic abuser, while the murderer is essentially an innocent pushed to a terrible act of violence by the discrimination he faces as a Catholic and a homosexual. McIlvanney reinforces this blending through skilful use of form. The narratives of *Laidlaw* and *The Papers of Tony Veitch* are noticeably unstable: they refuse to focus on and privilege one character alone and instead construct a shifting perspective by means of short, punchy chapters that allow us to see contrasting events focalised through different characters. This can have sometimes surprising effects, as when in *Laidlaw* we see the murderer at bay, Tommy Bryson, through the eyes of his lover Harry Rayburn and gain a very strong sense not only of Tommy's fear and vulnerability but also of the depth and tenderness of Harry's love for him. There is a good deal of homophobic banter traded between the novel's characters, but scenes such as this, taken alongside Laidlaw's own more understanding and humane attitudes towards so-called deviance, allow for a balanced and complex, but noticeably sympathetic treatment of what was, at the time, an issue that tended either to be ignored or subjected to casual prejudice and contempt.

Another formal device that reinforces sympathy is the use of a second-person address in the opening lines of *Laidlaw*:

> Running was a strange thing. The sound was your feet slapping the pavement. The light of passing cars batted your eyeballs. Your arms came up unevenly in front of you, reaching from nowhere, separate from you and from each other.[13]

In using this apparently casual idiom, McIlvanney places the reader, almost without realising it, into an empathetic relationship with the murderer. By this act of interpellation, hailing the reader and inviting him or her to imagine themselves into the panicking body of the criminal, McIlvanney signals one of the novel's main concerns – the potential interchangeability of the guilty and the innocent. His readers are, by implication, encouraged to think of themselves as like his characters, in the possibility they hold of unleashing 'this moment of ravening viciousness whose spores were in each of them'.[14] In denying the fleeing body agency and coherence and turning it instead into a blur of impersonal, instinctual flight, the narration is introducing a second issue that will be explored insistently throughout the Laidlaw novels – the question of whether we can ever properly be said to be the authors of our own actions. This question is one that hangs over Laidlaw and colours his approach to crime, leading him to interpret murder as a social as much as a personal act. It is, he tells Harkness, hypocrisy to believe that 'bad things can happen somehow of their own accord, in isolation. Without having roots in the rest of us.'[15] It also prompts him to a philosophy in which the individual is not so much the author of events as a subject created and defined by them. Laidlaw posits this in his own idiosyncratic reformulation of the Existentialist proposition that existence precedes essence: 'you don't know who you are until you happen'.[16]

Laidlaw is noticeably compassionate towards many of the criminals that come into his orbit. While he is quick to condemn some, especially those whose violence is unfocused or dishonourable or who have, like Matt Mason, betrayed the obligations they owe to their class, he is willing to stretch out a sympathetic understanding to the many caught in the flux of circumstances through which, according to a kind of chaos theory, small, ordinary impulses transform into criminal acts out of all proportion to their causes. 'It was', Laidlaw muses in *Strange Loyalties*, 'the crime beyond the crime that had always fascinated me, the sanctified network of legally entrenched social injustice towards which the crime I was investigating feebly gestured.'[17]

McIlvanney can't really be credited as the progenitor of the astonishing amount of Scottish crime fiction that has been written since the appearance of *Laidlaw*, even though writers like Ian Rankin have paid generous tribute to his influence. He is not, as journalists sometimes assert, the godfather of Tartan Noir, though he shares with the writers who have come after him a basic concern with the rootedness of Scottish crime in a long and unhappy history of economic inequality, sexual discrimination and religious and class prejudice. And this is principally because of his distrust of the detective genre itself, his reluctance to reduce the Laidlaw novels to a repeatable formula. Laidlaw is, like most fictional detectives, a fully paid-up member of the awkward squad, and one rather gets the impression that his creator feels he can really only honour that awkwardness in his character – that sense that the best defence against the modern world's criminality, mendacity and corporate bullshit lies in a recalcitrant individualism – by refusing to make him just another reproducible commodity in fiction's marketplace.

This is a concern that is shared by a number of the Scottish detective and thriller writers who have followed McIlvanney, even though some have been more content to write in a serial format. Frederic Lindsay first came to popular notice in 1984 with his political thriller *Brond* and has subsequently created a series of novels, beginning with *Kissing Judas* (1997), that follow the troubled development of his Lothian and Borders policeman D. I. Jim Meldrum. Like *Brond* these are dark pieces of fiction that engage the reader's morbid curiosity rather than sense of suspense, and in emphasis are more philosophical than procedural. They are literate, introspective and often rather oblique in their actions, tending to establish location without descriptive passages, and relying on a shifting free indirect voice that destabilises the authority of the narrative. Lindsay's fictions appear to have the intention to disturb rather than oblige, which does not make them particularly popular, but gives them the feel of serious, thoughtful literature. A similarly spiky, though less tortured, idiosyncrasy can be seen in Frank Kuppner's writing about crime in *A Very Quiet Street* (1989) and *Something Very Like Murder* (1994). In these books, which follow, rather digressively, the trials of the Glasgow criminals Oscar Slater and Bertie Willox, Kuppner wilfully resists literary categories and even consistency in tone, blending fact and fiction, apparently autobiographical speculation and historical recovery. He is perhaps not in the same league as W. G. Sebald, but Kuppner shares Sebald's eccentric, unresting curiosity about the manner in which his autobiographical narrator's life and personal experiences intersect with a national history chequered by crime and violence.

McIlvanney, Lindsay and Kuppner in their various ways use form to mimic the intractable nature of their subject matter, suggesting that individual acts of crime have roots so interwoven in a culture and a place that they can have no discernible beginning or end. Solving and understanding are two different things, and they are more concerned with the latter, knottier task. In doing this they stand outside the mainstream of a more market-friendly Tartan Noir which has often proved itself a little keener on appearing to solve its crimes or exploit them for sensational effect, and rather less willing to deal at anything more than a superficial level with ramifying, complex social and political issues that might clot its narrative flow and impair its orchestration of suspense. It is perhaps harsh to put into this category a series like Quintin Jardine's *Bob Skinner* books which, more so than his *Oz* (and now *Primavera*) *Blackstone* novels, are largely located in a recognisable and largely realistically portrayed modern Scotland and have often captured a strong flavour of Edinburgh crime and, sometimes, Scottish politics. But the demands of writing twenty Skinner novels in seventeen years are such that a number of often rather predictable Scottish themes and settings and even some rather unlikely ones (the Edinburgh Book Festival in *Fatal Last Words*, 2009) appear to be mined more for their opportunity to generate a sensational plot than to say anything pressing about the criminal mind, and Jardine seems rather too prone to granting his own and his characters' wishes: the villain is hit by a bolt of lightning in *Skinner's Round* (1995), Hibernian FC win the league in *Aftershock* (2008) and the often rather smug Skinner is elevated to Chief Constable in *A Rush of Blood* (2010).

The use of criminal violence as a form of entertainment, and its solving as a form of wish fulfilment, is also strongly present in the equally prolific Christopher Brookmyre. Brookmyre mixes an often brilliantly sardonic off-beat humour with scenes of graphic violence, seen to great effect in the series of gruesome comic thrillers beginning with *Quite Ugly One Morning* (1996) that feature investigative journalist Jack Parlabane. Brookmyre's novels take great delight in undermining the expected modes of Scottish criminal and investigative behaviour, as witnessed in *The Sacred Art of Stealing* (2002), which features a gang of international art thieves who stage bank robber-ies in the form of Dadaist happenings and an investigating policewoman, D. I. Angelique de Xavia, a Catholic Asian who supports Rangers Football Club. His novels' politics, such as they are, are of the irreverent, self-righteous left, and though his style is sophisticated and smart – often being compared to that of Elmore Leonard and Carl Hiaasen – his books sometimes suffer from the charmless sense of invulnerability that comes from always being in the right. They might be thought to challenge their readers, and perhaps do achieve this with their careless violence, but there is perhaps little in their casual cynicism really to shake the worldview of a generation acculturated to contemporary horror films and video games. In this Brookmyre might perhaps have taken account of some of the nuance and ambiguity found in Iain Banks, whose *Complicity* (1993) is often seen as a precursor to his work. *Complicity* is, to state it bluntly, a cautionary tale about the need to be careful what you wish for. Its story follows twin narratives: one is that of a sanctimonious, left-leaning and deplorably louche investigative journalist, Cameron Colley, written in the first person; the other, that of a mysterious murderer, written (as in the opening of *Laidlaw*, though to very different effect) in the second. The sense of complicity promised in the novel's title is manifested when it becomes apparent that the murders are enactments of some of Colley's less temperate and responsible journalistic opinions and are being performed on his behalf, so to speak, out of a twisted sense of gratitude, and even love. This ultimately prompts Colley to rethink his manner of living and ought, presumably, to encourage the book's readers to a similar revaluation – though there remains, perhaps, a nagging suspicion that in allowing ourselves to be titillated by the novel's graphic portrayals of sex and violence we have ourselves been complicit in its trivialising of such serious issues by treating them as subjects for recreational entertainment.

Val McDermid rarely shows such scruples in her work, which offers in place of ambiguity a series of absorbing, intricately engineered plots that have made her a major international bestseller. She resists the Tartan Noir tag, mainly because she writes only infrequently about Scotland in her three major crime series that feature Manchester private detective Kate Brannigan, Scottish lesbian journalist Lindsay Gordon and the Bradfield-based pair of psychological profiler Tony Hill and policewoman Carol Jordan. Her novels certainly deal with serious issues, particularly in relation to gender and sexual identity, and can at times involve subtle characterisations of individual vulnerability: for example, in the portrayal of Tony Hill's sexual dysfunction in *The Mermaids Singing* (1995). This is leavened in the Brannigan and Gordon books with a dark humour, but in the Hill and Jordan books the emphasis is on the blacker, more sustained criminal deviation expressed in serial killing. McIlvanney's Laidlaw doesn't believe in monsters and scorns those who do, like his competitor Milligan, for lacking perspective: 'Faced with the enormity, they lose their nerve, and where they see a man, they make a monster.'[18] McDermid's approach is quite different: her fiction does believe in monsters, and Tony Hill labours under 'no illusions about the extremes of evil that human beings were capable of'.[19] McDermid takes this assumption and builds on its foundation an elaborate, sophisticated mechanism for keeping the reader carefully under the control of her words. It is, like much good crime fiction, a form of hypnotism – not unlike that practised by Buchan's Dominick Medina – that employs its rhythms to suspend rational judgement and unlock the transgressive imagination. And then like all successful hypnotism, it clicks its fingers with the solving of the crime and returns us safely back to our lives. It is, in that sense at least, a worthy, if much more sophisticated, successor to the tradition of Conan Doyle and Stevenson. But, like the work of these predecessors, it tells us very little that is particular to Scotland, and returns us to what seems to be a fundamental incompatibility between the idea of a serious national literature which aims to illuminate the unique conditions of a particular people in a particular place, and an international genre that is concerned with entertaining a wider audience according to a limiting narrative of transgression and correction.

Two contemporary writers who have addressed these issues and have perhaps achieved the most success in synthesising them are Denise Mina and Ian Rankin. In her Maureen O'Donnell trilogy, *Garnethill* (1998), *Exile* (2000) and *Resolution* (2001), and the Paddy Meehan novels that begin with *The Field of Blood* (2005), Mina successfully balances the suspense narrative characteristic of McDermid and the debunking, plot-suspicious demotic of McIlvanney. Mina's O'Donnell is reluctant to think of crime as unspeakable monstrosity because she has lived much of her life in a forced intimacy with abuse and speaks as its victim. The trilogy is not without its monsters – principally and perhaps tellingly the hospital psychologist Angus Farrell – and is not without an element of righteous vengeance and wish fulfilment towards its close, but it is characterised for the most part by the ironising down-to-earth attitudes of Maureen and the community of vulnerable but articulate people with which she surrounds herself. Her status as a former psychiatric patient makes her suspicious of authority, and it is her awareness of the necessity of resisting totalising narratives and the categorising of others that makes her both a sympathetic and, in her own way, authoritative and strong central character.

Ian Rankin's D. I. John Rebus is undoubtedly the most commercially successful Scottish literary detective there has been. He has earned this status largely because of Rankin's skill in constructing compelling and, as the series developed over twenty years, increasingly complex plots that tied a strongly realised sense of place to a cast of largely credible characters led by the often refractory Rebus. There are ways in which the series, completed with the publication of *Exit Music* in 2007, appears a little too formulaic. Rebus's much-vaunted complexity seems to some readers of serious literary fiction to be a little gestural, to lack the real sense of psychological instability and vulnerability of Mina and Lindsay or the existential depth of McIlvanney. There is a sense, often in the early fiction, that the targets of Rebus's indignation are the soft ones of a somewhat conventional and unreflexive leftism: the professional classes, lawyers, businessmen, the men in suits who constitute a rather underdeveloped authority against which Rebus huffs and puffs. There are times, too, when a weakness for song titles and bad puns undermines the attempts to create a smart, streetwise style – the menu of the Heartbreak Café in *The Black Book* (1993), with its 'Blue Suede Choux' and 'Jailhouse Roquefort', springs to mind here, or the same novel's awful pun on the 'silence of the lums', or the neologised 'woolly suits' and 'biscuit tins' of *Black and Blue* (1997). But sitting alongside that is a writing that is persuasively local in its reference and tone, that paints for both its Scottish and international readers a convincing picture of contemporary Edinburgh at a number of levels and which responds to and develops the literary tradition out of which it comes. This tradition is perhaps intrusively apparent in the first two Rebus books, *Knots and Crosses* (1987) and *Hide and Seek* (1991), which employ Stevenson's *Jekyll and Hyde* as an intertext, but becomes more fully integrated as the series develops. Rankin began the Rebus books with the intention of writing 'something that was on the surface a crime novel that was going to sell loads of copies, but which would be accepted by my peers in academia as being serious Scottish fiction'.[20] In the eyes of many readers, he has successfully resolved this seemingly intractable problem, and has provided a series of books that sit comfortably in what had for a long time seemed the mutually incompatible categories of serious Scottish literature and popular crime.

Notes

1 Stephen Knight, *Crime Fiction since 1900: Detection, Death, Diversity*, 2nd edn (Houndmills: Palgrave Macmillan, 2010), p. 61.
2 Robert Louis Stevenson, *Memories and Portraits* (London: Chatto & Windus, 1919), p. 274.
3 *Ibid.*, p. 54.
4 See George Scott-Moncrieff (ed.), *James Mclevy: The Casebook of a Victorian Detective* (Edinburgh: Canongate, 1975), and James McGovan, *The Mcgovan Casebook: Experiences of a Detective in Victorian Edinburgh* (Edinburgh: Mercat Press, 2003).
5 John Buchan, *The Leithen Stories* (Edinburgh: Canongate, 2000), pp. 29, 28.
6 John Buchan, *Greenmantle* (Oxford: Oxford University Press, 1993), p. 79.
7 John Buchan, *The Three Hostages* (London: Thomas Nelson & Sons, 1926), pp. 22–3.
8 *Ibid.*, pp. 20–1.
9 Brian Docherty, 'Grace under Pressure: Reading Alistair Maclean', in Clive Bloom (ed.), *Twentieth-Century Suspense: The Thriller Comes of Age* (Houndmills: Macmillan, 1990),pp. 203–24.
10 Muriel Spark, *The Driver's Seat* (Harmondsworth: Penguin, 1974), p. 101.
11 William McIlvanney, *The Papers of Tony Veitch* (London: Coronet, 1984), p. 18.
12 William McIlvanney, *Laidlaw* (London: Coronet, 1979), p. 66.
13 *Ibid.*, p. 5.
14 *Ibid.*, p. 214.
15 *Ibid.*, p. 186.

16 *Ibid.*, p. 165.
17 William McIlvanney, *Strange Loyalties* (London: Hodder & Stoughton, 1991), p. 7.
18 McIlvanney, *Laidlaw*, p. 134.
19 Val McDermid, *The Last Temptation* (London: HarperCollins, 2002), p. 483.
20 Gill Plain, *Ian Rankin's 'Black and Blue': A Reader's Guide* (London: Continuum, 2002), p. 11.

Guide to further reading

Knight, Stephen, *Crime Fiction since 1900: Detection, Death, Diversity*, 2nd edn (Houndmills: Palgrave Macmillan, 2010)

Priestman, Martin, *The Cambridge Companion to Crime Fiction* (Cambridge University Press, 2003)

Rzepka, Charles J. and Lee Horsley, *A Companion to Crime Fiction* (Oxford: Wiley-Blackwell, 2010)

14

ROBERT ELLIS HOSMER, JR

Muriel Spark

In 1985, Muriel Spark was acclaimed 'the most gifted and innovative British novelist of her generation';[1] after her death in 2006, tributes and accolades multiplied, none, perhaps, more fitting than that of a fellow Scot, Ian Rankin, who deemed her 'the greatest Scottish novelist of modern times'.[2] Poet, playwright, editor, biographer, essayist, short story writer, most of all novelist, Muriel Spark achieved an eminence denied by few, but her work is often misinterpreted or misunderstood. Though she lived outside Scotland for most of her life, Spark was a Scottish writer, indelibly stamped by her first nineteen years in Edinburgh: she was 'Scottish by formation'.[3] And she was a theological writer, an artist of religious conviction and spiritual concerns, a Roman Catholic by conversion.

In Spark's first novel, *The Comforters* (1957), Caroline Rose labours to integrate the demands of her faith within the context of her own life as a fledgling novelist. In this novel of decided autobiographical import for Spark (in addition to her conversion and artistic calling, Caroline is part Jewish), Caroline achieves a personal integrity, rejecting the evils embodied in the self-righteous Georgina Hogg, the detached contemplation of Edwin Manders and the misguided charity of Helena Manders as well as the diabolism, hedonism and nihilism displayed by other characters. In the end Caroline accepts the reality of the supernatural voices writing her novel for her, and acquires a more charitable attitude towards others, however physically repulsive or morally repugnant she may find them. The outward conversion that took place before this novel began finds its necessary complement in this inward conversion, and *The Comforters* ends with Caroline's laughter echoing throughout a succinct parable of possibility. A lesser achievement in the canon of Spark's works, *The Comforters* sets out her enduring concerns with matters of faith and fictionality.

In *Robinson* (1958), January Marlow, stranded on an island after an aeroplane crash, struggles first for physical survival, then for a kind of spiritual survival. A recent convert, she encounters the forces of lapsed belief, magic, superstition, primitive nihilism and the occult. In the end she emerges as an integrated, functioning personality with a greater sense of charity, a sympathetic, if limited, artist. *Robinson* was followed by *Memento Mori* (1959), a novel in which several English geriatrics receive a puzzling telephone call with the same message, 'Remember, you must die.' Nearly all the recipients attempt to find a 'natural' explanation for the call, but several understand it quite otherwise: Charmian Colston and her former companion, Jean Taylor, both Roman Catholic converts, and Henry Mortimer, a retired police inspector and agnostic, all identify the caller as Death and accept the reality of the supernatural within the natural world. One of Spark's most overtly 'Catholic' novels, *Memento* is really a meditation on the first of the four last things in the form of a medieval mystery play. Jean Taylor is the perceiving consciousness who, at a moment of grace, identifies the caller, though she has never received a call herself. Taylor's detached perspective is both physical (she is an elderly arthritic confined to a nursing home) and spiritual. In casting off pride and accepting the gruesome realities of pain and death, she has opened herself to another reality: the grace to see ageing as part of a fulfilling process that leads through death to eternal life. Her life of prayer, sacrament, meditation and self-scrutiny constitutes a life well-lived, a death well-prepared for.

The *Ballad of Peckham Rye* (1960) presents a complementary reality: the diabolical in the world. But the greater sophistication of Spark's literary technique makes this a more difficult, indeed problematic, novel to consider. In some ways it stands in sharp contrast to its predecessors: there are no Catholics to speak of, unless one counts Nelly Mahone, a lapsed Catholic, and perhaps Dougal, who is never described as one, but does become a Franciscan novice for a period; there are no converts here, and the distinctly working-class ethos of this novel is a departure as well. Dougal does not introduce evil into the town of Peckham, he merely activates that potential inherent in some of its citizens. He breaks up relationships, he wreaks havoc and indirectly causes at least one murder. Though he can, on occasion, work good, this 'angel-devil' most often insinuates and manipulates toward evil ends. In the end, he slithers off, first to Africa, then to a monastery, before becoming a successful novelist. Spark's narrator delivers a final line conveying the groom's vision of 'the Rye for an instant looking like a cloud of green and gold, the people seeming to ride upon it, as you might say there was another world than this', giving spiritual proportion and perspective, even hope.[4] It's all a matter of choice and perspective, and Spark invites the discerning reader to share her perspective, to consider the possibilities: angel or devil; belief or unbelief.

In *The Bachelors* (1960), the battle is even more pitched, with Ronald Bridges, an epileptic Catholic, against Patrick Seton, a spiritualist medium of uncanny powers. Bridges has a clear, if unusual, sense of his vocation. Disqualified from holy orders because of his illness, he accepts his epilepsy as his vocation, using his fits as opportunities to cultivate greater self-awareness. These episodes let him know his strengths (analysis, definition, detachment) and his great weakness (a lack of charity). That knowledge challenges him to become more compassionate, to overcome his distaste for others, especially his co-religionists, and to become, unwittingly, an occasion of grace for others. Seton's seances, on the other hand, are sideshows staged for the manipulation of the innocent, guilty and gullible. While Ronald's fits bring true conversion, Patrick's seances effect fraudulent conversion. *The Bachelors* is a stunning technical accomplishment, contrasting true and false belief created by the use of true and false centres of consciousness.

Muriel Spark's preoccupation with manipulation and the themes of good and evil, particularly with the presence of evil as a paradoxical moment of grace for conversion, finds full expression in her next two novels, *The Prime of Miss Jean Brodie* (1962) and *The Girls of Slender Means* (1963). Jean Brodie is a developed treatment of the 'angel-devil' figure of Dougal Douglas, a dangerous and deluded woman, evil yet innocent, dedicated, she says, to her girls, and caught up in the struggle between the forces of good and evil warring for control of human souls. A mesmerising, unorthodox teacher at Edinburgh's Marcia Blaine School for Girls in the 1930s, Jean Brodie manipulates her students, creating a vicarious life for herself. This story of her impact on her special girls, 'the Brodie set', brought Spark fame and considerable wealth as the novel became a stage play, a popular film and a television project.

One of Miss Brodie's girls, Sandy Stranger, has particular difficulty in dealing with her spellbinding teacher. In the course of her two years under Miss Brodie in the junior school, then in the years beyond while in the upper school, Sandy gradually sees Miss Brodie in an entirely new light. The 'creeping vision of evil' that Sandy discerns in Miss Brodie causes her to turn on her teacher, thwart her plans and eventually to convert to Roman Catholicism before becoming a cloistered nun, Sister Helena of the Transfiguration. Flashes of Sister Helena clutching the grille punctuate and close the novel, providing its most enigmatic element: asked about influences on her during earlier years, Sandy responds, 'There was a Miss Jean Brodie in her prime.'[5] Why does the thought disturb her so? Perhaps because Jean Brodie has taken ultimate revenge? Perhaps because the battle for her soul, like that for all souls, continues in a fallen world? Perhaps because Sandy seeks the supreme confidence and self-defining authority Jean Brodie had, but cannot have since that authority belongs to God and the church?

In *The Girls of Slender Means* (1963), Nicholas Farringdon, in an epiphany atop a burning building, has a scorching vision of evil sufficient to move him toward conversion. Nicholas, a fledgling poet in wartime London, makes the acquaintance of a number of young women living at the May of Teck Club, a residence much like the Helena Club where Spark lived on her return to England in 1944. At the age of thirty-three and rather undecided about a number of matters (sexual preference, religion, suicide, pacifism), he embarks on an affair with the lovely Selina Redwood. When a number of the girls are trapped on the club's third floor during a bombing raid, the only escape route lies through a narrow window leading to the roof. The slender Selina escapes, then returns, not to rescue someone else but to save a Schiaparelli dress: at her reappearance with the dress, Nicholas 'involuntarily signed himself with the cross'. Years later one of the girls remarks about a note found in the manuscript of Nicholas's poems to the effect that 'a vision of evil may be as effective to conversion as a vision of good'.[6] Like Sandy Stranger, Nicholas Farringdon has received the gift of grace and been led to conversion and to the professed religious life: a Jesuit missionary priest in Haiti, he dies a martyr's death.

Conversion is also central to Spark's next novel, *The Mandelbaum Gate* (1965), with Barbara Vaughan, the daughter of a Jewish mother and Protestant father, on pilgrimage in the Holy Land. In terms of explicitly religious content, this is probably the richest of Spark's novels; in terms of autobiographical detail, it is certainly one of the most resonant. Spark uses the motif of the pilgrimage in a medieval way, viewing the experience in both literal and figurative terms. Barbara Vaughan's quest to find an integrated identity is simultaneously a pilgrimage towards an earthly city located in a land rent by strife and convulsed by the Eichmann trial (it is 1961), and towards a city which lies elsewhere. In the course of the novel, Barbara achieves a sense of her own identity, forging an integrated self from the disparate materials of her background. In the end she is a seriously religious woman, at home in the world, living according to the spirit, not the letter, of the law. Here, too, the vision of evil is catalytic: Barbara spends one day at Eichmann's trial, observing that the former SS colonel was answering 'for an imperative deity named Bureau IV-13-4, of whom he was the High Priest', and concluding, 'it was a highly religious trial'.[7] Spurred by this and by an English priest's remarks on faith in a sermon that begins in clichés and ends with insight, this young woman 'with the beautiful and dangerous gift of faith which, by definition of the Scriptures, is the sum of things hoped for and the evidence of things unseen', attains a mature religious vision, finally recognising that 'questions were things that sufficed in their still beauty, answering themselves', and that 'either the whole of life is unified under God or everything falls apart'.[8]

As demonstrated by her next four novels – *The Public Image, The Driver's Seat, Not to Disturb* and *The Hothouse by the East River*, published between 1968 and 1973 – Spark was influenced by the *nouveau roman* and its great exponent, Alain Robbe-Grillet. Robbe-Grillet's aesthetic can be summarised as an anti-realist, anti-romantic, anti-existentialist dogma grounded in the principle that literature is a search for an unknown, proceeding by means of rigorously objective description. Concern for traditional fictive elements like plot, character and setting are nullified. Often taking his subject matter from newspapers, Robbe-Grillet described personality and event with intense precision, from a very considerable distance. His viewpoint is an antiseptically neutral position in moral terms: 'the world is neither significant nor absurd: it simply is', he stated.

The Public Image (1968) is a fable, the story of Annabel Christopher, a very limited actress, who, under the tutelage of an Italian director, learns to play herself to a 't'. Her press agent creates both public and private images, for the actress and for her husband, Frederick. His attempt at scripting a counterplot including his own suicide, to ruin Annabel, fails. She resists further passivity, asserts her own centrality, takes her baby and leaves Italy for a new life. In *The Driver's Seat* (1970), Lise, a quite unremarkable young woman, 'neither good-looking nor bad-looking', searches for a young man who is her 'type', someone who will be her murderer. In the grip of delusion, Lise feels a sense of 'absolute purpose' and 'dominance over the situation'.[9] She has written her own death script and chooses everything carefully, from the clothes she wears to the place where she will be raped and bludgeoned so that what she has preordained will take place in the most grotesque, absurd, violent terms. Unlike Annabel's saga, Lise's story is a tragedy, made all the more poignant perhaps by her inability to control all its aspects. The novel chills the reader; Spark herself said that she became so frightened of Lise that she had to check herself into hospital to finish the novel.

Most reviewers of Spark's next novel, *Not to Disturb* (1971), were baffled. Auberon Waugh's verdict spoke for many: 'I have to admit that I could not make head or tail of it, it seems totally pointless.'[10] Others preferred to cite literary influences across a broad spectrum – Greek tragedy, Aristotle, Dante, Shakespeare, Proust, Pound, Ivy Compton-Burnett, Harold Pinter and Henry Green. Indeed, critics preferred to write of influences, since most had no idea of what to make of this fictional enterprise, with the exception of the astute Frank Kermode. Two other literary influences are of far greater significance, however: Eliot and Beckett. The world of the novel is etherised, and waiting is the essential activity (or non-activity) of the narrative. All the 'action' takes place on one night, in one place, a villa on the shores of Lake Leman. Baron Klopstock and his wife, along with their secretary, will die before first light. Confined to the library, the Baron will shoot the other two, then kill himself. A vivid cast of servants waits and waits for the carefully crafted scenario to be executed.

Though Prospero may come to mind in thinking about Lister, the butler and archmagician of this piece, Lister's means and ends differ radically from those of Shakespeare's magus as he manipulates a demonic cast into following his script. So clever and consummate an *auteur* is he that even the unexpected and unpredicted can be worked into the plan. Time has no meaning; as Lister says at one point, 'Let us not strain after vulgar chronology.'[11] Then the servants wait to cash in, selling their stories to press and film agents. One of the ironies of the novel lies in the servants' condition: they are as dead as the Baron and his companions. *Not to Disturb* presents as bleak a vision of life-in-death as Eliot or Beckett ever gave us.

The Hothouse by the East River (1973) is a surreal tale about Elsa, a woman whose shadow falls the wrong way, and her husband, Paul. When not out shopping or socialising or meeting with her psychiatrist, Elsa sits and stares at the East River, smiling with an air of expectancy. The novel captures the frantic world of the Upper East Side of New York in the 1970s, a world where everyone's 'into' analysis, disco parties, shopping at fashionable Madison Avenue boutiques and avant-garde theatre. The central characters move through a miasma of fears, hallucinations and flashbacks to Second World War horrors. Only late in the novel does the reader learn that these suffering, confused souls died thirty years earlier when their railway carriage was hit by a German bombing raid on England.

Each of these four novels is a parody of *le nouveau roman*. At the same time each is a rather savage satire directed not only at particular aspects of the contemporary world – the image-making industry, tourism, television journalism, psychiatry but also, and more importantly, at the moral nihilism and functional absurdity that pervade the contemporary ethos. In creating ghastly parodies, Spark co-opted a number of Robbe-Grillet's techniques (what she has referred to as his exactitude; his cinematic structural and narrative devices; his commitment to distance and detachment; his fondness for the present tense), while creating fictions which are deeply consistent with her long-standing, unremitting Catholic concerns. The perceiving consciousness of each of these novels blurs more than ever the distinction of past, present and future so that all the novels are told from an eschatalogical viewpoint, with death shaping the narrative focus to End Time. It is only the End that gives meaning and coherence, in aesthetic terms and in theological terms.

Despite frightening visions of damnation and suffering, every one of these novels manifests hope: Annabel departs with her baby at the end of *The Public Image*; Lise's wilful pursuit of her own end shreds the 'doctrine' of predestination; the graceful last line of *Not to Disturb*, 'While outside the house the sunlight is laughing on the walls', posits another world than this; and Elsa's expectant smile as she gazes east, the iconographic direction of the Resurrection, is a sign that Purgatory by the East River is but a liminal experience.[12]

In each of her next six novels, Muriel Spark reworked major ideas and concerns with fugal skill. *The Abbess of Crewe* (1974) is not just a satire on church politics loosely based on the Watergate episode of United States history. Spark's subtitle, 'A Modern Morality Tale', gives a clear indication of her intent: *The Abbess of Crewe* is a pointed exemplum on perhaps the 'deadliest' of the seven deadly sins: pride. Like Jean Brodie and Patrick Seton, Abbess Alexandra is a grand manipulator; like them she fosters a self-centred cult. But she goes beyond them in deception, cunning and perversion of the good with towering assertions like 'I'm your conscience and your authority. You perform my will and finish' and 'You cannot bring a charge against Agamemnon or subpoena Clytemnestra, can you?'[13] Unwilling to accept limitations and unable to locate herself within the dimension of sacred history, she declares, 'we are leaving the sphere of history and are about to enter that of mythology'.[14] Her own narcissistic personality is central to the mythology she spins: '"You know", she tells her sisters, "I am become an object of art, the end of which is to give pleasure."'[15] She mimics the divine, expecting that her word will order chaos and establish hierarchies. *The Abbess of Crewe* is more than a morality tale: it is simultaneously a parable of the deceptions of art and the evils of faith grounded in self, not other. At novel's end, Alexandra sails for Rome, summoned to explain herself. The novel's very last paragraph is not an 'endorsement' of the Abbess: actually, with its echoes of Prospero's conclusion to the masque within *The Tempest* ('our revels now are ended'), it establishes a contrast condemning her rank perversion of thought and language, while its beautifully wrought imagery crafted from traditional images of the Blessed Virgin Mary and the poetry of Thomas Traherne posits a world other than that consumed by grubby convent politics.

A number of critics saw Spark's next two novels, *The Takeover* (1976) and *Territorial Rights* (1979), as exclusively secular concerns but both novels condemn false mythologies and privilege true ones. At the centre of the former is Hubert Malindaine, who claims direct descent from the goddess Diana and the Emperor Caligula: like the Abbess of Crewe, Malindaine has entered the realm of mythology, though he has not become an object of art exactly: rather, he has woven a complex mythological web from filaments of pagan syncretism, solipsism, gross materialism and blackmail. At the novel's climax, a carefully choreographed cult observance in a garden at Nemi, presided over by Hubert as high priest, is disrupted by two women: Pauline Thin, a Roman Catholic, who arrests the congregation's attention by quoting St Paul, and Nancy Cowan, an Anglican, who joins in Pauline's condemnation of the cult of Diana and Hubert. *The Takeover* is a satire against materialism, church corruption, worldly Jesuits, the Children of God, Roman Catholic charismatics and much more, but it would be a mistake to consider its possibilities exhausted by satire. Several strategically placed references to eternal life coexisting with life in this world establish essential perspective on narrative events. The ease with which these references work may be a metaphor for the ease with which it is possible to miss the eternal while being consumed by the everyday.

Territorial Rights, set in Venice during the late 1970s, is a novel filled with evildoers: adulterers, liars, cheats, embezzlers, terrorists, blackmailers, drug dealers and more. Things have fallen to below canal level in this novel: guilt is largely unknown, the wicked prosper deliciously; in the words of one character, 'the really professional evildoers love it. They're as happy as larks in the sky.'[16] Demonic intelligence operates with startling efficacy in the absurd world of *Territorial Rights*, but the author, while detached and impersonal, has not failed to establish her customary perspective. She has aligned herself not with a particular character but with the great religious structures of Venice, monuments not of unageing intellect but of transcendent and enduring faith. As in so many of Spark's novels, the last paragraph is vital in creating meaning for the text: here the movement once again is clearly outward and beyond, to 'mosaics [that] stood with the same patience that has gone into these formations, piece by small piece'. This assertion of a different perspective from all those we have been party to in the novel offers Spark's affirmation of a patient biblical integrity, even in the smallest matters, not just because such structures rise on foundations often crafted of small pieces but because the whole process, witnessed from another world, creates enduring monuments.

In *Loitering with Intent* (1981), Fleur Talbot recounts the story of her nine-month stint working for Sir Quentin Oliver, an evil and deluded snob who has gathered a 'spiritual circle', called the Autobiographical Association, about him. A young woman of 'abounding faith', who writes poems and occasional articles for church newspapers, Fleur finds that her experiences editing and typing the memoirs of the association's members sharpen her perception of evil, confirm her vocation as an artist and strengthen her religious faith. Like Sandy Stranger, she discerns a creeping vision of evil in the person of the archmanipulator: unlike her, Fleur does not convert to Roman Catholicism (she is already a practising Catholic) but rather converts inwardly to a more charitable attitude, opening herself by deliberate choice to receive unmerited grace, should it come her way.

Fleur Talbot matures as an artist and as a believer. Spark delineates the process as Fleur writes her first novel, offering asides on character, motives, overheard remarks and the novelist's vocation ('Without a mythology, a novel is nothing. The true novelist, one who understands the work as a continuous poem, is a mythmaker.').[17] That mythology takes its inspiration, substance and direction from the novelist's abounding faith. Excerpts from the autobiographies of Newman and Cellini are woven into the text of *Loitering with Intent*, just as their very clear import is integrated within the personality of Fleur Talbot, who declares, 'How wonderful it feels to be an artist and a woman in the twentieth century.'[18] The novel's very last paragraph has her kicking a stray football 'with a chance grace'. Landing it in a 'small boy's waiting hands: the boy grinned. And so, having entered the fullness of my years, from there by the grace of God I go on my way rejoicing.'

An early Spark essay, 'The Mystery of Job's Suffering', appeared in the *Church of England Newspaper* in 1955. Her first novel, *The Comforters*, was inspired by it. She tried, unsuccessfully, to write her novel of Job more than once. Though every novel Spark wrote dealt with suffering, and in a particular way when the novel captures the experience of conversion, none until *The Only Problem* (1984) drew in such a straightforward manner on Job.

Harvey Gotham, a wealthy Canadian who has withdrawn to southern France to write a monograph on the Book of Job, is the novel's protagonist. A believer, Harvey seeks to reconcile the existence of a benevolent creator with the presence of unspeakable suffering. By novel's end, having suffered himself, he has ceased trying to find a rational solution; a man of 'abounding faith', he has accepted the limitations of his creaturehood, acknowledged that suffering is a mystery and learned that while suffering and art can illuminate Job (and life), that biblical text will never come clear, because it is a poem, not a scholastic argument. Harvey's conversion is perhaps even more profound than a change in religious affiliation, for he has turned away from the intellect and towards the heart as a guide for conduct; chastened and more deeply spiritual, the perpetually interrogative Harvey, like Barbara Vaughan in *The Mandelbaum Gate*, has realised that 'questions were things that sufficed in their still beauty, answering themselves'.[19] He now speaks in measured, declarative tones, turning outwards at the end, into the world of social responsibility; unlike Abbess Alexandra, Harvey has profited from the experience of withdrawal from the world, not so much from his own efforts as from an unexpected grace that touches suffering with insight.

A Far Cry from Kensington (1988) is another fiction with decided auto-biographical resonance. As in *Loitering with Intent*, a central Catholic char-acter achieves status as a mature believer and artist. And as in the earlier novel, a pitched battle between the forces of good and evil (here the evil is radionics, a pseudoscience that uses a black box to affect people's lives, for good or ill) rages in post-Second World War London. The conflict pits Nancy Hawkins, a young war widow in the publishing trade, against Hector Bartlett, a hack writer of extraordinary pretensions and execrable prose style. Here, as in other novels, evil effects a conversion, for Nancy's encoun-ter with radionics causes her to re-examine her religious practices; though convinced that 'it was a lot of rubbish', she reflects, 'But was it any more mad than my compulsive Hail Marys at 12 o'clock noon? … I decided then and there to give up those Hail Marys; my religion in fact went beyond those Hail Marys which had become a superstition to me.'[20] Like her creator, Nancy Hawkins accepts the absolute truths of doctrine, declaring, 'I can't disbelieve.'[21]

Though Spark's nineteenth novel, *Symposium* (1990), is set among the fashionable set of Tony Blair's Islington, it is a very Scottish undertaking riveted on Margaret Murchie, one of ten guests at a dinner party given by an American painter and his Australian companion. Originally from St Andrews, just recently married to William Damien, heir to several fortunes, Margaret is not the sort of woman to invite to dinner after all: she is a witch who, with the connivance of her 'mad' uncle Magnus, has brought about a number of deaths, quite gleefully. As Magnus tells her at one point, 'Here in Scotland people are more capable of perpetrating good or evil than any-where else. I don't know why, but so it is.'[22] And Margaret is her uncle's niece, announcing, 'I'm tired of being the passive carrier of disaster. I feel frustrated. I almost think it's time for me to take my life and destiny in my own hands, and actively make disasters come about. I would like to do something like that.'[23]

Symposium is a novel with characters who plan so carefully, whether a menu for dinner or an agenda for murder, and are deluded enough to think themselves in charge. But of course Spark knows better, even if they don't. The novel itself is the only plan that succeeds ultimately. Constructed with brilliant and elaborate plot lines that converge, *Symposium* is at once an edgy comedy of manners, a dexterous metafictional exercise and a sophisti-cated metaphysical meditation on evil itself. Evil exists and operates within this world, here and now; once asked if she believed in hell, Spark replied, yes, but all the devils are here, you know.

Reality and Dreams (1996) returns to the world of the film industry. This time, however, the focus is not on the star – as in *The Public Image* – but on the *auteur*, sixty-three-year-old Tom Richards, who has suffered a fall while directing his latest project from an elevated crane platform. Richards finds himself in hospital, then laid up at home, made painfully redundant by circumstances. He slips in and out of consciousness, mistaking his nurses for nuns and dream-plotting the murder of his wife, Claire. The narrative deals with Tom's slow recuperation and eventual return to his craft. It is the story of Tom and a number of women: the cast comprises Claire, a wealthy American, heiress to an upstate New York biscuit business; their daughter, Cora, an extraordinarily attractive young woman; and Marigold, Tom's daughter by his first wife, an unattractive woman described as 'a natural disaster'. Claire cares for Tom; Cora cares for Tom; Marigold hates Tom and tries to have him murdered. Read as a parable, *Reality and Dreams* repeats – that is, makes redundant – narrative and verbal instances. It may be a blistering comedy of errors – and the comedy is restorative, indeed Shakespearian.

For her twenty-first novel, *Aiding and Abetting* (2001), Spark fictionalised the sensational story of the 7th earl of Lucan. On 7 November 1974, Lucan allegedly entered the Lower Belgrave Street residence of his estranged wife, Lady Veronica, and bludgeoned his children's nanny to death, evidently having mistaken her for his wife, who was brutally beaten as well. Lucan promptly disappeared. A murder warrant, the first ever for a British peer, was issued. Though some claim that he killed himself that evening, others believed that he went on the lam, aided and abetted by wealthy friends who bankrolled a kind of Flying Dutchman existence for the peer. He was spotted everywhere – in Europe, South America, Australia and, most often, central Africa.

Spark doubles Lucan, with a 'Lucky Lucan' and a 'Walker', both claiming to be the real earl. Their story-line intersects with that of Hildegarde Wolf, a fashionable Parisian psychologist, who, like Lucan, has a past to hide, a new identity to perpetrate. The dominant metaphor of blood links the English lord and the Parisian shrink: the blood of the nanny and his wife defiles Lucan's hands, while menstrual blood smeared to replicate the five wounds of Christ (and used to bilk thousands of money in return for miracles) defiles Wolf, formerly known as Beate Pappenheim, as well. Wolf's prognosis of Walker's condition ('Your problem … is one of identity') binds all three together, hand and foot.[24] Spark's complicated narrative offers her ample opportunity for satire, directed particularly at upper-class attitudes and behaviours, as well as metaphysical speculation.

However, as one critic once noted about Spark's novels, 'ultimately the plot is an irrelevance'.[25] *Aiding and Abetting* is not just a study of the banality of evil (Lucan, capable of such violence and violation, is consistently boring; Hildegarde, capable of such fraud, is really so ordinary). Nor is it simply a critique of those who, like Lucan and Wolf, and all the aiders and abetters, practise 'a morality devoid of ethics or law'.[26] Behind the telling of this tale lurks a moral imperative, set forth by the narrator early on: 'Yes, in fact let us all hear about [the Lucan story] once more. Those who were too young or even unborn at the time should be told, too.'[27]

Certainly the cold, calculating exposure of moral frauds and blackmailers like these is vintage Spark; here we look in vain for the counterbalancing good *inside* the novel; *outside* perhaps, but not inside. Lucan, Walker and Hildegarde Wolf are all artists of a sort, creating themselves anew again and again as the occasion demands. They are figures of protean evil.

Spark's last published novel, *The Finishing School* (2004), was seen by some critics as illustrative of the aged writer's diminished powers. True, Spark returns to familiar territory as she tells a tale of the vicious and violent inroads made by jealousy – both sexual and artistic – among a small group. Rowland Mahler and his wife Nina Parker run a finishing school, College Sunrise, that caters to teenage children of the well-to-do. One student, Chris Wiley, is at work on a novel about jealousy in the world of Mary, Queen of Scots. He and the novel incur the jealousy of Mahler, himself at work, quite unsuccessfully, on a novel of his own. *The Finishing School* plots the arc of Mahler's rising jealousy, charting its intersection with murderous intention and obsession.

In typical fashion, Spark takes satiric aim at a number of targets, including creative-writing classes, the upper classes and publishers. But typically she is really only interested in the spiritual, and here she is unusually pointed, lest the reader miss her point. At one turn, the Narrator frankly informs the reader: 'According to the Roman Catholic faith, into which Rowland had been born, six sins against the Holy Spirit are specified. The fourth is "envy of Another's Spiritual Good," and that was the sin from which Rowland suffered.'[28] Later on, as if to underscore the point, we hear a conversation between Nina and her lover, Israel Brown: 'She had said, "He needs a psychiatrist," but Israel had said, "No, I think it is a spiritual problem."'[29] Indeed it is, and Spark not only diagnoses it but unusually provides the cure as well with a comic ending that turns the tables on everyone.

To read *The Finishing School* as a weak, late novel in Spark's *oeuvre* may well miss the point. Perhaps this is a deliberate parody? Or perhaps even closer to the mark is John Lanchester's contention; citing Edward Said on 'late' (that is, later in the artist's career) works of art, he asserts: '"Late" works are the pieces an artist produces toward the end of an *oeuvre*: they combine an absolute control and mastery with a kind of sketchiness, a speedy glossing-over of the aspects with which the artist can no longer be bothered.'[30] In the roundly comic ending, in the lightness of touch and tone, in the deft quickness with which character and episode are limned lies the sure hand of a master, one who perhaps felt 'Time's winged chariot' at her back and responded appropriately.

Spark was as assured, knowing, confident, discriminating and audaciously creative in the beginning as she was at the end. All that can really be made of the only salient shift, a tendency to write more succinctly, turning out slimmer but never anorexic texts, is perhaps an urgency that her point be taken; that paring down, in conjunction with ridicule, which she deemed 'the only honorable weapon we have left', and her typically devastating wit working towards ultimate ends.[31] Those ends have sometimes proved difficult to define: 'to give pleasure', she acknowledged, but there was far more to the game than that.

Spark was an acute diagnostician of the spiritual ailments of the human condition, but altogether so shrewd that she knew better than to be prescriptive. As James Wood has asserted, 'Whatever is at stake for her is not quite to be found in the novel one is reading, but is somewhat to the side of it, in a more permanent realm. The novel seems to be only the worldly annexe to this true realm.'[32] In a supreme compliment to the reader, Spark set things out, then said, in effect, 'you know what to do now'. Once asked what she thought she had done in her writing, Spark responded, 'I opened doors and windows in the mind so that people can see things in a new way.'[33]

Notes

1 David Lodge, 'Marvels and Nasty Surprises', *New York Times Book Review*, 20 October 1985, 38.
2 Ian Rankin, 'Dame Muriel Spark Dies Aged 88', *Scotland on Sunday*, 16 April 2006, www.scotlandonsunday.com/index.cfm?id=577502006.
3 Alan Taylor, 'Scottish by Formation', in Robert Hosmer (ed.), *Essays in Honor of Muriel Spark* (University of Notre Dame Press, in press).
4 Muriel Spark, *The Ballad of Peckham Rye* (New York: G. P. Putnam's Sons, 1982), p. 202.
5 Muriel Spark, *The Prime of Miss Jean Brodie* (New York: Harper Perennial, 1999), p. 137.
6 Muriel Spark, *The Girls of Slender Means* (New York: New Directions, 1998), p. 140.
7 Muriel Spark, *The Mandelbaum Gate* (London: Macmillan, 1965), pp. 189, 190.
8 *Ibid.*, pp. 18, 301–2, 308.
9 Muriel Spark, *The Driver's Seat* (New York: New Directions Press, 1994), pp. 8, 9.

10 Auberon Waugh, 'On New Novels', *The Spectator*, 20 November 1971, 12.

11 Muriel Spark, *Not to Disturb* (London: Penguin Books, 1974), p. 40.

12 *Ibid.*, p. 96.

13 Muriel Spark, *The Abbess of Crewe* (New York: New Directions, 1995), pp. 8, 20.

14 *Ibid.*, p. 87.

15 *Ibid.*, p. 105.

16 Muriel Spark, *Territorial Rights* (New York: Coward, McGann & Geohegan, 1979), p. 235.

17 Muriel Spark, *Loitering with Intent* (New York: Coward, McGann & Geohegan, 1981), p. 139.

18 *Ibid.*, p. 26.

19 Muriel Spark, *The Only Problem* (New York: Putnam, 1984), pp. 301–2.

20 Muriel Spark, *A Far Cry from Kensington* (New York: New Directions Press, 2000), p. 127.

21 *Ibid.*

22 Muriel Spark, *Symposium* (New York: New Directions Press, 2000), p. 159.

23 *Ibid.*, pp. 143–4.

24 Muriel Spark, *Aiding and Abetting* (New York: Anchor Books, 2001), p. 15.

25 Martin Stannard, 'Death, Love, and Filthy Lucan', *The Spectator*, 2 September 2000, 33.

26 *Ibid.*, 34.

27 Spark, *Aiding and Abetting*, p. 6.

28 Muriel Spark, *The Finishing School* (New York: Anchor Books, 2004), p. 93.

29 *Ibid.*, p. 100.

30 John Lanchester, 'In Sparkworld', *New York Review of Books*, 15 January 2004, 22.

31 Muriel Spark, 'The Desegregation of Art', in *Proceedings of the American Academy of Arts and Letters* (New York: The Blashfield Foundation, 1971), p. 22.

32 James Wood, 'Can This Be What Happened to Lord Lucan after the Night of 7 November 1974?', *London Review of Books*, 7 September 2000, 12.

33 Interview with Alan Taylor, 'The Elusive Spark', videorecording (Glasgow: BBC Scotland, 1996).

Guide to further reading

Gardiner, Michael and Willy Maley (eds.), *The Edinburgh Companion to Muriel Spark* (Edinburgh University Press, 2010)

Herman, David (ed.), *Muriel Spark: Twenty-First-Century Perspectives* (Baltimore, MD: Johns Hopkins University Press, 2010)

Hosmer, Robert (ed.), *Imagination: Essays in Honor of Muriel Spark* (University of Notre Dame Press, in press)

15

LIAM MCILVANNEY

The Glasgow Novel

In his landmark 1935 travelogue, *Scottish Journey*, the poet Edwin Muir finds himself daunted and perplexed by the tremendous fact of Glasgow. On the one hand, Glasgow's significance and scale are indisputable: the forces of industrialism that are transforming the country are most rampantly evident in the city on the Clyde, and a 'description of Scotland which did not put Glasgow in the centre of the picture would not be a description of Scotland at all'. On the other hand, Muir frets that Glasgow is un-Scottish, being shaped more by the homogenising, transnational processes of 'Industrialism' than by the customary folkways of the nation:

> In one way it may be said that this area *is* modern Scotland, since it is the most active and vital part of Scotland as well as the most populous ... But from another point of view one may say that it is not Scotland at all, or not Scotland in particular, since it is merely one of the expressions of Industrialism, and Industrialism operates by laws which do not recognize nationality.[1]

Should Glasgow engross or escape Muir's attention? Muir seems not to know, and his ambivalence reflects a sense of Glasgow as *sui generis* in the context of Scotland. Glasgow's economic take-off, rooted in the eighteenth-century tobacco and sugar trades, and its transformation by heavy industry in the Victorian era, made it a monstrous anomaly: by 1901 nearly half of Scotland's four and a half million people lived in the Clydeside conurbation.[2] Glasgow was a city with its face turned westward to America, and perhaps also to Ireland, rather than to the hinterland behind it. And it was a city with a raft of intractable social problems – slum housing and over-crowding being the most pernicious – of a scale and intensity unparalleled in the rest of the country. Glasgow was indeed a place apart.

But Muir's ambivalence is that of the poet and *littérateur* as much as the social commentator. Where strong Scottish traditions, both in poetry and

I am grateful to the Arts and Humanities Research Council for supporting the research on which this chapter is based.

the novel, have placed a premium on documenting and memorialising distinctively national customs – what Burns calls his 'manners-painting strain', and Scott 'the task of tracing the evanescent manners of his own country' – it is small wonder that a mushrooming industrial city should seem too generic, too 'universal' to warrant the writer's attention. A literature that valorises the small town and the rural, the burgh and the brae – whether in the post-Scott vogue for 'Highlandism', the prizing of the parish in the Kailyard fiction of the 1890s or the rural preoccupations of the interwar Scottish Renaissance – has struggled to accommodate Scotland's largest city. The very features of modern Glasgow – its crude commercial and industrial vigour, its inhuman scale, the ugliness of its slums, the coarseness of its vernacular – have suggested to many writers a basic incongruity between Glasgow and art. More than one of the novelists to grapple with Glasgow have done so in a spirit of paradox, writing novels about the impossibility of writing novels about Glasgow.

As the novelist James Robertson has observed, 'Scottish literature has had an uneasy relationship with both the concept and the reality of the city.'[3] Indeed it has sometimes seemed that, apart from a brief flurry of 'proletarian' novels in the 1930s, there has been, in literary terms, an 'urbane silence' about Scotland's largest city until the early 1980s, when the 'Glasgow Renaissance' galvanised contemporary Scottish literature with its potent fusion of vernacular energy, formal innovation and generic eclecticism.[4] Famously, in one of the towering achievements of that Renaissance, Alasdair Gray's *Lanark* (1981), a character in 1950s Glasgow dismisses his city's cultural heritage as 'a music-hall song and a few bad novels'.[5] In fact, by the time Gray's novel was published, novels lamenting the absence of a viable tradition had themselves become a tradition of sorts.[6] In seeking to qualify Duncan Thaw's gloomy assessment, this chapter contends, first, that there exists a significant if fitful body of novels about Glasgow stretching back to the early nineteenth century and, second, that the undoubted achievements of Glasgow fiction in the 1980s and beyond are better understood when we attend to that fiction's antecedents and exemplars. While there is not space here to attempt a comprehensive survey of Glasgow fiction,[7] I hope to outline the terrain and take notice of at least some of the more prominent landmarks.

'A city of business': Daniel Defoe and the early Glasgow novel

The earliest novelist to grapple with Glasgow is one of the earliest novelists in the English language. It is not in his novels, however, but in his travelogues and political journalism that Daniel Defoe confronts the city on the Clyde. Defoe's often-quoted encomium on Glasgow in his *Tour through the*

Whole Island of Great Britain (1724–7) – 'the cleanest and beautifullest, and best built city in Britain, London excepted' – is less the throwaway compliment of a literary tourist than the strategic flattery of a committed British Unionist and former government propagandist who views Glasgow as the key test case and proving ground for the benefits of Union. The Glasgow of Defoe's *Tour* is a 'city of business', the most flourishing commercial *entrepôt* in Scotland. The city's trade is 'new formed' by the Treaty of Union, which 'open'd the door to the Scots in our American colonies', allowing Glaswegians to anticipate a future of glorious prosperity on the back of the Virginian sugar and tobacco trades. The 'very fine city' growing up on the back of this trade is conspicuously modern, a planned space of broad, airy streets whose 'equal and uniform' buildings are supported by elegant neoclassical columns. From Defoe, we get the sense of Glasgow as a city defined by 'the rising greatness of [its] commerce', a city cut off from its medieval roots and – increasingly – from its immediate hinterland, a city created anew by the Union and leaving the rest of Scotland behind.[8]

At the same time, Defoe's Unionist boomtown is prey to dark, atavistic outbreaks of mob violence; the very Union that would bring the benefits of commercial modernity found its most inveterate and militant opponents among the Glasgow mob, who rioted against the measure in 1706. Defoe was in Scotland in 1706, an agent of the English ministry – an English spy, if you like – charged with promoting Union, and his letters to his political masters at this juncture ('All the west is full of Tumult. Glasgow is mad') record his terror of the 'Glasgow rabble'.[9] Defoe records that he must have been 'Torn to peices [*sic*]' if he had ventured into Glasgow while the Union was being passed.[10] In a little-known pamphlet entitled *A Short Letter to the Glasgow-Men* (1706), Defoe marvels that the law-abiding, Presbyterian inhabitants of Glasgow should collude with the Jacobites by rioting against a Union which will secure the Kirk, ensure a Protestant succession and promote the prosperity of their city: 'Dear MADMEN! where are you going? what Work are you doing?'[11] In his *History of the Union* (1709), Defoe devotes fifteen pages to the disturbances in Glasgow, recounting the provost's narrow escape from a furious anti-Union mob and comparing the rioters to the 'Men of *Sodom*' who would have 'Rabbled the Angels'.[12] Clearly, then, Defoe's Glasgow is a city of contradictions. If Glasgow was the place where a commercial British modernity reached its apotheosis, it was also the place in which that modernity was menaced by popular lawlessness. For Defoe, the city on the Clyde is both Jerusalem and Sodom, at once the greatest advert for Union and the greatest threat to Union, a baffling conjunction of modernity and atavism, of politeness and barbarity.

Defoe's vision of Glasgow casts a strong shadow over the early novelistic depictions of the city. Mat Bramble's panegyric in Smollett's *The Expedition of Humphry Clinker* (1771) – 'one of the prettiest towns in Europe ... one of the most flourishing in Great Britain ... The streets are straight, open, airy, and well paved' – mimics Defoe, as do the scenes of commercial bustle that animate Thomas Hamilton's *The Youth and Manhood of Cyril Thornton* (1827).[13] But the most ambitious of the early Glasgow novels engage Defoe's ambivalence. Walter Scott's *Rob Roy* (1817) takes us back, not merely to the era of Defoe – the novel is set in 1715 – but to the Glasgow of the *Tour*. Frank Osbaldistone's account of the city and its economy approaches at points a verbatim recapitulation of the *Tour*. And Defoe's analysis of the benefits of Union is voiced, in pithy Scots, by the novel's indefatigable Glasgow merchant, Bailie Nicol Jarvie:

> 'There's naething sae gude on this side o' time but it might hae been better, and that may be said o' the Union. Nane were keener against it than the Glasgow folk, wi' their rabblings and their risings, and their mobs ... But it's an ill wind that blaws naebody gude ... Now, since St Mungo catched herrings in the Clyde, what was ever like to gar us flourish like the sugar and tobacco-trade? Will ony body tell me that, and grumble at the treaty that opened us a road west-awa' yonder?'[14]

Nicol Jarvie, however, is not exclusively the calculating man of business. He is a kinsman of the novel's titular outlaw, Rob Roy MacGregor, and he takes a pride in his Highland lineage, his 'Hieland blude' warming at the tales of his outlawed kinsman's exploits (304). Jarvie is not averse to taking the law into his own hands when the occasion demands, and indeed the 'law' in this novel operates not simply as the 'civilising' replacement to a system of personal vengeance but as the very instrument of that vengeance: it is the law that has vindictively proscribed the very name of the MacGregors and obliged Rob Roy to become an outlaw.

For his part, and for all his plundering wildness, Rob Roy cuts a curiously 'civilised' figure. We encounter him first disguised as 'Mr Campbell', a cattle-trading businessman in England. Among his 'strongest characteristics' is 'courtesy' (22). As Murray Pittock observes elsewhere in this volume, Rob Roy – with his detailed knowledge of contemporary France – is more sophisticated and cosmopolitan than the self-declared 'man of the world' Osbaldistone. Daniel Defoe's attempt to locate civilisation and barbarity in separate social constituencies (the men of business and the 'Glasgow rabble') is, Scott's novel suggests, misguided. The same man will be civilized and barbarous in different measures at different times, just as the shaggy, armed-to-the-teeth Highlanders take their rightful place in the douce Presbyterian congregation of Glasgow Cathedral.

As with *Rob Roy*, John Galt's *The Entail* (1822) shows modernity and atavism coexisting in the same individual, as the grasping merchant Claud Walkinshaw puts his commercial fortune in the service of an obsessive quest to reclaim his family's country estate. *The Entail* may be the 'first real Glasgow novel', but Galt's most significant Glasgow novel – in the sense that it charts the transformation of lowland Scotland by globalised commerce and shows the pivotal role of Glasgow in that process – is set in rural Ayrshire.[15] *Annals of the Parish* (1821) is the chatty, engagingly idiosyncratic narrative of Micah Balwhidder, kirk minister in the fictional parish of Dalmailing. Spanning the momentous half-century between 1760 and 1810, during which modern urban Scotland came into being,[16] Balwhidder's chronicle shows his rural parish being steadily 'brought more into the world', becoming 'a part of the great web of commercial reciprocities'.[17] The catalyst here is Glasgow. It is the Clyde's Virginia trade that brings the first luxuries – limes, coconuts, a 'turtle-fish', sugar and coffee – into the parish. It is the burgeoning city that creates a market for the second Mrs Balwhidder's lucrative commerce in butter and cheese, and Glasgow is where Balwhidder's son becomes a flourishing merchant. The new toll road to Glasgow – and a thrice-weekly city-bound stage-coach – opens up the parish to new fashions, new ideas and the newspapers brought by the Glasgow carrier. It is Glasgow money (presumably the profits of the sugar and tobacco trade) that establishes a cotton-mill, with its politicised weavers, a bookshop and a sprawling new settlement. While 'all this commercing and manufacturing' brings improvements in Dalmailing's standard of living[18] – if not always in its quality of life – it exposes the parish to the vagaries of commercial fluctuations, as when the cotton-mill is briefly forced to close. The power of the novel lies partly in Balwhidder's beguiling voice, but also in the pathos by which Balwhidder records his own obsolescence. By the novel's close, we understand that the minister's parochial worldview, together with the old social system administered by the Kirk – what Tom Devine calls the 'Parish State' – and the familiar Scottish genre of the parish chronicle, as practised in the first *Statistical Account of Scotland* (1791–9), have been overtaken by events.[19] It is the very inability of Balwhidder's parish chronicle to contain and make sense of its 'global' material that lends the novel its power and point.

The Victorian period

Following Scott and Galt, a hiatus of sorts seems to settle on the Scottish urban novel. Where is the Scottish Dickens, the Scottish Zola, the Scottish Dostoevsky? For decades, Scottish critics have mounted the same complaint: in the era of Scotland's most intense industrial transformation the nation's novelists were looking the other way, retreating from the chaos on their doorsteps into the bucolic inanities of the Kailyard.[20] This critical orthodoxy was overturned in the 1980s by the researches of William Donaldson, who pointed out that, while such strictures may apply to novels published in book form, they traduce the much larger body of fiction – upwards of five thousand full-length novels – serialised in Scottish newspapers throughout the Victorian period. Often written in vigorous vernacular Scots, these novels deal routinely and robustly with the urban scene and the social traumas of the industrial city: 'there are cities and slums, factories, workers, capitalists, crime, poverty, disease, in short the whole urban gamut almost wherever one cares to look'.[21]

Donaldson's researches have not uncovered a neglected masterpiece, and the prospects of a Glaswegian *Germinal* or Clydeside *Bleak House* being redeemed from the archives of the *People's Friend* are, one must suppose, regrettably remote. Nevertheless, Donaldson has restored to critical attention some considerable Scottish novelists. David Pae (1828–84) was 'the leading serial novelist in Scotland' from the early 1860s to his death and 'probably the most widely read author of fiction in Victorian Scotland'.[22] His novel, *Lucy, The Factory Girl: Or, The Secrets of the Tontine Close* (1860), published first in book form before being serialised in the *People's Journal* and then reissued as a book, is a 'tale of humble life and crime-life' that explores the trope of the hidden city, the place of savage darkness in the heart of the commercial metropolis.[23] The Tontine Close, home to the novel's gang of burglars and cut-purses, is a close within a close, whose towering black cliffs echo to 'sounds of brawling and strife, laughter, shrieks, yells and imprecations' (100).

A firm of crooked lawyers, Shuffle and Sleek, is in league with the Tontine bandits, and throughout the novel Pae draws connections between the polite 'city of business' and the lawless 'Glasgow rabble'. The Captain, ruthless head of the Tontine gang, is a self-proclaimed businessman with a solid grasp of Smithian economics, who organises his gang 'on the division of labour principle' (25). Pae not only shows the city's respectable lawyers and bailies colluding with a criminal underworld; he also probes the roots of Glasgow's prodigious economic development in the chattel slavery that was a structural feature of the sugar and tobacco trades. When a down-at-heel actor, performing in a production of *Guy Mannering*, is jeered for being too drunk to remember his lines, he rebukes his audience of 'contemptible cotton-spinners' and informs them that 'There is not a stone in your dirty town but what is cemented by the blood of a negro' (185).

Correspondences between high and low life are again explored in *The Beggar's Benison* (1866), George Mills's two-volume *Bildungsroman*, the 'confession of a selfish man' who rises from the sin and squalor of the 'Goosedubbs' slum to the elegance and propriety of a West End mansion.[24] The strength of the novel lies in its 'vivid accounts of slum life about 1840',[25] and the sensory horror of tenement living assaults us from the opening page: 'Smoke, squalor, fumes, filth, vice, veniality, noise, nastiness – among these I first became sensitive of life' (vol. 1, p. 1). Like Pae's Tontine close, Mills's Goosedubbs is a 'little commonwealth of corruption' (vol. 1, p. 27): the hero's stepfather is a housebreaker, and the local children are beggars and thieves. The novel is unashamedly sensationalist – a long, unsettling account of a botched public hanging comes to mind – and Mills remains a 'middle-class Glaswegian displaying the slums for his reader's amazement and horror'.[26] His Goosedubbs is a kind of infernal Brigadoon, a perpetual sink of human misery to which the lexis of imperialism may be applied: the police, we learn, are 'actually afraid to penetrate its interior, in case of being murdered by its barbarous and savage inhabitants' (vol. 1, p. 289). Mills's repeated epithet for the Glasgow slum-dweller – 'civilised savage' – returns us to the dualisms of Defoe and Scott.

The 'Glasgow School' of the 1920s and 1930s

Despite the promise of Victorian novelists like Pae and Mills and the flourishing tradition of newspaper fiction, including the humorous 'urban kailyard' sketches of J. J. Bell and Neil Munro, offset by more grimly realist novels like John Blair's *Jean* (1906) and Patrick MacGill's *The Rat-Pit* (1915), it was the 1920s before a broad-based 'school' of serious Glasgow novelists began to emerge.[27] When C. M. Grieve ('Hugh MacDiarmid') discussed the 'new Glasgow School' in a somewhat disparaging 1926 article, his roster of emerging talents included Catherine Carswell, John Carruthers, Dot Allan, John Cockburn, George Woden, George Blake and J. M. Reid.[28] Of these names, only Carswell's and Blake's retain any resonance at all, but MacDiarmid altogether ignored – possibly because its 'popular' status placed it beneath his notice – the most compelling Glasgow novel of the 1920s.

Though described by its author as a 'Glasgow Fairy Tale', John Buchan's *Huntingtower* (1922) is a novel less of Glasgow than Glaswegians.[29] Retired city grocer Dickson McCunn is enjoying a walking holiday in the wilds of South Ayrshire when he uncovers an improbable Bolshevik plot involving imperial jewels and the kidnapping of a Russian princess. Aided only by a young poet and a gang of Glasgow street urchins (the 'Gorbals Die-Hards', modelled, it may be, on Sherlock Holmes's Baker Street Irregulars), McCunn proceeds to tackle the villains. Though the harmonious alliance Buchan sets up between McCunn and the Die-Hards (the 'city of business' and the

'Glasgow rabble') strikes some critics as implausible, it sits easily in a novel that gleefully reverses our expectations. A fat provision merchant is no one's idea of an adventure hero, but McCunn carries the day by treating the whole affair as a 'business proposition'.[30] Similarly, the slum-reared Die-Hards demonstrate excellent fieldcraft – bivouacking, conducting surveillance, fording rivers, scaling cliffs – precisely because of the operational training they have acquired through 'sleepin' in coalrees and dunnies and dodgin' the polis' (102). In the novel's dedication, Buchan identifies McCunn as a lineal descendant of Bailie Nicol Jarvie (and therefore of Rob Roy himself), and the portly grocer and kirk elder is as ready as his ancestors to flout the law, breaking into houses, resetting stolen goods and shooting at solicitors in the course of his adventures. 'Man, Dougal', he reflects to the Die-Hards' commander; 'isn't it a queer thing that whiles law-abiding folk have to make their own laws?' (101).

Buchan's Gorbals Die-Hards march into battle with their socialist Sunday-school hymns on their lips: 'Proley Tarians, arise! / Wave the Red Flag to the skies' (195). In the 1930s a whole slew of so-called 'proletarian' novels appeared, bringing news of the city's slums and shipyards, its football matches and picture palaces, its whist drives and socialist dances. The novels of this period have been characterised as a 'Glasgow school of crisis',[31] and many of these novels are indeed shaped and shadowed by cataclysm: the massive and disproportionate loss of Scottish life during the First World War; the collapse of Clydeside's heavy industries in the post-war Depression; and the city's acute and ongoing housing crisis, as depicted in journalistic exposés like William Bolitho's *Cancer of Empire* (1924).

In addressing such 'issues', one challenge for authors of 'proletarian' fiction is to avoid purveying propaganda or sociology. Another is to construct involving narratives from the experience of characters who remain, in the title of Samuel McKechnie's 1934 novel, *Prisoners of Circumstance*. In McKechnie's impassioned novel, as in other Glasgow fictions of this period, the characters' lack of agency is sanctioned and compounded by a narrative regime that addresses the reader over the heads of the unwitting characters: 'So much depended upon circumstances over which he had no control, and of which, indeed, he had no conception.'[32] This tendency to articulate *for* the characters, as Edwin Muir does throughout *Poor Tom* (1932), sits alongside the prevalence of intrusive social commentary and the practice of glossing Glasgow dialect in novels as disparate as John Macnair Reid's sensitive *Homeward Journey* (1934) and McArthur and Kingsley Long's sensational *No Mean City* (1935). Even when characters do assert their agency and attempt to impose themselves on their surroundings – like John Grant in Robert Craig's *O People!* (1932), an unemployed ex-soldier and would-be demagogue whose *idée fixe* is to secure independent representation for Scotland in the League of Nations – they cut a somewhat ridiculous figure.

One way to generate dynamism in the presentation of passive, power-less characters is through techniques of parallelism and juxtaposition. Both George Blake's *The Shipbuilders* (1935) and James Barke's *Major Operation* (1936) are constructed around the intertwining stories of a worker and a boss during the Great Depression. In *The Shipbuilders*, Leslie Pagan, a shipyard owner's son, and Danny Shields, a riveter and Pagan's former batman, face personal and marital crises when their shipyard closes down. Though weakened, as Blake acknowledged, by a sometimes condescendingly anthropological perspective on its working-class characters, the novel is redeemed by striking set-piece descriptions of Old Firm matches and city dance-halls, and by some resonant overviews of the urban scene, as in Pagan's 'sudden vision of the city's unwieldy vastness – of a hopeless complex of lives and interests all resting on heavy industry in decay, with a canker at its heart; perhaps a city doomed'.[33] In Barke's *Major Operation*, a socialist shipyard worker from the Partick slums and a failing city businessman share adjacent hospital beds. While their lengthy debates and arguments provide some insight into the *mentalités* of the 'Second City', they strain the reader's credulity and dissipate the novel's modest reserves of narrative tension. Barke is in any case liable to hold up the narrative to let a pompous authorial voice provide a sardonic field guide to the city in sections entitled 'The Smells of Slumdom', 'Erotic Nocturne over the Second City' and 'Pain in the Second City'. But there are also chapters, such as the vivid and Joycean 'Red Music in the Second City', in which the demotic voices of anonymous Glaswegians jostle for control of the narrative.

Welcomed by Edwin Muir as a 'novel of promise', Edward Shiels's *Gael over Glasgow* (1937) plumbs the anomie of a jobless young engineer during the Depression.[34] Abhorring the 'wasted days' of idleness, Brian O'Neill escapes to the Highlands, hiking the hills, traversing Loch Lomond in a canoe called *Gael* and musing on 'the bold, royal ideals of the Gael'.[35] He comes to view the city as a historical wrong turn, a place of darkness and squalor that has skewed the noble nature of the Highland and Irish Gaels. Through his sojourns in the Highlands, O'Neill learns 'the simple lesson that the hills were happy and the streets were sad' (235). Only when the Highlands are cultivated once more by those shipbuilding Gaels who devote more loving attention to their allotments than they ever did to the *Queen Mary* will Scotland be more than an 'industrial muckheap' (348). In a weakly utopian ending, Brian's uncle Patrick returns from Canada to buy a deserted Highland glen and persuades Brian to join him in a scheme to resettle the industrial unemployed on their 'ancestral' land. Like other 'proletarian' novels of the period, *Gael over Glasgow* suffers from a heavy-handed left-ist didacticism, though in this case the impetus comes from Catholicism as much as Communism: at one point Shiels quotes Leo XIII's demand in *Rerum novarum* that the working classes 'who contribute so largely to the advantage of the community may themselves share in the benefits which they create' (222).

In Frederick Niven's *The Staff at Simson's* (1937), the working classes certainly have their share in the narrative. A novel of commerce in which the firm itself – in this case a textile warehouse in Cochrane Street – is the hero, *The Staff at Simson's* is scrupulously democratic in distributing narrative space among each of the firm's employees, from partner down to office-boy. While this creates a sense of congestion and fragmentation, it nicely mirrors the rhythms of urban life. Itself a kind of textile machine, weaving a pattern from multiple strands, the novel hums with the 'murmur of the city faintly echoed, the murmur of the criss-crossing of many lives'.[36] If the Cochrane Street warehouse is 'the world in little' (316), Niven also has an eye on the world at large. Like Galt, Niven is keen to show how the 'great web of commercial reciprocities' implicates Glasgow in a wider world. At one point, during a royal visit to the city, one of the partners takes the firm's most valued buyers – an Australian, a New Zealander and a Canadian – to watch the royal procession from the vantage of his club: 'D'you realize, gentlemen', the partner enquires, 'that we bring the Empire together?' (40).

Dot Allan's *Hunger March* (1934) uses the occasion of a protest rally in George Square to present, in kaleidoscopic fashion, a day in the life of a provincial metropolis (it's no coincidence that one of the protagonists has the surname Joyce). We can speak of the 'architecture' of *Hunger March* in a particular sense: the novel is constructed around George Square, the city's central plaza. The square contains the offices of Joyce and Son, the Palatial Restaurant, the Cavendish Hotel, the City Chambers; it's the destination for the eponymous hunger marchers, and the square is what connects the large, multifarious cast of characters. The narrative switches between focalisers with tremendous rapidity, suggesting the random interconnectedness, the 'incessant yet futile movement' of the city streets.[37] But the square does not simply frame a slice of city life; it acts as a portal connecting the city to the world. At one point, Arthur Joyce envisages his office as the centre of a vast network of trading links, 'a world connected to his desk by the little wavering blue lines, like threads in a spider's web, that curvetted delicately across the map. Trade routes, these lines were called, but they were in reality tendrils springing boldly out of the seeds of male enterprise, male initiative here in the Square, and stretching out of sight to take root in other countries overseas.'[38] There is a telling ambivalence in this passage: the globalised system that permits Joyce to send his 'tendrils' overseas may also snare him like a fly in its 'web of commercial reciprocities'.

Post-war fiction

Like the 'proletarian' novels of the thirties, Glasgow's post-war novels purvey a bleak, infernal vision of the city. We have the city as labyrinth, as underworld, as necropolis and, in J. F. Hendry's powerful *Fernie Brae* (1947), the city as machine, a sordid contraption of iron and stone, crushing the life of its trammeled inhabitants. In Hendry's novel, the city is a parody of nature; its chimneys wag like 'wasted grain', its trains cross the landscape 'like black slugs'.[39] The hero, David Macrae, inhabits a tenement district penned in by a cemetery, a grassless park and two vast locomotive works. The irony here – that the locomotive workers rot in their places while the engines they fashion circle the globe – is dryly drawn: 'Engines from [the Cowlairs works] went to India, China and South America. The majority of the men who built them did not even go down town' (37). Hendry's city is a penitentiary, its spiked iron railings the symbol of its purpose. From the schoolroom, with its clangorous bell, to the factory, with its pitiless siren, the city is an instrument of subjection, a device for enforcing obedience to 'the mechanical cackle called civilisation' (81).

The old dichotomy between art and the industrial city – 'Is literature a life proved much too good / To have its place in our coarse neighbourhood?'[40] – is played out time and again in the novels of this period. The abortive *Künstlerroman* – the story of a sensitive would-be artist whose ambitions are crushed by the city's 'coarse neighbourhood' – is the dominant genre in post-war Glasgow fiction. Edward Gaitens's *Dance of the Apprentices* (1948) opens with a youth ecstatically reciting Robert Herrick's 'To Daffodils', only to be brought back to a consciousness of his brutalised surroundings – the rank back-courts, the drunken mother, the ill-nourished sister in the foul box-bed, the familiar Glasgow panoply of ravaged domesticity. In Robin Jenkins's *A Very Scotch Affair* (1968), insurance superintendent Mungo Niven (mockingly nicknamed 'Niven the Poet') longs to escape to a sun-kissed Mediterranean that might nourish his 'idealism', and can only reconcile himself to the Glaswegian streets by posing as an affluent Scots-Canadian businessman, home for a visit. Dunky Logan, the sensitive adolescent in Gordon Williams's *From Scenes Like These* (1968), learns to hate Catholics and snobs, broaden his accent so as not to sound like 'some English nancy boy on the radio' and abandon his 'daft notions' about education and books, in a novel whose title alludes bitterly to the pastoral idylls of

Robert Burns.[41] *Walk Don't Walk* (1972), Williams's study of another failed artist, has a prefatory poem deadpanning Scotland's dismal stagnancy:

> We knew our country was a smalltime dump
> where nothing ever happened and
> there was nothing to do.
> And nobody had a name like Jelly Roll Morton.[42]

Similarly disdainful of his native terrain is the shabby protagonist of George Friel's *Mr Alfred M. A.* (1972), an alcoholic schoolteacher vainly brandishing his clutch of unpublished poems amid the swaggering gang culture of a disintegrating city. For Mr Alfred, real life happens beyond the city limits, a perspective shared by the protagonists of Alan Spence's fiction, for whom an exotic, technicolour elsewhere throws into harsh relief the monochrome grimness of Glasgow.

Perhaps the most thoughtful and ambitious rendering of the 'failed artist' topos comes in Archie Hind's *The Dear Green Place* (1966), in which aspiring novelist Mat Craig works shifts in a slaughterhouse and tinkers with his Clydeside novel (his 'wee Glasgow opus'), while suspecting that 'Writers are always other people.'[43] As a novelist, Craig feels hampered, not just by the need to earn a living, or the call of his domestic duties, but by the 'Calvinist, Protestant city' in which he resides: 'A city whose talents were all outward and acquisitive ... its literature dumb or in exile, its poetry a dull struggle in obscurity.'[44] The paradox of the novel, of course, is that Archie Hind constructs a brilliantly realised fiction from the material Mat Craig finds so intractable. Hind finds something valid and venerable in the very waste lots and factories of 'the oldest industrial landscape in the world'. Tellingly, the novel alludes repeatedly to the glories of Dutch Golden Age painting – a body of work confirming that art can indeed flourish in a Calvinist, commercial culture. And Hind puts this lesson into practice in a bravura central chapter which describes, with extraordinary sensitivity and aesthetic discrimination, the labour processes in Mat's slaughterhouse. In showing how art can flourish in the 'coarse neighbourhood' of Glasgow, Hind pointed the way to the 'Glasgow Renaissance' of the 1980s.

The 'Glasgow Renaissance' and after

Scottish fiction in the 1980s was dominated by the emergence of two extraordinary talents whose fiction was overtly rooted in the 'magnificent city' of Glasgow.[45] In the frontispiece to Book 1 of *Lanark: A Life in 4 Books* (1981), Alasdair Gray revises the Glasgow city motto. 'Let Glasgow Flourish by the Preaching of the Word' becomes 'Let Glasgow Flourish by Telling the Truth' (119). Though no one is doing much flourishing in the full-page illustration – it depicts a Glasgow drowning in apocalyptic floods – Gray's amendment holds the key to his art. Throughout his fiction, the truth at which Gray worries is the old one – of exploitation, class brutality, man's inhumanity to man. 'Man is the pie that bakes and eats himself and the recipe is separation', as Monsignor Noakes puts it in *Lanark* (101). In *1982 Janine*, Jock McLeish is less enigmatic: 'The winners shaft the losers, the strong shaft the weak, the rich shaft the poor' (121). This is the truth which seeks out Gray's protagonists and shatters their complacency. This is the hell which underlies all life, and what obscures this truth is 'Preaching' – the lies of ministers, of politicians, of schoolteachers and, naturally, of novelists, whom Gray classes among the 'policemen and functionaries who keep society as it is'.[46]

In its politics, Gray's great novel is close to the 'proletarian' Glasgow fictions of the 1930s, but in its procedures – a realist *Bildungsroman* enclosed within a sci-fi political allegory, the whole thing written in a style of childish ingenuousness – it could hardly be more different. Around the same time as Gray galvanised Scottish literature with his 'blend of realism and fantasy',[47] his friend and contemporary James Kelman was announcing a new era in vernacular fiction with his demotic narratives of the Glaswegian working class. In novels like *The Busconductor Hines* (1984), *A Chancer* (1985) and *A Disaffection* (1989), Kelman broke down the traditional barrier between standard English narration and demotic Scots dialogue, developing a free, indirect style in which Scots pervaded both. This technique itself bespoke and begot a new confidence: no longer stuck in quotation marks, Scots was tackling narrative, 'the place where the psychological drama occurred'.[48] Not everyone was pleased. When Kelman won the Booker Prize with a challenging and humane vernacular novel about a jobless petty criminal, the sometimes scandalised reaction confirmed the book's significance; with *How Late It Was, How Late* (1994), the 'Glasgow rabble' was holding the floor.[49]

The formal trickery of Gray and the vernacular energy of Kelman instigated a 'Glasgow Renaissance' that continues to flourish. Janice Galloway manipulates typography, spacing, line breaks and marginalia in a 'concrete prose' that simulates Joy Stone's psychological fragmentation in *The Trick is to Keep Breathing* (1989), and combines techniques of *bricolage* with a forceful demotic voice in her feminist picaresque, *Foreign Parts* (1994). The sometimes narrowly masculine tradition of Glasgow fiction has been further breached and broadened by the carefully crafted fictions of Agnes Owens and by A. L. Kennedy's surrealist Glasgow love story, *So I Am Glad*

(1995). Perhaps the most significant post-Kelman vernacular performance is the exuberant, Runyonesque *Swing Hammer Swing!* (1992), in which Jeff Torrington sprinkles 'the slangy glitter of his lingo' over the adventures of Thomas Clay in a half-demolished sixties Gorbals.[50] The sound of the wrecking-ball is audible, too, in Andrew O'Hagan's masterful debut novel, *Our Fathers* (1999), a lyrical and sometimes acerbic family saga exploring masculinity, faith, politics and community through the perennial Glasgow topic of housing. As one might expect in a city of mythologised violence, crime fiction has been a vigorous strand of recent Glasgow writing, from William McIlvanney's Laidlaw novels, through Frederic Lindsay's accomplished *Brond* (1984) and Frank Kuppner's 'true crime' novel *A Very Quiet Street* (1989), to the contemporary noir of Christopher Brookmyre, Louise Welsh, Denise Mina and Caro Ramsay. At the same time, Mat Craig's 'Calvinist, Protestant' city has revealed its true diversity. The experience of the Glasgow Irish has been chronicled in the work of Thomas Healy and Des Dillon, while the city's long-standing Pakistani community finds limber voice in Suhayl Saadi's exhilarating *Psychoraag* (2004), whose Urdu-inflected Scots-English stages a bravura demonstration of cultural conjunction, 'the broiling confluence of the waters of the Ravi and the Clyde'.[51] Over the past thirty years, a city that had seemed almost incompatible with the novel has established itself as a 'city of literature' in a way that would have been unimaginable to Mat Craig or Duncan Thaw.

Notes

1 Edwin Muir, *Scottish Journey* (London: William Heinemann, 1935), p. 102.

2 T. M. Devine, *The Scottish Nation 1700–2000* (London: Allen Lane, 1999), p. 329.

3 James Robertson, 'The City in Scottish Literature', unpublished talk given on 9 February 2011 at Edinburgh Napier University.

4 Andrew Noble, 'Urbane Silence: Scottish Writing and the Nineteenth-Century City', in George Gordon (ed.), *Perspectives on the Scottish City* (Aberdeen University Press, 1985), pp. 64–90.

5 Alasdair Gray, *Lanark: A Life in 4 Books* (1981; repr. London: Picador, 1994), p. 243; further references will appear in the text.

6 Douglas Gifford, *The Dear Green Place? The Novel in the West of Scotland* (Glasgow: Third Eye Centre, 1985), p. 14.

7 Moira Burgess has in any case undertaken this task in *The Glasgow Novel: A Bibliography*, 3rd edn (Hamilton: The Scottish Library Association, 1999), and *Imagine a City: Glasgow in Fiction* (Glendaruel: Argyll, 1998).

8 Daniel Defoe, *A Tour through the Whole Island of Great Britain*, ed. P. N. Furbank, W. R. Owens and A. J. Coulson (London: Folio Society, 2006), pp. 415–20.

9 *The Letters of Daniel Defoe*, ed. George Harris Healey (Oxford: Clarendon Press, 1955), pp. 150–1. On the 'Glasgow rabble', see *ibid.*, pp. 148, 149, 168, 172.

10 *Ibid.*, p. 207.

11 Daniel Defoe, *A Short Letter to the Glasgow-Men* (Edinburgh, 1706), p. 6.

12 Daniel Defoe, *History of the Union of Great Britain* (Edinburgh, 1709), p. 64.

13 Tobias Smollett, *The Expedition of Humphry Clinker*, ed. Lewis M. Knapp, rev. Paul-Gabriel Boucé (Oxford University Press, 1984), pp. 245–6.

14 Sir Walter Scott, *Rob Roy*, ed. Ian Duncan (Oxford University Press, 1998), p. 312; further references will appear in the text.

15 Burgess, *Imagine a City*, p. 24.

16 Devine, *Scottish Nation*, pp. 105–23.

17 John Galt, *Annals of the Parish*, ed. James Kinsley (Oxford University Press, 1967), pp. 152, 197.

18 *Ibid.*, p. 128.

19 Devine, *Scottish Nation*, pp. 84–102.

20 See, for instance: George Blake, *Barrie and the Kailyard School* (London: Arthur Barker, 1951), pp. 80–1; David Craig, *Scottish Literature and the Scottish People, 1680–1830* (London: Chatto & Windus, 1961), pp. 13–14, 273; Tom Nairn, *The Break-Up of Britain: Crisis and Neo-Nationalism* (London: NLB, 1977), pp. 148–69; Noble, 'Urbane Silence'.

21 William Donaldson, *Popular Literature in Victorian Scotland: Language, Fiction and the Press* (Aberdeen University Press, 1986), p. 87.

22 *Ibid.*, pp. 77, 90.

23 David Pae, *Lucy, The Factory Girl: Or, The Secrets of the Tontine Close* (1860; repr. Hastings: Sensation Press, 2001), p. 63; further references will appear in the text.

24 George Mills, *The Beggar's Benison* (London: Cassell, Petter & Calpin, 1866), vol. 1, p. 272; further references will appear in the text.

25 William Power, *The Face of Glasgow* (Glasgow: John Smith and Son, 1938), p. 13.

26 Burgess, *Imagine a City*, p. 40.

27 The term was coined by Moira Burgess, *ibid.*, pp. 68–76.

28 Hugh MacDiarmid, *Contemporary Scottish Studies*, ed. Alan Riach (Manchester: Carcanet, 1995), pp. 342–51.

29 Andrew Lownie, *John Buchan: The Presbyterian Cavalier* (London: Constable, 1995), p. 169.

30 John Buchan, *Huntingtower*, ed. Ann F. Stonehouse (Oxford University Press, 1996), p. 86; further references will appear in the text.

31 Beat Witschi, *Glasgow Urban Writing and Postmodernism: A Study of Alasdair Gray's Fiction* (Frankfurt am Main: Peter Lang, 1991).

32 Samuel McKechnie, *Prisoners of Circumstance* (London: Sampson Low, 1934), p. 46.

33 George Blake, *The Shipbuilders* (London: Faber, 1935), pp. 21–2.

34 *Scotland*, 2:6 (Summer 1937), 66, quoted in Burgess, *Imagine a City*, p. 151.

35 Edward Shiels, *Gael over Glasgow* (London: Sheed and Ward, 1937), p. 298; further references will appear in the text.

36 Frederick Niven, *The Staff at Simson's* (London: Collins, 1937), p. 278; further references will appear in the text.

37 Dot Allan, *Hunger March* (London: Hutchinson, 1934), p. 57.

38 *Ibid.*, p. 239.

39 J. F. Hendry, *Fernie Brae* (Glasgow: William McLellan, 1947), pp. 63–4; further references will appear in the text.
40 Douglas Dunn, 'The Student', in *Barbarians* (London: Faber, 1979), p. 19.
41 Gordon Williams, *From Scenes Like These* (1968; repr. London: Allison and Busby, 1980), pp. 12, 22.
42 Gordon Williams, *Walk Don't Walk* (1972; repr. Glasgow: Richard Drew, 1988), p. 8.
43 Archie Hind, *The Dear Green Place* (1966; repr. Edinburgh: Birlinn, 2001), p. 81.
44 *Ibid.*, p. 61.
45 Gray, *Lanark*, p. 243.
46 Alasdair Gray, *Poor Things* (London: Bloomsbury, 1992), p. 176.
47 Gray, *Lanark*, p. 155.
48 James Kelman, *'And the Judges Said ...': Essays* (London: Secker & Warburg, 2002), p. 40.
49 On reaction to Kelman's Booker win, see Geoff Gilbert, 'Can Fiction Swear? James Kelman and the Booker Prize', in Rod Mengham (ed.), *An Introduction to Contemporary Fiction: International Writing in English since 1970* (London: Polity Press, 1999), pp. 219–34.
50 Jeff Torrington, *Swing Hammer Swing!* (London: Secker & Warburg, 1992), p. 385.
51 Suhayl Saadi, *Psychoraag* (Edinburgh: Black & White, 2004), p. 235.

Guide to further reading

Bissett, Alan, 'The "New Weegies": The Glasgow Novel in the Twenty-First Century', in Berthold Schoene (ed.), *The Edinburgh Companion to Contemporary Scottish Literature* (Edinburgh University Press, 2007), pp. 59–67

Burgess, Moira, *The Glasgow Novel: A Bibliography*, 3rd edn (Hamilton: The Scottish Library Association, 1999)

  Imagine a City: Glasgow in Fiction (Glendaruel: Argyll, 1998)

Gifford, Douglas, *The Dear Green Place? The Novel in the West of Scotland* (Glasgow: Third Eye Centre, 1985)

16

FIONA STAFFORD

'What is the language using us for?': Modern Scottish Poetry

Malcolm Mooney's question, posed at the beginning of W. S. Graham's late collection of verse, *Implements in Their Places*, articulates a concern shared by many modern Scottish poets.[1] All poets are sensitive to the complexities of their medium, but in Scotland language itself has been 'a question' for centuries. As the great poets of the 1920s and 30s locked horns over the proper use of Scots, English or Gaelic, issues of patriotic loyalty became inextricably bound up with linguistic choices. While many applauded Hugh MacDiarmid's resistance to what was often seen as the creeping, unavoidable incorporation of the Scottish languages into English, others debated Edwin Muir's view that Scots had survived largely as a medium for unsophisticated kinds of writing and had little future as a serious literary language. The notion that a poet's language was to be judged in terms of his national commitment, however, meant that the need to revive Scots and Gaelic was felt deeply – and widely. Graham's query, presented as both a title and a refrain half a century later, is in part reflective of a sense shared with numerous writers of his generation that their art was somehow determined by their choice of language. It also anticipates, however, the response of many younger poets to the language question, which has been chary of absolute choices and tending instead towards more exploratory, interrogative, ironic or wittily tangential approaches. It is not that the question has been forgotten, but rather that the modes of address have been transformed for a newly devolved, twenty-first-century Scotland.

When Maurice Lindsay introduced his anthology of *Modern Scottish Poetry* in 1965, he emphasised the 'variety of experience' and 'integrity of expression' that distinguished the poems he had gathered, arguing that 'these qualities, and not the question of which of Scotland's three languages her writers choose to use, are what constitute the real Scottish Renaissance'.[2] His very comment, however, reveals that in the 1960s it would generally seem strange to consider modern Scottish poetry without discussing the language question. Almost thirty years later, when Douglas Dunn turned his attention to editing another Faber collection, *Twentieth-Century Scottish Poetry*, he still found it necessary to address the implications of the linguistic choices represented in his anthology, observing somewhat drily that 'Scottish poetry has been steeped in politics ever since MacDiarmid's instigatory drum-beating back in the early 1920s.'[3] By the early 1990s, however, with the campaign for Devolution gathering momentum, it was possible to view the arguments between MacDiarmid and Muir with greater historical distance and to perceive Scottish poetry in a new, less internally conflicted, manner. For Dunn, the choice of language was not so much a considered political statement as an 'instinctive need', and his editorial introduction was more inclined to castigate fellow poets for producing artificial effects than for choosing an insufficiently Scottish poetic diction.[4] His own sense of Scotland is fundamentally forward-looking, and his anthology accordingly pointed to an underlying national unity, despite the obvious divisions – 'Scottish poetry has moved gradually into its liberty ... it is more and more the poetry in three languages of one nationality.'[5]

With the collapse of global binaries at the end of the Cold War, new models of unity were emerging in which numerous smaller parts could still make valid contributions to a larger, healthy whole. Power relations no longer seemed to involve the inevitable oppression of minorities, while increasing awareness of international diversity and voluntary economic union encouraged a more flexible understanding of national cultures. Instead of being signs of irreparable historical injury, internal differences of speech and tradition were coming to be seen as evidence of cultural richness. In the changing context of the 1990s, Scotland's language question need no longer prove paralysing or divisive, as Robert Crawford's new critical journal, with its Bakhtinian insistence on plurality, affirmed in its title – *Scotlands*. His 1992 volume of poems, *Talkies*, also began with Bakhtin's 'one's own language is never a single language', as if to problematise the very thought of choosing either Scots or English in modern society, where the daily condition of life meant 'Wearing something like a Sony Walkman, / Hearing another voice every time we speak.'[6]

The same willingness to celebrate rather than agonise over linguistic diversity characterised the new anthology which Crawford edited with Mick Imlah, *The New Penguin Book of Scottish Verse*, published in 2000, a few months after the opening of the Scottish parliament. Here the complexity of Scotland's linguistic heritage was foregrounded as a defining national feature, in a literary collection that began with St Columba's Latin hymn, before including poems from Welsh, Old English, Gaelic, Old Norse and

Old French. As the editors pointed out cheerfully in their introduction, 'If Columba is the A of Scottish poetry, B is for Babel' – for it was not until the fourteenth century that Scots became firmly established as the literary language of the Lowlands, with Gaelic still dominant in the Highlands.[7] Far from seeing the early confusion of tongues as a national punishment, however, they present the historical situation as being foundational for the later Scottish facility for translation and linguistic play.

Inclusion of Scotland's early languages in the Penguin anthology under-lined the idea that 'Scottish Verse' was not to be understood exclusively as 'verse in Scots'. Not only were the editors free to restore 'The Dream of the Rood' (a poem familiar to anyone who had grappled with Anglo-Saxon literature at university) to its origins in Dumfriessshire, but they were also able to begin their collection with a series of parallel texts. At once, the old anxieties about Scottish doubleness were aired and dismissed, since the ser-ies of translations from different languages into modern English diffused any sense of binary opposition, while rendering 'Scotland' excitingly various and full of unexpected delights. Scotland's 'multilingual background' was highlighted throughout the anthology, which made a virtue of translation and applauded the plurality of perspectives. Such national confidence had taken time to develop, however, and the editors of *The New Penguin Book of Scottish Verse* acknowledged the issues that had once proved so divisive as explicitly as any of the earlier anthologists, commenting that 'Choice of language continued to be a live issue for poets through the second half of the twentieth century.'[8] The fact that in the twenty-first century, it could be enthusiastically presented as a '*live* issue', however, suggests a rather more optimistic attitude to the language question than that of some in previous generations.

For those writing in the 1960s, like Maurice Lindsay, the argument over language seemed to have been played out exhaustively and yet remained unresolved. Battle-lines had been laid down between Scots and English which were difficult to ignore, however complicated the separation and however eager younger poets might be to find their own voices. The suc-cess of both Derick Thomson and Sorley MacLean had further demon-strated that Gaelic, apparently in retreat since the eighteenth century, was after all a viable language for the modern Scottish poet and therefore in need of more champions. A poet such as Iain Crichton Smith, who was brought up in Lewis, therefore had a choice of three languages – Gaelic, Standard English or Scots – but how free was the choice, when perceived as a national duty? As James Campbell pointed out in a retrospective assessment, Crichton Smith's ability to compose fine Gaelic poetry was compromised by his ambivalent feelings about the strictly Presbyterian

Hebridean culture of his youth, as expressed in his late poem, 'The Village':

> But I have to live
>   Where black Bibles
>   Are walls of granite,
> Where the heads are bowed
>   over eternal fire.[9]

If the uncongenial island, 'the anvil where was made the puritanical heart', seemed antithetical to artistic endeavour, however, it nevertheless continued to haunt his imagination, prompting new poems throughout his life.[10] A later section of 'The Village', for example, muses on 'the child who remembers / and the man who grieves', as the island moves away and yet remains forever in the mirror.[11] The experience of this modern Scottish poet was often figured in poems about exile, emigration and farewells.

Crichton Smith's sense of not belonging to any single culture informed much of his work, whether manifest in his frequent practice of translating his own Gaelic poetry into English, or in poems such as 'For Poets writing in English over in Ireland' that explicitly addressed the issue of bilingualism – 'I gaze at the three poets. They are me, / poised between two languages.'[12] In 'The Fool', he cast himself in harlequin red and black, 'the two colours that have tormented me – English and Gaelic', which seems a rather less comforting line on the language question than those presented by Crawford and Imlah twenty-five years later.[13] It is partly because of poets like Crichton Smith, however, whose serious confrontation of inner conflict is so illuminating, that Scottish poetry was gradually released from the painful association of language with torment. As 'a poet of question marks', Crichton Smith was tentatively opening up ways of approaching the fraught linguistic territory of his native culture, often producing work of striking beauty in the process.[14]

Paradoxically, Graham's image of the isolated Malcolm Mooney, moving 'slowly over the white language', thus has things in common with other Scottish writers of the 1970s.[15] Though resolutely set apart from his origins, the Arctic explorer, moving ever further away, preoccupied with both thoughts of home and the nature of language, reflects both the inner journeys of his creator and the problems of his contemporaries. Graham's explorations of language emerge in series of rhetorical questions, for no one can be expected to answer the man in the 'telephoneless, blue / Green crevasse'.[16] And yet, like Crichton Smith's endless endeavour, the journey is valuable despite the uncertainty: 'Where am I going said Malcolm Mooney' is answered by the poem itself. As Graham reflected at the time of composition, 'I think good things are coming out with strange, impossible, unpoetic beginnings like ... "What is the language using us for?"'[17]

Graham's persistent query, 'What is the language using us for?', is at once anxious and yet charged with possibility. For the neat reversal of traditional assumptions, which makes the *poet* rather than language an implement, was offering a way out of what seemed a potentially paralysing dilemma. If the image of Malcolm Mooney, surrounded by the frozen waste of language, is read not in terms of crippling alienation, but rather as an image of bleak literary freedom, it can be seen as a further step towards the linguistic liberty celebrated by the later generation of Scottish poets. Once the poet's inescapable subject is identified as language itself, then the urgency of settling on a particular language recedes. Does it matter if the medium is Scots, Gaelic or English, when what is under investigation – and what in fact determines any such enquiry – is the operation of language? Furthermore, concentration on words and grammar rather than the poet as the true source of meaning renders issues of biography and political commitments secondary to the workings of language. The influential ideas of French linguistic theorists dovetailed with Scottish literary concerns in the 1960s and 70s to open up the possibility of addressing the language question from an entirely new angle.

The title of Edwin Morgan's 1967 collection, *Emergent Poems*, suggests a similar movement from strange, unpromising beginnings into art, but it rapidly became apparent that his approach was to be rather more playful and inventive than that of his old friend, Sidney Graham. These were poems about language, sure enough, but 'Dialeck Piece' could hardly be more different in form and tone from 'Malcolm Mooney's Land'. Morgan's starting point, 'To a Mouse', becomes the end of his own emergent piece, which begins with scattered letters,

```
           i

    a      m
           m    ick     th      e
       d i      ck
           i              h    ave
        me
           m           a  t     e
```

before making its way irreverently towards one of Burns's famously Scottish lines – 'a daimen icker in a thrave'.[18] It was certainly a new look at the language question, and by placing Scots within a poem so unconventional in form and purpose, Morgan seemed to be shaking up the very paradigms of the old debate.

Choices between Scots and English seemed suddenly displaced by different questions about the constitution of words, grammar, poetic form and the way in which meaning emerges from the page. As he tore up newspapers, stanzaic forms and sentences in order to reassemble familiar letters into unfamiliar shapes, Morgan explored the social constructions of language and challenged Scottish poetry to embrace new methods of representation. Not only were his poems receptive to international influences, but they often self-consciously constructed from ludic cross-cultural dialogues, as in 'French Persian Cats having a Ball', which appeared in his much-admired volume of 1968, *The Second Life*,

> chat
> shah shah
> chat
> chat shah cha ha
> shah chat cha ha[19]

For Morgan, language never seemed primarily a matter of domestic politics, even though his attachment to his native land has always been abundantly evident in the numerous poems set in Scottish locations or addressing Scottish themes. His early work on *Beowulf* marked the beginning of his prolific output as a translator, which would subsequently take him to writers from Russia, Armenia, Hungary, Italy, Germany, Spain, France, Portugal, the Netherlands and Ancient Greece, as well as to those of multilingual, pre-Reformation Scotland.[20] The variety and sheer quantity of Morgan's work as a translator makes his attraction to other languages abundantly evident. The chunky Carcanet volume of his *Collected Translations* does not suggest the activity of a man forced into translation by painful cultural experience, but rather the chosen path of an enthusiast. The embrace of so many diverse foreign influences in Morgan's work conveys excitement rather than anxiety in the face of difference – and an instinctively multiple rather than binary understanding of the world.

Openness to the international has introduced an almost dazzling number of different perspectives into Morgan's extensive *oeuvre*, which plays instructively beside Crichton Smith's sense of unfulfilled yearnings – 'I should have loved Paris / when Picasso was there ... / when they stuck morsels of news / to their paintings: / when the concierge / was a cube.'[21] Like the Cubists, Morgan has been eager to break down conventional methods of perception and representation, collapsing deep-seated oppositions and seeking a new flexibility in his art. Resistant to prevailing ideologies, he drew on Russian and American, Protestant and Catholic poetry, while his own work explored the spaces between the spoken and written, pastoral and satirical, comic and tragic, country and city, earthly and terrestrial, masculine and feminine. It is not surprising that when younger Scottish poets were searching for work that might help them find ways of expressing the new attitudes of the late 1980s and 90s, they often turned to Morgan's example. When Liz Lochhead articulated her response to the collapse of the Berlin Wall in 'Five Berlin Poems', for example, she explicitly invoked Morgan's *Sonnets from Scotland*.[22] For he had, in a sense, already demonstrated how art could flourish in the rubble left behind after the demolition of great binary systems.

For women poets, especially, the breakdown of traditional contraries began to prove immensely liberating. Scottish poetry in the twentieth century had been largely dominated by male poets, whose confrontations had a distinctly masculine tone, but with the rise of international feminism in the 1970s, new questions began to erupt in Scotland, which cut across the differences between Scots, English and Gaelic. If linguistic theory had helped to open up the language question for all Scottish writers, it gave special impetus to the women poets who began to create a self-affirming literature of their own. Liz Lochhead's work often mimicked colloquial speech, but her choice of Scots seemed as much an attempt to give a voice to modern women as to articulate her commitment to the nation. Indeed, she has treated Scottish tradition with the same irreverence accorded to the cultural inheritance of the rest of the world, rewriting the old ballad of 'Tam Lin', for example, from the perspective of one of his lady's female friends, 'So you met him in a magic place? / O.K. / But that's a bit airy fairy for me.'[23] As the dramatic monologue unfolds, the old ballad emerges as the narrative of a young woman ensnared by masculine language, making 'Tam Lin's Lady' a cautionary tale for both teenage girls and modern women writers:

> He'd been talking in symbols (like
> Adder-snake, wild savage bear
> Brand of bright iron red-hot from the fire)
> And as usual the plain unmythical truth was worse.[24]

Lochhead's feminist critique of familiar myths revealed a similar impulse to fracture conventional binary thinking and create art from the demolition process.

If her poems often focused on female experience, however, she avoided any tendency to replace one binary view with another by acknowledging the oppression of women by other women. Elizabeth I's distinctly unsisterly attitude to her cousin, for example, featured prominently in Lochhead's well-known play, *Mary Queen of Scots Got Her Head Chopped Off* (1987), but she has also been alert to more understated, domestic conflicts, as depicted in poems such as 'Box Room', where a young woman makes her first week-end visit to her boyfriend's parents:

> First the welcoming. Smiles all round. A space
> For handshakes. Then she put me in my place —[25]

Here the neat binaries of the heroic couplet are disrupted by the internal breaks and enjambment, which register the resistance of both speaker and poet to the outward forms of polite convention. Like the speaker in 'Tam Lin's Lady', Lochhead deals in specifics and 'plain, unmythical truths', but ironically, her very skills in colloquial language have sometimes detracted attention from her accomplished use of traditional forms.

Lochhead's challenge to the maleness of Scotland's literary arena has been reinforced by the success of a new generation of women poets, including Carol Ann Duffy and Kathleen Jamie. Both have followed Lochhead's lead in making female experience central to their work, while sharing the more exploratory attitudes to language that have characterised later twentieth-century Scottish poetry in general. Jamie's 'The Queen of Sheba', for example, adopts colloquial idiom, but uses it to expose the way in which common speech can harden into conventional, repressive attitudes. Her uneasiness with certain aspects of contemporary Scotland is reminiscent of Crichton Smith, as she dwells on the disapproval of 'Presbyterian living rooms' and imagines the Queen of Sheba hearing the pejorative associations of her name among those for whom deep-rooted prejudice is part of the cultural inheritance:

> your vixen's bark of poverty, come down
> the family like a lang neb, a thrawn streak,
> a wally dug you never liked
> but can't get shot of.[26]

'The Queen of Sheba' answers the sense of limitation with a triumphant comic vision of emancipation: 'She's had enough. She's come.'

If the exotic Queen's welcome by 'a thousand laughing girls' is a telling image for modern Scotland, Jamie's use of Scots to attack the narrow-mindedness of some Scottish communities is a startling riposte to earlier champions of the language. At the same time, however, her own poem is dependent on the vitality of the spoken word and, like much of her work, draws subtly on the juxtaposition of the standard and colloquial. Jamie's vocabulary is hugely enriched by her evident ease in English and Scots, for while some of her poems exploit the difference between the two, many employ Scots words because they are the best for her purposes. In 'The Wishing Tree', for example, 'To look ... through a smirr of rain', seems the most natural expression, as does the description of 'A bletted fruit / hung through tangled branches' in 'The Tree House'.[27] Here the precision of the language reflects the clarity of the observation rather than any national agenda.

For Carol Ann Duffy, language is as important a subject as it was for Graham or Crichton Smith, though her poems often make its exploration intrinsic to other topics. In *Standing Female Nude*, published in 1985, the concern with language is part of the volume's broadly feminist stance, as evident in 'Alliance', where the misunderstandings in a marriage between an Englishman and French woman work as a metaphor for the failure of communication between the sexes. The observation that 'She is word-perfect' condenses the entire union – its prejudices and imbalance of power – with a laconic conciseness characteristic of Duffy's art.[28] The image of the French wife, 'dreaming in another language', is at once a literal representation of the experience of bilingualism and a metaphorical reference to the language of women identified by contemporary feminists. It also looks forward to poems such as 'Foreign', in *Selling Manhattan* (1987), and to the explorations in *The Other Country* (1990) of places visited in imagination – old love affairs, fantasies, visions of wealth and early memories.

Although the journeys in Duffy's poems are often metaphorical, the image of childhood as emigration in 'Originally', which provides the opening to *The Other Country*, draws on the poet's memories of her gradual assimilation into a new environment after the family's departure from Glasgow,

> I remember my tongue
> shedding its skin like a snake, my voice
> in the classroom sounding just like the rest.[29]

Duffy's bilingualism was not that of the modern Gaelic speaker, but rather of a child who felt compelled to adopt the Midlands accent of her school friends, even though her family continued to speak Scots. The use of simile seems an inevitable consequence of her early experience, for the slightly forced analogy of shedding an accent 'like a snake' in order to be accepted echoes through the collection, with its recurrent exploration of what things are like and which things are liked. In 'The Kissing Gate', the image of love, repeating words 'till they're smooth … like a small stone you sucked once', is followed by thoughts of 'the things you'd like to do to me / if you were here', while in 'The Way My Mother Speaks', a familiar phrase from home, 'what like is it', runs through the mind of a poet, 'homesick, free, in love / with the way my mother speaks'.[30] These poems speak of absence, but the effort to make connections through words, 'to spell them with love', as she later put it in 'Away and See', is often thwarted by doubt about the very nature of language.[31]

In 'Words, Wide Night', Duffy conjures up an image of the frustrated lover, 'singing / an impossible song of desire that you cannot hear', but as the speaker moves imaginatively towards her object, her declaration falters,

> For I am in love with you and this
> is what it is like or what it is like in words.[32]

As several critics have pointed out, Duffy's academic training in philosophy has made her especially alert to questions about the possibilities and limits of language explored in the work of Wittgenstein, Saussure and Derrida.[33] The workings of words are not treated in an abstract, objective manner in her poetry, however – even a poem such as 'The *Darling* Letters', which frankly acknowledges the mortality of language and inadequacy of cliché, also demonstrates their residual emotional power as it leaves 'the heart thudding / like a spade on buried bones'.[34] Whether or not Duffy's poetry exhibits what Stan Smith regards as a traditional longing for 'a fullness of self-presence in which sign and referent, language and things are one', there is little doubt that both language and desire have prompted her to poems of great vitality, which often counter apparent feelings of loss with their own unignorable sense of being.[35] 'Weasel Words', for example, may refer to 'words empty of meaning', as the epigraph makes plain, but it is difficult not to warm to the rhetoric of the Weasel and his obvious relish in sucking 'an egg. Slurp'.[36] This is a poem about the slipperiness of words, but it is also an accomplished sonnet, a dramatic monologue and a political satire, reminiscent of Burns's exuberant 'Address of Beelzebub'.

To see the preoccupation with language's inevitable limitation in terms of nostalgia for a lost unity may be illuminating for a poet influenced by early memories of an enforced bilingualism. However, in the context of modern Scottish poetry, it is possible to see Duffy's explorations as part of a bold challenge to conventional ways of thinking, which often results not in emptiness but plenitude. Indeed, it is largely her willingness to question conventional usage that allows her to revisit the past and acknowledge its continuing significance. As she explained in an interview in 1988, poetry can spotlight clichés, in order to show that 'although they look like a plastic rose in fact they've got roots underneath'.[37] So too, have modern Scottish poets, their sense of obligation eased by a positive pleasure in the workings of words, been able to revisit their cultural traditions and assess their continuing value. Jamie's 'Mr and Mrs Scotland are Dead' heaps up the clichés of her nation, the postcards from Peebles, Largs, Carnoustie, the cold weather, the anorak and the knitting pattern, but even as she half-mocks the redundant possessions of a lifetime, there is a deep pathos in the image of the 'stiff old ladies' bags, open mouthed' that spew them into the landfill site.[38]

Once shaken from their customary station, the objects lose their respect-ability and recover a new existence, which generates life, feeling and moral exploration. Like Lochhead confronted by the fragments of the Berlin Wall, Jamie's response to the collapse of old certainties is to turn her back on the past but to find new meaning from the unexpected chaos of images.

Liberation from the language question has not meant abandon-ing Scottish tradition, as Lochhead's reading of Morgan's *Sonnets from Scotland* makes clear. But just as Morgan's affirmation of the 'small and multitudinous country' involved being 'swung through centuries, ages, shifting geologies' and encountering figures as unexpected as Gerard Manley Hopkins in North Woodside Road or De Quincey in Rottenrow, so many of his younger contemporaries have delighted in Scotland's iron-ies, juxtapositions and miscellaneousness.[39] For contemporary poets, the old disputes over language are at once part of their nation's rich tradition and issues that still demand attention, though of a rather different nature. Mick Imlah's fine volume, *The Lost Leader*, for example, dares to take its epigraph from Edwin Muir:

> No poet in Scotland now can take as his inspiration the folk impulse that cre-ated the ballads, the people's songs, and the legends of Mary Stuart and Prince Charlie. He has no choice but to be at once more individual and less local.[40]

Imlah's collection then proceeds to confuse the old debate between Muir and MacDiarmid by presenting a series of highly sophisticated poems in English, inspired by many of the best-known Scottish legends. Deftly recouping 'The Lost Leader' from Browning for a poem on Charles Edward Stuart, Imlah explores questions of loyalty from the perspective of a defeated Jacobite, comparing his way along the Tromie to a poor, rain-soaked hiding-place with that of his leader:

> West down channels
> Of last-ditch loyalty;
> To France at last, your safety,
> Prince, your Highness,
> Your brandy, gout and syphilis.[41]

Although the poem could hardly be less like the popular Jacobite songs dis-missed in Muir's *Scottish Journey* and evoked here as an epigraph, Imlah's ironic representation of the Royal Prince is deepened by the evident sym-pathy for his follower. The brief closing stanza recalls 'the secret white of the rose' and the Jacobite's unreproachful confession, that 'all we did was sweet-ened by it'. Somewhere in the background of the title poem, with its com-plicated meditation on loyalty and exile, are the strains of MacDiarmid's 'little white rose of Scotland / That smells sharp and sweet – and breaks the heart'.[42] Whether this points to MacDiarmid as an inspiration for the volume, or casts him as another lost leader is open to debate, but Imlah's awareness of the complexity of representing Scotland's past is as evident in his own collection of poems as it was in *The New Penguin Book of Scottish Verse*.

Like so many modern Scottish poets, Imlah was fascinated by language and, like Duffy, his poems commented on the experience of being a Scot in the South. In 'Goldilocks', a witty revision of the familiar fairytale from a male perspective, the speaker who, finding on return to his Oxford rooms a homeless Scotsman in his bed, observes, 'Och, if he'd known *I* was Scottish! Then I'd have got it.'[43] Autobiographical reflections in *The Lost Leader* refer explicitly to the way in which a Southern education 'Had trimmed my Scottishness to a tartan phrase / brought out on match days and Remembrance Days', while the 'seemingly Islamical' name, Imlah, provokes assertions of Scottish roots and thoughts of 'what my family too had originally been'.[44] 'Originally' recalls Duffy's poem on her own emigration from Scotland, an experience indicated in Imlah's 'Namely' by a quotation from Angus Calder: 'Few people thought Mick Imlah, who teaches at Oxford, was a Scottish poet.'[45] After the publication of *The Lost Leader*, few people could remain in any doubt about Imlah's Scottishness, irrespective of his own mode of speech.

For Mick Imlah, the Oxford-educated, London-based, *TLS* editor who was also a modern Scottish poet, language was something to celebrate not contest. The opening poem of *The Lost Leader*, 'Muck', originally published in *Archipelago*, begins with a trip into Scotland's early history, landing in 'a rank bad place with no words at all'.[46] Although from here the future of Scotland is not without its dismaying developments, the history of its language and literature inspires admiration rather than lamentation. What emerges most clearly from the volume is Imlah's enjoyment of Scottish legends and cultural clichés, which, *pace* Muir, provide endless scope for the modern, urban poet. As he fused old and new, juxtaposing cairns and Thermos flasks, Orpheus and Girvan, the quartered Wallace and a hockey shirt, Imlah demonstrated the essential continuities of Scottish consciousness, even in its multiplicity.

The sequence that begins with 'Muck' concludes with 'Iona', but now attention is on the future, since the poem about Imlah's daughter is also a tender affirmation of words that had seemed worn out.

> Darling – 'little' – *Mädchen* – the same
> Suspicious argot I used to spy on.[47]

As Duffy has also recognised, words that seem lost can regain their power, once considered in a different context. Imlah's celebration of familiar things suddenly made marvellous is characteristic of contemporary Scottish poetry, in which even sentiment has been recovered as intrinsic to the national culture. His celebration of fatherhood, like that of his contemporaries, Robert Crawford and Don Paterson, emphasises that his work was forward-looking even while being drawn to the past. The willingness to look backwards and forwards without anxiety, to embrace the complexity of language and human experience, and to find the right words from the masses available, makes the future of Scottish poetry seem bright, even though Imlah himself is a prematurely lost leader.

Notes

1 W. S. Graham, 'What is the language using us for?', in *New Collected Poems*, ed. M. Francis (London: Faber, 2004), p. 199.

2 Maurice Lindsay (ed.), *Modern Scottish Poetry: An Anthology of the Scottish Renaissance* (London: Faber, 1966), p. 19.

3 Douglas Dunn, 'Language and Liberty', in Dunn (ed.), *Twentieth-Century Scottish Poetry* (London: Faber, 1992), p. xxvii.

4 *Ibid.*

5 *Ibid.*

6 Robert Crawford, 'Simultaneous Translation', in *Talkies* (London: Chatto & Windus, 1992), p. 14.

7 Robert Crawford and Mick Imlah (eds.), *The New Penguin Book of Scottish Verse* (London: Penguin, 2000), p. xvii.

8 *Ibid.*, p. xxv.

9 Iain Crichton Smith, 'The Village', in *Collected Poems* (Manchester: Carcanet, 1992), p. 289, cited in James Campbell, 'Iain Crichton Smith 1928–1998: A Celtic Undertow', *Times Literary Supplement*, 30 October 1998, 16.

10 Iain Crichton Smith, 'Lewis 1928–1945', in *Collected Poems*, p. 245.

11 Crichton Smith, 'The Village', p. 299.

12 Crichton Smith, *Collected Poems*, p. 239.

13 Iain Crichton Smith, 'The Fool', in *Collected Poems*, p. 196.

14 Campbell, 'Iain Crichton Smith', 16.

15 Graham, 'What is the language using us for?', p. 199. The poem revives the eponymous persona of Graham's *Malcolm Mooney's Land* (1970).

16 Graham, 'What is the language using us for?', p. 199.

17 W. S. Graham to Elizabeth Smart, 22 July 1973; repr. in M. and M. Snow (eds.), *The Nightfisherman: Selected Letters of W. S. Graham* (Manchester: Carcanet, 1999), pp. 267–8.

18 Edwin Morgan, *Collected Poems* (Manchester: Carcanet, 1990), p. 134.

19 *Ibid.*, p. 161.

20 Edwin Morgan, *Collected Translations* (Manchester: Carcanet, 1996). See also Peter McCarey, 'Edwin Morgan the Translator', in Robert Crawford and

Hamish Whyte (eds.), *About Edwin Morgan* (Edinburgh University Press, 1990), pp. 90–105.

21 Crichton Smith, *Collected Poems*, p. 288.

22 Liz Lochhead, 'Five Berlin Poems', in *Bagpipe Muzak* (London: Penguin, 1991), pp. 77–84.

23 Liz Lochhead, 'Tam Lin's Lady' from *The Grimm Sisters* (1981), in *Dreaming Frankenstein and Collected Poems 1967–1984* (Edinburgh: Polygon, 1984), p. 93.

24 *Ibid.*, p. 94.

25 Liz Lochhead, 'Box Room' from *Memo for Spring* (1972), in *Dreaming Frankenstein*, p. 176.

26 Kathleen Jamie, 'The Queen of Sheba' (1994), in *Mr and Mrs Scotland are Dead: Poems 1980–1994* (Tarset: Bloodaxe, 2002), p. 111.

27 Kathleen Jamie, 'The Wishing Tree' and 'The Tree House', in *The Tree House* (London: Picador, 2004), pp. 3, 41.

28 Carol Ann Duffy, 'Alliance', in *Standing Female Nude* (London: Anvil, 1985), p. 26.

29 Carol Ann Duffy, 'Originally', in *The Other Country* (London: Anvil, 1990), p. 7.

30 Duffy, 'The Kissing Gate' and 'The Way My Mother Speaks', in *Other Country*, pp. 46, 54.

31 Carol Ann Duffy, 'Away and See', in *Mean Time* (London: Anvil, 1993), p. 23.

32 Duffy, 'Words, Wide Night', in *Other Country*, p. 47.

33 See, for example, Jane E. Thomas, '"The Intolerable wrestle with words": The Poetry of Carol Ann Duffy', *Bête Noire*, 6 (Winter 1988), 78–88; Stan Smith, '"What like is it?" Duffy's *Différance*' and Michael Woods, '"What it is like in words": Translation, Reflection and Refraction in the Poetry of Carol Ann Duffy', in Angelica Michaelis and Antony Rowland (eds.), *The Poetry of Carol Ann Duffy* (Manchester University Press, 2003), pp. 143–68, 169–85.

34 Duffy, 'The *Darling* Letters', in *Other Country*, p. 48.

35 Smith, 'What like is it?', p. 163.

36 Duffy, 'Weasel Words', in *Other Country*, p. 14.

37 *Bête Noire*, 6 (Winter 1988), 75–6, cited by Smith, 'What like is it?', p. 143.

38 Jamie, 'Mr and Mrs Scotland are Dead', in *Mr and Mrs Scotland are Dead*, p. 134.

39 Lochhead, 'Five Berlin Poems', p. 78.

40 Mick Imlah, *The Lost Leader* (London: Faber, 2008), p. v, quoting Edwin Muir, *Scottish Journey*, ed. T. C. Smout (1935; Edinburgh: Mainstream, 1979), p. 94.

41 Imlah, 'The Lost Leader', in *Lost Leader*, p. 43.

42 MacDiarmid's 'The Little White Rose' is quoted in the introduction to Crawford and Imlah's *New Penguin Book of Scottish Verse*, p. xxix, and included again on p. 422.

43 Mick Imlah, 'Goldilocks', in Dunn (ed.), *Twentieth-Century Scottish Poetry*, p. 401.

44 Imlah, 'Stephen Boyd' and 'Namely', in *Lost Leader*, pp. 98, 61.

45 *Ibid.*

46 Imlah, 'Muck', in *Lost Leader*, p. 3.

47 Imlah, 'Iona', in *Lost Leader*, p. 109.

Guide to further reading

Brown, Ian and Alan Riach (eds.), *The Edinburgh Companion to Twentieth-Century Scottish Literature* (Edinburgh University Press, 2009)

Crawford, Robert, *Identifying Poets* (Edinburgh University Press, 1993)

Crawford, Robert and Mick Imlah (eds.), *The New Penguin Book of Scottish Verse* (London: Penguin, 2000)

Crawford, Robert and Hamish Whyte (eds.), *About Edwin Morgan* (Edinburgh University Press, 1990)

Dunn, Douglas (ed.), *Twentieth-Century Scottish Poetry* (London: Faber, 1992)

McGuire, Matt and Colin Nicholson (eds.), *The Edinburgh Companion to Contemporary Scottish Poetry* (Edinburgh University Press, 2009)

Whyte, Christopher, *Modern Scottish Poetry* (Edinburgh University Press, 2004)

17

MATTHEW WICKMAN

The Emergence of Scottish Studies

Analyses of origin are always complex – or, as Edward Said would have it, 'beginnings' are always 'uncanny', or unsettling.[1] For one thing, their object is multiple: to recount the rise of Scottish Studies, for example, one must also account for the field's *prehistory* – what was there before it developed into its modern, recognisable form. Then there are questions of *territory*, that is, of the place of individual works within the field and of the field itself relative to some larger academic terrain. And in the case of *Scottish* Studies in particular, this generic complexity is compounded by the extent that the discipline involves a nation composed of multiple languages and cultures, an ambiguous relation to conventional statehood and a significantly diasporic history.

Hence, to discuss the rise of Scottish Studies is to evoke a great many things besides, so that no short essay can do the subject justice. Of course, to some extent, the field is a monument to the purported injustice it has perpetually done itself – or so it would appear from a certain branch of its history. In 1919, G. Gregory Smith observed that Scotland's relatively small size and coherent languages should lend themselves to 'a general estimate' of the nation's literature. However, he continued, close engagement of the material reveals contrary propensities toward realism and fantasy which, 'under the stress of foreign influence and native division and reaction', spawn 'a zigzag of contradictions'.[2] But then, in a gesture befitting Hegel or Renan, or perhaps Blake, Smith unified these contraries under a banner he labelled the 'Caledonian Antisyzygy', a portrait of the national spirit as Jekyll and Hyde. For both good and ill, Smith's vision left a lasting impression. As Gerard Carruthers has shown, Smith's 'quasi-racial musings set Scottish criticism off on the path of mass-psychology, which led later Scottish critics into absolute pessimism about the viability of Scottish literature and culture'.[3] While the poet, critic and political activist Hugh MacDiarmid embraced Smith's notion of cultural bifurcation in the 1920s, seeing it as a symbol of national energy, others who conceded Smith's central claim were far less sanguine. Indeed, Edwin Muir in the 1930s, John Speirs in the 1940s, Kurt Wittig in the 1950s, David Craig and David Daiches in the 1960s, Tom Nairn in the 1970s and Kenneth Simpson in the 1980s all perceived the divisions of Scottish culture as debilitating. In the 1980s and 90s, however, a group of scholars including Cairns Craig, Craig Beveridge, Ronald Turnbull, David McCrone and Lindsay Paterson began arguing that Scotland's cultural fault lines made up an important part of its history, and that, in any event, national traditions inherently entail complex processes of cultural negotiation. As Craig puts it, 'nations have never been pure', and so national identities derive from 'the dialogue between alternative possibilities of the self'.[4] When these convictions began to hold sway in the 1990s and early 2000s, they refashioned the image of a fatally divided Scotland into a figure (not unlike MacDiarmid's) of galvanising diversity.

One way to tell the story about modern Scottish Studies is simply to trace the development of this dialogical paradigm. There is much here to tell, not only of important work within distinct branches of the field – literature, history, philosophy, geography and more – but also of expansive institutional developments (such as, for instance, the founding of the Research Institute for Irish and Scottish Studies at the University of Aberdeen, home for many years to the AHRC's largest grant in partnership with Queen's University, Belfast, and Trinity College, Dublin, or the Scotland's Transatlantic Relations (or STAR) project run out of the University of Edinburgh). However, two wrinkles in the narrative of burgeoning diversification prompt a slightly different approach. Craig presents one himself in extending the argument I cited above, adding that precisely because of its dialogical history, 'Scotland might stand as an exemplar of the fact that nationalisms and national cultures are always multiple' and that such 'pluralism is not a denial of national "identity."'[5] An 'exemplar[y]' Scotland is neither essentialised (*pace* Smith) nor mass-psychologised (in the mode of his followers), but it does convert the nation into a category, in this instance in a larger project of cultural criticism. 'Scotland' becomes not just a place, but also a way of relating, which means that, consistently with the long history inaugurated by Smith, the imperative to *think* – and not simply to *document* – Scotland remains a feature of the discipline. And yet, and this is the second wrinkle (with which I suspect Craig would concur), the narrative of the nation's pluralistic coming of age, and the role of Scottish self-consciousness in shaping that narrative, suggests that Scotland's status as a cultural category may be not merely exemplary but also critically instructive – not merely affirming, but also unsettling or difficult. I say this because any story which begins in schizophrenia, then passes through a dialectic of uneven national development and eventually leaves off with a Bakhtin-enfranchised cultural heteroglossia inverts the conventional course of cultural history which proceeds from 'modernism' to 'postmodernism'.[6] In Scottish Studies, the postmodern moment in some ways comes first; and, while the dialogic emphasis of the current era in some ways conserves traditional (or, here, phase two) categories like nationhood, it also potentially threatens its own grand narrative of enlightened diversity with the spectre of dissolution, specifically by admitting a 'cosmopolitan' criticism which vacates the nationalist paradigm altogether.

In short, as much as the field has evolved, it may not entirely have left Smith behind. If it had, it might be impossible to tell the story of how it did so, or to tell it in a way which still bespoke 'Scottish Studies', since the discipline would already be defining itself as something else. And while it is a truism that cultural categories bear the aura of their own history, this phenomenon carries special significance in Scottish Studies, in part because the field has traditionally devoted a good deal of attention to the task of self-examination, or to asking what it means to engage in Scottish Studies in the first place. In that spirit, what follows here is less a comprehensive than a critical history of the field. I will focus particularly on the rise or emergence of the field in its current or dialogical phase, playing off an intrinsic tension between the terminology of a rising discipline (which suggests a linear narrative of progress) and the more radical implications of the field's dialogism (which would appeal less to a 'rising' discipline than to an 'emergent' one, which is to say, to notions of being more consistent with a virtual, non-linear, even 'schizophrenic' cultural poetics). As I hope to show, the presence of the past in contemporary Scottish Studies – of earlier incarnations of the field in its later developments – does not inhibit as much as it provokes dynamic thinking, not only with respect to Scottish culture, but also to the wide world of 'studies' discourses.

First, it may be helpful to chart some key historical landmarks in the field of Scottish Studies as we currently recognise it. Carruthers, who has written very helpfully on this subject, observes that 'Scottish Literature as an academic discipline ... has really only come into being since the 1960s. G. Ross Roy ... founded its first journal, *Studies in Scottish Literature*, in 1963; the Association for Scottish Literary Studies (ASLS) was formed in Scotland in 1970; and the autonomous Department of Scottish Literature at the University of Glasgow came into being in 1971.' These institutional inroads were themselves laid across important earlier developments, like 'the founding at the University of Glasgow in 1913 of the Chair of Scottish History and Literature', the organising of the Glasgow Ballad Club in 1908 and the forming of the Scottish Text Society in 1882.[7] But Scottish Studies really came of age in the last decades of the twentieth century, with the surge of national consciousness in the wake of the failed devolution referendum of 1979, and with the watershed scholarship which appeared across a range of disciplines in the 1980s and 90s. Key texts here include (but are by no means limited to) Alexander Broadie's *The Tradition of Scottish Philosophy* (1990), Duncan Macmillan's *Scottish Art* (1990) and John Purser's *Scotland's Music* (1992) and, in literary studies, Cairns Craig's four-volume edited set *The History of Scottish Literature* (1987), his monograph *Out of History* (1996), Robert Crawford's *Devolving English Literature* (1992) and Douglas Gifford and Dorothy McMillan's edited collection *A History of Scottish Women's Writing* (1997). Such work formed a scholarly corollary to the oft-noted outburst of creative energy in Scottish literature, headlined by novelists like James Kelman, Janice Galloway and Alasdair Gray, and by poets like Crawford, Kathleen Jamie and Don Paterson (to name only a few). The establishment of Scotland's devolved parliament via the Scotland Act of 1998 both formalised and further underscored the nation's resurgence. And all this growth in the cultural and political sectors fuelled expansion within the universities as the natural home for Scottish Studies, fostering new research centres, book series, conferences, courses and journals (most pertinently, at least in name, the *Scottish Studies Review* in 2000).

The field's development – indeed, one reason why scholars employ the term Scottish *Studies* – owes much to its historical coincidence with British Cultural Studies. The latter arose during the 1950s as a 'subjective' and politically engaged (as opposed to a 'positivist' and disinterested) method of inquiry.[8] Originally drawing heavily from Frankfurt School, Marxist-inflected engagements of culture, the movement today preoccupies itself less with Marxian topics like hegemony and uneven development than with post-modern (or post-postmodern) categories like ontological intensities (which is to say, with internally rather than externally configured networks of power). Whereas hegemony traditionally operates under the auspices of state institutions like schools and churches, generating normative ideals and behaviours, intensities arise more spontaneously from sub- or counter-cultural media, as in cyberspace communities formed through Facebook or Twitter. Scott Lash describes this evolution from hegemonic power-from-above to intensified power-from-below as a move from a regime of representation to one of communication, a shift which corresponds with the difference between, on the one hand, a 'rising' and fundamentally linear field and, on the other, an 'emergent' and essentially chaotic one.[9] This transformation follows almost logically (and, ironically, in linear, 'rising' fashion) from the historical impetus of Cultural Studies, which Stuart Hall says originated as a partial response to the social crisis which emerged after the Second World War: 'The vocation of cultural studies has been to enable people to understand what is going on, and especially to provide strategies for survival, and resources of resistance, to all those who are now – in economic, political, and cultural terms – excluded from anything that could be called access to the national culture.'[10]

This credo manifests itself in Scottish Studies in two principal ways. There is, first, an 'emergent' tendency there towards cosmopolitanism, or towards a concept of 'the world as a network of interdependencies' created from the refuse of old nation states.[11] Here, Hall's 'access' evokes images of cultural hybridity (not to mention online shopping franchises like eBay and Amazon: identity constituted by the click of a mouse). Scholars of an 'emergent' consciousness in Scottish Studies occasionally express frustration at the recalcitrance of the 'rising', comparatively staid quality of the national model.[12] But here, and second, it may be useful to think of the post-war history of which Hall reminds us, and to recall that the question of national culture bore heightened significance in Scotland during the onset of the Cultural Studies era, not least because, as T. M. Devine observes, that 'linchpin of the union, the British Empire, was disintegrating at remarkable speed', providing Scots with less 'access' not to culture per se, but to imperial markets.[13] The assertion of a cultural-nationalist identity – *Scottish* Studies – thus represents, after a fashion, a residually political remnant of a Cultural Studies movement whose politics are increasingly virtual and diffusive.

But this raises a more basic question than whether Scottish Studies are national or cosmopolitan, 'rising' or 'emergent', namely: what do we mean by 'Scottish Studies'? Even if we define the term tautologically as 'studies of Scotland', what does that mean? What is 'Scotland'? Pursuing a purely anecdotal heuristic, a keyword search of 'Scotland' at Brigham Young University's library for the year 2008 retrieves 146 items. While some of these texts, like Murray Pittock's *Scottish and Irish Romanticism*, seem clearly central, others, like *Advances in Mathematical Modeling for Reliability* (which shows up because a 2007 conference on this subject happened to be held at the University of Strathclyde), appear negligible. A little deconstruction may be in order, however, for the graphical methods and Bayesian networks which the latter book discusses represent the increasingly popular means whereby scientists chart statistical frequencies and, by extension, the identity of objects. Elsewhere in literary studies, statistical models are reconfiguring historical and national fields, so much so that one can imagine making the case that such metrics may eventually enable us to push beyond a nominal 'Scottishness' and help us determine more precisely just what the fields – plural – of a diversifying-and-already-eclectic Scottish Studies are.[14]

To be sure, statistical approaches invite scepticism from traditional scholars of literary studies, for whom Bayesian networks represent a foreign (if not a downright intergalactic) language. But before dismissing them altogether, and staying within the parameters of 'Scotland 2008' at BYU's library, consider the debatable land of Scottish Studies between the (apparent) extremes of *Scottish and Irish Romanticism* and *Advances in Mathematical Modeling*. A project like Louisa Gairn's *Ecology and Modern Scottish Literature* seemingly fits squarely within the field, and yet it more or less presupposes the 'Scottish' aspect of Scottish literature – discussing a range of writers without probing the question of their identity per se – because its aim is to take familiar material and open it to new (in this case, eco-critical) perspectives. By contrast, the posthumous book by a long-standing goad to the field, H. R. Trevor-Roper's *The Invention of Scotland*, takes 'Scottishness' as its direct object of reflection. A third book, Penny Fielding's *Scotland and the Fictions of Geography*, takes a middle path, showing how Scottish literary self-consciousness (specifically of itself as the product of historical rather than organic sensibilities) served an instrumental role in fashioning Britain's sense of its own modernity.[15] All these projects fall under the broad heading of Scottish Studies, though what is 'Scottish' about them differs, appearing by turns contingent (in Gairn), essential (in Trevor-Roper) and historically self-conscious (in Fielding). And so, to draw an accurate map of a truly 'diverse' field, we almost *need* the statistical methods discussed by the seemingly *least* 'Scottish' book of the 146-item sample.

Let me emphasise that I am not on a quest here for the golden fleece of a pure or even an 'improved' field of Scottish Studies. But as we see in the intrinsic dialectic between Gairn and Trevor-Roper (in which the text which appears more germane to Scottish Studies, Gairn's, is actually less concerned with Scotland per se), diversity is probably less a hard-won than an inherent and inexorable feature of the field. Then again, who, other than some Bayesian analyst, can say just what diversity means, or what forms it takes, in Scottish Studies or any other field? The imponderability of the category helps explain why scholars like Christopher Whyte advocate eschewing the self-congratulatory (or sometimes -flagellating) cultural-nationalist paradigm in favour of other – especially formal, or aesthetic – interpretive criteria in which the Scottish Question does not even appear.[16] Reminiscent of Paul de Man's crusade for a 'formal materialist' poetics in the early 1980s, what de Man contemptuously labels the 'humanist' aspects of a field of 'rising' diversity would give way to an 'emergence' of such chaotic intensity that we would lose sight of the field 'as such' altogether.[17]

And yet, it is via the aesthetics of form that we behold a curious and, at times, seemingly unintentional recrudescence of the narrative of a 'rising' nation, or what de Man would call a chiastic reversal (if not an outright deconstruction) of the categories of cultural nationalism and cosmopolitanism. MacDiarmid set an important precedent here by juxtaposing the ideal of an imminently independent (and internationally minded) Scotland with the effigy of a degenerate North Britain (or of what his colleague Lewis Grassic Gibbon called 'Scotshire'), an intellectually and politically bankrupt province of England sustaining itself culturally on the pap of such debased stereotypes as 'Kailyard' fiction.[18] MacDiarmid's scathing assessment of aspects of the Scottish past laid the groundwork for the narrative of a nation rising from its own detritus. Some cultural historians, however, shared MacDiarmid's distaste for the past without catching his vision of the future. In 1961, for example, the philosopher George Davie articulated an influential narrative of national decline, arguing that Scotland's eighteenth-century educational programme, which privileged general education and critical thinking, both resisted the English emphasis on early specialisation and also furnished 'a distinctive code regulating the Scottish way of life'. In essence, he claimed, the universities had enabled the nation to retain a measure of cultural autonomy even in the wake of the 1707 Union; they were the first home to a 'Scottish Studies' which extended across the curriculum, less as content – Scotland as object – than as form – Scotland as a way of thinking. However, he continues, parliamentary reform in the 1830s 'shook to its foundations the interlocked network of institutions on whose co-operation depended whatever was distinctive in Scottish society', eventually corroding the system which had enabled Scotland's world-renowned 'Enlightenment'.[19] In the mid 1970s, the proto-cosmopolitan Tom Nairn took Davie's story of Scottish abjection one step further, essentially impugning the 'studies' model of the Enlightenment as an appeasement strategy exploited by the British state.[20]

These arguments of Scotland as a nation which either fell from enlightened grace or which was already corrupted at the outset have certainly not gone unchallenged over the past two or three decades, but they have not exactly disappeared, either. For instance, they take a modified, uncanny form in Cairns Craig's Preface to the important 1990s-era 'Determinations' book series at Polygon:

> Scotland's history is often presented as punctuated by disasters which over-whelm the nation, break its continuity and produce a fragmented culture. Through the 1980s such conceptions have been challenged by a wide range of critical and analytical works that have shown just how profound the tradition of Scottish culture has been, and how dynamic the debates within it have remained – even in those periods (like the period after 1830) which cultural history usually looks upon as blanks in the nation's achievement.[21]

Craig's manifesto all but denounces Davie by name. However, it does not dispel the darkness of the Scottish past as much as it displaces it from the mid nineteenth century to the mid twentieth. But this means that narratives like Davie's and Nairn's not only provide the impetus for the revisionist histories which refute them, but they also uncannily inform the logic of their own repudiation even as they become the image of the past they had renounced. Past and present enter into a strangely, and provocatively, mimetic relationship with each other.

To appreciate why this reflexivity matters, we might consider the further example of Duncan Macmillan's magnificent study *Scottish Art, 1460–2000*. In a discussion of Scottish Presbyterian iconoclasm, Macmillan aims his own rhetorical weapon at traditional assumptions concerning the 'fundamental incompatibility between Protestantism and painting', a canard which historically places 'visual art in Scotland at a permanent disadvantage'. The cultural allergy to artistic representation which is part of the legacy of John Knox

> prevents the Scots from seeing that their contribution to the humanising of western culture – the philosophy of Hume, the portraits of Ramsay, the poetry of Burns, the novels of Scott, the paintings of Wilkie or the town planning of Patrick Geddes, to name just a few examples – has not been achieved in spite of the Reformation, but is in fact an integral extension of their profound involvement in that event which was where this humanising process began.[22]

Deconstruction of the Presbyterian/Humanist binary has since become more prominent in Scottish Studies, but the history of which Macmillan writes is less at issue here than the circuit of his reasoning: (a) Scottish culture bears Knox's burden even though (b) Scots have actually made, in concert with this legacy, a series of important contributions to the West. Sadly (c), this fact has gone largely unrecognised, but (d) not in a study like this one, not in our present era. The message is inadvertently mixed: the splendour of Scotland's history – the revisionist claim – has too long escaped our dim gaze – the defeatist line. In one sense, then, Macmillan's argument readmits the cultural desuetude it renounces; in another, however, it also makes itself a part of the history it revitalises.

The point worth underscoring here is that it is not the content of history alone (for example the Knoxian legacy) which Macmillan revises, but also the *form* of that history, which is less chronological than performative. In discussing history, that is, Macmillan effectively makes history. And he is not alone. The journalist Neal Ascherson does something similar in his remarkable historical memoir as he recounts the after-effects of the failed devolution referendum on the morale of his friends and associates. Calling the years after 1979 'bleak', he claims that, prior to this disappointment, people 'had grown accustomed to the idea that Scotland was to become an exciting, lively little country'. But when the referendum dashed those hopes, Ascherson struck a dour note in his diary: 'The future existed for many years; people became used to it as a background; now it has vanished and there is a blankness only.'[23] The 'blankness' to which he refers, anticipating Craig's Preface to the 'Determinations' series, alludes to Edwin Muir's scathing indictment of the nation in Muir's 1936 treatise *Scott and Scotland*. Walter Scott, Muir writes, 'spent most of his days in a hiatus, in a country, that is to say, which was neither a nation nor a province, and had, instead of a centre, a blank, an Edinburgh, in the middle of it'.[24] Muir's point is that Scotland's historical self-division across languages (Scots and English, to say nothing of Gaelic), religions and national identities had riven the national spirit and the organic sensibilities of its inhabitants. But, of course, Muir traffics here in myth himself, and self-consciously so. By the time he reached his maturity as a writer in the 1920s and 30s, Muir viewed his native Orkney as a kind of Edenic paradise set against the lapsarian Glasgow of his teens – a place where tragedy had struck his family (claiming the lives of his parents and two older brothers), and which seemed to Muir to symbolise the dire consequences of industrialisation. Glasgow thus became a metonymic figure of the modern forces dragging Scotland – or, really, for Muir, all of humanity – into its vortex.[25] Muir interpreted Scottish literary history backwards from this fallen condition, reading into Scott what Muir's friend T. S. Eliot labelled the 'dissociation of sensibility', the rupture between thought and feeling which personified the pervasive sense of alienation to which so many early twentieth-century writers were attuned.

That Scotland should have become for the Eliot-influenced Muir a lens through which to interpret modernity seems appropriate inasmuch as Eliot's own mythic appraisal of the modern world as a wasteland was itself partly founded on the formulations of Herbert Grierson, Professor of English Literature at the University of Aberdeen (and then, later, at the University of Edinburgh). So claims Craig, who argues persuasively that Grierson's Introduction to his 1912 edition of the poems of John Donne provided Eliot with the theoretical armature for his locution of 'the dissociation of sensibility' in his 1921 anthology *Metaphysical Poetry*.[26] In a sense, then, Muir finds in Scottish culture the form as well as the substance of his jeremiad; his ascription of 'blankness' to his place of inspiration thus indicates an innovative (albeit deeply conflicted) spirit in Muir's historiography – an impulse so famously lacking in his early poetry.[27] Tellingly, Ascherson, to return to our example, manifests this same innovative impulse in the way he deploys Muir's trope. He recalls how Scottish political sentiment in the 1970s was rife with a spirit of unrealised ('exciting … lively') possibility.[28] The 'blankness' to which Ascherson gave momentary and frustrated expression in 1979 ('now [the future] has vanished and there is a blankness only') was thus a way to capture the contrast between expectation and outcome. Indeed, his screed directs itself at the prolonged dissociation of *political* sensibility (that is Scottish societies, Westminster government), which he sees more as a problem for Britain (as an increasingly uneasy conglomerate of ill-fitting parts) than for Scotland as such.

Ascherson's account, evocatively building on Muir even as it exhibits Macmillan's historiographical reflexes (by making itself a part of the history it recounts, overtly, in memoir form), instructively reveals that there is more to the alleged vacuity of Scottish history than first meets (or, as it were, escapes) the eye. As such, it implicitly links what we might call first- and second-generation Scottish modernism – MacDiarmid and Davie – with scholarship from the era of 'rising', 'dialogical', 'diverse' Scottish Studies. My point is not that the field is compelled to repeat its past, but rather that it bears a dynamic relation to that past, even (or perhaps especially) when it affects to renounce it altogether. Indeed, and to bring my argument full circle, this is where the clarion call for a more cosmopolitan Scottish Studies, or for a field which abdicates an allegedly bankrupt nationalist paradigm in favour of a more 'emergent' and culturally hybridised approach, begins to sound suspiciously, or alluringly, like Muir's mythic ruminations on Scottish blankness.[29] After all, if emergent criticism is what is happening 'now', then such criticism is also (or perhaps merely) rising, even as it represses whatever it was that preceded it. But by this same token, and precisely because a 'rising' model of Scottish Studies self-consciously places itself in relation to its own past (whether rich or 'blank'), it elicits a more 'intensified' space of being and history – one which is both empty *and* full, progressive *and* non-linear, objective *and* performative. Odd as it may at first appear, the more traditional (that is, the *merely* diverse, *merely* dialogical) field already exhibits the complex state of cultural being to which its cosmopolitan variant aspires.[30]

We might say, then, that in Scottish Studies, contrary to a presumably more radical Cultural Studies, nationalism does not precede but rather proceeds from its own supposed dissolution in the cultural infernos of schizophrenia and 'blankness'. In an odd way, in the logic of its articulation if not in its historical conditions, Scottish Studies began in the brave new world where Cultural Studies is now venturing. Hence, while scholars continue to grow in their understanding of the Scottish past (like Scottish art, thanks to Macmillan), the *meaning* of that history (in Muir as in Ascherson, in Davie as in Craig) tells a rather different story – one in which the field of Scottish Studies constitutes a kind of revenge against the presumptions of its own recovery, its own 'rise'. Indeed, to recount the rise of Scottish Studies is to reinforce the field's connection to the deep history (and historiography) it purportedly supersedes. And this makes Scottish Studies uncanny not only with respect to themselves, but also relative to the 'studies' of culture more generally.

Notes

1 See Edward Said, *Beginnings: Intention and Method* (New York: Columbia University Press, 1985), pp. xi–xiv.
2 G. Gregory Smith, *Scottish Literature: Character and Influence* (London: Macmillan, 1919), p. 4.
3 Gerard Carruthers, *Scottish Literature* (Edinburgh University Press, 2009), p. 13.
4 Cairns Craig, 'Scotland and Hybridity', in Gerard Carruthers, David Goldie and Alastair Renfrew (eds.), *Beyond Scotland: New Contexts for Twentieth-Century Scottish Literature* (Amsterdam: Rodopi, 2004), pp. 229–53.
5 *Ibid.*, pp. 250–1.
6 On the 'schizophrenic' critique of an all-too-linear 'modernism', see Gilles Deleuze and Félix Guattari, *The Anti-Oedipus: Capitalism and Schizophrenia*, trans. Robert Hurley, Mark Seem and Helen R. Lane (Minneapolis: University of Minnesota Press, 1983). Conversely, on the comparatively more restrained function of Bakhtinian dialogism in Scottish Studies, see Alastair Renfrew, 'Brief Encounters, Long Farewells: Bakhtin and Scottish Literature', *International Journal of Scottish Literature*, 1 (2006), www.ijsl.stir.ac.uk/issue1/renfrew.htm.
7 Carruthers, *Scottish Literature*, pp. 25, 24.
8 See Simon During, Introduction to Simon During (ed.), *The Cultural Studies Reader*, 2nd edn (New York: Routledge, 1999), pp. 1–2. I am especially grateful to my research assistant, Drew Hausen, for helping me scale the mountain of material on the history of Cultural Studies.
9 For an overview of this shift, see Scott Lash, 'Power after Hegemony: Cultural Studies in Mediation', *Theory, Culture & Society*, 24:3 (2007), 55–78. N. Katherine Hayles specifies that 'Emergence implies that properties or programs appear on their own, often developing in ways not anticipated by the person who created the simulation'. *How We Became Posthuman: Virtual Bodies in Cybernetics, Literature, and Informatics* (University of Chicago Press, 1999), p. 225.
10 Stuart Hall, 'The Emergence of Cultural Studies and the Crisis of the Humanities', *October*, 53 (1990), 11–23.
11 Berthold Schoene, 'Cosmopolitan Scots', *Scottish Studies Review*, 9:2 (2008), 71–92.
12 See, for example, Eleanor Bell, *Questioning Scotland: Literature, Nationalism, Postmodernism* (Houndmills: Palgrave Macmillan, 2004), and Cairns Craig's rejoinder in *Intending Scotland: Explorations in Scottish Culture since the Enlightenment* (Edinburgh University Press, 2009), pp. 55–60.
13 T. M. Devine, *The Scottish Nation 1700–2000* (New York: Penguin, 1999), p. 578; cf. Murray Pittock, *The Road to Independence? Scotland since the Sixties* (London: Reaktion, 2008), pp. 15–16. On the term 'national culture', see Murray Pittock, 'What is a National Culture?', *Litteraria Pragensia*, 19:38 (2009), 30–47.

14 The most influential manifesto for a statistical approach to literary studies is probably found in Franco Moretti's *Graphs, Maps, Trees* (London: Verso, 2005).

15 See Louisa Gairn, *Ecology and Modern Scottish Literature* (Edinburgh University Press, 2008), H. R. Trevor-Roper, *The Invention of Scotland: Myth and History* (New Haven: Yale University Press, 2008) and Penny Fielding, *Scotland and the Fictions of Geography: North Britain, 1760–1830* (Cambridge University Press, 2008).

16 See Christopher Whyte, *Modern Scottish Poetry* (Edinburgh University Press, 2004), pp. 7–16; cf. Berthold Schoene's discussion of Whyte's position in 'Going Cosmopolitan: Reconstituting "Scottishness" in Post-Devolution Criticism', in Schoene (ed.), *The Edinburgh Companion to Contemporary Scottish Literature* (Edinburgh University Press, 2007), pp. 7–8.

17 See, for example, Paul de Man, 'Kant and Schiller', in *Aesthetic Ideology* (Minneapolis: University of Minnesota Press, 1996), pp. 129–62. For a discussion of the ethics of diversity in Scottish Studies, see James McGonigal and Kirsten Stirling, Introduction to McGonigal and Stirling (eds.), *Ethically Speaking: Voice and Values in Modern Scottish Writing* (Amsterdam: Rodopi, 2006), pp. 9–15.

18 On MacDiarmid's complex relation to questions of Scottish history and reform, see Scott Lyall, *Hugh MacDiarmid's Poetry and Politics of Place: Imagining a New Republic* (Edinburgh University Press, 2006), esp. ch. 1, and Margery Palmer McCulloch, *Scottish Modernism and Its Contexts, 1918–1959: Literature, National Identity and Cultural Exchange* (University of Edinburgh Press, 2009), esp. chs. 1–2. Gibbon employs the term 'Scotshire' in describing the novelist Neil Gunn in his essay 'Literary Lights', in Hugh MacDiarmid and Lewis Grassic Gibbon (eds.), *Scottish Scene, or The Intelligent Man's Guide to Albyn* (London: Jarrolds, 1934), p. 200.

19 George Davie, *The Democratic Intellect: Scotland and Her Universities in the Nineteenth Century* (Edinburgh University Press, 1961), pp. xi, xvi.

20 Tom Nairn, *The Break-Up of Britain: Crisis and Neo-Nationalism* (1977; Altona, Vic.: Common Ground, 2003).

21 Cairns Craig, cited in Craig Beveridge and Ronnie Turnbull, *Scotland after Enlightenment* (Edinburgh: Polygon, 1997), p. 7.

22 Duncan Macmillan, *Scottish Art, 1460–2000* (Edinburgh: Mainstream, 2000), p. 8.

23 Neal Ascherson, *Stone Voices: The Search for Scotland* (London: Granta, 2002), p. 108.

24 Edwin Muir, *Scott and Scotland: The Predicament of the Scottish Writer* (New York: Robert Speller, 1938), pp. 11–12.

25 Muir expresses this angst most completely in his *Autobiography* (Edinburgh: Canongate, 1993).

26 Cairns Craig, 'Tradition and the Individual Editor: Professor Grierson, Modernism and National Poetics', *Times Literary Supplement* (in press).

27 On the poetic conservatism of Muir's early poetry, see McCulloch, *Scottish Modernism*, pp. 169–70.

28 For some, this feeling held even after the defeat of 1979. 'At some point [the] afternoon [of the election, Ascherson] rang Tom Nairn, Scotland's most

influential political philosopher and one of [Ascherson's] former flatmates ... Tom was astonishingly cheerful', given that the working class had supported the referendum. 'It was the middle class which had ratted. And this ... ensured that when self-government did come, it would be in a more radical form, not merely a painless removal of the Establishment into a new building.' Ascherson, *Stone Voices*, pp. 105–6.

29 For example, Berthold Schoene cites the edited volume *Cosmopolitan* in asking '[w]hy ... so many nationalists appear so slow to realise that at last we live in "an interdependent world in which the nation-state faces imminent obsolescence as a viable economic unit, a politically sovereign territory, and a bounded cultural sphere"[.] How come the national ideal is proving so persistent, when it might best be understood as an historical aberration?' ('Cosmopolitan Scots', 71).

30 Gavin Miller also analyses the residual features of the new Scottish pluralism. See 'Scotland's Authentic Plurality: The New Essentialism in Scottish Studies', *Scottish Literary Review*, 1:1 (2009), 157–74.

Guide to further reading

Bell, Eleanor, *Questioning Scotland: Literature, Nationalism, Postmodernism* (Houndmills: Palgrave Macmillan, 2004)

Carruthers, Gerard, *Scottish Literature* (Edinburgh University Press, 2009)

Craig, Cairns, *Intending Scotland: Explorations in Scottish Culture since the Enlightenment* (Edinburgh University Press, 2009)

'Scotland and Hybridity', in Gerard Carruthers, David Goldie and Alastair Renfrew (eds.), *Beyond Scotland: New Contexts for Twentieth-Century Scottish Literature* (Amsterdam: Rodopi, 2004), pp. 229–53.

18

CAIRNS CRAIG

Otherworlds: Devolution and the Scottish Novel

The central figure in Allan Massie's *One Night in Winter* (1984) is Fraser Donnelly,[1] putative leader of a Scottish Nationalist movement which he claims will bring about 'a real revolution, a revolution of consciousness, a revolution of morals', one that will allow Scots to escape 'the auld Scotland of kirk and kailyard' and produce a country 'that's free and rich too' (43). What Donnelly actually surrounds himself with, however, is not a modern political machine but 'a Court' (124), as full of intrigue and sexual corruption as any in Renaissance Italy. That archaic social structure is gateway to even more atavistic emotion – 'sometimes you have to go back in time to make the next leap' (124), he tells one of his courtiers, Jimmy, who later explains its significance:

> As for what he meant by a' that going back in time, well, he'd been doing an awfy lot of reading – that surprises you, that Fraser's a great reader, it shouldna – about old religions, the Ancient Greek Mysteries, and he'd got haud of the notion that they offered the sort of transcendental experience you needed for real sexual liberation. (125)

In Fraser Donnelly, nationalism is figured as a return to paganism, as an invitation to the dark gods of the primitive to erupt again into the modern world. This Fraser re-enacts the return to the past that J. G. Frazer had undertaken in *The Golden Bough* at the beginning of the twentieth century:

> It was impossible not to feel that Fraser had given them something of profound reminiscent appeal; that the Buick had carried them like a chariot across the gulfs of history, back to the dawn, to a time when the bonding of flesh and spirit was natural to man, before sense was dulled by moral convention, to a time when the primal moving forces of the world acted directly on tingling nerves. (126–7)

Nationalism is a release of archaic energy that appears to be creative but proves to be profoundly destructive both of self and society.

It is a version of nationalism shaped by Nazism's ideology of blood and soil, but by 1984 such views had, as a result of the work of Ernest Gellner, been largely displaced by an account of nationalism as the political medium by which modernisation was managed. Nationalism was a necessary – though nonetheless unpleasant – stage in the progress towards some more civilized form of global society. Massie's use of the earlier conception of nationalism was not, however, entirely inappropriate since, according to Gellner, nationalism ought not to exist in a country which had been one of the earliest to industrialise and had been a participant in the state that was the very exemplar of modernity. The rise of nationalism in Scotland from the 1960s was a historical anomaly with threatening implications. At a political level, the lexicon of 'home rule' last heard in relation to Ireland in 1914 had to be brought back into debate, while the paradigms by which the development of modern societies had been understood had to be re-examined, whether in the neo-Marxism of Tom Nairn's *The Break-Up of Britain* (1979), or the neo-liberalism of the Adam Smith Institute, founded by St Andrews graduates Madsen Pirie and Eamonn Butler in 1977. Ironically, it was the foundering of the Labour Party's devolution strategy in the referendum of 1979 – in which a small majority voted in favour of devolution but not enough to achieve the 40 per cent required by the government's legislation – and the subsequent withdrawal of support for the minority Labour government by the Scottish Nationalists, that allowed Mrs Thatcher to take power in 1979 and to implement the neo-liberal agenda that made devolution politically irrelevant at a UK level but a simmering issue in Scotland itself – as Elspeth Urquhart notes in Candia McWilliam's *Debatable Land*:

> Things are bad. There could be a split. People want it. They sing about it. There was the fish, there is the oil. The stupidity of the South has hurt, the tactlessness that has looked like pillage, the willingness to treat the place like a plaid, to throw on for its ancient rustic glamour and to throw over puddles to save them from getting their feet wet. I fear for the border.[2]

In Massie's *One Night in Winter*, what is revealed by Fraser Donnelly's search for liberation, and his eventual murder by his wife Lorna, is a Scotland which cannot be liberated or regenerated by any political action, as Donnelly himself is allowed to state: 'Scotland's a douce, canny shy place. The mair it's a failure, and by God it's a failure, the mair loth it is to turn to anything new' (142). All efforts at transformation founder in a culture whose capital city has 'the atmosphere of the undertaker's parlour' (199); whose bars 'were in the kingdom of limbo, the never-never land of those lost girls and boys who had been caught half-way out of their prams' (65); whose efforts at modernisation showed 'the poverty of imagination ... of a denatured and broken culture' (32). Donnelly will be killed as much by Scotland as by Lorna, since her nature is so shaped by the country: 'Lorna's damnable timidity, her inability to choose, her damn fatalism; that was Scots. She was in love with defeat, with a Fate that had singled her out as a victim. It's in the air there. It chokes you' (158). As one old relative tells Dallas: 'Let Scotland be as independent as they wish, it will not alter the fact that there's little ... to keep talent here', with the result that 'Scotland will grow ever less Scottish and ever less stimulating; we live in a withered culture. Sounds of energy are the energy of the death-rattle' (112).

At the climax of his narrative, Dallas has to be dismissed (by himself) because 'he was on the sidelines' (123): it might almost describe the condition of the novel in Scotland in the period after the Second World War. The nationalist upsurge had been fuelled by and, in turn, fed into a cultural revivalism whose impact was felt across a wide range of artistic activities. Poetry, which had dominated the nationalist 'Literary Renaissance' pioneered by Hugh MacDiarmid in the 1920s, saw a new upsurge of writing based on the literary Scots of pre-Reformation Scotland; traditional music received academic acknowledgment through the work of the collectors of the School of Scottish Studies, established at the University of Edinburgh in 1951, which brought to prominence 'tradition bearers' such as Jeanie Robertson of Aberdeen and inspired a new generation of folk-artists such as Ewen MacColl and Jean Redpath, and later groups such as the Corries and the McCalmans; theatre was revitalised by plays in Scots, whether the historical Scots of Donald Campbell's *The Jesuit* (1976), or the working-class Scots that was used in 'workplace' dramas such as Bill Bryden's *Willie Rough* (1972) and Roddy McMillan's *The Bevellers* (1976). Theatre was particularly prominent in engaging with politics through the work of the 7:84 company, combining Brechtian techniques with Scottish pantomime traditions in plays such as *The Cheviot, the Stag and the Black Black Oil* (1974), which proposed socialist solutions to Scottish problems but raised nationalist issues to public prominence.

To this cultural ferment, the novel remained stubbornly marginal. Promisingly talented writers like Alan Sharp (*A Green Tree in Gedde*, 1965; *The Wind Shifts*, 1967) decamped to alternative careers in Hollywood; Archie Hind's influential *The Dear Green Place* (1966) was followed by an almost lifelong silence; Jessie Kesson's *The White Bird Passes* (1958) and *Glitter of Mica* (1963) received none of the attention they deserved and Kesson focused on producing scripts for the BBC; and James Kennaway's death in 1968 at the age of forty cut short a talent which, in *Tunes of Glory* (1956) and *Household Ghosts* (1964), had promised more than it had delivered, as he too had been sucked into the film industry. Even major contributions in the 1970s, such as William McIlvanney's *Docherty* (1975), set in a Scottish mining town around the First World War, seemed like a farewell to a Scotland which had passed into history, and the same author's turn to crime fiction with *Laidlaw* (1977), though it would set a pattern for the Tartan Noir genre of the 1980s, tended to confirm that Scotland was a challenge to the novelist.

The fundamental resistance of Scotland to the form of the novel was the conclusion of Francis Russell Hart's ambitious account of *The Scottish Novel*, published a year before the first devolution referendum. Having traced the Scottish novel to 'Kennaway, Spark and After', he concluded that 'there is still much truth in Edwin Muir's gloomy diagnosis of the novel in Scotland',[3] a diagnosis which led Muir to believe that there was 'an emptiness and unreality quite peculiar to Scotland', which infected the writing of its greatest novelist, Walter Scott.[4] Muir's book-length analysis of Scott's failings – *Scott and Scotland: The Predicament of the Scottish Writer* – was first published in 1936 but reissued in 1982 with an 'Introduction' by Allan Massie which suggested that, post the failure of devolution, everything remained pretty much as Muir had painted it. Indeed, in a review of Hart's book published in the *London Magazine*, Massie agreed that Hart had indeed identified the 'real problem which nobody in Scotland has answered satisfactorily. How do you write about a second-hand society?'.

If, as contemporary theory insisted, nationalism in Scotland was a belated version of a nineteenth-century political ideology, the rise of nationalism in Scotland simply confirmed that Scotland was trapped in the narrative loop of its own irrelevance to the processes of history. Since the exploration of the 'intricate mechanism' that was 'human society as a whole' was, according to classics of contemporary criticism such as Ian Watt's *The Rise of the Novel* (1957), the very purpose of the novel,[5] it was a task made impossible if Scotland was not a 'whole society', because many of the levers which controlled it were not part of its own social fabric. That is why, perhaps, Massie has written only occasionally about contemporary Scotland and made his reputation with a series of large-scale historical novels, set both in the ancient world (beginning with *Augustus*, 1986) and at crisis points in the twentieth century (*The Death of Men*, 1981; *A Question of Loyalties*, 1989; *Sins of the Father*, 1991). But in 1981 Massie had also written a small critical book on Muriel Spark, in which he had presented her as a novelist in the tradition of 'Waugh, Firbank, Henry Green and Powell, who have attempted to understand the world by cultivating detachment'.[6] He pointedly avoided dealing, however, with Spark's second novel, *Robinson*, which appeared in 1958, the year after the publication of Watt's analysis of the origins of the novel. Spark's novel deliberately situates itself inside Watt's conception of the tradition of the novel – *Robinson Crusoe* is the first novel in Watt's account – but only in order to disrupt its insistence on the forces of progressive history and of the understanding of a whole society. Everything in *Robinson* is double – Robinson himself shares his name with the island on which he lives, just as the heroine, January Marlow, is confused both with the month whose name she bears and with Conrad's voyager into the heart of darkness. Nothing on Robinson can be proved real, since the events that the novel recounts are recorded in a diary of which the novel itself gives us only occasional – and unconfirmable – specimens. Spark's *Robinson* deconstructs the tradition of the realist, masculine, social novel to produce a novel no longer tied to probability but one in which, as the novel's final words declare, 'all things are possible' (185).

Hart deals extensively with Spark's novels in his account of the Scottish novel but remains uncertain of how a writer who deals so little with Scottish society – *The Prime of Miss Jean Brodie* (1961) is her only novel set primarily in Scotland – can be a contributor to an ongoing tradition of the Scottish novel: 'Can the most eminent living novelist nurtured by Scotland be recognised, then, in her eminence, in her eccentricity, as a Scottish novelist?'[7] And yet by 1979 Spark was publishing her fifteenth novel, entitled *Territorial Rights*, set in modern Venice, in which a group of characters – all exiles – struggle to control the power that the past has to disrupt the present. At the centre of the plot is the body of Victor Pancev, a Bulgarian executed towards the end of the Second World War, whose corpse was cut in two so that each half could be buried separately and his grave(s) tended by two sisters, both of whom had been his lovers. It is the image of a Europe torn apart – and yet now supported – by American and Soviet 'great powers' who compete for ownership of its past as foundation for their own future ambitions. But running through the narrative is another intrusive voice from the past that comes from much closer to Spark's original home:

> Anthea fell asleep in her chair. She did not dream of the book but of her grandmother from Scotland who used to chant to her:
>
> > For her I'll dare the billow's roar,
> > For her I'll trace a distant shore,
> > That Indian wealth may lustre throw
> > Around my Highland lassie, O.[8]

It is as though the Scottish folk voice is itself a ghostly disruption – or prefiguration – of modernity, offering a choric reflection on the novel's action. That voice is allowed the last word in the penultimate chapter before the novel officiously tidies up and packs away all its puppets: 'The pennie's the jewel that beautifies a"', it ironically chants.[9] Confronted by a world of chaotic international corruption, in which only material values count, Spark implicitly asserts, through Scottish balladry, her own territorial rights – the right to refuse simply to imitate the narrative of the modern world. It is, for Spark, modernity as a whole which is a 'second-hand world', one which the novelist can only approach by a radical subversion of the realist tradition which would give primacy to the narrative trajectory of that modernity. It is a strategy she had used in *The Ballad of Peckham Rye* (1960), in which Dougal Douglas is a Scottish devil set loose in London, and in *The Hothouse by the East River* (1973), in which J. M. Barrie's *Peter Pan* becomes the intertextual Scottish commentary upon the action of a novel set in a purgatorial New York, and she was to use it later in *The Takeover* (1976), which takes place in Nemi, the setting of the opening of J. G. Frazer's *Golden Bough*, and again in *Symposium* (1990), in which Margaret Murchie and her Uncle Magnus are carriers of the magical powers invoked by old Scottish ballads:

> Magnus lowered his voice. 'Who do you have,' he said, 'but me? Out of my misfortune, out of my affliction I prognosticate and foreshadow. My divine affliction is your only guide. Remember the ballad:
>
>> As I went down the water side
>> None but my foe to be my guide
>> None but my foe to be my guide.[10]

Such a shift, from the 'probable' of realism to the 'possible' of a fabulatory fiction, foregrounds the artifice of the novel: like some of the characters in *Symposium*, it is as though Spark has 'skipped the nineteenth century in our genes' and gone back to the playfulness of the pre-realist tradition of the novel initiated by Cervantes.[11]

In Spark's ambitious refusal of realism, and in the increasingly fairytale structures of a novelist like Robin Jenkins, whose *Fergus Lamont* (1979) parodied the 'predicament' of the Scottish writer, Scottish novelists had begun to challenge the limitations which Francis Russell Hart still felt beset the Scottish novelist in 1978. Hart identified three characteristics of Scottish novel writing, each of which had posed profound problems to Scottish novelists. First, 'in every phase of the novel's Scottish history can be seen a fidelity to local truth, to the particulars of communal place and time; at the same time an intention to represent national types and whole cultural epochs; and finally an impetus to transcendent meaning. With such scope', Hart suggested, 'one sometimes finds the tendency to force implication, to make the particular mean too much on too many levels.'[12] Second, there is 'a swithering of modes', the 'antisyzygy', the 'dissociation of sensibility', all indicative of the problem of whether 'such switherings or radical conjunctions can be successfully assimilated into narrative art'.[13] Third, was the 'problem of uncertain narrative voice', caught between various possible 'English' styles and the vernacular speech of local communities.[14] In the following ten years, Scottish novelists grasped each of these supposed deficiencies as a creative opportunity to analyse the weaknesses of a culture which had failed to accept the opportunity to govern itself. That the novel was to be central to this analysis was defiantly asserted by the publication in 1981 of Alasdair Gray's *Lanark*, a novel which had been at least twenty years in the making. Gray's novel self-consciously situates itself within a history of the novel which refuses the traditions of realism: its 'Index of Plagiarisms' notes that the 'device of giving a ponderous index to a work of ponderous fiction is taken from *Sartor Resartus*', while footnote six in the same chapter, 'Epilogue', tells us that 'the index proves that *Lanark* is erected upon an infantile foundation of Victorian nursery tales'.[15] In fact, *Lanark* combines Hart's 'fidelity to local truth' in two of its four books, focusing on the realistic portrayal of Duncan Thaw's failure to become a successful artist, while the other two books implement through fantasy and science fiction the representation of 'national types and whole cultural epochs', both in the character of Lanark himself and the various archetypal characters whom he encounters. In its conjunction of these different generic possibilities, *Lanark* joyfully exploits Hart's 'swithering of modes' as an answer to the 'dissociation of sensibility' from which its hero suffers. In its epic ambition to defy the traditional structure of the novel (Book Three precedes Book One, the 'Epilogue' intercedes between chapters forty and forty-one), *Lanark* showed how realism cannot explain the Scottish condition because the Scottish condition is part of a power structure whose sources are lodged beyond the reach of realism's 'fidelity to local truth'.

Lanark was a weird kind of novel about a country which had itself, apparently, become a weird anomaly among nations. The trauma of political failure was mirrored in a sequence of novels that followed Gray's lead in having as their central character someone who has lost track of his or her identity: in Iain Banks's *The Bridge* (1986), the central character is in a coma, his life being imaginarily continued on an endless version of the Forth Bridge; in Janice Galloway's *The Trick is to Keep Breathing* (1989), the protagonist has been reduced to near non-existence by society's refusal to acknowledge her place in her dead lover's life; A. L. Kennedy's *So I Am Glad* (1995) is narrated by a character whose 'peace and calmness is, in fact, empty space',[16] and Roy Strang in Irvine Welsh's *Marabou Stork Nightmares* (1996) survives 'down here in the comforts of my vegetative state, inside my secret world'.[17] The world that surrounds these traumatised characters becomes surreal, a place of strange encounters, where a drug-taking dropout can be the resurrected spirit of Cyrano de Bergerac (*So I Am Glad*); where a daughter can be drugged by her father into believing she is a castrated boy (Iain Banks, *The Wasp Factory*, 1984); where a Catholic cleric can attend a doctor's surgery because he has flowers blossoming from his backside (Christopher Whyte, *Euphemia MacFarrigle and the Laughing Virgin*, 1995); where a journey from Edinburgh to Glasgow goes via Salerno and Vladikavkaz, in each of which the protagonist encounters the same characters he has been trying to escape in Edinburgh (James Meek, *Drivetime*, 1995); and where a girl struggles to get a pizza into the oven because the dead body on the floor 'caused the usual hassles' (Alan Warner, *Morvern Callar*, 1996).[18] It is a place where alternative otherworlds become visible, as in James Kelman's *The Busconductor Hines*:

> There is a crack in the pavement a few yards from the close entrance: it has a brave exterior: it is a cheery wee soul; other cracks can be shifty but not this one. Hines will refer to it as Dan in future. Hello there Dan. How's it going?[19]

Hines releases an alternative reality by simply naming it differently. In Iain Banks's *Walking on Glass*, on the other hand, Stephen Grout believes that in the 'static' of tape recordings he can hear the engines of bombers from another world: this apparently mad belief that he has discovered 'a Leak, a tiny slip they had made which let part of reality slip through into this prison of his life', becomes, however, the reality of a second narrative of a future world which has invented a technology allowing its inhabitants to enter the heads of people in the past – like Grout – and control them for their own pleasure.[20] As though in defiance of the historical reality in which it is trapped, the Scottish novel of the 1980s and 90s drew its energy from discovering a variety of routes into alternative ontologies where the imaginary can become real, from the mind-bending effects of drugs in Irvine Welsh's *Trainspotting* (1993) to the body-bending of Joss Moody, female impersonator of a male trumpeter in Jackie Kay's *Trumpet* (1998), from the space opera epic of sci-fi games in Iain Banks's *The Player of Games* (1988) to the laconic absurdities of the 500 chapters of Frank Kuppner's *The Concussed History of Scotland* (1990).

The political significance of such otherworlds was itself the theme of Alasdair Gray's *1982 Janine* (1984), in which the central character, Jock McLeish, escapes the boring reality of his life as a salesman through a novelful of fantasy sexual characters with names like Superb and Janine. The alternative world which he invents for them is explicitly driven by the failure of devolution:

> Then came cuts in public spending, loss of business and increased unemployment and now Westminster has decided to spend the North Sea oil revenues building a fucking tunnel under the English Channel. If we ran that race again [the devolution referendum] we would win by a head and a neck so we won't

be allowed to run it again, cool down cool down you are goading yourself into a FRENZY my friend, think about fucking Superb, think about fucking Janine, don't think about fucking POLITICS.[21]

Jock's dilemma is the dilemma of the novel itself: its otherworlds are providing an escape from a failed reality, reinforcing the very failure from which it is in flight: 'if I am wrong about my past, WHO AM I? If the reality I believed in is wrong, how can I right it?' (329). If the novel is to re-engage with reality it must first, self-reflexively, address its own falsehoods: it does so in part by having Janine realise she is a character in a story – '*She realises it is her inescapable fate to be a character in a story by someone who dictates every one of her movements and emotions, someone she will never meet and cannot appeal to*' – while Jock declares that in this 'she is like most people, but not like me. I have been free for nearly ten whole minutes' (332). The irony, of course, is that Jock too is a character in a story, but in his insistence that a human being is not a character in someone else's story he gestures to the possibility of an escape from an apparently predetermining narrative, a gesture which is as valid for a nation as for an individual. That gesture is taken up and elaborated by Gray within the typography of the novel: at the moment of Jock's nervous breakdown, his psyche fragments into a series of voices which are typographically represented by having a variety typefaces and typesizes travelling in different directions across the page, and between which he is

'*SUFFUFFUFFUFFUFFUFUCKUCKUCKUCKATING*'. (184)

Jock's loss of control is encased in and balanced by the book's own typographic precision. Each page has a subtext beneath the page number at the head of the page, predicting, commenting on and elaborating the contents of the page – when Jock seeks the escape of his sexual fantasies for a final time the subtext announces 'SEXIST CRAP'. The novelist is not only able, therefore, to comment on the action of the novel but the novel can never be published in anything except the exact form invented by the author: through typography he asserts a control over the novel that is the antithesis of the loss of control of both character and nation.

Gray acknowledges his indebtedness to the typographic experiments of Scottish poets Ian Hamilton Finlay and Edwin Morgan, but his experiments with typography were rapidly taken up by other writers and their publishers: James Kelman's *The Busconductor Hines* (1984) separates sections of its chapters with a row of three slightly eliptical 'o's

whose effect is to reduce to nothing the moments when its central character's thoughts are not being presented to the reader. The same visual image is used to separate the sections of Janice Galloway's *The Trick is to Keep Breathing*, which also has comments in the margin of the text that bleed off the page, like a voice incapable of getting itself fully into the narrative, and even page numbers that sometimes disappear, as though they have been erased along with the character's sense of self.[22] Such typographic play resisted the very form in which the novel was normally encased and this foregrounding of the book as object was to reach its culmination in Gray's *Poor Things* (1992), subtitled *Episodes from the Early Life of Archibald McCandless M.D. Scottish Public Health Officer*, which claims to be a reprint of a publication of 1909 by Glasgow publisher 'Robert Maclehose & Company, Printers to the University 1909'. The elements of this 'complete tissue of facts' are distinguished by different typefaces, interlaced with illustrations and with six pages which are supposed 'photogravures' of handwriting.[23] The typography and the illustrations underline the multiple ways in which information about the past can be presented: the novel concludes with a letter from McCandless's wife denying the story which he has told of her life, for 'there can be no doubt', she claims, that her version is the 'most probable', while her husband's 'stinks of all that was morbid in that most morbid of centuries, the nineteenth' (272). The 'probable', however, is precisely what is at issue: Gray's narrative is grafted on to classic elements of the 'morbid' imagination of the nineteenth century, such as the Frankenstein myth, in order to explore the 'unconscious' of the city of Glasgow, a city whose nineteenth-century wealth, world-wide connections and architecture (all visually presented in the book's final pages) are, quite literally, fabulous from the perspective of the late twentieth century. The 'radical conjunctions' which gave Hart concern in 1978 have, by 1992, become the very basis of Gray's ambitious reworking of what, in his introduction, he acknowledges as a central tradition of the Scottish novel: 'a blackly humorous fiction into which some real experiences and historical facts have been cunningly woven, a book like Scott's *Old Mortality* and Hogg's *Confessions of a Justified Sinner*' (xi). Gray's interest in this tradition was also taken up by Allan Massie in *The Ragged Lion* (1994), a novel about Walter Scott and his 'uncanny' imagination, and by a whole series of novels which drew inspiration from the narrative complexities of Hogg's work – Emma Tennant's *Bad Sister* (1978), Brian McCabe's *The Other McCoy* (1990) and Iain Banks's *Complicity* (1993), as well as James Robertson's *The Fanatic* (2000).

The most radical change in the Scottish novel in the aftermath of devolution was, however, in its attitude to language. In Iain Banks's *The Bridge* (1986), the protagonist is accompanied by a 'familiar' who speaks in broad Scots, defying Hart's insistence that vernacular produced a 'problem of uncertain narrative voice':

Misty an dark on the uthir side ov the rivir as wel. Left Karen stannin in his boat an went off up the roade towards this big sorta palace thing on a cliff, keepin an eye open for this big dug Serry-Bruce. Just as well ah did; basturt jumpt me in this big coartyard place right on the clifside. Fukin thing had had three heids! Snarlin and droolin it wiz.[24]

In *The Bridge*, Banks was rapidly responding not only to Alasdair Gray's *Lanark* but to the impact of James Kelman's *The Busconductor Hines*, published in 1984. Instead of treating Scots as the language spoken by characters who were sympathetically – or condescendingly – represented by an English-writing narrator, Kelman produced a novel in which narrator and character became one, and in which the literary and class relations of literate English and vernacular Scots were inverted. The implicit instruction to working-class Scottish authors, Kelman insisted, was 'write a story wherein people are talking, but not talking the language they talk':[25]

> In prose fiction I saw the distinction between dialogue and narrative as a summation of the political system; it was simply another method of exclusion, of marginalising and disenfranchising different peoples, cultures and communities. I was uncomfortable with 'working-class' authors who allowed 'the voice' of higher authority to control narrative, the place where the psychological drama occurred. How could I write from within my own place and time if I was forced to adopt the 'received' language of the ruling class?[26]

Kelman's answer was to present characters who existed primarily in and through the vernacular patterns of their speech, a speech rendered without any apparent authorial voice to set an alternative 'standard':

> There are parties whose attention to a variety of aspects of existence renders life uneasy. It cannot be said to be the fault of Hines that he is such a party. A little leeway might be allowed him. A fortnight's leave of absence could well work wonders. A reassembling of the head that the continued participation in the land of the greater brits
>
> Fuck off.
>
> Hines is forced into situations a dog wouldn't be forced into. Even a rat. It is most perplexing. Hines has a wean and he treats this wean as a son i.e. a child, a fellow human being in other words yet here is he himself being forced into a situation whence the certain load of shite as an outcome, the only outcome, an outcome such that it is not fair. It is not fucking fair. Hines is fucking fed up with it.[27]

Hines is his own third-person narrator; the voice which describes him has the linguistic structure of his own interior monologues. Each of Kelman's subsequent novels – *A Chancer* (1985), *A Disaffection* (1989) and *How Late It Was, How Late* (1994) – explored the world as defined by the unique language of its central character. In language, however, there are no impossibilities – the improbable is just as *sayable* as the probable, and even that which is discovered to be non-existent, as Patrick Doyle in *A Disaffection* discovers, continues to subsist: 'That poor old nonentity Vulcan, being once thought to exist, and then being discovered not to. Imagine being discovered not to exist! That's even worse than being declared fucking redundant, irrelevant, which was the fate of ether upon the advent of Einstein.'[28] The language which apparently locks us into the limits of the local is also the language in which all things – even the non-existent – are possible.

Kelman's experiments with vernacular voice opened a floodgate of Scottish creativity in which novelists sought to explore and exploit the linguistic possibilities of the local. If no one, in 1979, would have predicted that in 1994 a novel in a Scottish vernacular would win Britain's major literary prize – as Kelman did with *How Late It Was, How Late* – no one would have predicted that in the same year a novel in the vernacular of the Edinburgh working classes would become an international best-seller, but that indeed was the case with Irvine Welsh's *Trainspotting* (1993):

> Aw ah did wis put a pint ay Export in front ay Begbie. He takes one fuckin gulp oot ay it; then he throws the empty gless fae his last pint straight ower the balcony, in a casual backhand motion. It one ay they chunky, panelled glesses wi a handle, n ah kin see it spinnin through the air oot ay the corner ay ma eye. Ah look at Begbie, whae smiles, while Hazel n June look disoriented, thir faces reflecting ma ain crippling anxiety.[29]

Begbie may be the moral antithesis of Burns's 'man of independent mind' but the language in which he is rendered insists that the authentic rendering of Scotland can only be done in and through an acceptance of the cultural equality of the language of the working classes. It is a language which was often, at the time, described in terms of a raw realism – a realism which could indeed be found in the works of Agnes Owens, Jeff Torrington, Duncan Maclean – but it was also the language of an alternative social reality and of an alternative literary tradition. This was the argument of Robert Crawford's *Devolving English Literature* (1992), which reread Scottish literature both as a strategic occupation of the centre of English culture – Scotland, as Crawford's later book insisted, *invented* English literature – and as an encouragement to the resistance to English hegemony by its colonial offsprings' exploitation of the vernacular possibilities of local language.

The adoption of Scots in poetry in the 1980s and 90s would have been nothing new; its adoption in the novel, in the very form which had represented the fundamental problems of Scottish culture since Sir Walter Scott, was an act of defiance which retrospectively transformed the whole status of Scottish culture since the Union. It was an 'otherworld' than that which the nation's cultural histories had described – not one of decline and oblivion but of energy and creativity, not one of submission and defeat but of potential and liberation. When the end of communism in 1989 allowed the nations of Eastern Europe to recover their ancient identities, Scotland's nationalism was no longer an exception to the rules of history but a revelation that history's rules do not conform to the order of the probable.

Notes

1 Allan Massie, *One Night in Winter* (1984; London: Bodley Head, 1985); further references will appear in the text. For a general account of the novel in the second half of the twentieth century, see Douglas Gifford, 'Breaking Boundaries: From Modern to Contemporary in Scottish Fiction', in Ian Brown, Thomas Owen Clancy, Susan Manning and Murray Pittock (eds.), *The Edinburgh History of Scottish Literature*, vol. III, *Modern Transformations: New Identities (from 1918)* (Edinburgh University Press, 2007), pp. 237–53.

2 Candia McWilliam, *Debatable Land* (1994; London: Bloomsbury, 1995), pp. 135–6.

3 Francis Russell Hart, *The Scottish Novel: A Critical Survey* (London: J. Murray, 1978), p. 407.

4 Andrew Noble (ed.), *Edwin Muir: Uncollected Scottish Criticism* (London: Vision; Totowa, NJ: Barnes & Noble, 1982), p. 106.

5 Ian Watt, *The Rise of the Novel* (London: Hogarth Press, 1987), p. 301.

6 Allan Massie, *Muriel Spark* (Edinburgh: Ramsay Head Press, 1982), p. 94.

7 Hart, *Scottish Novel*, p. 295.

8 Muriel Spark, *Territorial Rights* (London: Macmillan, 1979), p. 172.

9 *Ibid.*, p. 237.

10 Muriel Spark, *Symposium* (1990; repr. London: Penguin, 1991), p. 81.

11 *Ibid.*, p. 64.

12 Hart, *Scottish Novel*, p. 406.

13 *Ibid.*

14 *Ibid.*, p. 407.

15 Alasdair Gray, *Lanark: A Life in 4 Books* (1981; repr. London: Picador, 1994), pp. 487, 489.

16 A. L. Kennedy, *So I Am Glad* (London: Vintage, 1995), p. 5.

17 Irvine Welsh, *Marabou Stork Nightmares* (London: Vintage, 1996), p. 17.

18 Alan Warner, *Morvern Callar* (London: Jonathan Cape, 1995), p. 50.

19 James Kelman, *The Busconductor Hines* (Edinburgh: Polygon, 1984), p. 168.

20 Iain Banks, *Walking on Glass* (London: Abacus, 1986), p. 113.

21 Alasdair Gray, *1982 Janine* (London: Jonathan Cape, 1984), p. 66.

22 Janice Galloway, *The Trick is to Keep Breathing* (1989; repr. London: Vintage, 1999), pp. 79–80.

23 Alasdair Gray, *Poor Things* (London: Bloomsbury, 1992), pp. 145–50.

24 Iain Banks, *The Bridge* (1986; London: Abacus, 1987), p. 160.

25 James Kelman, *'And the Judges Said ...': Essays* (London: Secker & Warburg, 2002), p. 65.

26 *Ibid.*, p. 40.
27 Kelman, *Busconductor Hines*, pp. 181–2.
28 James Kelman, *A Disaffection* (London: Vintage, 1989), p. 252.
29 Irvine Welsh, *Trainspotting* (London: Vintage, 1993), p. 79.

Guide to further reading

Brown, Ian, Thomas Owen Clancy, Susan Manning and Murray Pittock (eds.), *The Edinburgh History of Scottish Literature*, vol. III, *Modern Transformations: New Identities (from 1918)* (Edinburgh University Press, 2007)
Craig, Cairns, *The Modern Scottish Novel* (Edinburgh University Press, 1999)
Wallace, Gavin and Randall Stevenson (eds.), *The Scottish Novel since the Seventies* (Edinburgh University Press, 1994).

19

GERARD CARRUTHERS

Scottish Literature in Diaspora

Between the 1820s and the Second World War, around 2.3 million Scots emigrated.[1] Pre-nineteenth-century Scottish emigration included, variously, a significant mining community which went off to ply its trade in Poland, pedlars and merchants across the Baltic states, the plantation of Ulster and Catholics and Jacobites exiled in France, Germany, Italy and Spain. From the nineteenth century two principal phenomena accounted for Scottish emigration: the British Empire and the Clearances. One interesting pre-Clearances moment in Scottish literature is provided by Robert Burns in his poem, 'Address of Beelzebub' (1786). Here, satirically, Burns's diabolic narrator salutes the earl of Breadalbane, president of the Highland Society. This had supported landlords such as Mr Macdonald in maintaining his people in abject poverty through preventing their projected emigration from his estates of Glengary to Canada. Burns's knowledge of diaspora was of largely exciting greater potential abroad. This too, however, was not without a darker side, as Burns seems for a period in 1786 to have contemplated going to Jamaica to work as an official in the slave plantations. This route to greater prosperity was a well-trodden journey for hundreds of Scotsmen of good education but limited prospects at home in the latter half of the eighteenth century. Burns in the end did not go, but his possible alternative life in the West Indies is well imagined in a modern novel by Andrew Lindsay, *Illustrious Exile* (2006).

Tobias Smollett responds to another strong element of pre-nineteenth-century Scottish diasporic experience in his novel *Roderick Random* (1748), partly dealing with life on board a Royal Navy ship as a surgeon (along with the tobacco and slave trades, the military was the means by which many eighteenth-century Scots were introduced to, and frequently settled in, the New World). Although not without criticism of practices in the British navy, *Roderick Random* is generally enthusiastic about the imperial enterprise in which Britain is involved. Smollett himself had served on a man-o'-war and he is Scotland's first major writer to live for a large part of his life abroad, not only in England, but in the West Indies (1741–4) and in France and Italy from 1766, Smollett dying in the latter country in 1771. Smollett is perhaps Scotland's first 'travel writer' in the modern sense, producing *Travels through France and Italy* (1766), a work that Robert Louis Stevenson has explicitly in mind in his voluminous travel writing undertaken from the start of his career as a published writer. Smollett's final novel, *The Expedition of Humphry Clinker* (1771), which features a touring party in Wales, England and Scotland, is, largely, a Unionist novel. Its thesis is that the different parts of the British Isles must understand one another for the greater good of the United Kingdom and British Empire. Among its most striking material is the recounting of the adventures of the former British Army lieutenant, Lismahago, among the native peoples of North America, amidst whom he experiences both brutality and hospitality. In one of the best fictional accounts in English of 'going native' in this situation, Lismahago reports on the incredulity and sense of shocked piety among the native peoples in the face of proselytising Christian missionaries and their outlandish theology. Smollett's account, then, is not blind to failings in Western colonisation, though by no means condemnatory in general. One further interesting nuance is Lismahago's contention that Scottish military personnel are less likely to obtain advancement in service than Englishmen owing to the greater wealth existing in England. The background here is a situation where military commissions were purchased, and the unstated implication is that imperial service for Scottish military men might sometimes bring greater opportunity for advancement through merit, or, put another way, heroic deeds. In the same year that *Humphry Clinker* appeared, another Scottish novelist, Henry Mackenzie (1745–1831), offered in *The Man of Feeling* a depiction, fairly graphic for its time, of British cruelty in India, though not from the position of particularly cogent critique and rather in the context of one of numerous situations exemplifying an unfeeling world. We begin to see here at least, however, nascent troubled conscience over empire.

The most 'rooted' part of Scottish Diaspora literary culture has featured less than any other in accounts of Scottish literature, no doubt because it represents Scotland's earliest imperial success. Most especially in the late eighteenth and early nineteenth centuries, Ulster-Scots writing features several poets of note including James Orr (1770–1816), Hugh Porter (*fl.* 1780) and Samuel Thomson (1766–1816). Born in Ulster, these poets were strong heirs to traditions of the Scots language and Scottish forms (including the 'Habbie Simson' and 'Christ's Kirk' stanzas). There has been a revival of interest in Ulster in such writers since the late 1940s, and an increasing body of criticism during the past decade or so, first of all by Liam

McIlvanney and then by critics from Northern Ireland, has begun to create a much richer critical context for Ulster-Scots writing.[2] However, several factors continue to militate against the reception of Ulster-Scots texts. In the case of the poets mentioned, there has been a still-current tendency to see these individuals as historically interesting rather than in literary terms. Their reception as 'folk poets' or 'rhyming weavers' has tended to emphasise their value, undoubtedly present, as documenters of social and cultural reality. Such labels, however, have tended to underplay the individuality of the likes of Orr, Porter and Thomson. Another impediment to their evaluation has been the estimation of Orr and Thomson as largely derivative disciples of Robert Burns. In the present there exists also a suspicion of Ulster-Scots writing as a confection of dubious political motivation. One of the most successful Scottish diasporic communities which settled the north of Ireland from the time of the seventeenth-century Plantations, as part of the British strategy to colonise the island of Ireland, the Ulster-Scots clearly lack the glamorous, downtrodden motivations – famine and dispossession – propelling abroad other waves of Scottish emigration. Irish literary anthologies, such as the Field Day anthologies, have included, albeit in rather limited fashion, Ulster-Scots writing. We also have the interesting anomaly that the Monreagh Ulster-Scots Heritage Centre is in County Donegal in the Republic of Ireland, with funding from the government in Dublin. So far Scottish literary studies has shown absolutely no desire to anthologise Ulster-Scots writing in spite of the encouraging signs that Scottish criticism is beginning to accommodate its discussion.[3] The fraught canonicity of Ulster-Scots writing, which does not admit of easy description as either a majority or minority culture, or as an indigenous or satellite one, represents a highly problematic but potentially very fruitful future area in the theorising (post-colonial and otherwise) of both Irish and Scottish literatures.

James Orr was also part of a significant grouping of writers from the British Isles in the 1790s who took up residence in North America as refugees of republican political stamp. Again some significant Scots therein are not well treated in histories of Scottish literature.[4] Among this number are James Thomson Callender (1758–1803), James Tytler (1745–1804) and Alexander Wilson (1766–1813). Threatened with prosecution over his reformist tract, *The Political Progress of Britain* (1792), Callender fled Edinburgh for Ireland in 1793, shortly thereafter sailing for Philadelphia and becoming in that city part of a vibrant British émigré literary and journalistic scene. Callender is sometimes seen as the inventor there of tabloid journalism, as his writings exposed alleged sexual impropriety in high political places of the American republic as well as the supposed corruption of

Thomas Jefferson. His writerly tussles with English exile William Cobbett mark out a fascinating episode in late eighteenth-century American letters which is commemorated in a remarkable modern novel by William Safire, *Scandal-Monger* (2000). Like Callender, Tytler fell foul of the authorities in Scotland for his pro-reform activities and escaped to Belfast, before emigrating to Salem, Massachusetts. In America his career in journalism was much less incendiary than Callender's, and his text of most enduring historical interest is a poem celebrating the United States as the true home of revolutionary liberty. 'The Rising of the Sun in the West' was penned while Tytler voyaged across the Atlantic, though published in Salem in 1795. Alexander Wilson was the most politically radical Scots-language poet *in situ* in Scotland in the 1790s. He was accused in his hometown of Paisley of attempting to extort money through using his poetry to slander a manufacturer as an under-payer of the weavers who worked for him. As a result, Wilson served the first of several prison sentences. Seeking a better life in America he wrote there poetry of a pro-Jeffersonian and anti-Federalist nature, which represents highly interesting source material for American politics of the period.

Nineteenth-century Scottish émigré writers are altogether more politically ambiguous than the likes of Callender, Tytler and Wilson. Glaswegian Thomas Campbell (1777–1844) pens *Gertrude of Wyoming* (1809), a long adventure poem paying sustained tribute to the natural beauty of North America, to where he had relocated (in pursuit of his personal economic interest rather than as result of the Clearances). A vocabulary of 'freedom' forged in the 1790s may be attendant on his text but so too is one of 'empire':

> Alas! poor Caledonia's mountaineer,
> That wants stern edict e'er, and feudal grief,
> Had forced him from a home he loved so dear!
> Yet found he here a home and glad relief,
> And plied the beverage from his own fair sheaf,
> That fired his Highland blood with mickle glee:
> And England sent her men, of men the chief,
> Who taught those sires of empire yet to be,
> To plant the tree of life, – to plant fair Freedom's tree![5]

Optimistic opportunity rather than disadvantage has been the emphasised keynote of nineteenth-century Scottish emigration, and this facet is certainly to the fore in the life of novelist John Galt (1779–1839). Galt enjoyed highly successful years in Canada in the 1820s, where he founded the town of Guelph in 1827 and was superintendent of the Canada Company, charged with developing the British controlled territories. Always intensely interested in the wider world, his novel *Annals of the Parish* (1821) observes the way in which a rapidly globalising world has its impact upon an Ayrshire parish. One vividly depicted character is Mr Cayenne, who has made his fortune across the Atlantic, returning to Scotland, black servant in tow, and proceeding to behave towards his mill workers and those he judicially tries (in his capacity as Justice of the Peace) with the same insensitivity we are supposed to infer he has also employed in amassing his fortune abroad. Politically conservative, Galt is exercised across his *oeuvre* by those who attain and abuse power, especially among the bourgeois class from which he himself springs. Drawing directly on his colonial experience, Galt pens *Lawrie Todd or the Settlers in the Woods* (1830) and *Bogle Corbet* (1831). The former is typical of Galt's historical verisimilitude in drawing upon the memoirs especially of a New York merchant, his fellow Scottish émigré, Grant Thorburn, as well as his own experiences. The novel's focus shifts from the eastern seaboard, westwards beyond the city of Utica and the opening up of the great American forest lands. The novel celebrates American expansionist energy and a society less encumbered than Britain by staid political control, somewhere that is conducive to capitalist enterprise, albeit that we glimpse also less scrupulous hustlers. *Bogle Corbet* features a central character from the west of Scotland whose business dealings in his native land fail, with the result that, at the behest of his creditors, he journeys to Jamaica, from where he returns but continues trading with the West Indies. Historically accurate, documenting declining Scottish profit from tobacco and interlinked slave trades following the American and French revolutions, Corbet soon finds himself yet again in financial trouble and emigrates to Canada. Corbet's experiences there become a platform for the novel's criticism of British rule in Canada, which is seen to inhibit improvement, especially in comparison to the United States, though the latter too is seen as a place not without its problems of rampant individualism, sometimes all too excessive. The novel essays the difficulty of community, a value on which Galt places a high premium, in two very different social outlooks on the North American continent, as well as in Britain. As with all of Galt's fiction, there is much honestly inquisitive and nuanced treatment of the character of Western humanity, though little real consideration of indigenous peoples and environment.

John Galt is among various candidates for the authorship of 'The Canadian Boat-Song', published in 1829. Allegedly from an authentic Gaelic text, it was a song supposedly part of the repertoire of Scottish fur-traders as they navigated Upper Canada by canoe.[6] One of the most explicit contemporary texts about the Highland Clearances, there is something of an air of aggressive rage that also extends to life in the new world:

> When the bold kindred, in time long-vanish'd,
> Conquer'd the soil and fortified the keep, –
> No seer foretold the children would be banish'd,
> That a degenerate Lord might boast his sheep:
> *Fair these broad meads – these hoary woods are grand;*
> *But we are exiles from our fathers' land.*
>
> Come foreign rage – let Discord burst in slaughter!
> O then for clansman true, and stern claymore –
> The hearts that would have given their blood like water,
> Beat heavily beyond the Atlantic roar:
> *Fair these broad meads – these hoary woods are grand;*
> *But we are exiles from our fathers' land.*[7]

Alternatively argued to have been produced in Canada or in Britain, in addition to the uncertainty about its authorship, 'The Canadian Boat-Song' reflects the shadowy cultural terrain where Scots in less than propitious circumstances go on to inflict dubious circumstances on other peoples overseas. In the nineteenth century a significant number of Scottish writers fled hardship and emigrated to Canada, where their attitudes became unmistakeably imperial. Alexander McLachlan (1818–96) left Johnstone in Renfrewshire in 1840. A minor part of the West of Scotland radical political scene, overseas McLachlan was soon adapting a Burnsian idiom associated with dissent to suit the chest-puffing pride of a nation that ruled the waves. His 'Britannia' (1864) precisely inhabits the cadences of 'Scots wha hae', with a hymn to his nation, 'Great Mother of the Mighty Dead', for which 'Sir Walter sang, and Nelson bled'. There is more transmogrification in 'The Anglo-Saxon' (1874), as this text subsumes the myth of the sturdy, martial Scot within the wider racial identity of the enterprising, conquering Briton. It features an opening of crude intent: 'The Anglo-Saxon leads the van, / And never lags behind, / For was not he ordain'd to be / The leader of mankind?'[8] More innocuous perhaps, another Scottish-born Canadian poet, James Anderson (1842–1923), wrote poems of genuine energy, sometimes in the Scots language, depicting the difficult graft of prospecting and mining. Among numerous Canadian writers of Scottish descent or connection, the earliest of genuine artistic significance is probably Robert Service (1874–1958), born in England, brought up in Scotland and living in British Columbia from 1896. Although not exactly Whitman-like stylistically, his poetry, such as that in the volume *Songs of a Sourdough* (1907), displays a finely particular realism about the physicality of human life that owes something to the American poet and looks towards the Modernist movement. His *Rhymes of a Red Cross Man* (1916) extends the same unsentimental objectivity to the awful conditions and carnage of the Great War. Service's fiction remains underappreciated, among it *The Roughneck, A Tale of Tahiti* (1923), one of a number of texts where he reflects on the conditions of both colonised and colonising races in places other than Canada, including, as well as the South Seas, South Africa.[9]

It is in the South Seas where diasporic Scottish literature, arguably, scores its greatest achievement. From 1890 until his death, Robert Louis Stevenson (1850–94) lived in Samoa in the Southern Pacific. His initial motivation for settling there was in finding a climate more amenable to his fragile health, but he soon became absorbed in the local culture. *A Footnote to History* (1892) saw Stevenson depict dangerous recent fractures in Samoan society that the Americans, the British and others were doing too little to heal. This appeal to what he hoped might be an enlightened Western paternalism fell, however, on deaf ears, and civil, or tribal, war broke out. Stevenson's novel *The Wrecker*, published in the same year, is a rather light-hearted satire featuring as main character a *flâneur* abroad in Europe, the United States and the South Seas who leaves mild chaos in the wake of his travels. From 1892, Stevenson's fiction set in Samoa generally takes on much darker notes. One of Stevenson's finest short stories is 'The Beach of Falesà', which appeared in serialised form in the *Illustrated London News* through July and August 1892. The London periodical refused to publish in full a 'marriage contract' near the start of the text where its narrator, John Wiltshire, is 'illegally married [to Uma of Falesà island] for one night, and Mr John Wiltshire is at liberty to send her to hell next morning'.[10] The sexual licence depicted therein was too much for the editor of the *Illustrated London News* to stomach unlike the equally flagrant and larger-scale colonial immorality which this passage also metonymically embodies. 'The Beach of Falesà' depicts white men performing a number of cheap tricks, of which the marriage 'contract' is merely one, on the Samoan people of Falesà. Through mechanical machinations, the 'villain' of the story, Case, persuades the islanders that the interior of their domain is haunted by malevolent spirits so as to harness for his own commercial gain the natural resources of the island. Case is exploiting not only the Samoans but his 'fellow' white men. He has also been the architect behind Wiltshire's marriage to Uma, who is shunned by the inhabitants of Falesà for reasons that remain obscure, but with whom dealings are believed to bring bad luck, as her husband gradually realises. Wiltshire turns out to be only the latest in a sequence of white competitors who have been damaged, perhaps even murdered, by Case. A 'heroic' quest and battle ensues as Wiltshire penetrates the interior of the island and exposes Case's malevolent secrets, the former killing the latter after a fierce struggle. Clearly, what we have here is a kind of standard 'romantic adventure', where evil is trumped in the end. However, from the beginning and Wiltshire's collaboration in the outrageous 'terms' of his marriage to Uma, we have a character who is more piratical freebooter than conventional 'hero'. At the end of the story, we see Wiltshire having remained with Uma, briefly perhaps giving the reader the hope that a kind of good has prevailed, contemplating and worrying over the lives of his daughters:

> [W]hat bothers me is the girls. They're only half-castes, of course; I know that as well as you do, and there's nobody thinks less of half-castes than I do; but they're mine, and about all I've got. I can't reconcile my mind to their taking up with Kanakas [indigenous Samoan], and I'd like to know where I'm to find the whites?[11]

To modern eyes it is remarkable that the readership of the *Illustrated London News* could be thought comfortable with such a passage while being discomfited by Wiltshire's marriage contract. Obviously Wiltshire's statement exposes a naked racism that was fairly easily accommodated by late nineteenth-century Western society. Stevenson's ending inhabits the 'moral' outlook of that society, even as the author is ironically signalling actual moral muddiness in the white mentality. As well as its awkward journey fully into print (the censored *Illustrated London News* version long prevailed in many quarters), 'The Beach of Falesà' was a story that was difficult for Stevenson fully to complete, but the creative process excited him greatly. As he wrote of it in a letter to Sidney Colvin, 'I never did a better piece of work, horrid and pleasing, and extraordinarily *true*.'[12] Stevenson's difficulty and satisfaction with 'The Beach of Falesà' shows him at the cutting edge, as one of the earliest European fictional dissectors of the racism, and the lack of moral superiority generally, inherent in Western colonial advancement.

One might argue that in his South Seas fiction Stevenson finds liberation from the historical fiction with which he was also associated. His subversion of 'adventure' and 'romance' forms, as Penny Fielding explains elsewhere in this volume, 'degenerates' completely in *The Ebb-Tide* (1894). This novella is Stevenson's most explicitly searing condemnation of the Westerners as bringers of disease, intolerance and hypocritical Christianity to the South Seas, and represented a rather difficult reading experience for its 'home' readership in its own day with its portrayal of a paradisaical Polynesian setting rendered nightmarish thanks to the incursions of white civilisation. In spite of sophisticated critical advances in recent years, the popular profile of Stevenson remains that of an adventure writer rather than as a path-breaking commentator on colonialism whose withering depiction of

Western interference in the third world paves the way for such writers as Joseph Conrad and Graham Greene.[13]

In South Africa, the story of Scottish diaspora writing is earlier on a little different from that elsewhere in the colonies, in the powerful presence of one individual at least. Born in the Scottish borders, Thomas Pringle (1789–1834) left behind the maudlin and popularly well-received poem 'The Emigrant's Farewell' (1819), and farmed and became a man of letters around Cape Town from 1820. He was outspoken against slavery, producing for instance his powerful 'Letter from South Africa' on this theme. This was published by Thomas Campbell, mentioned above, also to his credit an abolitionist. Interestingly, like Campbell, a predominant note in his poetry, written *in situ* in a colonial place, is pride in his own race. However, unlike Campbell, there is much more of the beginnings of a critique of white dispossession of the natives. A later South African poet of Scottish ancestry, Roy Campbell (1901–57), perhaps unsurprisingly given the fact that twentieth-century South African racism becomes if anything worse, brings much more trenchant critique of the society in which he lives.[14]

It can be argued that, generally, writers of the Scottish diaspora significantly come of age in the later twentieth century. One of Canada's finest essayists has been Hugh MacLennan (1907–90). An accomplished writer of fiction also, he was an even-handed portrayer of the tensions between English-speaking and French-speaking Canada. Of particular note is his novel *Each Man's Son* (1951), a tense family drama against the backdrop of the Cape Breton mining community which acutely observes rapid social change after the Second World War. MacLennan's essay 'Scotchman's Return', which gives the title to his volume of collected prose from 1960, sees him critically, but not without some wry affection, dealing with the foundation myth of 'the Scotchman' in British and British colonial culture. Similarly, in New Zealand, James K. Baxter (1926–72) exemplifies a more complex relationship to his Scottish background than most previous poets of the southern hemisphere. Named in his middle name (Keir) after Keir Hardie, Baxter inherited the left-leaning politics of his family, upon which fell suspicion of pacifism or even outright disloyalty to the state during the Second World War. Baxter was an admirer of Robert Burns, battled with alcoholism, was sporadically successful and disastrous in his educational achievement, converted to Roman Catholicism and espoused the culture and rights of the Maori people. It was particularly through Burns, whom he read as a 'tribal' poet, that Baxter found a means of engagement with Maori culture.[15] Baxter's story is the fairly typical story of the post-Romantic artist, alienated from 'modern' civilisation. His poetic landscapes are those of his unsentimentally rendered home city, Dunedin, of powerful Scots heritage, which is often cold and austerely presented, as well as a sometimes rather sinister New Zealand countryside, which has had its Maori culture scandalously submerged. As with many later twentieth-century poets, Baxter sees nature and (Western) humanity often at cross purposes, though in much of his work there is clearly too a Catholic (married sometimes to a Maori) mysticism that in its universalism removes him as far as possible, it might be argued, from his own (or any) historical, ethnographical roots.

'Scottishness' remains very apparent, though not necessarily central, in a range of writers who are impressively to the fore in recent critical accounts of 'post-colonial literatures in English'. Like most such writers, however, for New Zealand poet Bill Manhire (b.1946), his Scottish note is not in any way a predominant one amidst his *oeuvre*. It arises incidentally or as part of the contingent circumstances of his wider life experience. Typical of the Scottish-themed poems that crop up in his work is 'The English Teacher' (1996). The poet depicts his mother teaching Polish soldiers in Scotland during the Second World War and the sadness of one man, particularly, whose family has possibly been murdered by the Russians. At this point the poet's father, a man as yet unknown to his mother, is in America; the Polish soldiers about to be part of the Allied invasion of Europe; and the poet's parents' eventual settlement in faraway (from Scotland) New Zealand remains unexplained. Long after all these events, the poet addresses his mother: '"Give me more detail," I say. "You know, to put in the poem."'[16] The point, of course, is that 'detail' is not the point. It is not the physicality, the precise historicity of facts, that matters so much, but rather the human life and emotion that is the outcome of the turbulent historical winds which sweep people hither and thither. Manhire's poem is a wryly gentle chiding of history, in the case of New Zealanders of Scots descent as with many others, of people who have clung too fast to tradition, to genealogy at the expense, perhaps, of wider, less certain, messier human reality. Notable in this connection too is another New Zealander, Keri Hulme (b.1947), one of her nation's finest novelists. Of highly heterogeneous ancestry, including Orcadian and Maori, Hulme draws liberally on Celtic and Maori mythology in her work. Not primarily backward-looking, Hulme is strongly contemporary in her feminism and in the sophisticated interplay in her work with Modernist and Postmodernist impulses; most controversially she has been attacked for her identification with Maori culture, her critics accusing her, in effect, of a kind of revisionism of her own predominantly 'white settler' heritage. Among Australian poets two particularly prominent individuals, Chris Wallace-Crabbe (b.1934) and Les Murray (b.1938), are also periodically drawn to the Scottishness that is in their lineage. Wallace-Crabbe's 'The Last Ride'

(1990) depicts a nineteenth-century exodus on a Scottish sabbath of a fairy-like folk, 'The People of Peace [who] shall never more / Be seen on the braes of Scotland', observed only by a herdboy and his sister.[17] Obviously and with a seductive beauty, the text inhabits 'traditional' Scottish natural and supernatural landscapes, with subtexts too of the Clearances and large-scale emigration. The strikingly anachronistic performance of this surface text in the late twentieth century, however, brings the reader up sharp. History and myth are hopelessly entwined in Scotland, and for its émigré peoples across the globe, the poem suggests. Scotland never was simply a static place, visited by catastrophic calamity. It was always a place in flux, in history, as other places; the myth is one of resistant beautiful elegy, but which ought, precisely, to be resisted in the end. Les Murray speaks to something of the same conclusion in his insightful essay 'The Bonnie Disproportion' (1981), which makes plain his choice to pay some serious historical regard to his Scottish heritage, even as in unregretful manner he sees myths of ancestry recede in importance, the 'only real option' to be Australian. Murray's strongly anti-elegiac note occurs, paradoxically enough, in his 'Elegy for Angus Macdonald of Cnoclinn' (1977):

> my fathers were Highlanders long ago
> then Borderers, before this landfall
> – 'savages' once, now we are 'settlers'
> in the mouth of the deathless enemy –
> but I am seized of this future now.
> I am not European. Nor is my English.
> And perhaps you too were better served here
> than in Uist of the Sheldrakes and the tides
> watching the old life fade, the *toradh*,
> the good, go out of the island world.
> Exile's a rampart, sometimes, to the past,
> a distiller of spirit from bruised grains;
> this is a meaning of the New World.[18]

Here Murray's attitude is poised; there is ambiguity about what has been lost (both a previous life in Scotland and the indigenous, pre-white world of Australia). The only certainty is change, the creation of new things (such as 'non-European' English), the previous Scottish 'savages' have become 'settlers' (with the newly negative 'white' connotations of the word) and good and bad remain constantly in exchange in the wide world, in Australia as everywhere else. If we are alert, we catch a glimpse here too of Murray the convert to Roman Catholicism, the biggest area in which he has rejected elements of his ancestral heritage, in which a sense of the eternal temporal battle between good and evil is to the fore.

Of modern Canadian fiction writers of Scottish descent, the most famous is Alice Munro (b.1931). A wide and appreciative critical literature, on one of the technically finest feminist short-story writers in the world, had not made much of Munro's ancestral origins. This is perhaps not surprising, since she herself did not foreground these much in her work until comparatively recently. The collection *The View from Castle Rock* (2006) mixed fiction with her own family history, in which she pointed to James Hogg as being among her forebears. Appropriately enough, then, given the thematic terrain of Hogg's *Confessions of a Justified Sinner*, repressive Calvinist-tinged religion and maleness predominate in a series of writings about crossing and living on the other side of the Atlantic. As the title of Munro's book suggests, the hard, lofty 'view' of the Scottish émigré takes a long time to shift, if ever, in North America. Of all books by those of Scots descent, *No Great Mischief* (1999) by Nova Scotian Alistair MacLeod (b.1936) has perhaps been most fêted in Scotland (as well as being critically acclaimed in Canada and many other places too). A historical novel, based to some degree on MacLeod's own Catholic clan and family, which had suffered during the Jacobite rebellions and the Clearances, it is a text that, even as it deals with such cataclysmic historical occurrences, sees the eventual possibilities for his family probably as propitious in exile as if they remained in the motherland. At the same time, the nicely casual irony of the title indicates the innocence of his people even as they begin to supplant and alter indigenous North American culture. MacLeod's is a novel that, even as it is clear-sighted about the bad things that humans do to one another, sees this humanity as less wholly motivated by evil than might be thought. Again, MacLeod's religious perspective, Catholicism, might here be glimpsed, an outlook that links him with the likes of Les Murray, much more so than any ethnic kinship. 'Scottish literature' in diaspora and in writers of Scottish origin represents a patchy story that remains inadequately narrated in any systematic way.

Notes

1 For discussion of emigration figures from Scotland, see T. M. Devine, *The Scottish Nation 1700–2000* (London: Allen Lane, 1999), esp. pp. 279–85.

2 See Liam McIlvanney, 'Robert Burns and the Ulster-Scots Literary Revival of the 1790s', *Bullán: An Irish Studies Journal*, 4 (1999/2000), 2, 125–43; Carol Baraniuk, 'Ulster's Burns? James Orr, the Bard of Ballycarry', *Review of Scottish Culture*, 19 (2007), 54–62; Jennifer Orr, 'Samuel Thomson's Poetic Fashioning of the Ulster Landscape', *Scottish Literary Review* (Spring–Summer 2010), 41–58.

3 See Frank Ferguson (ed.), *Ulster-Scots Writing: An Anthology* (Dublin: Four Courts Press, 2008) for the most comprehensive guide to Ulster-Scots writing from the seventeenth century to the present.

4 The best account of exiled Scottish writers of the 1790s remains Michael Durey, *Transatlantic Radicals and the Early American Republic* (Lawrence: University Press of Kansas, 1997).

5 Thomas Campbell, 'Gertrude of Wyoming', in *The Poetical Works of Thomas Campbell*, ed. Rufus W. Griswold (New York: Leavitt & Allen, 1865), part 1, lines 46–54.

6 See www.electricscotland.com/poetry/canadian_boatsong.htm.

7 Carole Gerson and Gwendolyn Davies (eds.), *Canadian Poetry* (Toronto: McLelland & Stewart, 1994), p. 72.

8 *Ibid.*, p. 93.

9 The situation of nineteenth-century Scottish, or at least Scottish- (often) Burns-influenced, poetry is no more inspiring in the USA or New Zealand. See Gerard Carruthers, 'Burns's Political Reputation in North America', in Sharon Alker, Leith Davis and Holly Faith Nelson (eds.), *Robert Burns and Transatlantic Culture* (Aldershot: Ashgate, 2012), and Alan Riach, 'Heather and Fern: The Burns Effect in New Zealand Verse', in Tom Brooking and Jennie Coleman (eds.), *The Heather and the Fern: Scottish Migration and New Zealand Settlement* (Dunedin: University of Otago Press, 2003), pp. 153–71. Thanks to Alan Riach for bibliographical help here.

10 Robert Louis Stevenson, *South Sea Tales*, ed. Roslyn Jolly (Oxford University Press, 1996), p. 11.

11 *Ibid.*, p. 71.

12 Ernest Mehew (ed.), *Selected Letters of Robert Louis Stevenson* (New Haven and London: Yale University Press, 2001), p. 464.

13 Roslyn Jolly's *Robert Louis Stevenson in the Pacific: Travel, Empire and the Author's Profession* (Aldershot: Ashgate, 2009) brings Stevenson's life and career in the South Seas into fuller focus than ever before.

14 A useful anthology including both Thomas Pringle and Roy Campbell is Stephen Finn and Rosemary Gray (eds.), *Broken Strings: The Politics of Poetry in South Africa* (Cape Town: Maskew Miller Longman, 1992).

15 For discussion of this area, see Liam McIlvanney, Editorial – 'Burns and the World', *International Journal of Scottish Literature*, 6 (Spring–Summer, 2010), www.ijsl.stir.ac.uk/.

16 Bill Manhire, *My Sunshine* (Wellington: Victoria University Press, 1996), p. 54.

17 Chris Wallace-Crabbe, *For Crying Out Loud* (Oxford University Press, 1990), p. 49.

18 Les Murray, *Collected Poems* (Manchester: Carcanet, 1991), p. 156.

Guide to further reading

Devine, Tom, *Scotland's Empire, 1600–1815* (London: Penguin Allen Lane, 2003)

Fry, Michael, *The Scottish Empire* (East Linton: Tuckwell Press; Edinburgh: Birlinn, 2001)

Leask, Nigel, 'Scotland's Literature of Empire and Emigration, 1707–1918', in Susan Manning (ed.), *The Edinburgh History of Scottish Literature*, vol. II, *Enlightenment, Britain and Empire (1707–1918)* (Edinburgh University Press, 2007), pp. 153–62

Mack, Douglas, *Scottish Fiction and the British Empire* (Edinburgh University Press, 2006)

Pearce, G. L., *The Scots of New Zealand* (Auckland: William Collins, 1976)

Reid, W. Stanford (ed.), *The Scottish Tradition in Canada* (Toronto: McClelland and Stewart, 1976)

Wannan, Bill (ed.), *The Heather in the South: Lore, Literature and Balladry of the Scots in Australia* (Melbourne and London: Landsdowne Press, 1966)

INDEX

Cambridge Companions to ...

AUTHORS

Edward Albee *edited by Stephen J. Bottoms*

Margaret Atwood *edited by Coral Ann Howells*

W. H. Auden *edited by Stan Smith*

Jane Austen *edited by Edward Copeland and Juliet McMaster* (second edition)

Beckett *edited by John Pilling*

Bede *edited by Scott DeGregorio*

Aphra Behn *edited by Derek Hughes and Janet Todd*

Walter Benjamin *edited by David S. Ferris*

William Blake *edited by Morris Eaves*

Brecht *edited by Peter Thomson and Glendyr Sacks* (second edition)

The Brontës *edited by Heather Glen*

Bunyan *edited by Anne Dunan-Page*

Frances Burney *edited by Peter Sabor*

Byron *edited by Drummond Bone*

Albert Camus *edited by Edward J. Hughes*

Willa Cather *edited by Marilee Lindemann*

Cervantes *edited by Anthony J. Cascardi*

Chaucer *edited by Piero Boitani and Jill Mann* (second edition)

Chekhov *edited by Vera Gottlieb and Paul Allain*

Kate Chopin *edited by Janet Beer*

Caryl Churchill *edited by Elaine Aston and Elin Diamond*

Coleridge *edited by Lucy Newlyn*

Wilkie Collins *edited by Jenny Bourne Taylor*

Joseph Conrad *edited by J. H. Stape*

H. D. *edited by Nephie J. Christodoulides and Polina Mackay*

Dante *edited by Rachel Jacoff* (second edition)

Daniel Defoe *edited by John Richetti*

Don DeLillo *edited by John N. Duvall*

Charles Dickens *edited by John O. Jordan*

Emily Dickinson *edited by Wendy Martin*

John Donne *edited by Achsah Guibbory*

Dostoevskii *edited by W. J. Leatherbarrow*

Theodore Dreiser *edited by Leonard Cassuto and Claire Virginia Eby*

John Dryden *edited by Steven N. Zwicker*

W. E. B. Du Bois *edited by Shamoon Zamir*

George Eliot *edited by George Levine*

T. S. Eliot *edited by A. David Moody*

Ralph Ellison *edited by Ross Posnock*

Ralph Waldo Emerson *edited by Joel Porte and Saundra Morris*

William Faulkner *edited by Philip M. Weinstein*

Henry Fielding *edited by Claude Rawson*

F. Scott Fitzgerald *edited by Ruth Prigozy*

Flaubert *edited by Timothy Unwin*

E. M. Forster *edited by David Bradshaw*

Benjamin Franklin *edited by Carla Mulford*

Brian Friel *edited by Anthony Roche*

Robert Frost *edited by Robert Faggen*

Gabriel García Márquez *edited by Philip Swanson*

Elizabeth Gaskell *edited by Jill L. Matus*

Goethe *edited by Lesley Sharpe*

Günter Grass *edited by Stuart Taberner*

Thomas Hardy *edited by Dale Kramer*

David Hare *edited by Richard Boon*

Nathaniel Hawthorne *edited by Richard Millington*

Seamus Heaney *edited by Bernard O'Donoghue*

Ernest Hemingway *edited by Scott Donaldson*

Homer *edited by Robert Fowler*

Horace *edited by Stephen Harrison*

Ted Hughes *edited by Terry Gifford*

Ibsen *edited by James McFarlane*

Henry James *edited by Jonathan Freedman*

Samuel Johnson *edited by Greg Clingham*

Ben Jonson *edited by Richard Harp and Stanley Stewart*

James Joyce *edited by Derek Attridge* (second edition)

Kafka *edited by Julian Preece*

Keats *edited by Susan J. Wolfson*

Rudyard Kipling *edited by Howard J. Booth*

Lacan *edited by Jean-Michel Rabaté*

D. H. Lawrence *edited by Anne Fernihough*

Primo Levi *edited by Robert Gordon*

Lucretius *edited by Stuart Gillespie and Philip Hardie*

Machiavelli *edited by John M. Najemy*

David Mamet *edited by Christopher Bigsby*

Thomas Mann *edited by Ritchie Robertson*

Christopher Marlowe *edited by Patrick Cheney*

Andrew Marvell *edited by Derek Hirst and Steven N. Zwicker*

Herman Melville *edited by Robert S. Levine*

Arthur Miller *edited by Christopher Bigsby* (second edition)

Milton *edited by Dennis Danielson* (second edition)

Molière *edited by David Bradby and Andrew Calder*

Toni Morrison *edited by Justine Tally*

Nabokov *edited by Julian W. Connolly*

Eugene O'Neill *edited by Michael Manheim*

George Orwell *edited by John Rodden*

Ovid *edited by Philip Hardie*

Harold Pinter *edited by Peter Raby* (second edition)

Sylvia Plath *edited by Jo Gill*

Edgar Allan Poe *edited by Kevin J. Hayes*

Alexander Pope *edited by Pat Rogers*

Ezra Pound *edited by Ira B. Nadel*

Proust *edited by Richard Bales*

Pushkin *edited by Andrew Kahn*

Rabelais *edited by John O'Brien*

Rilke *edited by Karen Leeder and Robert Vilain*

Philip Roth *edited by Timothy Parrish*

Salman Rushdie *edited by Abdulrazak Gurnah*

Shakespeare *edited by Margareta de Grazia and Stanley Wells* (second edition)

Shakespeare and Popular Culture *edited by Robert Shaughnessy*

Shakespeare on Film *edited by Russell Jackson* (second edition)

Shakespeare on Stage *edited by Stanley Wells and Sarah Stanton*

Shakespeare's History Plays *edited by Michael Hattaway*

Shakespeare's Last Plays *edited by Catherine M. S. Alexander*

Shakespeare's Poetry *edited by Patrick Cheney*

Shakespearean Comedy *edited by Alexander Leggatt*

Shakespearean Tragedy *edited by Claire McEachern*

George Bernard Shaw *edited by Christopher Innes*

Shelley *edited by Timothy Morton*

Mary Shelley *edited by Esther Schor*

Sam Shepard *edited by Matthew C. Roudané*

Spenser *edited by Andrew Hadfield*

Laurence Sterne *edited by Thomas Keymer*

Wallace Stevens *edited by John N. Serio*

Tom Stoppard *edited by Katherine E. Kelly*

Harriet Beecher Stowe *edited by Cindy Weinstein*

August Strindberg *edited by Michael Robinson*

Jonathan Swift *edited by Christopher Fox*

J. M. Synge *edited by P. J. Mathews*

Tacitus *edited by A. J. Woodman*

Henry David Thoreau *edited by Joel Myerson*

Tolstoy *edited by Donna Tussing Orwin*

Anthony Trollope *edited by Carolyn Dever and Lisa Niles*

Mark Twain *edited by Forrest G. Robinson*

John Updike *edited by Stacey Olster*

Mario Vargas Llosa *edited by Efrain Kristal and John King*

Virgil *edited by Charles Martindale*

Voltaire *edited by Nicholas Cronk*

Edith Wharton *edited by Millicent Bell*

Walt Whitman *edited by Ezra Greenspan*

Oscar Wilde *edited by Peter Raby*

Tennessee Williams *edited by Matthew C. Roudané*

August Wilson *edited by Christopher Bigsby*

Mary Wollstonecraft *edited by Claudia L. Johnson*

Virginia Woolf *edited by Susan Sellers* (second edition)

Wordsworth *edited by Stephen Gill*

W. B. Yeats *edited by Marjorie Howes and John Kelly*

Zola *edited by Brian Nelson*

TOPICS

The Actress *edited by Maggie B. Gale and John Stokes*

The African American Novel *edited by Maryemma Graham*

The African American Slave Narrative *edited by Audrey A. Fisch*

Allegory *edited by Rita Copeland and Peter Struck*

American Crime Fiction *edited by Catherine Ross Nickerson*

American Modernism *edited by Walter Kalaidjian*